E467.1.E86 A4 2012
The letters of General Richard S.
 Ewell :
33663005153545
PIN

D1272742

DATE DUE

BRODART, CO.   Cat. No. 23-221

The Letters of General Richard S. Ewell

The Letters of General Richard S. Ewell
Stonewall's Successor

Edited by Donald C. Pfanz

Voices of the Civil War • Peter S. Carmichael, Series Editor

The University of Tennessee Press / Knoxville

The Voices of the Civil War series makes available a variety of primary source materials that illuminate issues on the battlefield, the home front, and the western front, as well as other aspects of this historic era. The series contextualizes the personal accounts within the framework of the latest scholarship and expands established knowledge by offering new perspectives, new materials, and new voices.

Copyright © 2012 by The University of Tennessee Press / Knoxville. All Rights Reserved. Manufactured in the United States of America. First Edition.

The paper in this book meets the requirements of American National Standards Institute / National Information Standards Organization specification Z39.48–1992 (Permanence of Paper). It contains 30 percent post-consumer waste and is certified by the Forest Stewardship Council.

Frontispiece: Richard S. Ewell. The only known photograph of the general. (Courtesy National Archives)

Library of Congress Cataloging-in-Publication Data

Ewell, Richard Stoddert, 1817–1872.
[Correspondence]
The letters of General Richard S. Ewell : Stonewall's successor / edited by Donald C. Pfanz. — 1st ed.
        p. cm. — (Voices of the Civil War)
Includes bibliographical references and index.
ISBN-13: 978-1-57233-873-9 (hardcover)
ISBN-10: 1-57233-873-3 (hardcover)
1. Ewell, Richard Stoddert, 1817–1872—Correspondence.
2. Generals—United States—Correspondence.
3. Generals—Confederate States of America—Correspondence.
4. United States—History—Civil War, 1861-1865—Sources.
5. United States—History, Military—19th century—Sources.
  I. Pfanz, Donald.
 II. Title.

E467.1.E86A4 2012
355.0092—dc23
                                2012005296

ACC LIBRARY SERVICES AUSTIN, TX

To Betty,
whom I shall always love

Contents

Illustrations

Figures

Maps

Series Editor's Foreword

Of all of Robert E. Lee's lieutenants, Richard Stoddard Ewell is usually put at the far end of the bench, sitting behind the Army of Northern Virginia's "first string": Thomas "Stonewall" Jackson, James Longstreet, Jeb Stuart, and John B. Gordon. If only Michael Shaara had given Ewell a historical facelift similar to the one he gave Longstreet in his novel *The Killer Angels*. Instead, Shaara parroted the popular line that the newly minted Second Corps commander squandered the Confederacy's best chance of victory at Gettysburg. Indecisiveness, vacillation, and a paralysis of the mind are again and again rolled out by Shaara and like-minded critics to explain why the Southern assault stalled at the base of Cemetery Hill on the evening of July 1. Such criticisms have a direct lineage to the Lost Cause exoneration of Lee at Gettysburg, even though Lee himself took full responsibility for the army's defeat. Wartime sources affirm Lee's claim of culpability while also revealing that Ewell was actually open to taking Cemetery Hill. Through another subordinate, Ewell suggested a joint assault with A. P. Hill, but the final push never materialized, largely because orders never came from above. Only Lee had the authority to coordinate his two army corps. He was on the field, standing at Seminary Ridge with a panoramic view of Gettysburg before him, watching disordered Federal troops flee toward a final defensive position. Why Lee did not bring unity to his command is one of the great imponderables of the battle, but rather than admit to the unknowability of the past, too many historians have turned Ewell into a scapegoat for Confederate defeat.

Ewell was certainly no Napoleon in the rough, but he was an exceptional combat officer, especially at the divisional level, until his wounding at Groveton on August 28, 1862. His subsequent promotion to corps commander brought uneven results to be sure, but the shadow of Gettysburg has obscured fine performances at a number of fields, including the Wilderness and Fort Harrison. Unfortunately, the entirety of Ewell's career is rarely considered, and facile generalizations persist to this day that Ewell could never shake his case of the "slows" after Gettysburg. Such simplistic thinking is turned upside down by Donald Pfanz in *Richard S. Ewell: A Soldier's Life* (1998), a superb piece of scholarship and by far the finest biography we have of the general. He breaks from the official line that Ewell was simply a bizarre and emasculated soldier, utterly helpless before an overbearing wife, timid before ambitious subordinates, and a victim of delusional bouts who supposedly thought of himself as a bird! Pfanz brings much-needed balance to the general's war record, and his assessment draws heavily from Ewell's own correspondence, a body of papers the author has superbly edited for the Voices of the Civil War series. Stonewall Jackson and Ewell are the only corps commanders in Lee's army to have had their letters published, and this edition includes much more of Ewell's correspondence than did Percy Hamlin's 1935 volume, *The Making of a Soldier: Letters of General R. S. Ewell.*

As presented here, Ewell's letters are remarkable for their breadth, covering his time at West Point, his prewar career in the U.S. Regular Army, his rise in the Army of Northern Virginia, and his life after Appomattox. His letters rarely chronicle daily life in humdrum fashion. Ewell was too cranky, too irreverent, too ironic, and too smart not to stand back and expose the absurdity of the human condition. Joining the Confederacy did not mute Ewell's contrarian voice. Although he prospered as Stonewall's subordinate, he felt estranged from his superior's plans and was not afraid to tell the world that he felt as though he was fighting with blinders on. "Genl Jackson is off possibly 'Somewhere,'" Ewell wrote Jeb Stuart on May 14, 1862, "and leaves me standing gaping at the gap while he is after the Yankees." In politics, Ewell was also outspoken, believing that the Southern nation needed to marshal all of its resources, even if that meant tinkering with the system of human servitude. He was one of the first Southern officers to suggest that Confederate forces arm slaves, a position that apparently did not hurt his professional aspirations as it did with other officers. When defeat descended upon the Confederate nation and Ewell was a captured officer, sequestered in a Northern prison camp during the spring and summer of 1865, he did not fantasize about a resurrection of the Southern cause. He was clear-eyed about the totality of defeat. Slavery was gone forever, taking his social class down as well, and Ewell the realist understood that he and his fellow ex-Confederates were in no position to shape the terms of Northern victory. Above all else he worried about the possibility of property confiscation, a fear that prompted him to propose limited African American suffrage, an unusual suggestion even among moderates. But, like the vast majority of former slaveholders, Ewell found it difficult to negotiate around the ground truth of

Reconstruction. Ultimately, the desire for a cheap and dependent labor force prompted landowners to strip freed people of their political rights. The general's postwar letters from his farms in Mississippi and Tennessee expose how former slaveholders, when confronted by a black labor force demanding higher wages and better conditions, dismissed African Americans as being racially unfit for a supposed free-labor system of wages.

The Letters of General Richard S. Ewell provides a sweeping view of the nineteenth century. Such chronological breadth makes this volume truly exceptional and important. Through Ewell's eyes we see the many worlds of an American people at war. His thoughtful observations, biting wit, and ironic disposition offer readers a chance to rethink the paper-thin generalizations of Ewell as a quirky neurotic who simply crumbled under the legacy of Stonewall Jackson. Historical redemption in the popular mind still awaits Ewell, as does a new monument at Gettysburg.

Peter S. Carmichael
Gettysburg College

Preface

Of all the armies that took the field during the Civil War, none gained greater renown than General Robert E. Lee's Army of Northern Virginia. For four years it battled against great odds, earning for itself a name of imperishable glory. Just six men held the rank of lieutenant general in that army. Two of them, Richard H. Anderson and A. P. Hill, left little in the way of written records. Two others, James Longstreet and Jubal A. Early, wrote memoirs. Only Thomas J. "Stonewall" Jackson and his successor, Richard S. Ewell, left sizable bodies of personal correspondence. Jackson's letters were published in 1895 by his wife in a book called *Memoirs of Stonewall Jackson by His Widow*. Ewell's letters remained out of the public eye until 1935, when Dr. Percy G. Hamlin published *The Making of a Soldier: Letters of General R. S. Ewell*. Longstreet's and Early's memoirs, while helpful in understanding the workings of the army, were written many years after the war with an eye toward publication and vindication. Jackson and Ewell, by contrast, wrote during the war to family and friends. They had no axes to grind, no reputations to defend. Unguarded in style and untainted by hindsight, their letters offer an honest and instructive commentary on contemporary events.

This volume represents a new edition of General Ewell's personal correspondence. But why, after three-quarters of a century, is such a book needed? First, there is the discovery of new letters. Hamlin's book contains 49 letters that had been passed down to his wife through her grandmother, Lizzie Ewell. Since then, many additional letters have come to light. Thus, this volume, in contrast to Hamlin's, contains 173 personal letters (complete or partial), 7 letters of a more official cast, 4 battle narratives, and 2 memoranda of incidents that took place during the Civil War. Half of these documents were written during the Civil War.

A second reason for publishing this volume is that Hamlin's book made little effort to explain comments made by General Ewell in his correspondence.

In *The Making of a Soldier* Hamlin provided just fifty-four footnotes—approximately one per letter. Of those, most were one-line identifications and at least two were patently wrong. By contrast, this edition contains approximately fifteen hundred footnotes to help illuminate the general's words.

Finally, I produced this new edition to improve the accuracy of the transcriptions. Hamlin thought it best to tidy up Ewell's letters for the benefit of his readers. To that end, he eliminated abbreviations, corrected spellings, removed duplicate words, and added punctuation. While his corrections make Ewell's correspondence easier to read, they dilute the letters of their original flavor. This edition leaves the letters closer to their written form. Spellings and abbreviations have been left as Ewell wrote them; punctuation marks and extra letters, when added, are enclosed in brackets; and duplicate words, when eliminated from the text, are cited in the footnotes.

However, to render Ewell's correspondence intelligible to modern eyes some editorial work was necessary. The general ended sentences in every way imaginable: with commas, semicolons, colons, and dashes. Often he would end a sentence with no punctuation at all, and simply start the following sentence with a dash. I have chosen to end all of his sentences with periods. Likewise, Ewell often used dashes in place of commas and semicolons. In some cases, I have left these as he wrote them, but when a comma or a semicolon is clearly called for, I have changed it. Conversely, Ewell almost always used commas as a substitute for apostrophes. These too I have changed. On rare occasions, he would leave a long gap between the end of one sentence and the beginning of the next rather than start a new paragraph, and often when he did start a new paragraph, he failed to indent it. I have eliminated such idiosyncrasies. Similarly, I have standardized as much as possible the irregular alignment and spacing of the elements with which Ewell began and ended his letters—dates, names of persons and places, salutations, complimentary closings, and signatures. Also, Ewell followed a common practice of his time in rendering abbreviations: he typically included the first three or so letters of a word while expressing the final letter as an underscored superscript. Thus, in abbreviating "General," he would usually write, "Genl"; for "February," he would write, "Feb^{y}"; and so on. To avoid typesetting problems and ensure a cleaner appearance, I have eliminated the superscripts and underscoring. Therefore, with the examples just cited, "Genl" becomes "Genl" and "Feb^{y}" becomes "Feby." Where the meaning of an abbreviation might be unclear, I have supplied omitted letters in brackets or clarification in a footnote. Finally, words that Ewell underlined, usually for emphasis, have been italicized.

In preparing these letters for publication, I have received help from various quarters. First and foremost I wish to thank members of the Ewell family who have supported me in this project. Stan Aylor and Kenton McCartney kindly provided me with photographs of Ewell's brothers and sisters for this volume, while Mildred Ewell provided valuable assistance in identifying family members mentioned by the general in his letters. I have greatly benefited from their help and support. No less helpful were Wayne and Noel Garland, Bill Toomey, Noel Harrison, Carolyn Parsons, Robert Krick, Eric Mink, Douglas Murphy, Jim Holmberg, and Terry Jones, each of whom, in one way or another, assisted me in my research.

For the use of General Ewell's letters I am indebted to the staffs at a number of repositories, including the Library of Congress, the United States Military Academy, the College of William and Mary, the University of North Carolina, the University of South Carolina, the Museum of the Confederacy, the Filson Historical Society, the Huntington Library, Duke University, the Virginia Historical Society, the Western Reserve Historical Society, the Alexandria Public Library, the Maryland Historical Society, and the Tennessee State Library and Archives. In addition, Mildred Tyner and Jerry Wilbourn kindly allowed me to use letters from their personal collections. To all these people and institutions, I offer my sincere thanks.

To Scot Danforth, Thomas Wells, Gene Adair, Pete Carmichael, Robert E. L. Krick, and others associated with the publication process at the University of Tennessee Press, I extend my gratitude for making this book a reality.

Abbreviations

BSE	Benjamin Stoddert Ewell.
CB	Campbell Brown.
ESE	Elizabeth Stoddert Ewell Jr.
F	Frame(s).
FHS	Brown-Ewell Family Papers, Filson Historical Society, Louisville, KY.
LC	Richard Stoddert Ewell Papers, Library of Congress, Washington, DC.
LCB	Lizinka Campbell Brown (Ewell).
LE	Lizzie Ewell.
M	Microcopy.
NA	National Archives, Washington, DC.
OR	United States War Department. *The War of the Rebellion: A Compilation of the Official Records of the Union and Confederate Armies.* 128 vols. Washington, DC: U.S. Government Printing Office, 1880–1901.
PBE	Polk, Brown, and Ewell Family Papers (#605), Southern Historical Collection, Wilson Library, University of North Carolina at Chapel Hill.
R	Roll.
RG	Record Group.
RLE	Rebecca Lowndes Ewell.
RSE	Richard Stoddert Ewell.
TSLA	Campbell Brown and Richard S. Ewell Papers, Tennessee State Library and Archives, Nashville.

TTG   Thomas Tasker Gantt.

USMA   Special Collections, Manuscript Collection, Richard S. Ewell, USMA 1840, United States Military Academy Library, West Point, NY.

WM   Benjamin Stoddert Ewell Papers, Special Collections Research Center, Swem Library, College of William and Mary, Williamsburg, VA.

Letter Sources

The numbers following each of the sources listed below refer to the numbers assigned to the letters in the main text of this volume.

Bonham, Milledge Luke, Papers. South Caroliniana Library, the University of South Carolina, Columbia, SC: 80.

Brown, Campbell, and Richard S. Ewell Papers, Tennessee State Library and Archives, Nashville, TN: 157, 174, 186.

Brown-Ewell Family Papers, Filson Historical Society, Louisville, KY: 79, 81, 83, 120, 122, 127, 136, 138–40, 147, 149, 151, 152, 163, 165.

Confederate Military Leaders Collection, Eleanor S. Brockenbrough Library, Museum of the Confederacy, Richmond, VA: 85, 90, 113.

Early Family Papers. Mss1 Ea765 b 11–72, Virginia Historical Society, Richmond, VA: 105.

Early Papers. Library of Congress, Washington, DC: 107.

Ewell, Benjamin Stoddert, Papers. Special Collections Research Center, Swem Library, College of William and Mary, Williamsburg, VA: 24, 28, 30–32, 110, 133.

Ewell, Benjamin Stoddert, and Richard Stoddert Ewell Papers. Manuscript Department, William R. Perkins Library, Duke University, Durham, NC: 94.

Ewell Letter Book, 1862–1865. Rare Book, Manuscript, and Special Collections Library, Duke University, Durham, NC: 112, 129, 131.

Ewell, Richard S., compiled service record. M331, R89, NA, Washington, DC: 108.

Ewell, Richard S., file. United States Military Academy Cadet Application Papers, 1836, M688, RG94, R103, National Archives, Washington, DC: 1.

Ewell, Richard S., to J. E. B. Stuart, 14 May 1862. Huntington Library, San Marino, CA, SA 17: 97. (This item is reproduced by permission of the Huntington Library.)

Ewell, Richard Stoddert, Papers. Library of Congress, Washington, DC: 4, 6–10, 12–23, 25–27, 29, 33–37, 39–50, 52–56, 58–77, 82, 86–89, 91–93, 96, 99, 102–4, 106, 111, 117, 119, 126, 137, 141, 145, 154, 158, 160, 161, 168, 172, 173, 175, 179, 181, 182, 185.

Ewell, R. S., to James Lyons, 25 May 1863. Huntington Library, San Marino, CA, BR Box 36: 109. (This item is reproduced by permission of the Huntington Library.)

Fredericksburg and Spotsylvania County Battlefields Memorial National Military Park, Fredericksburg, VA: 183.

Hamlin, Percy G., ed. *The Making of a Soldier: Letters of General R. S. Ewell.* Richmond, VA: Whittet & Shepperson, 1935: 5, 146.

Harris, David B., Papers. Rare Book, Manuscript, and Special Collections Library, Duke University, Durham, NC: 84.

Johnson, Bradley, Papers. Rare Book, Manuscript, and Special Collections Library, Duke University, Durham, NC: 101.

Johnson, John Lipscomb. *The University Memorial: Biographical Sketches of Alumni of the University of Virginia Who Fell in the Confederate War.* Baltimore: Turnbull Brothers, 1871: 100.

Lossing, Benjamin J. *Pictorial History of the Civil War in the United States of America.* Hartford, CT: T. Belknap, Publisher, 1868: 180.

Milligen Collection. Manuscript Division, Maryland Historical Society, Baltimore, MD: 177.

New York Herald, 26 June 1865: 135. (Also published in James D. McCabe Jr., *Life and Campaigns of General Robert E. Lee* [Atlanta: National Publishing Company, 1866].)

Palmer, William P., Collection. Mss. 3194, Civil War Miscellany, Western Reserve Historical Society, Cleveland, OH: 118.

Polk, Brown, and Ewell Family Papers (#605). Southern Historical Collection, Wilson Library, University of North Carolina at Chapel Hill: 51, 57, 78, 95, 98, 114, 115, 121, 123–125, 128, 132, 134, 142–44, 150, 153, 155, 156, 159, 162, 164, 166, 167, 169–71, 176, 178, 184.

Roche, Thomas T. "The Bloody Angle," 3 September 1881, *Philadelphia Weekly Times:* 130.

Special Collections, Manuscript Collection, United States Military Academy Library, West Point, NY: 2, 3, 11.

Tyner, Mildred: 116.

United States War Department. *The War of the Rebellion: A Compilation of the Official Records of the Union and Confederate Armies.* 128 vols. Washington, DC: U.S. Government Printing Office, 1880–1901: 148.

Wilbourn, Jerry: 38.

Introduction

It is the fate of some men to be remembered for the triumphs in their lives; it is the fate of others to be remembered for their failures. Richard Stoddert Ewell falls into the latter class of men. Despite many notable successes in his career, first as a United States dragoon and later as a Confederate general, he is largely remembered for the role he played in a rare defeat: Gettysburg.

By then, Ewell had been an army officer for nearly a quarter century. His military career had started in 1836 when he accepted an appointment to the United States Military Academy. Although not as well prepared as classmates such as George Thomas and William Tecumseh Sherman, Ewell performed capably, and at the end of four years he stood thirteenth in his class. Even at that young age, he had the makings of a soldier, a fact recognized by the academy staff, who appointed him an officer in the cadet corps.

Upon graduation Ewell became a lieutenant in the 1st United States Dragoons and was sent to Arkansas and Missouri, where he learned the nuts and bolts of running a military post. He also learned how to command men. At first, he demanded obedience and enforced it with iron discipline and sharp rebukes, but in time he came to learn "that kindness gives a far more perfect control over the human, as well as brute races, than harshness and cruelty."[1] Many officers never learn that lesson.

As an officer at a small frontier post, Ewell shouldered a multitude of responsibilities, not the least of which was dealing with contractors looking for work. Patience was not one of Ewell's virtues, and the contractors' impertinence pushed him to the limit of his endurance. "They will sit in my room for hours at a time very often before they will tell their business and quit although I have an office for their express benefit," he complained to his sister Rebecca. "As for hints you might as well try them upon a runaway horse. Take up a book or leave the room they will wait as cool as a cucumber untill you are through with the book, or for that matter inter[r]upt you with some such question as

'Well do you know any news about more forces coming out here' repeated for perhaps the twentieth time. The brutes actually put me in a furor sometimes."[2]

The letters that Ewell wrote in the 1840s devote far more ink to social outings than to military matters, however. While on duty at Jefferson Barracks, he accompanied his superior, Colonel Stephen Kearny, to a party in St. Louis. "[I]t was one of those assemblages that very properly are called . . . Tea fights," he explained to his sister, "that is to say there was no dancing but the company was expected to amuse itself by flirtations &c &c. Very much contrary to my expectations the evening instead of being dull & tiresome was to me directly the reverse and I regretted very much when a few drops of rain dispersed the company at 12 o'clock at night."[3]

As a cadet at West Point Ewell had vowed never to marry, but life on the frontier undermined that conviction. After just a few months at an isolated post, he was writing to Rebecca: "I really think if you can find any person about Stony Lonesome who would like a military life and who is fair to look upon that I would quit the lonesome life of a bachelor. Should you find one that you think will answer and that you can recommend you can give a letter of introduction and send her out. Maybe as there is a large lot to pick from you had better send half a dozen so I can take my choice."[4] Although he was being facetious, thoughts of marriage had obviously entered his mind. Unfortunately, there were few women in the territories from which to choose. Even at St. Louis, Ewell found the pickings slim. "This is the worst Country for single ladies I ever saw in my life," he complained to his brother Ben. "They are hardly allowed to come of age before they are engaged to be married however ugly they may be. . . . I have not seen a pretty Girl or interesting one since I have been here."[5]

Recruiting duty in Louisville, Kentucky, afforded Ewell the opportunity to meet a wider circle of women. The letters he wrote from that city early in 1845 reflect a young man intoxicated by romance. "There are a number of *beautiful* women in this place," he confessed, "and as unsophisticated a personage as myself would most certainly fall a victim were it not, that one heals the wounds left by another."[6] Despite meeting a number of eligible ladies, Ewell returned to his company no closer to marriage than before.

With the coming of the Mexican War in 1846, the young officer's thoughts abruptly turned from love to war. By then he had been in the army for six years, and he was eager to taste combat. By pulling a few strings, he managed to have himself transferred to Company F, commanded by First Lieutenant Philip Kearny, which had orders to proceed to Mexico. Kearny's company served briefly under General Zachary Taylor in northern Mexico before joining General Winfield Scott's army in its march on Mexico City. At a mountain called Cerro Gordo, Scott routed the Mexican army under General Antonio Santa Anna, clearing the road to Mexico City. Like many in the army, Ewell thought the victory signaled the end of the war. "This country is to all intents & purposes conquered," the young imperialist wrote. "We have only to send home the volunteers & keep possession for a year or two & extend our laws to make this a part of the United States."[7]

However, much hard fighting still lay ahead. Scott unwisely halted his army short of the capital and opened negotiations with the Mexican government, giving Santa Anna time to raise another army. Scott had no choice but to resume offensive operations. Before doing so, he sent Captain Robert E. Lee of his staff on a reconnaissance to the Pedregal, a large lava bed south of the city. Kearny and Ewell accompanied Lee, engaging the Mexicans in a brief nighttime skirmish. It was Ewell's first time under fire, and he seems to have relished the experience: "Some 200 rancheros fired upon [us] from the crevices of the rocks &c. but we dismounted & soon convinced them it was no place for Mexicans," he wrote his mother.[8]

As a member of General Scott's headquarters guard, Ewell had ample opportunity to observe Lee in action, and for the man who would be his future chief he had only praise. "By his daring reconnois[s]ances pushed up to the cannon's mouth he has enabled Genl Scott to fight his battles almost without leaving his tent," Dick told Ben. "His modest, quiet deportment is perfectly refreshing compared with the folly & bombast of the Genls & Officers made by Mr Polk."[9]

Lee's reconnaissance prompted Scott to order a turning movement. In the heavy fighting that followed, the Mexican army was routed. Kearny and Ewell pursued the fleeing enemy down a narrow causeway, directly toward a Mexican fort. A blast from a cannon greeted the horsemen as they reached the works. Kearny pitched to the ground with a canister ball in his arm, while Ewell lost two horses. Disregarding the danger to himself, Ewell grabbed his chief by the waist and helped him to the rear.

Kearny would survive his wound, but others were not so lucky. Ewell's younger brother Tom died leading an attack at Cerro Gordo, while his cousin Levi Gantt fell in the final attack at Mexico City. For Ewell, it was a tragic introduction to war.

With the capture of its capital city, the Mexican government sued for peace. By 1848 the American army was heading home. Ewell returned to duty on the frontier, manning forts in territories recently ceded by Mexico to the U.S.

government. For the next twelve years he struggled to maintain the national authority in a lawless, often violent land. Clashes between Native Americans, Mexicans, and Americans were commonplace and frequently led to bloodshed. "They murder, each the other . . . without the slightest remorse and as if they wanted to see which was the most atrocious," Ewell informed his niece, Lizzie.[10]

Ewell often found himself in the saddle for days at a time chasing down murderers, thieves, and deserters. On one occasion, he helped rescue a young Mexican girl from the Apaches. In response, the territory's grateful settlers proclaimed him a hero. "The people made a great fuss about the child," Ewell told Lizzie, "and not knowing how to thank Providence for the safe recovery, vented their gratitude in making a fuss over me. I was marched into the convention, had a county called after me, and a public hall, all of which under a different description, would appear very ridiculous."[11]

Such events were unusual, however. For Ewell, most days consisted of dry routine. In an effort to combat boredom, he tended a garden, hunted game birds, and poled for fish. He encouraged others to do the same. As he explained to his brother, Ben: "Unless one drinks or gambles it is necessary to keep from absolute stagnation that interest should be taken in something. . . . it is necessary to get up some outside humbug to take interest in & not to let yourself know that it is humbug."[12]

Ewell devoted a great deal of time to the pursuit of wealth. Having grown up in poverty, he placed a high value on financial security. In an effort to gain fiscal independence, he raised sheep and cattle, invested in stocks, and contemplated driving dray horses to California for sale to prospectors. His most promising venture, though, was investment in a silver mine. "The Pa[t]agonia mine (so they call the one in which I am interested) is fast sinking towards the centre of the earth," he fairly chortled to Lizzie. "It is the darkest, gloomiest looking, cavern you can imagine—about 50 feet deep with prospects looking quite bright—I have been offered $1000, for my interest, having at that time expended about $100, so if we fail, the croakers cant say it was an absurd speculation."[13]

Such activities did not cause him to neglect his social obligations. As a post commander, Ewell was expected to play host to passing travelers, a duty that was always more of a burden to him than a source of pleasure. "I have been entertaining for the last week a French Priest and would rather have the 7 year itch than see him come around again," he complained in a letter to Lizzie. "The fact is my house is a sort of tavern & I am annoyed to death at the impudent & unblushing pushing of these people."[14]

America was then a hodgepodge of ethnic and racial groups. Few escaped Ewell's notice—or his censure. He described Indians as "compounds of children & foxes," Irish and Germans as "low foreignors," and Mexicans as "barbarians." His criticism frequently extended to his superiors. "Maj. Steen who commanded for two years is the greatest liar & scamp in the world & a miserable old setting hen," he told Lizzie, "& his successor is too much of an invalid to attend[,] as he ought, to his duties."[15]

The Civil War forced aside older men such as Steen and gave younger and more enterprising men, like Ewell, an opportunity to advance. Ewell viewed the coming war with trepidation, however. Like many Virginians, he was a political moderate and viewed the prospect of Civil War with horror. "Every one here is on the tenter hooks of impatience to know what the Southern States will do," he informed Lizzie. "Officers generally are very much averse to any thing like civil war, though some of the younger ones are a little warlike. The truth is in the army there are no sectional feelings and many from extreme ends of the Union are the most intimate friends."[16]

Although Ewell had grown up in a slave society and had owned at least two slaves prior to the Civil War, he bitterly regretted the South's decision to secede. He had devoted his entire adult life to the service of the United States; he had fought and bled under its flag. He later wrote that he "clung to the last ray of hope like a drowning man to straws." Yet, when forced to take sides, Ewell reluctantly cast his lot with the South. He did so neither for money nor the hope of advancement but from what he described as "a painful sense of duty" toward his family, his neighbors, and Virginia. Of his decision, he would later write: "It was like death to me."[17]

Because of his military experience, Ewell received a commission in the Confederate army. In just nine months, he went from being a captain in charge of a one-hundred-man company to being a major general in charge of a ten-thousand-man division. Battles were frequent and on a scale unmatched in American history. Although Ewell had seen his share of combat in the Mexican War, the carnage that he witnessed between countrymen sickened him. "It may be all very well to wish young heroes to be in a fight, but for my part I would be satisfied never to see another field," he lamented to Lizzie. "What pleasure can there be in seeing thousands of dead & dying in every horrible agony—torn to pieces by artillery &c. many times the wounded being left on the field for 24 hours before they can be cared for? I wish this war could be brought to a close, but except by the hands of providence I can see no way of its coming to an end."[18]

Ewell blamed the war on "fanatical abolitionists & unp[r]incipled politicians, backed by women in petticoats & pants and children." As he reminded his niece, "Such horrors as war brings about are not to be stopped when people want to get home. It opens a series of events that no one can see to the end."[19] Ewell fought for the Confederacy out of a sense of duty, but he never became a Southern radical. Indeed, he found secession and the bloodshed and destruction it spawned distasteful.

Thousands of Southerners had to flee their homes to escape the destruction. Among them was Ewell's cousin and fiancée, Lizinka Campbell Brown. Ewell had loved his winsome cousin since they were children, and in December 1861 she consented to be his wife. Ewell was delighted. "To this time I feel as though all human calculations were overthrown and I have hope & faith in the future," he told her. "At all events it seems to me that the future has more to look forward to than I ever thought possible."[20]

But while Ewell's future looked bright, the future of the Confederacy did not. Union victories in Tennessee and Kentucky in 1862 threatened to bring a quick end to the rebellion. The Confederate armies simply needed more soldiers. To help compensate for the thousands of German and Irish immigrants who were fighting for the North, Ewell advocated that the South arm its slaves. "[T]hey would be a fair offset & we would not as now be fighting kings against men to use a comparison from Chequers," he told Lizzie.[21] The suggestion, though pragmatic, was far too revolutionary for the time. It would be three more years before Southern leaders would even consider such a radical step. By then it was too late.

Meanwhile Ewell was making a reputation for himself as Stonewall Jackson's right-hand man. Initially, Ewell had a low opinion of his fellow Virginian, but that changed during the 1862 Shenandoah Valley Campaign. When the campaign commenced, Ewell thought Jackson crazy, but as he told a fellow officer, "before he ended it I thought him inspired."[22] Jackson's opinion of Ewell rose in like measure. In battle after battle, Jackson found his eccentric subordinate to be brave, judicious, and energetic—an officer who could be trusted to carry out an assignment, no matter how difficult. The fighting in the Valley created a bond between the two generals that ended only with Jackson's death at Chancellorsville.

Ewell was not with Jackson at his death, having been absent from the army since the Battle of Groveton in August 1862, when a Union bullet shattered his left knee. By the time he was able to return to duty, Jackson was dead. Lee appointed Ewell to take his place as commander of the Second Corps.

Before rejoining the army, Ewell and Lizinka became husband and wife. Some officers claimed that the loss of a leg and the accession of a wife sapped Ewell of his fighting spirit, but nothing in Ewell's subsequent record bears that out. He was the same man after his marriage that he had been before. What had changed was his situation. In 1862 Ewell had been a division commander under Jackson; in 1863 he was a corps commander under Lee. In the latter capacity, Ewell enjoyed far more independence of movement and received far less explicit instructions.

Critics claimed that he was not up to independent command, but the record clearly proves otherwise. At the Battle of Second Winchester, during the march through Pennsylvania, and on the opening day at Gettysburg, Ewell's leadership was able—even brilliant. Only when directly under Lee's supervision and subject to his discretionary orders did Ewell falter. That first came to light on July 1, 1863, at Gettysburg when Lee ordered his subordinate to capture Cemetery Hill "if practicable." Without reinforcements, Ewell deemed that it was not practicable and therefore did not attempt it, a decision for which he has been unjustly condemned. It mattered not that Ewell was hampered by restrictive orders, false information, and a lack of support by his fellow officers, nor that the Union forces occupied an unusually strong position bolstered by stone walls and massed artillery. The army needed a scapegoat, and Ewell fit the bill.

Lee's confidence in Ewell markedly diminished after Gettysburg, a trend accelerated by defeats that autumn at Bristoe Station and Rappahannock Station. A poor showing at the Battle of Spotsylvania Court House in May 1864 sealed his fate. From then on Lee sought to replace him, an opportunity that came two weeks later when the Army of Northern Virginia faced the enemy across the North Anna River. Ewell fell ill and had to temporarily relinquish command to his subordinate, Major General Jubal Early. Lee seized the occasion to make the change permanent. He had Ewell transferred to the Department of Richmond, a desk job that the old dragoon considered tantamount to being "laid on the shelf."[23]

As the city's military commander, Ewell had the responsibility of supporting Lee's troops north of the James River. His finest moment of the war came on September 29, 1864, at Fort Harrison, when he held twenty-five thousand Union soldiers at bay with a ragtag force until Lee arrived from Petersburg with reinforcements. A Confederate soldier who fought at Fort Harrison remembered that Ewell led from the front "and by his cool courage and presence wherever the fight was hottest, contributed as much to the victory gained as any one man could have done."[24]

That was Ewell's way. A brilliant combat general, he could always be found where the fighting was most fierce, rallying troops, giving orders, and leading charges. He had an excellent eye for terrain and possessed military instincts that at times seemed inspired. Only a few weeks earlier, on July 30, 1864, he told his wife that he had an uneasy feeling that the enemy was about to "try some previously unheard of plan of taking Richmond."[25] That very day Union troops detonated a mine under Lee's lines at Petersburg, resulting in the Battle of the Crater.

The Confederacy, low in both men and supplies, collapsed in 1865. On April 2, Union forces broke Lee's lines, forcing the Army of Northern Virginia to evacuate both Petersburg and Richmond. Secretary of War John C. Breckinridge ordered Ewell to burn the capital's tobacco warehouses to prevent them from falling into Union hands. Although Ewell saw the danger in such a measure, he carried out the distasteful order. A general conflagration ensued, and much of the city went up in flames. Many held Ewell responsible for the destruction, a charge the general vehemently denied.[26]

Turning his back on the burning city, Ewell joined Lee's army in its retreat toward Appomattox Court House. He never made it. On April 6, Union cavalry severed Ewell's and Lieutenant General Richard H. Anderson's corps from the rest of the Confederate army. Union infantry closed in for the kill. Outnumbered and surrounded, Ewell had no choice but surrender. For the first time in his career, he was a prisoner. To the end, he blamed the South's demise neither on its citizens nor its soldiers but on the politicians in Richmond.

For the next three months, Ewell languished behind bars at Fort Warren in Boston Harbor. Although the war was over, the passions incited by Abraham Lincoln's assassination remained fresh. Until they subsided, all that Ewell and other imprisoned Confederate officers could do was wait. Ewell helped pass the time by writing to Lizinka, who was herself a prisoner in St. Louis. The many letters he wrote to her discussed important issues, such as the propriety of Southern officers taking the Oath of Allegiance while Confederate troops were still in the field, the prospect of black suffrage, and the question of whether Southern leaders should remain in the United States or move overseas.

Ewell had opinions on all these matters. As for supporting the United States government, he was clear. "I for my part am heartily anxious to become a law-abiding member of the community," he asserted, "if allowed & would be the best one to be found." In fact, he vowed "to put down guerillas or stop the mouths of demagogue talkers of sedition—the worse of the two—provided the govt establishes such an office." "I am sick of halfway men," he growled. Ewell was as good as his word. For the rest of his life he was a model American citizen.[27]

Ewell gained his freedom in July 1865. He spent his remaining years managing farms in Tennessee and Mississippi. His postwar letters touch on problems common to Southern planters in the Reconstruction Era: the high cost of supplies, adverse weather, broken machinery, insect infestations, and falling cotton prices. Securing reliable workers at a reasonable price was Ewell's most vexing problem. "I am as usual fretting my soul away because of the darkies who wont see that 12.50 & rations are any particular reasons for working hard," he fumed to Lizzie. "In fact they think they are conferring a favor on us. . . . The fact is they are crazy half the time and are constantly apparently trying to see if they are really free."[28] Like most Southern planters, Ewell had never had to negotiate with blacks for their labor, and it would take time to adjust to the change. Time, however, was not on Ewell's side. He died just seven years after the war, on January 25, 1872. He was not yet fifty-five.

History has not been kind to Ewell's memory. The Army of Northern Virginia's foremost historian, Douglas Southall Freeman, drawing on biased accounts, portrayed Ewell as a feisty but hesitant general entirely unsuited for independent command.

Later writers picked up on Freeman's themes. One modern biographer has characterized the general as hopelessly indecisive; another portrays him as a borderline psychotic. A third writer chose to focus on Ewell's more obvious traits, titling his article, "One-Legged Dick Ewell, Lee's Cussin' General." Ewell deserves far better. Competent and energetic, enterprising and brave, he was worthy of the high rank he attained, a fact he demonstrated time and again at places such as Front Royal, Port Republic, Gaines's Mill, and the Wilderness. As for his capacity for independent command, one has only to examine his record. Of the four battles in which Ewell commanded, he won three: Cross Keys, Second Winchester, and Fort Harrison. The only battle as a commander that he lost was Sailor's Creek. Even then, he surrendered only after being surrounded by a vastly superior foe. It was a record of which any general might be proud.

Ewell's record as a man is more difficult to assess. He had a sharp tongue and could be as prickly as a porcupine. He was highly critical of others and expressed no reservations about the institution of slavery. But he was also a kindhearted, generous, modest man, hardworking and truthful, who possessed a keen sense of humor and who was always upright in his dealings with others.

Such traits are evident in his letters. In them, we see the man himself—sometimes admirable, sometimes flawed, but always interesting. No one who reads them will ever view Ewell the same way again.

Notes

1. RSE to Joseph Lewis, 13 June 1865, Box 1, Folder 15, PBE (letter 153, this volume).
2. RSE to RLE, 13 Nov. 1841, LC (letter 12).
3. RSE to RLE, 25 Oct. 1844, LC (letter 20).
4. RSE to RLE, 13 Nov. 1841, LC (letter 12).
5. RSE to BSE, 9 Aug. 1844, LC (letter 18).
6. RSE to BSE, 28 Feb. 1845, LC (letter 22).
7. RSE to BSE, 3 May 1847, LC (letter 26).
8. RSE to Mother, 1 Sept. 1847, LC (letter 27).
9. RSE to BSE, 25 Nov. 1847, LC (letter 29).
10. RSE to LE, 26 Oct. 1859, LC (letter 73).
11. RSE to LE, 2 May 1860, LC (letter 75).
12. RSE to BSE, 28 July [1856], PBE (letter 57).
13. RSE to LE, 10 Aug. 1858, LC (letter 64).
14. RSE to LE, 21 Dec. 1858, LC (letter 67).
15. RSE to LE, 16 May 1858, LC (letter 63).
16. RSE to LE, 22 Jan. 1861, LC (letter 77).
17. RSE to Joseph Lewis, 13 June 1865, Box 1, Folder 15, PBE (letter 153); RSE to Lizinka Ewell, 11 June 1865, FHS (letter 152).
18. RSE to LE, 20 July 1862, LC (letter 99).
19. RSE to LE, 14 Aug. 1862, LC (letter 102).
20. RSE to LCB, undated letter fragment (ca. 10–11 Jan. 1862), FHS (letter 88).
21. RSE to LE, 20 July 1862, LC (letter 99).
22. Jackson, *Memoirs,* p. 287
23. RSE to BSE, 20 July 1864, LC (letter 126).
24. Johnson, "Fort Gilmer," 499.
25. RSE to LCB, 30 July 1864, PBE (letter 128).
26. McCabe, *Life and Campaigns,* 612n.
27. RSE to LCB, 12 May 1865 and 8 June 1865, FHS (letters 138 and 151).
28. RSE to LE, 7 Jan. 1866, LC (letter 172).

Ewell Family Chart

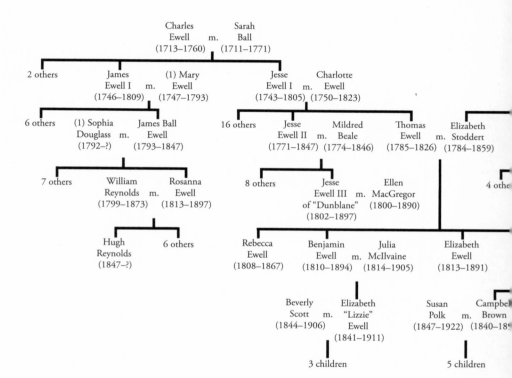

Charles Ewell m. Sarah Ball
(1713–1760) (1711–1771)

2 others

James Ewell I m. (1) Mary Ewell
(1746–1809) (1747–1793)

Jesse Ewell I m. Charlotte Ewell
(1743–1805) (1750–1823)

6 others

(1) Sophia Douglass m. James Ball Ewell
(1792–?) (1793–1847)

16 others

Jesse Ewell II m. Mildred Beale
(1771–1847) (1774–1846)

Thomas Ewell m. Elizabeth Stoddert
(1785–1826) (1784–1859)

7 others

William Reynolds m. Rosanna Ewell
(1799–1873) (1813–1897)

8 others

Jesse Ewell III of "Dunblane" m. Ellen MacGregor
(1802–1897) (1800–1890)

4 othe[rs]

Hugh Reynolds
(1847–?)

6 others

Rebecca Ewell
(1808–1867)

Benjamin Ewell m. Julia McIlvaine
(1810–1894) (1814–1905)

Elizabeth Ewell
(1813–1891)

Beverly Scott m. Elizabeth "Lizzie" Ewell
(1844–1906) (1841–1911)

Susan Polk m. Campbel[l] Brown
(1847–1922) (1840–18[ ])

3 children

5 children

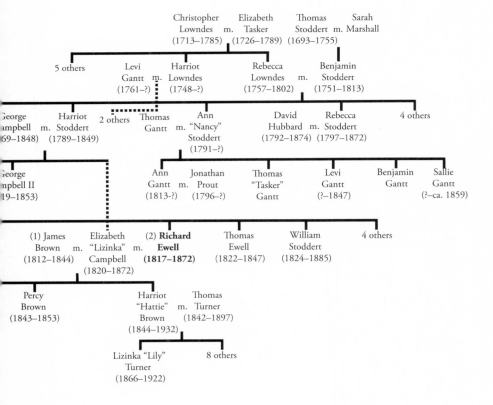

Christopher Lowndes (1713–1785) m. Elizabeth Tasker (1726–1789)   Thomas Stoddert (1693–1755) m. Sarah Marshall

5 others   Levi Gantt (1761–?) m. Harriot Lowndes (1748–?)   Rebecca Lowndes (1757–1802) m. Benjamin Stoddert (1751–1813)

George Campbell (1769–1848) m. Harriot Stoddert (1789–1849)   2 others   Thomas Gantt   Ann m. "Nancy" Stoddert (1791–?)   David Hubbard (1792–1874) m. Rebecca Stoddert (1797–1872)   4 others

George Campbell II (1819–1853)   Ann Gantt (1813-?) m. Jonathan Prout (1796–?)   Thomas "Tasker" Gantt   Levi Gantt (?–1847)   Benjamin Gantt   Sallie Gantt (?–ca. 1859)

(1) James Brown (1812–1844) m. Elizabeth "Lizinka" Campbell (1820–1872) m. (2) **Richard Ewell** **(1817–1872)**   Thomas Ewell (1822–1847)   William Stoddert (1824–1885)   4 others

Percy Brown (1843–1853)   Harriot "Hattie" Brown (1844–1932) m. Thomas Turner (1842–1897)

Lizinka "Lily" Turner (1866–1922)   8 others

The Letters of General Richard S. Ewell

April 13th 1862

Dear Lizinka;

I write after three days of
intense suspense – Contradictory reports have been
in circulation in regard to our affairs out west –
But a mulatto spy sent into the enemy's lines
has just reported that he has been in Washington
and that it is reported there among them
that Beauregard has been defeated with a loss
of 17000 prisoners. his own arm shot off &c. &c –
– I have not yet told this to b nor will I do so
untill there is some confirmation or better news
over the wires – My first care in this is for
our country. but who in the country will suffer more than you & in whose suffering will
I feel more sympathy than in yours – I do
not feel for myself for all of my cares are absorbed in others – While I write I have to be
annoyed by staring stupid boors – who are satisfied to be in the room with an officer of
high rank, although he may be a mere ephemeral production of the Prest, and who do not
care if they bore him or not, so they are not

A sample of Ewell's handwriting. (Polk-Brown-Ewell Papers, Southern Historical Collection, University of North Carolina)

Chapter 1

West Point, 1836–1840

Richard S. Ewell was born on February 8, 1817, at "Halcyon House" in the District of Columbia, the Georgetown home of his grandfather Benjamin Stoddert. A man of substance, Stoddert had been one of the young nation's leading merchants and its first secretary of the navy. Richard's mother, Elizabeth, was the secretary's eldest daughter and through her mother's side of the family claimed ties to many of Maryland's foremost families.

Dick Ewell's father was a Virginian. Thomas Ewell had grown up at "Bel Air," a Prince William County plantation two dozen miles southwest of the capital city. He married Elizabeth in 1807 and fathered ten children by her, eight of whom survived infancy. Thomas supported his growing family by practicing medicine. A brilliant man, he wrote several books prior to his death in 1826. By then the family had fallen on hard times. Alcoholism had cost Thomas both his medical practice and his reputation, and at the time of his death his family was reduced to scratching out a living at a farm called "Stony Lonesome" in Prince William County.

Thomas's death in 1826 plunged the family still deeper into poverty. To put food on the table, Mrs. Ewell taught school while Dick and his brothers worked the farm. Although Elizabeth Ewell could not give her sons ease or material possessions, she did everything in her power to secure them professions. For her eldest son, Benjamin, she wrangled an appointment to West Point; she scraped together enough money to put another son, Paul, into medical school; and she sent a third son, Thomas, to study law with relatives in Tennessee.

Dick followed Ben into the army. Thanks to the influence of a prominent uncle, George W. Campbell, Dick received an appointment to the United States Military Academy in 1836. He thrived under the school's strict military regimen and in his final year was appointed a lieutenant in the cadet corps. He graduated in 1840, thirteenth in a class of forty-two cadets.

His letters from this period reflect a serious student, determined to make the most of the educational opportunity West Point afforded. But beneath the boy's austere facade one can also see the wry sense of humor that in later years became his trademark.

1. *To Lewis Cass*

Virginia March 28th 1836

Sir,

I accept with pleasure the appointment of Cadet, as tender'd to me by you.[1] Should further instructions be sent, they will reach me, if directed to Greenwich, Prince William, Va.[2] Respectfully

Richard S. Ewell[3]

to the hon.
Lewis Cass
Secretary of War.[4]

I consent to my son's signing articles by which he will bind himself to serve the United States, five years.

Elizabeth Ewell

1. According to Chief Engineer Joseph G. Totten, Ewell was appointed by President Andrew Jackson "in consequence of the revolutionary services of his Grandfather." Ewell's appointment, following that of his brother Benjamin eight years earlier, violated Secretary Cass's policy of appointing no more than one member of each family to the academy. Ewell's uncle George Washington Campbell (1769–1848) undoubtedly imposed upon his friend Jackson to bend the rules in Ewell's favor. Having served at different times as a judge on Tennessee's Supreme Court of Errors and Appeals, as a senator and United States Congressman, as secretary of the treasury, and as minister to Russia, Campbell was one of America's wealthiest and most powerful citizens. John G. Totten to ?, 4 Dec. 1839, M91, R27, NA.

2. The village of Greenwich, Virginia, stood five miles north of Catlett's Station and as many miles west of Bristoe Station. The Ewells' farm, "Stony Lonesome," was slightly more than two miles east of Greenwich.

3. Interestingly, the handwriting of this letter, including Dick's signature, seems to be that of his mother.

4. Lewis Cass (1782–1866) had a long and distinguished public career. A major general of volunteers in the War of 1812, he went on to become governor of the Michigan Territory, secretary of war, minister to France, United States senator, and secretary of state. In 1848 he ran for president on the Democratic ticket but lost the election to Zachary Taylor.

2. To Rebecca Ewell

West Point August 29th 1836

Dear Becca

You must excuse my not writing to you sooner which I would certainly have done but I expected to go into Barracks every day and in Camp we have nothing to write on but the floor not being allowed to keep trunk or table in the tents.[1] The duties here are much more arduous than I had any idea of. We have to walk post eight hours out of the 24, 4 in the day and 4 in the night, and if we do not walk constantly or if we speak to any person while on post we are reported and get 8 or 10 demerit. You are much mistaken when you suppose that I was hurt at your not coming home to help about my clothes. I can't see what right I had to expect anything of the kind and I think I would have been very unreasonable if I had. I wish you would send me the way in which Tasker[2] gave you if you have not forgotten it. they do it here by another way which I do not think is right.[3] You were very cautious about letting it be known that Ben was engaged in Civil Eng. but I had heard it from the Cadets long before I received your letter.[4] Ben appears to be a great favourite with the Cadets, at least I should judge so by what they say of him. They consider him the best Mathematician on the Point and the most intelligent man. They told me that I ought to stand high because I am so much like him. We were often taken for each other before I put on my uniform. On one occasion he was ordered to his quarters in no very gentle terms by one of the Cadet Officers who supposed that it was me. There was a splendid ball given here on the 28th. It was given in the Mess Hall which was adorned with wreaths[,] flags of the different European nations, muskets and swords and presented a most beautiful appearance. The Hall is very large as you may suppose for the whole Corps to dine in at once but it was crowded to overflowing with visitors. I was on guard and of course could not attend and would not if I could. Fire works were kept up untill a late hour, some of which were most beautiful. It was a close[5] night and the rockets would often go above the clouds before they burst giving them the same tints as the sun in the morning. I have no hopes of getting a good standing at this place. The Plebe class consists in all off [*sic*] nearly 150 and is said to be the most intelligent class that has been here for many years. There are several Yankees here who know the whole mathematical course; of course they will stand at the head of the Class. A person who comes here without a knowledge has to contend against those who have been preparing themselves for years under the best teachers and who have used the same class books. The Yankees generally take the lead in almost every class. How are all the good folks in Va? Is old Jim Ball[6] married yet? A certain young lady at Stony L fancied he was paying her attentions. if so she had [better] take him, for then she will have horses to ride about after the parsons whenever she pleases.[7] All of your letter except about 15 lines was taking up in visits. I do not think that you can make any crop [but] grass and weeds. I wrote home some time ago and have not received an answer and begin to feel uneasy. I have no society here yet and a letter gives me more pleasure than anything else. Tasker is the only person who treats me decently. The first thing I knew of Tom's[8] going to the West was your asking me my opinion of it. I had no idea of his going before that.

R S Ewell

Write soon and give me the problem & let me know what is become of Ben. Do you intend remaining at home yourself? It is time for you to rest in your old age.[9]

1. During the summer months, West Point cadets camped outside on the academy's parade ground.
2. Thomas Tasker Gantt was Ewell's first cousin through his mother's younger sister Nancy. He attended West Point from 1831 to 1834 but did not graduate.
3. Ewell seems to be referring to clothing that Rebecca was making for him.
4. Ewell's older brother Benjamin Stoddert Ewell (1810–1894) graduated third in his class in the U.S. Military Academy's Class of 1832. After graduation, he returned to West Point as an assistant professor in mathematics. He resigned his commission in September 1836, shortly after this letter was written, to accept a position as assistant engineer for the Baltimore and Susquehanna Railroad.
5. "Close"—i.e., humid.
6. A neighbor of the Ewell family.
7. Here Ewell is probably referring to his older sister, Elizabeth, who was then twenty-three years old. Rebecca Ewell was not living at Stony Lonesome at this time, and Ewell's younger sister, Virginia (who died one year later), was just sixteen years old.
8. Because she did not have money to give him an education, Elizabeth Ewell Sr. in 1836 sent Dick's younger brother Thomas (1822–1847) to live with her brother William Stoddert in Jackson, Tennessee. Thomas graduated from Nashville College in 1840, pursued a career in law, and eventually ran for the Tennessee state legislature.
9. Ewell was teasing his sister, who was just twenty-eight years old.

United States Military Academy, West Point, as seen from Constitution Island, ca. 1820, from a painting by John R. Smith. (Library of Congress)

3. To Benjamin Ewell

Milty Acdy W. P. Nov 6th 1836

Dear Ben

I have delayed writing to you so long that I am almost ashamed to begin. To tell the truth, there is little or nothing to write about. I have got along pretty well so far in my studies, the knowledge I had of Algebra being of considerable service to me. At least I have not found it necessary to study hard untill within the last week or two. But during the last week I have found it no joke. I was obliged to sit up more than half the night several times or go to the Section room without knowing anything of my lesson. Lt. Bliss[1] is my Proffessor of Math. I like him extremely[—]not the most dignified person though that I have ever seen; he sometimes sets the whole Section to laughing at his grimaces. There are some excellent Mathematicians in the 4th Class; one from Massachusetts has studied the whole course under Ross.[2] I got a letter out of the office for you the other day (which I redirected to York Pa.)[3] dated Camp Leavenwo[r]th, which I suppose you have received before this. Reynolds[4] desires to be remembered to you. Several of the first Class[5] have desired me to ask you for information about Engineering. they wish to enter into something of the kind. It has been the most fortunate thing for me in the world that I did not room with any old Cadets. there are several here who will be deficient on that account.[6] they are always frolicking and spreeing instead of studying. I do not think I am more than 4 or 5 $ in debt owing to the things you gave me.[7] I like W. Point much better than I did some time ago and shall be very well contented if

I get along in my studies. If I do not get along the fault will not be in my not studying. I have seen very few handsome ladies since I have been here and have had nothing to do with them, which I believe is a very good thing as I am apt to think of them rather than of Algebra. Major Alden[8] died last Saturday the 6th and was buried on Sunday with the honours of war. His son had left the week before for Europe on account of his health. I admired the procession very much, but there appeared to be none who cared [in] the least for the deceased. How do you like Engineering? I hope you continue to be pleased with it. They say here if a person wants to make money and is not afraid of giving up the ghost that he can make more money in the south than any where else in the United States. But then he is very apt to catch his death just in time to leave a good sum to his heirs.[9] Eliz. wrote me from home the other day that Miss L. Carter[10] is to be married. I hope you sustain yourself as becomes a man under the affliction. What do you think of Mr Ewell's marriage?[11] I expect there will be another lot of young cousins in a few years. I'll bet the lady has twins the first offstart. The old man had lived single so long when I left home he could not come within 20 steps of a lady without grinning from ear to ear and "casting sheep's eyes at her." (People said his negroe women were the better by it several dollars.)[12] He used to lecture me about going to see the ladies so often (and said it would put bad notions in my head.) What do you think of Tom's going to Uncle William's?[13] Mother wrote to me that she had not heard from Uncle William since early in the summer and that he wanted her to send Tom and William.[14]

Richard S Ewell

1. William Wallace Smith Bliss (1815–1853) graduated from West Point in 1833 and was assistant professor of mathematics there from 1834 to 1840. A gifted linguist, he was said to be fluent in thirteen languages. Bliss was promoted twice in the Mexican War. He later wed Mary Elizabeth Taylor, youngest daughter of General Zachary Taylor. When Taylor became president, Bliss became his private secretary. Following Taylor's death in 1850, Bliss returned to military duty, serving as adjutant general of the army's Western Division. He died of yellow fever during a visit to New Orleans in 1853.
2. Unidentified.
3. Ben was then living in York.
4. Alexander W. Reynolds of Virginia (1817–1876) was then in his fourth year at West Point. He served as an officer in the 1st United States Infantry until the

Mexican War when he became a captain in the Quartermaster Corps. At the outbreak of the Civil War, he joined the Confederate army and commanded a brigade in the Western Theater. After the war, he moved to Egypt, where he served as a colonel in the army of the Khedive.

5. Then and now, fourth-year cadets were members of the First Class. Plebes, by contrast, were in the Fourth Class.

6. Deficient in their studies. A cadet found deficient in his studies might be dismissed from the academy or held back for a year.

7. Ben handed down to his brother books, equipment, and other articles that he had used as a cadet. Even so, Dick found it hard to stay out of debt.

8. Major Roger Alden (?–1836) had served as an officer in the American Revolution. He resigned from the army in 1781 but reentered the service forty-four years later as the military storekeeper. He died on November 5, 1836.

9. The fear may have been of malaria and other fevers.

10. Unidentified.

11. James Ball Ewell Sr. (b. 1793) was a first cousin of Ewell's father. In 1836 he took Emily Matthew Gwynn to be his wife.

12. Ewell seems to be suggesting that James Ewell rewarded his female slaves for sexual favors.

13. William Stoddert (1796–1839) was the younger brother of Ewell's mother, Elizabeth. Stoddert had a law practice in Jackson, Tennessee. He kindly agreed to take his sister's son Thomas under his roof and train him in the law.

14. Ewell's two younger brothers.

4. To Rebecca Ewell

Dear Rebecca,[1]

I may be mistaken but I have been under the impression that you've owed me a letter for the last year instead of my owing[2] you, and think I've documentary evidence to that effect. I always keep a list of my numerous correspondents and[3] answer their letters as soon as recd. I am very glad that Mother has sold Charley. It was certainly the best thing she could have done with him. The price appears to me to be very high; you forget he was getting well stricken in years and was too small to be of any essential service.

You appear to like a horse that cuts capers with you. The rolling feat ought to have given you enough of Charley. You didn't become perfectly infatuated with Dick untill after he tried to run away with you.[4] May be you expect to be so much better off in the next world than in this that you think to be sent there would be the most fortunate event that could happen to you.

There is no probability of my going home next summer. A leave for two months is generally given from June to members of my Class (the third) but being considerably in debt and as it would be very expensive with but little profit I have thought it best to stay here. I should have to spends [*sic*] a good deal of money in clothes, which would be useless after the summer is over. Besides two yrs are not long enough to "forget the little Plough boy that whistled on the lea."[5]

I don't remember the anecdote to which you refer in your last but I assure you I've no idea of making any mystery about the matter. Anything of the kind appears to me to be very silly and affected. The circumstances you mention about the slave must be provoking to Aunt Nancy. All that's wanting to make the story complete is that they should both (Aunt Nancy and Aunt Campbell)[6] dispose of their respective purchases at the same time. Uncle Campbell didn't act with his usual *judgement* to have two persons buying the same thing in different parts of the country. But the blame of course will be laid on the ladies as it generally is whenever anything goes wrong.

Your idea of farming on your own account is capital; but take care lest you give way to avarice. I am afraid you are so much occupied with your privy purse that you will forget to lay up treasures where moth & rust etc.[7]

You[r] letter was almost entirely taken up with slander; you were much mistaken if you supposed such a worldly and yea sinful subject could be purefied by the short text with which you closed. It is very evident that you devote hours and indeed days to your worldly accounts where you give moments to your Heavenly ones. I am sorry Mother thinks me such a Yankee as not to write on account of the postage. I recd a letter from Eliz today; well the first since 17th Jany although I have written twice since.[8] To prove to you that the postage has nothing to do with my wrinting [*sic*] I'll send this unpaid.

Yrs   R S Ewell

P.S. Liz[9] is very much afraid Ben is going to be married.[10] he had better and settle into a steady member of society.

Dear Aunt,[11]

I expect you hardly supposed I would have impudence enough to write to you on the little encouragement you gave me, but give the devil an inch etc. Becca appears to take more interest in scandal than she does in the welfare of the nation. I was quite shocked at the amount of it in her last. I knew she was addicted to it before leaving home[12] but supposed six month[s'] residence with you would have cured her. Remember me to Ben.[13]

Levi[14] says that as you have not answered his last letter he will not send you any message. He has been studying hard lately but will not have to keep it up much longer as the Academic year has nearly expired. His course has been as long as any section of his Class. The sections are made much smaller than they used to be and of course the same numbered section now is higher than when Tasker was here. Then they had but 4 now there are 8.[15]

Yrs   R S Ewell

1. The envelope for this letter is postmarked May 6, suggesting that the letter was written on May 5, 1838.
2. Ewell repeated the word "owing" in the original text.
3. Ewell repeated the word "and."
4. Charley and Dick were horses.
5. This sentence appppeared in the margin of the page and was undoubtedly added as an afterthought to this paragraph. The phrase in quotation marks is a reference to "The Ploughboy," an English folksong that pokes fun at social advancement. The first stanza and chorus of the song are as follows:

    > A flaxen-headed cowboy, as simple as may be,
    > And next a merry ploughboy, I whistled o'er the lea;
    > But now a saucy footman I strut in worsted lace,
    > And soon I'll be a butler, and whey my jolly face.
    > When steward I'm promoted, I'll snip the tradesmen's bill,
    > My master's coffers empty, my pockets for to fill;
    > When lolling in my chariot, so grand a man I'll be;
    >
    > *Chorus:*
    > So great a man, so great a man, so great a man I'll be!
    > You'll forget the little ploughboy, that whistled o'er the lea,
    > You'll forget the little ploughboy, that whistled o'er the lea.

6. Ewell's aunt Harriot Stoddert married George Washington Campbell of Tennessee. Nancy Stoddert, her sister, was married to Thomas Gantt of Maryland.
7. Here Ewell quotes Jesus, who said, "Do not store up for yourselves treasures on earth, where moth and rust destroy, and where thieves break in and steal. But store up for yourselves treasures in heaven, where moth and rust do not destroy, and where thieves do not break in and steal. For where your treasure is, there your heart will be also." Matt. 6:19–21 (New International Version).

8. A small portion of this page was torn out. The editor has supplied the words "account of," "today," and "I have" in these sentences, based on their context and on fragmentary spellings.

9. Ewell's sister Elizabeth.

10. Ben married Julia McIlvaine on April 19, 1839.

11. Nancy Stoddert Gantt.

12. Rebecca Ewell was then living with the Gantt family at "Brook Grove" near Bladensburg, Maryland.

13. Nancy Gantt's younger son.

14. Ewell's cousin Levi Gantt was one year behind Ewell at West Point. He graduated in 1841, near the bottom of his class.

15. Cadets from each class were divided into sections, the brighter students being grouped together in the First Section, the next brightest comprising the Second Section, and so on. By 1838 the number of sections had doubled, reducing the number of cadets in each section by half.

5. To Elizabeth Ewell Sr.

West Point,
October 3, 1839.

Dear Mother:

It has been so long since I have written home that I am actually ashamed to commence a letter. You, however, cannot blame me when you call to mind that two of your consecutive letters last year had their dates, the one in January, the other in June, although I wrote two letters within that time.

Levi appears to be perfectly infatuated with Prince William,[1] which is not to be wondered at as almost any place would be a Paradise to one who had stayed here two years without entering into any of its amusements. Miss Gray[2] must have made a good impression on him; he has not done talking of her yet. I would not have believed that any woman could have made such a change in him. It looks more like magic than anything I ever saw. Formerly, the only way in which he ever showed his admiration for one of the fair sex was by abusing the fortunate lady most unmercifully. But Miss Gray appears to have lighted a flame which he does not try to conceal, with even this artifice.

I am very much obliged to you for your information and advice concerning Miss Susan Macrae,[3] but unfortunately I made a vow many years ago that I would never marry, and my resolutions have been confirmed by my maturer deliberations. You know there are two kinds of persons who never get married; one kind includes those who never "fall in love," the other (to which I belong) those whose hearts are very susceptible, yet owing to this quality are too tender to retain an impression long enough for it to lead to any dangerous consequences.

You expressed a wish in your last letter that I should not remain in the army after graduating, but did not say what you would prefer. I think I have nearly as much aversion to that life as yourself, but you know that the education that we get here does not qualify us for any other than a military life, and unless a man has money, he is forced to enter the army to keep from starving. I am very anxious to ascertain the best Corps of the three (Artillery, Infantry, or Dragoons), which I will be entitled to enter. My inclination would lead me to select the Dragoons since, being stationed in the West, I should have opportunities of resigning and entering upon some more independent way of getting my living.[4] There are so many contradictory accounts of this Corps (the Dragoons) and its duties, that it is necessary to be cautious in selecting it; some make it the most desirable, and others the worst in the army. What would you think of the Marines? I have heard they have three years furlough for three years of duty. The Ordnance (Colonel Bomford's Corps)[5] would be the most desirable on every account, but this requires friends at Washington. The officers receive a third more pay, have nothing to do, and have more privileges than any others in the army.

I wish you would give me Ben's address. I have owed him a letter for a long time, thinking that he would be so much occupied with his wife that a letter would be a bore. However, as he must now be at "leisure," I should like to atone for my neglect as soon as possible.

Levi is too prudent to give me any information on the subject concerning which you referred me to him. There was an advertisement of Ben's in the Alexandria Gazette some time ago for pupils.[6] Do you know whether he has succeeded in obtaining any or not? Don't you think it would be best for a person to stay in the army where he is always sure of a competence, than to be changing his pursuits so many times, and get a situation at last which is scarcely as good as the one he resigns, and which there is little or no chance of bettering? For my part, I like the old saying, "A rolling stone gathers no moss," and shall look well before I give up the bird in the hand for the one in the bush.

It is a pity that Mrs. Dade[7] has left the neighborhood. She was one of the most ladylike and agreeable of the place. I am afraid that all of my old acquaintances will have left the country before I get home again, that is if I ever get home at all, which I am sometimes inclined to doubt. Harrison[8] was delighted with that neighborhood. He says he never enjoyed himself more than he did last summer.

I hope you will excuse any bad spelling and faults in perspicuity that may occur in this as it is my first effort in three months. I have nothing but a French dictionary to correct my spelling with, and it is so much trouble to use it that I am afraid that I have spelled many words improperly, rather than take the trouble to look for them. Major Delafield[9] would not give me a dictionary because I am in debt, although it would be of immense advantage to me. Remember me to all. I have been nearly a week spending all my leisure time on this, and think you ought to reward my industry by a speedy answer.

Yours,
R. S. Ewell.

P.S.:

If I have made any gross blunders in spelling, do tell me what they are. I have been seized with a wish to improve lately. I never thought of thanking you for the shirts, because I have not felt sufficiently estranged from home to enter upon a regular form of thanks. I never thought of expressing my thanks before leaving home and do not now.

1. Prince William County, Virginia, the location of Ewells' home. Ewell's cousin Levi Gantt visited the Ewell family there during the summer furlough that followed his second year at West Point.
2. Unidentified.
3. James W. F. Macrea and his family lived near the Ewells in Prince William County. Susan was probably his daughter.
4. Ewell's original letter has been lost. The text has been taken from Percy G. Hamlin's *The Making of a Soldier*, 26–29. Hamlin cut this sentence in two whereas Ewell obviously intended it to be kept as one.
5. George Bomford (d. 1848) had graduated first in West Point's Class of 1808. He became the Army's chief of ordnance in 1832.
6. The advertisement, found on page 3 of the September 14, 1839, edition, reads as follows:

> THE SUBSCRIBER
>
> Having been appointed Professor of Mathematics in Hampden Sydney College, Virginia, will in addition to his other duties, instruct a small class in the science of Civil Engineering. Having been for four years, an Assistant Professor of Mathematics and Natural Philosophy at West Point, and subsequently, for nearly three years, engaged in the practical duties of a Civil Engineer, he hopes to be able to render his instructions to a high degree,

useful. The location of the College is, in every respect, excellent. Board may be had at it for $10 per month. There is no more healthy spot in the State. Letters, (post paid) addressed to the subscriber, before the 1st of October, at Buckland, Prince William County, Virginia, and, after that time at Prince Edward Court-House, Virginia, requiring further information, will be promptly attended to. BENJ. S. EWELL.

7. Charles E. Dade was living in Prince William County with his family at the time of the 1830 census. His wife's name is not listed.
8. Marylander Masillon Harrison graduated third in West Point's Class of 1841. He served as an officer in the engineers prior to his death in 1854.
9. Richard Delafield (1798–1873) attended West Point at the age of sixteen and served in the United States Army as an engineering officer for forty-eight years. He served two terms as superintendent of the United States Military Academy, from 1838 to 1845 and again from 1856 to 1861. In 1864 he became a brigadier general and was appointed commander of the Corps of Engineers. He retired in 1869.

6. To Benjamin Ewell

Milty Acdy W.P. N.Y. Jany 10th 1840

Dear Ben

I have delayed writing to you so long that I am almost afraid to commence a letter.

I hardly knew where to direct untill I learnt from Mother a few days ago. Besides I thought you would be so occupied with the increase of business & cares attendant upon the change in your situation that you would be bored by a letter & worse than all I thought I would have to congratulate & wish you joy &c. all which would be got over by delay, as writing anything of the kind would be a moral impossibility for me.[1] Levi brought me your Uniform coat; it does not fit me well enough for it to be worn without some alterations which Mother said you had vetoed.

I expect at present to go into the 1st Dragoons unless I learn something which may make me change my mind, & as the Unif. of the two Corps is diff[eren]t your coat would not be of any service. One of my Classmates who only wishes to stay a short time in the army & does not like to go to the expense of buying a new coat offered to purchase. I have no idea of its value & did not tell him what I should do with it.[2] It would be better for you to let me know as soon as possible the least you will take for it, as I expect he is not the only one who would like to buy. I have taken every care of it, not allowed it to be opened. I would be much obliged to you if you could give me some advice as to my future path. I am at present in rather a disagreeable situation unable to decide firmly between the Drag, Marines or Infty. I am prejudiced against the Art[illery] and decidedly opposed to applying for it (almost the only point on which I have made up my mind). Very flattering accounts are given of the 1st Dragoons. Their duties are said to be more pleasant than those of most reg. in the service and the Officers are reported to be some of the best specimens of the Army. Tasker advises me to go into that Corp by all means. The Inf are stationed in the west and on that account would suit me better than the Art'y at the same time not so far as to be out of the world which I am afraid is the case with the Drag. I have always had an inclination for the sea and on that account should prefer the Marines. Henderson[3] (the Col of the corps) is said to be anxious to get graduates to enter and, I have heard, says he will give them their choice of ship or station. You may see I am like an ass between 3 bundles of hay and all light on the subject would be of invaluable service to me. It is very difficult to get information here as all those to whom I apply are interested and of course give colored images & it is difficult to judge for one['s] self when hearsay and misrepresentation form almost the only data. The thoughts of graduating give me any thing but pleasure. although I have suffered some pain and mortification since I have been here yet the pleasures have more than counterbalanced the sorrows & it is hard to leave forever those with whom (in the language of one of our 4th of July toasts) we have shared the hardships of the camp and the terrors of the Black-board. Is there a Newton from Norfolk Va at H & S. College? There is one in the Corps who told me he had a brother there.[4] The one here is a protégé of Pro. Mahan,[5] one of the most promising members of the Corps. He stood head last June in everything 4th Class but the cursed demerit. Bliss has been made assist Adj't Gen'l with the rank of Captain, his place filled by Lieut. Shiras.[6] There have been many changes since you were here; Major Delafield seems to pride himself upon having every thing different from what it used to be. Some of his changes have been certainly for the better. the Mess hall which used to take from 12 to 14 $ per month now scarcely amounts to half that much and affords much better fare. If we had always had him I would be out of debt which I am far from being as it is. The people about here are as much afraid of him as if he had absolute authority; none of the old women will make pies for Cadets, within 5 miles around. some of them are even afraid to make them for their own use lest they should be suspected. Godfrey our shoemaker refused the other day to make three holes in a leather strop for pants, because it was customary to make but two. Money is of less service here than any place I ever saw inasmuch as nobody will sell without the permission of the Supt. "A new broom sweeps clean." I expect after a while things will go on in the old way. It is better for the inst[itution] that the Supt should have a character for strictness; under DeRy[7] administration it was going down hill with increasing velocity. Delafield is trying to make the examinations much stricter than they used to be; he has divided the Board into three committees and keeps them all at work at the same time; making the ex[amina]t[io]n 3 times as long as it used to be.[8] I heard from Mother a few days ago—all well. she says they have made 40 lbs of corn, but nevertheless complains more than she did when they did not make as many pints.

Mother wants me to resign and teach school in the neighbourhood. Unfortunately our ideas on that subject don't exactly agree. How are you pleased with the country you are in? Mother says it is a very religious neighbourhood. Give my respects to Mrs Ewell. I find that I have violated the rules of Blair[9] but if I don't send this another would not be written this side of June.

Yrs

R S Ewell

1. Ben had taken a wife eight months earlier. About that same time he accepted a position as professor of mathematics and natural philosophy at Hampden-Sydney College.
2. Ben had received a commission as a second lieutenant in the United States Army on July 1, 1832, upon his graduation from the United States Military Academy, but within two months he was appointed assistant professor of mathematics at the academy. He had therefore rarely, if ever, worn the expensive garment.
3. Brevet Brigadier General Archibald Henderson (1783–1859) served as commandant of the United States Marine Corps from 1820 to 1859, longer than any other man. Born in Fairfax County, Virginia, he joined the Marine Corps in 1806.
4. John Newton (1822–1895) graduated second in West Point's Class of 1842. Although a Virginian, Newton remained loyal to the Union and rose to command a corps in the Army of the Potomac.
5. Dennis Hart Mahan (1802–1871) graduated from West Point in 1824 and immediately joined the academy staff as an assistant professor of mathematics. Later, as professor of civil and military engineering, he wrote several textbooks relating to engineering and field fortifications.

6. Alexander E. Shiras (d. 1875) had graduated from West Point in 1833. During the Civil War, he served the Union army as a commissary officer, ultimately becoming commissary general in 1874.

7. René E. DeRussy had graduated from West Point in 1812 and was brevetted for gallantry at the Battle of Plattsburg, New York, during the War of 1812. After working as an engineer on the New York Harbor defenses, he was appointed superintendent of the United States Military Academy, a position he held from 1833 to 1838. He retired from the army as a brevet brigadier general in 1865 and died later that same year.

8. At the semiannual examinations, cadets were questioned by a board consisting of the superintendent, faculty, board of visitors, and prominent guests. Delafield divided the board into three bodies, or committees, which conducted their examinations simultaneously, thereby tripling the examination time.

9. The Reverend David Blair published the book *Models of Familiar Letters in English, French, and Italian for the Exercise of Students* in 1827.

7. To Benjamin Ewell

West Pt March 29th 1840

Dear Ben

I am very sorry not to be able to give you any information concerning the price of the books you mentioned in your last letter. They are in the Library but their cost is not given. I spoke to Pro. Bartlett[1] concerning the latest publications in Nat[ural] Phil[osophy], but could not get any satisfaction from him. he did not seem to know what the newest works were. Lube's Int. and Diff'l Cal. is said to be one of the best math'l works that has appeared lately. It is a German (Lube's) work translated into English. Another work of the same kind by the same author is expected to make its appearance shortly. Among the works in the Library Young & Ivy have a great many examples of max. & min. If I learn any thing of importance I shall let you know.[2]

You asked in your last if I should like to remain at W.P.? I should not like to stay in any Dept. but that of Chemistry, as that is the only branch I should like to teach and indeed the only one I would venture upon. My standing in Chem. was quite resp[ec]t[able], and should have been better but it would have been contrary to the nature of things to put the "big bugs" down for one whose standing in other branches was as low as mine. This however did not give me much uneasiness as I studied it rather to gratify my inclination than for standing. This Dept is full and I should not like to return in any other. I have no particular wish to stay in the army but a positive antipathy to starving or to doing anything for a living which requires any exertion of mind or body. I am so unluckly [*sic*] as to be in the Hospital at this time with a trifling but painful aff[l]iction of the upper part of the throat brought on by the weather changing from disagreeably warm to far below freezing. What with the pain on the inside, the remedy (Cayenne pepper & spirits of turpentine) on the outside and being obliged to keep up a conversation with my room-mate[3] I should not be at all surprised if you are not able to read this or having read not be able to understand. The worst of the scrape is that with an appetite which would enable me to give a good account of an ox I am not able to eat any thing but spoon victuals and not enough of that. If I don't raise the price of board when I recover the use of my jaws, it will not be for want of good will. The news from Wash'tn is so very warlike at present that I should not be at all surprised if I cannot get a Furlough next summer. fortunately I am not homesick. If I do go home contrary to my expectations I may possibly pay you a visit; but this chiefly depends on the state of my funds. I am afraid my graduating account will be so heavy that I shall have to pay much more attention to economy than I like.

I am glad you think my choice of the Dragoons a judicious one. I do not think that I have any choice in the matter. the fact is since I have been here I have found it difficult to ascertain what my inclinations are on any subject. It seems that a person after being subjected to orders for a long time loses all will of his own.

Levi told me that Aunt Gantt had gone to Stony Lonesome; her health is as good as it has been for some time. I hope this visit may be beneficial to both her & mother, of which there can be but little doubt unless there happen[s] to be a scarcity in the eating line; which you know[4] is apt to be the case there in the spring.[5]

March 31st I feel so much better that I expect to go to Barracks shortly so I shall send this up for Levi to seal & direct. Remember me to Mrs Ewell[6] & to William.[7]

Yrs   R S Ewell

1. Professor William H. C. Bartlett (d. 1893) had graduated from West Point in 1826 and entered the army as an engineer. He joined the West Point faculty in 1836 and retired from the army in 1871.
2. John Radford Young (1799–1885) was a prominent nineteenth-century mathematician and author.
3. Ewell may be referring to classmate Reuben P. Campbell, with whom he shared a room at West Point. During the Civil War, Campbell commanded the 7th

North Carolina Infantry. He died while leading his regiment in a charge at the Battle of Gaines's Mill on June 27, 1862.

4. This word was torn out of the original letter and has been supplied by the editor.

5. Ewell was not exaggerating. Later in life he remembered that his family was so impoverished that as a boy he sometimes went to bed with nothing to eat but a piece of cornbread.

6. He is referring here to Ben's wife, Julia.

7. William Stoddert Ewell (1824–1885), Ewell's youngest brother, was then a student at Hampden-Sydney College. In 1840, about the time this letter was written, William dropped his Ewell surname. From then on, he went by the name of William Stoddert.

Chapter 2

Dragoon in Training, 1840–1846

Dick Ewell graduated from West Point in 1840 and began his career as an officer in the 1st United States Dragoons. Forerunner of the cavalry, so famous in later wars, the dragoons typically occupied posts on the western frontier. Before being assigned to such duty, however, recruits and new officers had to undergo training at Carlisle Barracks, a military installation in south-central Pennsylvania. The commander at Carlisle was Captain Edwin V. Sumner, a forty-three-year-old veteran of the Black Hawk War who later became a major general in the Union army. Under Sumner's tutelage Ewell learned the nuts and bolts of military life.

After six months, Second Lieutenant Ewell and other new officers received orders to report to their commands. The War Department assigned Ewell to Company A, which was then on duty at Fort Gibson in Cherokee Territory, near modern Muskogee, Oklahoma. By the time the Virginian reached Fort Gibson, however, his company had transferred to Fort Wayne, seventy miles farther north. Ewell joined it there on December 19, 1840. Less than two years later the company moved again, this time to Fort Scott, a new post just west of the Missouri border and located roughly one hundred miles south of Fort Leavenworth, Kansas.

While stationed at Fort Scott, Ewell took part in two notable expeditions: Captain Philip St. George Cooke's 1843 trek down the Santa Fe Trail and Colonel Stephen W. Kearny's 1845 journey down the Oregon Trail. The expeditions tested Ewell's mettle and sparked his sense of adventure. He saw herds of buffalo, battled prairie fires, and learned to survive in harsh conditions imposed by the desert and the prairie. They were times to remember.

Between expeditions Ewell was assigned to the less exciting task of enlisting new soldiers for the regiment. His recruiting duty took him first to Fort Leavenworth and later to Louisville, Kentucky, and Madison, Indiana. At these places the young officer indulged his social appetite, paying visits to young ladies at their homes and attending dances and teas. The grim business of war lay in the future; for now Ewell enjoyed the fruits of peace.

Julia McIlvaine was Benjamin Ewell's wife and the mother of his daughter, Lizzie. Julia possessed an uneven temperament, and she and her husband separated when Lizzie was still a child. (Courtesy Stan Aylor)

8. To Benjamin Ewell

Carlisle Barracks Oct 21st 1840

Dear Ben

I recd your letter this evening and applied to Capt Sumner[1] sur le Champ[2] who gave me leave without the slightest hesitation to go to York on the 26th. I am very sorry to learn that you are disappointed as to the College.[3] Alvord[4] is the last man I should suppose to be Prof. as he can scarcely be understood when he is talking common sense & must be perfectly unintelligible when he undertakes Math or Phil.

When I was coming here I met Lieut Robertson[5] an Officer of my Regt in the D.C.[6] who advised me[,] as I was not certain at what time my uniform would be here to hasten on so that I might go to N.Y. for it if it were not here which made me unable to spend more than 30 min in York instead of the 24 hrs I intended otherwise to have staid there so that I only had time to take leave of Julia.[7] I was disappointed in not finding my uniform here but the Capt prefered my staying as it made but little difference so that my leave. . . . [I am more pleased][8] than otherwise with my situation though I am working harder than I ever did in my life having to be in the stable from Reveille to Breakfast, then drilling & reciting Tactics untill Dinner and drilling & stable duty untill Retreat. So far from disliking the duties I would not care if they were increased

As a captain, Edwin V. Sumner trained Ewell in the duties of a dragoon at Carlisle Barracks. Later, as a major general, he led a grand division in the Army of the Potomac. (Library of Congress)

as I spend the time more agreeably. Thus far I am very much pleased with Capt Sumner who is strict with himself as well as with us. Tattoo is sounding and this must be in the office to night.

I congratulate Mr Snap[9] upon his prowess.

Respects to Julia & family.

Yrs &c

Rich S Ewell

I shall be down early; Should I not get your watch I shall some other so do your will[10]

1. Edwin V. Sumner (1797–1863) had a long and honorable career in the United States Army. Twice brevetted during the Mexican War, he was in command of the 1st United States Cavalry when Confederate forces fired on Fort Sumter. Brought east in 1861, he led a corps and later a grand division in the Army of the Potomac. He died on March 21, 1863, of natural causes.

2. French, "on the field."

3. Hampton-Sydney College.

4. Benjamin Alvord (1813–1884) graduated from the United States Military Academy in 1837, after which he remained for three years as an assistant professor of

mathematics. During the Civil War, Alvord served as the army's chief paymaster in Oregon, and from 1872 until his retirement in 1880, he was paymaster general of the army.

5. Possibly a reference to William Robertson, a classmate of Ewell's at West Point, who was then a lieutenant in the 2nd United States Dragoons.

6. District of Columbia.

7. Ewell traveled to York, Pennsylvania, to visit Ben's wife, Julia McIlvaine, and her family.

8. Several words were cut out of the letter at this point. The words set off in brackets were inserted by the editor.

9. Unidentified.

10. The import of this last sentence seems to be: "Should I not get your watch, I will get another one and therefore accomplish what you ask of me."

9. *To Rebecca Ewell*

Carlisle Barracks Nov 12th 1840

Dear Becca

I have delayed answering your last letter so long that I am almost ashamed to commence one to you now and quite ignorant where to direct. As I intend however to write a pretty long one in a[n]swer to your dozen lines you may alter the date of the first half so as to make quite a punctual letter of it and the other part you may have gratis. I paid a very agreeable visit to York on the 26th of last month[,] the first time I had seen any of Dr McIlvaine's family as I only staid a few minutes there when on my way here and did not see any one but Julia. My short stay was caused by my learning from an Officer whom I met at the Depot the day you left me in Wat[ingto]n that there was a strong probability of my having to go to New York for my uniform. Julia has two most strikingly pretty sisters I have ever seen. Jane the oldest of the three is the handsomest lady I ever saw. Ben however thinks Sarah the most captivating of them all but Doctors you know will differ.[1] I was a good deal disappointed not to find Ben in Yk when I got there but as he arrived there the next day I had no reason to find fault with his want of accuracy[;] indeed it required considerable judgement to make an appointment of that kind a week beforehand where the weather, roads &c had to come into account. The first day I got to York I found myself in a most filthy hog hole of a German Dutch tavern and not seeing any of the attractions at Dr McIlvaines you may depend I was disgusted but after changing my lodgings and seeing the ladies I would have been willing to have remained there a week instead of the day to which I was limited. I am sorry to say in answer to your inquiries concerning waltzing that I have not had that pleasure since I left Stony Lonesome.

Capt Sumner our Commandant gave us a party soon after we reached [here] which is the only opportunity I have had of dancing since I have been here. On that occasion I was near shocking the delicate nerves of one of the young ladies past recovery by asking her to waltz.[2] She told me with quite a tragedy queen air that the ladies of Carlisle never waltzed. I came within an ace of telling her the anecdote in Peter Simple where the breast of the turkey would not go down.[3]

The young ladies here are too puritanical to dance though they have no objection every now and then to a little flirtation and gossip. I had not a very high opinion of the people here from the very first. No place could be much with 2 Presbyterian churches and but few inhabitants to share the qualities which such places of resort alway[s] impart to those who frequent them.[4]

There are some very pretty women among them and quite the first circles too. If it were not for an insurmountable prejudice I have to every thing which has the smallest claim to be called Dutch I should certainly fall in love with some of their pretty faces.

I received a letter from Levi the other day. he appears to be better pleased with this year's course than the last as well he may be. His letter contained an account of an unfortunate accident which happened to an Officer on the Point a few weeks ago. Lieut Bransford[5] in company with some Officers was riding around the plain when his horse took fright and ran off with him for nearly half a mile throwing his head against a tree which caused his death in about 12 hours. I cannot imagine what could have been the matter with him that he did not stop the horse. he must have been frightened out of his presence of mind. I find Mother has stopped sending my paper to Milford[6] and sends it on direct to me. I thought so by receiving it so quickly but believe I am mistaken after examining the handwriting of the direction. I hope she has suited her own convenience by doing so as it is a matter of indifference to me whether I get it a week sooner or later. As for the Chronicle[7] it is such a complete humbug that I am anxious for the subscription to be out just to have the pleasure of putting a stop to it.

There is a Lieut West[8] here from Md whose family I think it likely you or Mother may know. He is Nephew to Uncle Dick's widow[9] and is related to the Ogle family and to some Lloyds, not those we knew however.[10] I forget whether his Mother or Father is related to Aunt Lowndes;[11] his name is Richd West. I presume you can get all his history from Mother (which I confess I have some curiosity to learn). I think it likely that I shall remain here untill some time in the Spring and then go to the West with a detachment of recruits.

Duties here are more constant and laborious than I believe they are at my Post. We never think of stopping our drills for the cold. Capt Sumner says for his own comfort he wishes the thermometer would always remain 20° below zero so that common mortals have no chance with him. Thus far thank my stars I have been able to stand as much cold as others and think I can continue to do so.

Yrs &c   R. S. Ewell

Tell Elizabeth whenever I wish to be in a good humour with myself I read her clause in Mother's letter.[12]

1. The United States census shows the McIlvaine household in 1840 as consisting of Dr. William McIlvaine (fifty-six years old); his wife, Juliana (forty-six years old); two sons; and three daughters. Jane and Julia, the two eldest daughters, were between sixteen and twenty years old, while Sarah, the youngest, was fifteen years old.

2. Ewell visited Stony Lonesome in the summer of 1840 immediately after graduation. He had learned to waltz at the United States Military Academy, where, according to his sister Elizabeth, the dancing instructor had proclaimed him "the best waltzer at the Point!" ESE to CB, 2 Mar. 1874, TSLA.

3. Peter Simple was the protagonist of an 1834 novel of that name written by Frederick Marryat about a young British seaman in the Napoleonic Wars. In chapter 11, the protagonist asks his dinner partner whether he could help her to a piece of turkey breast. The offended woman upbraided him for his bad manners in saying "breast" rather than "bosom" in a lady's presence.

4. In this letter, Ewell voices two prejudices that he harbored throughout his life: a dislike of the "Dutch" (i.e., German-Americans) and Presbyterianism. Ewell himself had been raised in the Episcopal Church.

5. Samuel J. Bransford of Virginia had graduated from West Point in 1836 and was serving as a first lieutenant in the Second United States Artillery when he was accidentally killed on November 3, 1840.

6. A village near Ewell's boyhood home, Stony Lonesome.

7. A Washington, D.C., newspaper.

8. Richard West Jr. had become a second lieutenant in the 1st Dragoons on January 25, 1837, and was promoted to first lieutenant on January 29, 1839. He died on July 19, 1844.

9. Unidentified.

10. Ewell was related to the Ogle and Lloyd families of Maryland through his mother, Elizabeth Stoddert Ewell.

11. "Aunt Lowndes" may refer to the granddaughter of Ewell's great-grandfather, Christopher Lowndes. If so, she was Ewell's first cousin, once removed.

12. Not found.

10. To Benjamin Ewell

Fort Wayne[1] Cherokee Nation
Feby 2d 1841

Dear Ben

Enclosed are thirty dollars leaving me twenty in your debt if I recollect the amount due correctly. You can imagine my astonishment at Carlisle on the 20th of Nov. when orders were received for all of us with 2 exceptions to scatter to the four winds of Heaven. I should have been very glad to have remained there untill my debts were paid and I had accumulated sufficient funds to purchase a fine horse and bring him out here. It is impossible to procure as good a horse out here as can be had in Va for 150.$. The best horses here would scarcely bring more than from 50 to 70 $ there & they ask from 100 to 250 just in proportion as the man is a greater or less rogue and they all have more or less of that development which leads to cheating.

I thought my sufferings and privations between Car & Pittsburgh were unequalled in the annals of man untill unfortunately I remembered that hundreds went the same journey every day. My trip was particularly agreeable as it rained the whole time and we had 9 passengers and one squalling brat. I went to the Theatre in Pittsburgh the most blackguard hole I ever saw of the kind. I had quite an agreeable voyage down the Miss and Ohio except that one old merchant from Pitts bamboozled about 20 passengers myself included to take passage on a particular boat promising to get our fare cheap when the old fox merely made use of our names to the Capt to secure a good bargain for himself and left the rest in the lurch.

I had to wait several days for a boat at the mouth of White River at a place called Montgomery's Point[2] (boats have to go through the White into the Arkansas river) where I had to sleep in my clothes and go pretty much on the fasting principle without even the consolation of saving cash as they charged 2$ per diem. I was forced to take a wagon when I had steamboated within a few miles of Fort Gibson[3] making a two days journey across the country thereby acquiring a very goodly idea of Western travelling as we had to swim a stream and were forced to leave wagon and baggage behind and ride on the horses going into the Fort in style as you may suppose. I soon found out however that appearances were of less consequence than any place I had ever yet seen. My company was stationed at Fort Wayne a collection of huts about 70 miles to the North West of F. G. nearly on the line between Ark[ansas River] and the Ch[erokee] Nation. A site was selected near this some years ago and government went to considerable expense erecting a steam saw mill &c. c. That Post was abandoned on account of ill health and this site selected, which proved to be very eligible and large beginnings were made, frames set up and everything progressing in fine style when orders were received from Head Quarters for the works to be abandoned thus leaving a vast amount of public property exposed if Gen. Arbuckle[4] had not thought proper to disobey the order and have my Co left here, which accounts for my finding it here instead of at Fort Gibson where I was ordered. When I arrived I found Chilton[,][5] my Capt (Simonton)[6] and Dr Simpson[7] the only Officers here. Chilton was left here there being no subaltern of my Co to act as Qr Master and Commissary of subsistence both of which duties I now perform as well as my comp[an]y duties and am half the time commanding the Post so that you see I am pretty well in for it.

I like the duties very well except that my time hangs heavy on my hands and I am sometimes a little in the humour for society although the last penchant comes less often every day.

I am more troubled for a servant than [any]thing else. A soldier costs $16 per m[o]nth and [I] dont have the use of him more than half [the] time. The Cher[okees] about here own slaves but they are worthless and moreover cost double. They are rather whites than Cherokees, men who have Cherokee wives and are settled in the Nation, generally speaking a most worthless pack. Many of the Officers have Cherokee Mistresses, a scrape I intend to keep out of both on account of my purse and taste. Occasionally a good looking half breed may be seen but generally they are a dirty set and all have a smoky odor about them which is particularly disagreeable to me at the distance of ten yards for I was never closer. There are one or two wealthy men in the immediate vicinity of the post who are trying every thing they can do to have the post removed but without success. They are driven from their homes which galls them though they will be well paid for their property. I believe the Nation[8] have had a Councill and pet[it]ioned Congress on the subject. They are all very well disposed and friendly towards the whites and it would be much better to have the Post in Arkansas where the people are cutting each others throats ad libitum.[9]

Respects to Dr McIlvaine's family[10] first opportunity. I saw Lieut. Haller at Gibson[—]very kind & polite.[11] Saw his brother in York. Address me at Fort Wayne, Cherokee Nation via Sylvia Post Office.

I understood from an Officer a short time since that Lieut. Alvord was still at Fort Gibson and did not intend to take the Professorship. Good authority. Please answer as soon as possible as I shall be uneasy about the money. Remember me to all.

Yrs   Richd S. Ewell

I send 30 thirty $ on second thoughts. write to me the state of the bank. nothing else passes here but the silver.

I have not written half as much as I intended but this is pretty well for the present. answer this and I will send the other 20.

1. Fort Wayne stood in what was then Indian Territory, near the point where the states of Missouri, Arkansas, and Oklahoma now meet. Established in July 1840, the fort protected a military road that ran through the area. The army abandoned the post two years later because of its unhealthy location and moved the garrison to Fort Scott.

2. The White River flows into the Arkansas River at the Norell Lock and Dam near the town of Nady, Arkansas.

3. Established in 1824, Fort Gibson stood on the left bank of the Neosho River, three miles above the point where it emptied into the Arkansas. The army placed it there to check the aggressions of the Osage tribe.

4. Mathew Arbuckle of Virginia received a second lieutenant's commission in the infantry in 1799. He rose steadily through the ranks and thirty-one years later was brevetted a brigadier general. He died in 1851.

5. Robert H. Chilton (1816–1879) was an 1837 graduate of West Point and an officer in the 1st Dragoons. During the Civil War, he served as General Robert E. Lee's chief of staff and later became the adjutant and inspector general of the Confederate army.

6. Isaac P. Simonton of Ohio had graduated from West Point in 1827 and was promoted to captain of the 1st Dragoons in 1836. He died in 1842, just one year after this letter was written.

7. Richard F. Simpson of Virginia had been an assistant surgeon in the army for one year. He died in 1861, just a year after being promoted to full surgeon.

8. Cherokee Nation.

9. *"Ad libitum"*—i.e., just as they please.

10. Ewell inadvertently repeated the word "family" here.

11. Granville O. Haller was then a second lieutenant in the 4th United States Infantry. He served with distinction in Mexico and rose to become major of his regiment by the time of the Civil War.

11. To Charles Wickliffe

Fort Wayne C.N[1]

May 14th 1841

Dear Charley[2]

I send down by the bearer receipts for $50. please return the receipts you have for $100. You can date receipts for yourself. You are a "nice un" to talk about any person's writing. I am sure I beat you in that respect as far as one Pole is from the other. I have no doubt my epistles will be held up in after ages as models of fine writing and be used in the schools as copies. As for yours we have bought a telescope to read it with and have to call a Council of War over every letter. If you will come down here I will give you the whole art of penmanship in 6 lessons. I never heard anything to match your giving yourself airs about my writing since I have been in the country.

Tuesday Morning. I have concluded to send the money by Mr West[3] who goes down in a few days, and will be likely to return in a shorter time than the teams. Genl Arbuckle wrote us that we must do our own hauling which accounts for our teams going down. G-d knows when they will return.

Yrs

R. S. Ewell

I leave the receipts blank that you may fill them up as you please. Make has[t]e as it is almost time to sent [*sic*] accts off.

R. S. Ewell

P.S.

I brought no sword from the East with me and had to use one out of the Company & happening to break the Scapbard on drill, I could not replace it but by using an old one without a sabre which I found in your store room when I was looking for the clothing you sent for the other day. I forgot to mention it before.

I have been living in hopes of getting a saddle by these recruits from Carlisle but have been mistaken and will have to get one made here. Can you let me pay for one and get some man of your Company to sign for it?

I mean that I want the time to have it fixed. there is a saddler's shop to be established in the neighbourhood. I do not like to ask Capt Simonton as I have had many things from him and he does not like to do those things.

R[es]p[ect]s

R. S. Ewell

1. Cherokee Nation.
2. Kentuckian Charles Wickliffe graduated one year ahead of Ewell at West Point. Upon graduation, he accepted a commission in the 1st United States Dragoons. Dropped from the army's rolls in 1842, he briefly returned to duty during the Mexican War as a captain of infantry. When the Civil War began, Wickliffe became colonel of the 7th Kentucky Infantry (CSA) and was mortally wounded at Shiloh.
3. Unidentified.

12. To Rebecca Ewell

Fort Wayne

Cherokee Nation Monday Nov 13th 41

Dear Becca

A few day[s] since I recd a letter from Mother containing a few lines from y[ou]rself stating that you had written to me last Spring without recg an an-[s]wer which I am inclined to believe is a foul slander; but however I shall make security doubly sure by taxing you with the present. In the first place I must premise by demanding free liberty to spell as I choose seeing that Capt Simonton has borrowed my dictionary and left it locked up in his qu[a]rt[er]s.

You may remember my writing home some time since that we had had some little difficulty with the Indians around here in consequence of one of the soldiers killing an Indian in a drunken brawl at a miserable little assemblage of grog shops near here for which 4 of our soldiers have been in jail in Ark. for nearly 4 m[o]nths. I have been for the last eight days attending their trial at Bentonville a little county seat near the frontier and am very sorry to have it to say that all of them were acquitted as differing from the mass of Dragoon soldiers they are most worthless vagabonds. It was truly mortifying to see the neglect and nonchalance with which I was treated by the good people of Bentonville and its environs. The poor ignorant devils are not half so well informed as the Indians (who are in the constant habit of seeing military Posts &c) but look upon an Officer as something infinitely below themselves unless they want to get a contract or something of that sort in which case their attentions and civil[i]ty become almost aweful. I have the misfortune to be actg Quartermaster and have to make purchases &c and I assure you I find their impertin[an]ce at times unbearable. They will sit in my room for hours at a time very often before they will tell their business and quit although I have an office for their express benefit. As for hints you might as well try them upon a runaway horse. take up a book or leave the room they will wait as cool as a cucumber untill you are through with the book, or for that matter inter[r]upt you with some such question as "Well do you know any news about more forces coming out here" repeated for perhaps the twentieth time. The brutes actually put me in a furor sometimes.

I am just in the same situation with regard to a Post as I was a year ago. No one can tell how long they will keep this one up. We expect to be ordered away every mail and are in a most disagreeable state of uncertainty.

I found not long since that all my hair was coming out and was obliged to shave my head to keep what little I have left from following suit with I believe the desired effect. As there are no wigs to be had I am obliged to wear a black silk scull cap. It would have made you laugh to have seen the people in the Court house stare when I took off my hat. I really believe they thought I had been shaved for some misdemeanor or other. I understand the society of the Post[1] is about to be improved and enlarged by the addition of an Officers family who are daily expected. I really think if you can find any person about Stony Lonesome who would like a military life and who is fair to look upon that I would quit the lonesome life of a bachelor. Should you find one that you think will answer and that you can recommend you can give a letter of introduction and send her out. Maybe as there is a large lot to pick from you had better send half a dozen so I can take my choice. I must however except Miss So & Miss H[2] for reasons that you may possibly guess. I suppose Mr Dubuessor[3] has made Catholics of you all ere this. I heard a Campbellite[4] last night at Fayetteville where I staid 35 miles distant and had a great mind to join the Brethering and Sistering just for the sake of shaking hands [with] the girls which is the first ceremony but was deter[r]ed because some of them had been crying and I believed wiping their noses without their h[and]dk[erchief]s. which is considered quite the thing here. One of the lawyers was a methodist Preacher who had beat his own wife half to death some where in the East and then ran off with another Mans. (E. Pluribus Unum).[5]

A[n]swer this if you think it worth one and believe me Yrs

R. S. Ewell

1. A hole in the paper destroyed this word, which the editor has supplied.
2. Unidentified.
3. Unidentified.
4. Alexander Campbell (1779–1857) was a founder of the Restoration Movement, an early-nineteenth-century religious movement that sought to eliminate denominational barriers that divided Christians, uniting believers into a single church whose sole authority was the Bible. Ironically, the movement resulted in the creation of three new denominations: the Christian Church, the Church of Christ, and the Disciples of Christ.
5. Latin, "from many, one." This motto appears on the official seal of the United States.

13. To Rebecca Ewell

Fort Wayne
C.N. April 10th 1842

Dear Becca

Yours of Dec 31st came duly to hand. I delayed answering it longer than I should have done as this Post is about being moved into the Indian Country back of Missouri & I thought I would wait until I could tell you where to direct. The Osages[1] a pack of sheep stealing vagabonds cannot agree with the[2] people on the frontier (who are a good match for the Osages in rascallty generally) and we must be set to work building log cabins & government must be put to an expense of some $4 000 on acct of transportation instead of shooting the Indians like beasts as they are. I did not like to postpone writing longer but will let you know where the Post Office will be as soon as possible. The orders are to select a site about 100 miles south of Fort Leavenworth[3] about 10 miles inside of the Indian country. Capt Moore[4] is now absent looking for a site & will return in a few days when we will make preparations for a move. As we will have to carry all our provisions, clothing &c &c it will be no trifling move I assure you, requiring a train of about 40 wagons. This will be a perfect God-send for the miserable poor devils about here as it will give them an opportunity to make a little money by the hire of their teams. The only money (except shin-plasters[5]) they ever see is what comes from the Fort & the chance of getting their teams employed seems to run them almost crazy. Scarcely a day passes but they are in to see me about "a Chance for hauling" & this is just the season too that farmers ought to be employed about their corn.

I am about purchasing a Negro boy for $600.[6] He is about 14 yrs old & is able to cook & take care of my horses for me. I get him rather cheaper than the common price here as I have to leave it optional with his owner to redeem him at the end of two yrs for what I give. A servant costs me about $12 a month so, that you see I shall get at the rate of 25 per ct for my money & will make $300 by the transaction even if the negro is redeemed which is hardly probable as I think times will [be] harder even, than they are now. I am not able to more than half pay for him now & will borrow the rest. One good effect of the purchase will be that I shall live more economically than I can when I have no object in view. I have been trying for the last six months & have scarcely made both ends meet whereas now I shall be able to lay up more than half my pay as I have an object in view. At least such was the case when I had my graduating debts to pay.[7] As soon as I shall have squared myself with reference to the boy I believe I shall endeavour to purchase a woman & as I won't want her out here will transmit the money home for that purpose. I believe this is the best investment & one that will return a larger interest than any other.[8] I recd two Intelligences from home the other day. There were so many interesting articles in them that I could not be certain what you had reference to in sending them. You have never yet told me who it was with Mrs Dade in the Herald[9] you sent me some time ago.

I am just on the eve of riding about 40 miles into the country so that as I will be at the Office I must draw this to a close observing that though I expect an answer to it yet I do not consider this as a good specimen either of spelling or diction. I shall write to Mother as soon as I hear of the new Post Office.

Yrs &c   R. S. Ewell

1. The Osage people at one time lived along the Ohio River. By 1800 they had migrated west into what is now southern Missouri, northern Arkansas, and eastern Kansas, becoming the strongest tribe in that region. As American settlers moved onto their lands, the Osage withdrew into what would become Oklahoma. In 1870, they were put on a reservation in the northeastern corner of the state.
2. In the original letter, Ewell wrote the word "the" twice.
3. Established in 1827, Fort Leavenworth stood on the right bank of the Missouri River, near the mouth of the Little Platte River. Located near the beginning of the Santa Fe Trail, it was the Army's most important frontier post prior to the Civil War.
4. Captain Benjamin D. Moore began his military career in the United States Navy but quickly transferred to the mounted rangers and then to the dragoons.

Promoted to captain on June 15, 1837, he died in 1846 at the Battle of San Pasqual in California.

5. Shinplasters were privately issued currency, often poorly secured and depreciated in value.

6. Ewell sold the boy, whose name was Arthur, in the winter of 1844–45. See RSE to RLE, 3 Oct. 1845, LC (letter 23, this volume).

7. Ewell's "graduating debts" refer to the debts he amassed at West Point, particularly those he incurred in properly equipping himself for future service in the 1st Dragoons.

8. When Ewell was growing up, his family had owned a slave named Fanny Brown, whom the children familiarly called "Mammy." Ewell continued to own slaves in small numbers through the Civil War. He never expressed any moral reservations about buying or selling other humans beings; rather, the economics of the transactions were his primary consideration.

9. Presumably the *New York Herald*.

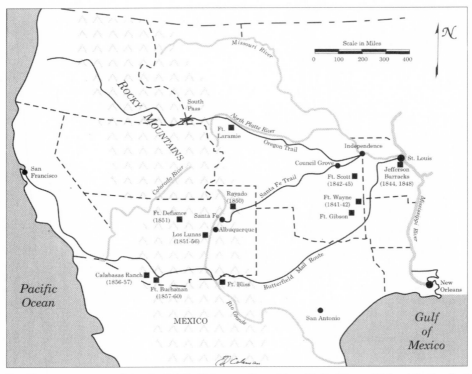

Ewell's western posts. (Map by Ed P. Coleman, from Donald C. Pfanz, *Richard S. Ewell: A Soldier's Life* [Chapel Hill: University of North Carolina Press, 1998].)

14. To Benjamin Ewell

Fort Scott Mo. Ter.[1]
Nov 5th 1843

Dear Ben

The last time I wrote to you I was in somewhat of a hurry being on the eve of a trip to the Prairie.[2] I fully expected at that time to go all the way to S[an]t[a] Fe. I joined Capt Cooke[3] the Commander of the escort at Council Grove[4] about 150 miles from here & found him under orders to escort the traders to Santé Fé or untill the traders would dispense with his services. As there was no chance of the latter alternative our spirits were raised to many degrees above boiling. We fully expected to spend a month or so in St Fé[,] dance the Spanish dance with the loveliest & kindest (so those who pretend to know say) of the human race[,] visit Towse [Taos] & all the villages about there[,] & proceed to Bent's Fort[,][5] a trading establishment under the mountains[,] where we were to spend the winter & return next spring through the Valley of the Platte. We reached the crossing of the Ark. River with this impression & six day[s] more would have made surety doubly sure by placing us so far b[e]yond the crossing that we could not have returned on account of the lateness of the season, when as if the devil had placed them there for our sins we found about 50 Mexican troops forming the adva[n]ce guard of about 500 Drag sent from St. Fé to escort the traders & who reached the crossing the evening previous to our doing so. The main body was left back at the Semerone[6] 70 miles distant. This party was under command of a Lieut. Capt Cooke sent his Ad'jt[7] over with an invitation to this Officer to cross the river (they were on the Mexican[,] we on the U.S. side) but he ret[urne]d for answer that he was under positive & particular orders not to cross the river. The Adjt who crossed over said they were indifferently mounted but well armed & accout[e]red somewhat like our Drag[oons]. Orders were recd at St Fé by express at 8 o clock in the evening & they were ready to start at 3 o.clock next morning. Pretty well for Barbarians. I was so full of St Fe that the Buffaloe &c of the wilderness did not make as lasting an impression on me as they would otherwise though at the time I was much more astonished with the novelty & grandeur of the sight than I conceived possible for a person of my phlegmatick disposition. If you stand in the back door at home (whence there is the largest view) you cannot see land enough whereon to place the buffaloe I have seen at one Coup d'oeil.[8]

You are aware that on the Prairie you can see at times ten or fifteen miles from the effects of Mirage, but there were points on the trail whence the bare Prairie could not be seen, hill after hill covered with buffaloe ad infinitum.

I enclose a draft payable to your order on New York for $100 (Bank of America) No 9 signed by Maj. Walker[9] Paymaster. I cannot conveniently send you a larger amount of cash at present. Our Paymaster comes but twice a year & has been here this Fall. If you wish more money & if a Pay Account would answer I can spare you what you want in a small way without trouble. I would send you $200 but it is necessary to keep some funds on hand to last untill the Paymaster returns (6 months). As you see I do not put myself to any inconvenience. I hope you will not hesitate to call on me. Drafts on Bk. Mo.[10] are easily had if they will suit.

Yrs &c

R. S Ewell

Lt Dgs[11]

1. Missouri Territory.
2. In September–October 1843 six companies of the 1st U.S. Dragoons led by Captain Philip St. George Cooke escorted a train of merchant wagons down the Santa Fe Trail as far as the Arkansas River. It was one of the earliest mounted military expeditions along that route. For Cooke's report on the expedition, see Connelley, ed., "A Journal of the Santa Fe Trail."
3. Philip St. George Cooke (1809–1895) was a captain in the 1st United States Dragoons at this time and became its colonel in 1858. When the Civil War began, he became colonel of the 2nd United States Cavalry. He led a cavalry division on the Peninsula and later commanded a military district in Louisiana. Both his son, John R. Cooke, and his son-in-law J. E. B. Stuart became generals in the Confederate Army.
4. Council Grove was a wooded area on the Neosho River, approximately 120 miles northwest of Fort Scott and fewer than 50 miles southeast of Topeka, Kansas.
5. Bent's Fort was a walled adobe trading post located on the Mountain Route of the Santa Fe Trail near the modern town of La Junta, Colorado. Constructed in 1833, it remained in operation for sixteen years before being abandoned in 1849 due to disease and other calamities.
6. Cimarron River.
7. Ewell's abbreviation for "adjutant," an officer who served as the regimental clerk.
8. "*Coup d'oeil*"—i.e., stroke of the eye. Here the phrase may be translated as "glance."
9. Major Benjamin Walker had served in the Ordnance Department, the artillery, and the infantry before becoming a paymaster in 1839. He died in 1858.

10. The Bank of Missouri.

11. Lieutenant, Dragoons.

15. To Benjamin Ewell

Fort Scott
Feb. 18th 1844

Dear Ben

Your last letter came duly to hand & would have been ans[were]d before but that having nothing to do I put off writing from day to day. I recd a very bad piece of news by last week's mail. A man named Schaumburg[1] who resigned from this regiment some years ago and who has been since, for the purpose of getting back again, Loco foco,[2] Whig[3] & Tylerite,[4] has succeeded in getting reinstated by the Pres[iden]t to his former rank, which will bring him in as 8th Captain.[5] he is to take his place on the first vacancy among the Caps. or if one should occur among the 1st Lt sooner to come in at the head of the list until a vacancy among the C. shall occur. This man once belonged to the Marines I understand where he could not stay, was appointed to the Drag's & resigned *under charges,* fought a duel in N.O.[6] on horseback with broadswords & killed his own or his opponents horse I forget which & was carrying on a blackguard correspondence with an Editor of a paper in Phil. called the Forum in which he is used up. An Officer sent me the papers containing the cor[respondence], in which Ruffian &c &c are favourite expressions. He was taking Capt Stockton[7] of the Navy's part calling upon the people of Phil. to give him a dinner & I expect it is through his influence he is thrust upon us. He wrote to Capt. Terrett[8] of my comp'y last Fall saying he expected to come back & wishing to know how he would be recd & hinting he would mak[e] those, who, were not disposed to receive him politely, do so. A protest was going the rounds of the regt a few m[o]nths since against his coming back which was signed by all who saw it. Our only hope now is that he may be rejected by the Senate which I am sure he would be if they knew the circumstances of the case. Turner[9] has taken an active part in the affair. I do not know when I have been so disgusted. I would not mind it were he an acquisition but his reputation is so bad that Maj. Graham[10] is as much excited as any of the Drgs.

I find it next to impossible to get a good horse out here. the horses of the country are so flat footed & poorly bred that they cannot stand anything. I have 3 now & have but one[11] for service. I was after a wolf some time & the horse I was on though not going at more than half speed let down in one leg & will never be of service to me. Another one (cost me $165[)] had a disease called big head last summer (an enlargement of the bones of the head) and I would have shot him but I wished to see the course of the disease & to my surprise cured him. he had his back hurt on the Prairie last fall which has not healed since. My third horse is a pony which has done me more servic[e] than all the horses I have ever had. Lt Love[12] last Fall had 7 horses—using two. Col. Kearney[13] is in command of the Dept. & stationed at St. Louis where he has his Adjt. He has opened a recruiting Rendezvous there & expects to supply the Regt so that my hopes of going on that duty are quashed. If there had been a detail from the 2d Lieuts I should have had the best chance. I thought some time ago of applying for a furlough this year but the 1st Lieut (Eustis)[14] of my comp'y being on sick leave I could not get one were I to apply.

Yrs &

R. S. Ewell

Lt Dgs

I cannot agree with your views in regard to joining the church.[15] I doubt if a person would show much respect by join[in]g some cir[c]uits out here. The only civilized Indians (Cherokees) have just passed a law expelling missionaries. Q[uestion]. I say Indian is that a white Child? Ans[wer]. This Child is part missionary & part Indian.

1. James W. Schaumburgh of Louisiana had a checkered career. Appointed second lieutenant in the Marine Corps in 1829, he was cashiered three years later. He subsequently joined the mounted rangers before switching to the 1st Dragoons in 1833. Promoted to first lieutenant in March 1836, he resigned four months later. Reinstated in July 1844 over the objections of Ewell and other officers in the regiment, he was dropped from the rolls less than one year later. During the Civil War he served as a paymaster in the Union Army, but he left the service in March 1862 when the Senate refused to confirm his appointment.

2. The term "Locofoco," referring to a brand of radical Democrat, dates to an 1835 New York convention. When conservatives attempted to shut down the gathering by turning off the gaslights in the convention hall, participants kept the meeting going by striking locofoco matches.

3. The Whig Party was created in 1834 from a coalition of groups opposed to Andrew Jackson and the Democratic Party. The Whigs advocated the "American System," a platform that favored internal development, protective tariffs, and the creation of a national bank. Divided over the issue of slavery, the party dissolved in 1856.

4. A supporter of John Tyler (1790–1862), who was president of the United States from 1841 to 1845.

5. At that time, promotion within a regiment was based on seniority. Schaumburgh's reinstatement as captain would have placed him ahead of Ewell on the promotion list.

6. New Orleans.

7. Robert F. Stockton (1795–1866), the grandson of a signer of the Declaration of Independence, served with distinction as a naval officer from 1811 to 1850. During the war with Mexico, he helped seize California, declaring the former Mexican province a territory of the United States. After resigning from the navy, Stockton served in the United States Senate and was a delegate to a peace conference held in Washington, D.C., in 1861 aimed at averting civil war.

8. Like many officers, Burdette A. Terrett began his military career in the mounted rangers, only to transfer to the dragoons a few months later. Promoted to captain in 1842, he died in 1845 of a gunshot wound thought to have been accidentally self-inflicted. However, a letter to Ewell by Private Joseph Lewis written in 1865 casts doubt on whether Terrett died by accident or by design. Lewis left the service in 1843 after Terrett struck him across the skull with a saber, a "cowardly and murderous blow" that fractured Lewis's skull. As soon as he was back on his feet, Lewis recalled lying in wait for Terrett "with a loaded Rifle, in hopes of obtaining Satisfaction for the wrong he had done me, when my hands were tied." Although he did not admit to killing his cruel commander, Lewis certainly would have liked to have done so. Others may have harbored similar grudges. See Joseph Lewis to RSE, 20 June 1865, FHS.

9. Brevet Captain Henry S. Turner (1811–1881) of Virginia was the adjutant of the 1st Dragoons. Pioneer Susan S. Magoffin considered Turner "a gentleman of extensive information, and exceedingly polite." Drumm, *Down the Santa Fe Trail*, 125.

10. Lawrence P. Graham had been appointed a second lieutenant in the 2nd United States Dragoons in 1837. He rose quickly through the ranks and was brevetted major in May 1846 for gallantry at Palo Alto and Resaca de la Palma. He served as a brigadier general in the Union army during the Civil War.

11. Ewell repeats the word "one" here.

12. John Love was one of Ewell's closest friends. Graduating from West Point in 1841, one year after Ewell, he followed his friend into the 1st Dragoons and in 1849 became the regiment's quartermaster. During the Civil War, Love became a major general of militia in Indiana.

13. Stephen W. Kearny (1794–1848) joined the army in 1812 as a first lieutenant in the 13th United States Infantry. He remained in the army after the war, serving at various frontier posts. By 1844 he was colonel of the 1st Dragoons. As a brigadier general in the Mexican War, he would capture Santa Fe and assist in the capture of California. He died in 1848 of a tropical disease contracted during the war.

14. William Eustis of Rhode Island had graduated from West Point in 1830. Originally assigned to the infantry, he switched over to the dragoons in 1833 and became a captain in March 1845. He resigned four years later.

15. Ewell's years at West Point and in the army, coupled with abuses that he witnessed among missionaries on the frontier, had made him a religious skeptic. He returned to his Christian faith during the Civil War.

16. To Rebecca Ewell

Fort Scott March 2d 44

Dear Becca

I received your letter by the last mail but one and am glad to find that although tardy in paying yr debts you have not repudiated them entirely. As your letter has been due for almost 3 yrs you should have paid interest. It seems to me that persons when they commence a correspondence have a certain amount of Capital to dispose of (like the spider who only spins a certain amount) & after that they break down. My theory also is that the more affectionate & highflown the letters are & the oftener they are written the sooner the supply is exhausted; reasoning thus you ought to keep up a correspondence for an indefinite period. I received letters from Tom & Ben a short time since. they as studiously avoid anything touching themselves in their letters as if they were fearful of committing their characters to the Public. I do not believe I have ever recd a letter from either by which their respective professions could be ascertained. Has Tom joined the Church[1] as well as the rest? If so I think I have reason to congratulate myself for I ought of course to be the focus for all your prayers & think I have a pretty good chance to get to Heaven without any exertion of my own. I was strongly tempted a few days ago to subscribe to the Pictorial Bible, which is so lauded but I was afraid Congress might reduce our pay so much that I could not spare the money $12.50. Besides I am the only member of the family who by individual exertions ever gained a Bible[2] & being sent to West Point & then sent here without one I do not think in justice to y[our]self that I ought to subscribe. I went to Fort Leavenworth last Ch[r]istmas with Lt Love & another Officer who Paid us a visit. I went across the Missouri River while there to a ball[—]a pretty unique sort of affair it would be thought in Va. but quite elegant out here. There was hardly a single girl over 13 in the room so fast the[y] get married out her[e]. I did not feel in a very good humour that night. somebody asked me to let them introduce me to a partner & marched me up to a Mrs Pye[3]—& a most excessively heavy one she was. I got so mad before we sat down that I was in a perfect fever. She would not begin to dance untill I would tell her what to do & then she would keep dancing untill the musick began for the next couple. It was just as much as I could do to keep myself from shoving her along & I have no doubt she thought she was quite a Fan[n]y Elssler.[4] We have three ladies at present here[,] two married. A person would think they ought to be very intimate whereas they do not visit. Napier[5] says war is the natural state from man to the lowest insect. it seems to apply most particularly to the womenkind. Mrs Terrett,[6] a Creole from La is at present on a visit to her relations. I was much amused at her fears of returning. She told me she had been brought up a strict Catholic by her Sister & that since she left her home she had lost faith & was afraid her apostasy would be severely taken to task by the Orthodox one. I have some curiosity to see if she sticks to the heresy acquired according to her own account by reason & observation. She says she will never believe however in the miracles that were performed at boarding school again. Have you seen a controversay [sic] between Dr Wainwright & Dr Potts Episcopal & Presbyter[ian]?[7] I was sorry to see the first gentleman rather getting the worse of it[—]not that I care for the creed so much but I have a sort of friendly feeling for [the] Church I was brought up in. Besides I detest the sour Presbyterians. I was quite shocked at the thought of William's turning Missionary.[8] I have seen so much injury done the Indians here by them that I am rather skepti[c]al as to their utility. some of the greatest scamps we have are[?] Missionaries. Methodists are the favourites in the country here. One Parson was employed here to plough the garden & used to Preach[;] however he is not in good repute as it is said he stole some hogs. he wished to be made chaplain for the Post. I would study Spanish & Italian could I procure the books. Maybe you think I had better study spelling.

A gentleman in Phil. sent me some pamphlets[:] Loitering of Arthur O'Leary & some by the swedish woman Mrs Bremer.[9] I receive[d] the [?].

1. Although they were raised in the Episcopal Church, both Rebecca Ewell and her sister, Elizabeth, converted to Catholicism at this time. Their brother William Stoddert became a Presbyterian divine. Benjamin and Dick Ewell

remained in the Episcopal Church. For evidence of Rebecca's conversion to Catholicism, see CB to LCB, 3 July 1862, PBE.

2. Percy G. Hamlin, an early Ewell biographer, recounts an episode in Ewell's youth when he was presented with a book by his Sunday School teacher. When her son accepted the gift without comment, his mother prompted: "Aren't you going to thank Mr. Lloyd for it?" To this Ewell replied, "I never asked him for it." The book in Hamlin's story may be the Bible to which Ewell refers here. Hamlin, *"Old Bald Head,"* 6–7.

3. Unidentified.

4. Fanny (Franziska) Elssler (1810–1884) was a famous Austrian ballet dancer and choreographer who performed throughout Europe. She had toured America in 1840.

5. Unidentified.

6. The wife of Captain Burdette A. Terrett.

7. Jonathan M. Wainwright (1893–1854), a graduate of Harvard University, was consecrated provisional bishop of New York in 1852. In 1844 he engaged his friend Dr. George Potts (1802–1864), minister of the Duane Street Presbyterian Church in New York City, in a discussion on the subject of Episcopal ordination. Their lengthy discourse appeared in the *New York Commercial Advertiser* and was later published as a pamphlet.

8. Ewell's younger brother William Stoddert became a Presbyterian and attended Union Theological Seminary. In 1845, Ewell's mother noted that William was a minister and was handing out religious tracts and teaching Sunday school.

9. Fredrika Bremer (1801–1865) was born in Finland and raised in Sweden. She wrote several books, the most influential being *Herta* (1856). Bremer traveled throughout Europe and Palestine from 1856 to 1861 and published accounts of those travels. *The Loiterings of Arthur O'Leary* was the work of Irish novelist Charles James Lever (1806–1872).

17. To Rebecca Ewell

Jeff. Brrks[1]
July 30th 1844

D[ea]r Becca

I recd your letter about a week ago from Fort Scott where I suppose it had been lying for a month, the stupid Postmaster not thinking of sending it here.

I recd rather an unwelcome piece of news a few days since to wit that I might expect orders to rejoin my Comp'y, at Ft Scott or wherever it might be, within a week. When I first came here they told me I would in all probability remain here for a year & it is most disgusting to return in less than 3 months.[2] The reason I am sent back is, that they have made so many more recruits than might have been expected that the regiment is full & there is no longer any necessity for so many Officers on that duty. So that untill you hear from me again do not write as I cannot at Present give you my direction. It is an ill wind that blows no person any good. I shall be able by returning to economize which I stand in need of at present as I had many expenses to incur when I came here which I would not have had had I remained at Ft Scott & which have left me under the weather a little.

I do not know when I have been more surprised, than I have been since being at this Post, at the want of accommodation shown by the ladies towards each other. There are six or eight families left here without protectors[,] there Husbands being with their regiments encamped at Fort Jessup,[3] and of course are rather helpless but to my surprise I may say, they shew anything but a disposition to oblige each other. One family yesterday had made up their minds to go to town (about ten miles off) & in an unguarded moment offerred two seats in their carriage to a neighbour who had none & who were anxious to go to town, but they repented of their offer & changed their minds about going alleging the sickness of one of their family as an excuse who was at least as well yesterday as she has been for a month. I was to have driven the establishment to town but was so much disgusted with their meanness that I have been running about since sunrise trying to get a horse & carriage for the second set. As soon as these come back the others will wish to go when of course I will be too much engaged. I would see them at the devil first.

Mrs Terrett is far from affording a specimen of the kind of miracle that you seem to suppose. She rather appeared on her return to be more inclined the other way than ever. The fact is I believe the part of the world, she came from, being chiefly settled by ignorant French & Spanish requires a very different method of teaching from the more enlightened Anglo Saxon race & Mrs Terrett having opportunities of hearing others has opened her eyes. I am afraid if I am to continue much longer I should forfeit your thanks for forbearance on the subject of Catholicism, but you have no right, as in your last letter, to say anything for or against them without being willing to have a return.[4]

August 1st I stopped just above because the former mentioned horse made his appearance & I had to start up to town[5] but such a horse! He was a most pensive looking affair that seemed to be aware one of the ladies weig[h]ed at least 200. I took good care before I started to remove all signs of the Military so that I might not be recognized. The ladies insisted to my great joy upon coming back last night so about an hour after dark we left town an awfull looking cloud overhead & about 3 inches of mud beneath. The horse stopped on the first hill we came to & I had to jump out & lead him up the hill. you may depend I cut a fine figure in the way of muddy pants by the time I reached home but anything rather than try it again in the day time. Elizabeth in a Postscrip[t] to one of Mothers letters spoke of a young man Thornton[6] who had enlisted in the Dragoons & whose sister[,] a Nun[,] had made enquiries about him. I have not time now to hunt up the letter but tell her that the result of my enquiries is that he is still at Fort Atkinson[7] but not worth his sister's anxiety. He deserted about 6 m[o]nths ago and was sentenced to be whipped but was let off that part of his punishment.

Should his sister wish to hear anything about him she should address Capt. E. V. Sumner & state what she wishes plainly. he is an excellent man & [will] take interest in it. It is as far from here almost as from you—direction Capt. E. V. Sumner.

1st Drags

Fort Atkinson

Via Prairie du Chien

W. T.

P.S. Yrs &c
 R. S. Ewell

I will write as soon as my destination is fixed. I may have to go to the Prairies yet. I have not heard from home for more than a month.

1. Jefferson Barracks was a large military post located south of St. Louis, Missouri. Created in 1826, the post became the birthplace of Ewell's regiment, the 1st United States Dragoons, seven years later.
2. Ewell had been ordered to Jefferson Barracks on recruiting duty in May 1844.
3. Fort Jessup was constructed in 1822, roughly halfway between Natchitoches, Louisiana, and the Texas border. Commanded by General Zachary Taylor, the fort was designed to protect America's border with Mexico and to provide law and order in that region. After the Mexican War, the U.S. Army no longer needed the post and abandoned it.
4. Mrs. Terrett, the wife of Ewell's commanding officer, was a Louisiana Creole. Raised a Roman Catholic, she had recently left the church and was consequently apprehensive about returning home on a visit. Rebecca Ewell, herself

a Catholic, apparently thought Mrs. Terrett might return to the faith of her childhood after spending time with her family, but Dick informed her that the trip had only strengthened Mrs. Terrett in her new beliefs.

5. This word is missing due to a tear in the page. It has been supplied by the editor.
6. Unidentified.
7. Fort Atkinson had been established by the army in the Wisconsin Territory during the Black Hawk War. It was located in what is today Jefferson County, Wisconsin.

18. To Benjamin Ewell

Jeff. Brrks August 9 1844

Dear Ben

I recd your letter in due course of mail & shall go to the business Part &[c] first. When I read your letter the other day I thought you said you wished to give Becca & Elizabeth $50. apiece which I hestitated to do as I thought the money might be better used than by trying to get rid of their sins.[1] I just now saw that your letter read $5 or $10. I will tell you what I wish to do—my trunk having been broken open & some money taken out I have been temporarily embarrassed as I have undergone expenses on having that money I would otherwise have not incurred. If you could send me fifty dollars of the amount so as to reach me by the end of this month (about) the balance you can dispose of as you please either by letting them[—]Becca & Eliz—have it or what would be better[,] using it yourself. I expect to go to Fort Scott before the end of Septr and do not wish to incur any debts I cannot liquidate before that time. I shall have to buy one or two horses (used) to take back with me & shall have other expenses to incur. Now if you cannot conveniently send me the money it makes but little difference as I shall only have to leave a pay out which is almost as good as gold. When I return to Fort Scott I shall live economically enough to save $2 or 300 by next spring when I shall apply for a furlough. You see I have no urgent necessity for money not owing but in perspective. I did not reach here untill after the troops had all left & a most disagreeable Post it is. I am glad that recruits have been made so fast that Col. Kearney thinks one of the Officers can be spared from the duty. I did not reach here in time to see Mrs Alden. When the 4th left[,] Capt Alden[2] was on furlough. he left Mrs A. in Newport R. I. & passed here a few days since on his way to join the 4th at Fort Jes[s]up. There is no garrison here but a few grass widows[3] belonging to the 4th Regt & very poor company[,] as the crackers say[,] they make always grumbling about their Husbands. I never saw a place so well calculated as Jeff. Brrks is, at present to cure an Officer of a matrimonial disposition. I must however except the Miss Garlands[4] from the number of antidotes as they are so dev[i]lish pretty they have rather a tendency the other way. Fortunately one of them is to be married in Sept. to Lieut Deas of the 5th Infy & the other to Brevet 2nd Longstreet as soon as she is old enough.[5] This is the worst Country for single ladies I ever saw in my life. They are hardly allowed to come of age before they are engaged to be married however ugly they may be. Except the Miss Garlands I have not seen a pretty Girl or interesting one since I have been here. I have seen a good deal of Tasker[6] since being here who has treated me with a great deal of kindness indeed. for the last ten days however he has been in Jefferson City up the Missouri River attending the Courts of law. He seems to have a great deal to do & I have been afraid of intruding on his business hours. 6th I was in St Louis yesterday & found Tasker there who had just retd & glad enough he seemed to be to get back from the wilderness. Col. Kearney told me that as my company[7] has started for the prairie I should remain where I am untill it returns which will be in about eight weeks. In the mean time all recruiting for my regiment is stopped it being full while other regiments in service are just beginning to be recruited for. Lieut Philip R. Thompson[8] is here of my regiment who has been recruiting in Louisville. he requested me a few days since when I next wrote to you to give his respects. I hope you understand that I am in no need at present of the $50. & would not have mentioned it at all but from the tenor of your letter I thought you seemed to want to settle the matter. I shall have to buy a horse before the end of September & can do so whether you send me the money or not. I wrote to Tom last Feby since which time I have not heard of him. Tasker told me he had written twice to him recently but had recd no answer. Tasker had heard of a fine opening for a lawyer which he had offered to Tom. Capt Irwin[9] went on a trip to Fort Leavenworth a few days ago & I went with him to the steamboat. He told me when he retd that a young man on board asked him if my name were not Ewell & said that he had been to Hampden Sydney & recog[nized] me by my likeness to yourself.[10] The Capt. was struck by the peculiar Virginian appearance of the carriage & horses. He said the young gentleman regretted much not having introduced himself to me. Capt Irwin forgot his name.

Yrs &

R. S. Ewell

Lt 1 Dr[11]

---

1. Ewell is probably referring to indulgences, the practice of paying money to receive forgiveness of sins.

2. Bradford R. Alden of Pennsylvania had graduated from West Point in 1831 and became captain of the 4th United States Infantry in June 1842. He resigned from the service in 1853.

3. The term "grass widows" refers to women temporarily separated from their husbands. It can also refer to divorced women, but the first meaning is probably the one Ewell had in mind.

4. John Garland, a Virginian, joined the army during the War of 1812 and by this time was lieutenant colonel of the 4th United States Infantry. Garland had two daughters: Mary Elizabeth (1825–1899) and Marie Louise (1827–1889).

5. George Deas of Pennsylvania was then a second lieutenant in the 5th United States Infantry. Brevetted to major during the Mexican War, he resigned his commission in 1861 and cast his lot with the Confederacy, becoming a lieutenant colonel. Deas married Mary Elizabeth Garland just months after Ewell penned this letter. James Longstreet (1821–1904) was a brevet second lieutenant in the 4th United States Infantry. Like Ewell, he became a lieutenant general in the Army of Northern Virginia during the Civil War. Longstreet married Marie Louise Garland on March 8, 1848, a union that produced ten children.

6. Ewell's cousin Thomas Tasker Gantt practiced law in St. Louis, Missouri.

7. Company A, 1st United States Dragoons.

8. Philip R. Thompson of Georgia had graduated from West Point in 1835. Brevetted to the rank of major for gallantry in the Mexican War, he was cashiered in 1855 and died two years later.

9. Captain James R. Irwin of Pennsylvania was an officer in the 1st United States Artillery. He died in 1848.

10. For Ewell's similarity in appearance to his brother Ben, see RSE to RLE, 29 Aug. 1836, USMA (letter 2, this volume).

11. Lieutenant, 1st Dragoons.

19. To Benjamin Ewell

Jeff. Brrk Oct 17th 1844

Dear Ben

I have negletted [*sic*] answering your last letter because I have ever since its receipt been in daily & hourly expectation of going to Fort Scott again & disliked writing before I was settled down. I was told yesterday in a kind of half official way that It was the intention of Col. Kearney to keep me here all winter. I should like it well enough if it were not for playing 2d fiddle to Thompson. The only way we have here to pass off time is to go to St. Louis occasionally

Ewell was assigned to duty at Jefferson Barracks, Missouri, in May 1844. He found it both expensive and devoid of society, "a most disagreeable Post." (Library of Congress)

which, being attended at all times with a certainty of spending a small amount & the possibility of spending a good deal, is not always agreeable.

I have been very much disappointed with Jeff. Brrks. instead of being the pleasant Post I had anticipated it is as lonesome as Fort Scott excepting The City of St. Louis. Several families of the 4th were left here, when the Regiment went to La, expecting the Regt to return soon but their absent Husbands & lovers occupy the thought & conversation so much when one visits them that it is quite a bore to call. I have been for a long time trying to purchase a horse here & did not succeed untill a few days since when I bought on[e] for $100. that would not in any respect compare with the little bay called Charley[1] that you had at Stoney Lonesome some time ago.

I was very glad at receiving the $50. you sent me. By an act of the last Congress Forage Officers have to muster their horses at the end of each quarter. Had I not bought a horse in September I should have lost $24.00 & have had to buy a horse besides in a short time. I am now economising as much as possible in order to lay up some money to go on furlough next Spring. Had I been left at Fort Scott I would have been able to save by that time nearly if not quite $800. I have seen a good deal of Capt Cram[2] of the Topog's since last August. he is in St Louis on duty connected with the harbor of the Town which is in some danger of being left by the Mississippi above instead of underneath the water. The Capt often enquires about you & has several times requested to be remembered to you. The Captain is engaged in a most important work here & one that requires an entirely different plan from any operation in the water that I ever heard of before.

The Captain showed me some of his reports on the St Louis harbour which interested me very much. I have made some very pleasant acquaintances in St Louis chiefly however among the Officers families. Major Lee[3] has treated me with as much kindness as any person that I have met with, out of my own Corps. Capt Turners wife is a remarkably fine woman & does not seem to have the smallest idea that she is or will be immensely rich. To tell the truth I like her much better than I do the Captain. Schaumburg a man appointed from civil life to my Regt in 34 & who resigned under charges of ungentlemanly conduct in 38 has been re-appointed to come into the regiment with his original rank. Thanks to Capt Stockton of the Navy All the Officers of the regiment who can exert any influence either directly or indirectly have been called upon to do so to resist his confirmation by the Senate. Do you know any[4] way in which you can be of service to your humble servant? Of all things promotion downwards is the most disagreeable.[5]

R. S. Ewell

Mrs Turner says she is going to Va with me next Spring—which by the way I much doubt.

1. For an earlier reference to Charley, see RSE to RLE, ca. 5 May 1838, LC (letter 4, this volume).
2. Thomas J. Cram of New Hampshire rose through the ranks of the Artillery before transferring to the Topographical Engineers in 1838. He was promoted a brevet major general in 1866 for faithful and meritorious service in the Civil War.
3. Richard Bland Lee of Virginia had graduated from West Point in 1817, the year Ewell was born. At this time he was serving as an officer in the Commissary Department. He later served in the Commissary Department of the Confederacy with the rank of colonel. He died in 1875.
4. Ewell repeated the word "any" twice.
5. Schaumburgh's appointment made him senior to Ewell. As promotion in the army was generally based on seniority rather than merit, Schaumburgh's appointment effectively knocked Ewell down one notch on the promotion list.

20. To Rebecca Ewell

Jeff. Brrks Octr 25th 1844

Dear Becca

After remaining for two months in a state of perfect doubt as to my winter quarters I have at last within a few days been informed that I might consider myself as fixed at this Post for the Winter—an arrangement which but for the expense I should consider as very fortunate. The only thing that I care about is that I shall not have as much money to spend when I have a furlough as I would had I remained at Fort Scott. I have now the first chance, I may say, since graduating for entering civilized society & if possible I shall take advantage of it. Col. Kearney the chief of my regiment was so kind a few days since as to offer to take me to a Mr O'Follan's[1] with him who (Mr. O.F.) was to give a party last night. I went up yesterday evening and drove out with the Col. & I assure you spent a most delightful evening. What seems strange it was one of those assemblages that very properly are called by Mrs Turner[,] a lady of my Regt[,] Tea fights, that is to say there was no dancing but the company was expected to amuse itself by flirtations &c &c. Very much contrary to my expectations the evening instead of being dull & tiresome was to me directly the reverse and I regretted very much when a few drops of rain dispersed the company at 12 o'clock at night. The only addition to conversation that we had during the evening was a most excellent supper, accompanied by Champagne & other wines in abundance. The ladies present did not give me a very exalted idea of the beauty of St Louis for I do not think I ever saw a more homely set together. The daughter of our Host though ought to be excepted from the crowd, for whether it was because her father was immensely wealthy or she really was so, I thought I had not seen a more interesting looking young lady for a good many years. An Officer of my regiment was married a few days ago to a lady of St Louis who, of all the indifferent looking ones that I have seen[,] struck me as the Queen, & strange to say he is one who has seen as much or more society than a majority of the Dragoon Officers. He was caught last Winter at Fort Leavenworth where the lady was spending a short time & where he could not compare her with any others so as to be able to form a just estimate of her charms. It is the fate of many Officers who pass the ordeal of the world to fall a victim at an isolated Post to very inferior stock.

It reminds me of a saying that Renoe's Bob[2] used to make use of to wit, "Who knows the luck of a lousy Calf that lives all the Winter but to die in the Spring"? Tell Elizabeth that I received her letter a few days since and will answer it in a short time. I have seen Mary Lee[3] of whom she speaks, very often but must say I do not admire her much. She is quite plump & (but I just remembered she has relations there and you always make a point of repeating, so I must praise her) and lively and is said to be a good deal admired. Anyhow some of the ladies here were quite piqued at her offering to spare some of her beaux for them she having such a surplus of them. Tasker is a warm admirer of the Father & I believe visits there oftener than anywhere else in town. I have been to the Catholic Church in town with Mrs Turner but have always been disappointed in my hopes of hearing a good sermon. The Bishop of whom Mrs Turner is very fond of bragging being sick and of course having his place filled by a more indifferent. Mrs T. is very fond of talking about going to Va with me next Spring which I hope she may do though I am afraid she is jesting. This place is so expensive that I am sometimes afraid I will not have money enough to pay my expenses next Spring though I think I can afford to live on bread & water for one month.

Yrs &   R. S. Ewell

1. John O'Fallon (b. ca. 1792), a native of Kentucky, owned a farm near St. Louis.
2. Strother Renoe owned a house near Stony Lonesome in Prince William County, Virginia. Bob may have been one of his slaves.
3. The words "and" and "Mary" in this sentence were torn out of the original letter, but were supplied by Percy G. Hamlin in his book *The Making of a Soldier*, 54–56. Mary Lee was the daughter of Major Richard B. Lee.

21. To Rebecca Ewell

Louisville Ky Jany 14th 45

Dear Becca

Yesterday evening about dark a man brought me a bill of lading from a Steamboat for a box from St Louis. To my great joy this morning I found it to be the "long-expected" box of shirts from home which had been sent here from St Louis by Maj. Mackay.[1] I am now writing with one on and I assure you that it fits me better than any I ever wore. They are so neatly made & so much better than any I can get out here that I do not intend to have but a few done up for grand occasions. They were all present Towels &c. &c. I thought however that Mother had put a purse in for me—if so I cannot find it. I was just resolving myself into a committee of the whole on ways & means to buy half a dozen from some shop when these came. I believe there is no pleasure without alloy. the boat bringing these shirts passed within a mile from here the boat taking Tom away who had been on a visit to me.[2] I should have rejoiced very much to have given Tom 6 or 8 shirts as they would have been of as much service to him as to me & have left me with 2 yrs supply on hand. Tom came here about the 16th of last month & was attacked almost as soon as he came with Erysipelas or as it is called by these people "black tongue"—A swelling & inflam[m]ation of the face & scalp &c. Tom's face was swelled so much that he could not see & from the constant application of diluted lunar caustic, was as black as Othello. The attack was accompanied with delirium & for several days while at its worst he was in great danger of his life. He left perfectly recovered but weak from abstinence during the attack. It was to me like meeting with a stranger in whom one is interested & whose character is a matter of interest. I passed him in the streets without either recognising the other. I saw his name on the books & was told he had stepped out to look after his trunk. I walked down the street scrutinizing all I met & made up my mind that one person was him & was correct, but was not certain enough to stop him. He is nearly 6 feet tall, but stoops a little has very fine eyes, (if you remember it) his peculiar manner of wiping his nose has given it a slight bend downwards that is not unbecoming as it makes it look a little aquiline. His old habit of putting out his lips when drinking with a spoon still remains to a slight degree. It is singular that these little peculiarities should have struck me after so long a time & after such great changes in other respects.

He is a noble minded fellow & as talented [as] Mother ever anticipated he would be in her most sanguine moments. He excels in conversation & I should think must be a most excellent speaker. I think in all probability he will settle in Memphis[,] a much better field than Jackson can open to him & if he be patient cannot but succeed. His exceedingly youthful appearance I should think must prevent him from succeeding as quickly as he would if he looked older.[3] By the by an old gentleman asked which of us was the younger. I had plenty of offers of service from the people here when he was sick but[4] did not require any as he was not in want of sitting up with. I employed a Dr Powell[5] from the neighbourhood of Haymarket[6] formerly I believe who managed his case very well. did you ever hear of him? Tom was in a great quandary when he left as to what should be done with the medicine over & above what he had taken & I believe would have bribed the waiter to take them if he could. I wrote home more than a month ago. what is the reason I have not got an answer? It only requires 10 days for a letter to go. I called to day on one of the belles of this place & spent quite an agreeable 2 hours (the first visit). One of her beaux was amusing her with extracts from "Desdemonia"[7] very much to her edification.

Nice girl but too much rouge. I am invited to a ball there day after to-morrow when I anticipate much pleasure. There are some beautiful girls in this place & nothing but poverty prevents my falling desperately in love. I regretted very much that Toms Phis,[8] did not recover suifficiently [*sic*] for him to visit some of the ladies as his wit would have delighted them.

I received a letter from Tasker this morning who speaks in glowing terms of the gaieties of St Louis enough almost to make a person wish themselves back there again. He says Ben is enjoying himself very much indeed.

Yrs &
R S Ewell

I wonder if you all have got over the bad habit of extracting from one correspondents letters to write to another?

1. Aeneas Mackay of New York began his military career during the War of 1812 and in 1838 was promoted to major in the Quartermaster Corps. He died in 1850.
2. Dick had last seen his brother Tom in 1836, when Dick left Stony Lonesome to attend West Point. A short time later, Tom went to study law in Jackson, Tennessee.
3. Tom was then approaching his twenty-third birthday.
4. The page was torn here. The editor has supplied the word.
5. Unidentified.
6. A village near Stony Lonesome.
7. Desdemona was the wife of the title character in William Shakespeare's play *Othello*. In the play, Othello becomes convinced, wrongly, that his wife had been unfaithful and murders her.
8. Face, perhaps short for physiognomy.

22. To Benjamin Ewell

Louisville Kentucky
Feby 28th 1845

Dear Ben

In looking for something (somebody rapped at my door just then & lo and behold a waiter came in with a bouquet of the finest flowers with a card on which was written in a *female* hand "From a friend, a Cincinnati bouquet". These ladies do certainly plague one out of his life) else this morning among my papers I came across a letter of yours with the enclosed note which I send to you requesting that you would do with the amount whatever seems most proper. if you think it would do you as much good as it would Becca & Elizabeth to give to the Priests pray keep it, otherwise lay it out for Miss Betty.[1] I assure you there is little necessity for the lecture on economy in your last letter. I have suffered from stoppages robberies &c and instead of being in debt as any person else would have been am square with the world even while living in cities. I am perfectly delighted with Louisville & the only drawback to my pleasure is the anticipation of having to return to the frontier to fried bacon and Indians. There are a number of *beautiful* women in this place and as unsophisticated a personage as myself would most certainly fall a victim were it not, that one heals the wounds left by another. The bouquet mentioned above came I presume from a widow whom I have, or rather, who has been sparking me & who at present is on a visit to Cin'i. She is rich and is engaged to be married but like most Widows is fond of a flirtation.

Do your remember Saunders[2] who graduated at West Point in 37 & belonged to your section? He was regularly victimized by this same widow & served as a warning to myself to keep out of danger; which warning I have profited by. He often speaks of you (he is living next door to me) and desired to be remembered. Henry Clay Jr[3] was in town a few days since and enquired particularly after yourself.

Tom was about a month here this winter part of the time dangerously ill; so much so that his physician was almost in despair. I haven't seen him since he was a boy 9 yrs ago and did not recognize him though I met him in the streets knowing he was in town and of course looking out for him. I never saw a per-[s]on whose colloquial and other talents made a stronger impression on me. He possessed [*sic:* impressed] the Dr and all who came about him, very much indeed. He is entirely undecided as to his future course. in his last letter he speaks of applying for an Office (Consul) & in case of failure to go to Louisiana to practice his profession. He is determined not to remain in Jackson.

In the new Army Register I see Schaumburg is placed at the head of the 1st Lieuts from which I infer that the Senate contrary to all our hope has confirmed his re-appointment over the heads of those who have been in service & who have not been forced to resign from their own acts of the basest fraud. He has written if the Officers of the regt do not respect him that he will make them—a task which I think will give him some trouble if he attempts to try it.

I have received three congratulations at intervals of nearly a month from Col. Kearny on the improvement in my hand, but I am so pushed for time it being the last of the month I cannot take time to give you a specimen of my improvement.

Yrs &c

R. S. Ewell

1. Ben's four-year-old daughter.
2. Franklin Saunders of North Carolina graduated last in West Point's Class of 1837. Like Ewell, Saunders joined the 1st Dragoons. He left the Regular Army in 1838 but fought in the Mexican War as a captain in the 1st Kentucky Volunteers. He died in 1856.
3. Henry Clay Jr. (1811–1847) was the second son of Kentucky statesman Henry Clay. An 1831 graduate of West Point, the younger Clay raised and led the 2nd Kentucky Volunteer Regiment in the Mexican War. He died at the Battle of Buena Vista.

23. To Rebecca Ewell

Fort Scott October 3rd 1845

My Dear Becca;

I received your two letters last Sunday, for which I assure you I feel very much obliged indeed though I cannot help thinking if postage had not been reduced you would not have written them. I expected ere this to be on my way to Va. but for some quibble my application was returned from St Louis to have some change made in its form, thereby causing me to lose 20 days. it is now 17 since it has been sent off a second time & I shall receive an answer, whether favorable or not, in about 20 more. Should I get the leave & Tom be in Tenn. I intend at present to go through Nashville to see him & then on home. I beg you would correct that mistaken notion, twice mentioned "the disease he (Tom) caught while in Louisville" referring to his throat. He went to Louisville in very cold weather with a stock on that was not actually 1 inch wide (George Campbell[1] who has not more neck than a bullfrog had persuaded him that such was "bon just")[2] with his glands swollen from an attack of some weeks standing & complaining of a sore throat. I persuaded him to throw the thing away & put one on a little more suitable to circumstances but it was too late, for though he got better while there it broke out as soon as he left.

One would suppose from your letter that people only went there to eat. you make so many lamentations over the garden now I wish you to understand that when I get there the eating part must be left to me alone. Are any of those blue cylindrical looking cups with a handle (I was going to say on one side) left yet? I am using a set that [cost] 37 1/2 cents out here which are much more fashionable looking. I do not often drink as good coffee as I got out of those; when I was lucky enough to get the first fillings. We have a N.E. rain to-day & a married Officer called in just before dinner to spend [a] tiresome hour & in the mean-time my dinner was brought in, which, as he had the bad taste to eat of, I must describe. Two raw tomatoes cut up with 1 onion in one of the 3 bit (bit = 12 1/2 oz) saucers neatly covered by another, some salt in a cup, 6 cold sweet potatoes & two little pieces of beef *dried* on the gridiron. When the table was set I asked him to set up, as a matter of course, thinking he would be as likely to sit in the fire but, for some cause, inexplicable to me, he took a seat, and dived at the tomatoes. Married men, on all such occasions, generally hurry off, on the first intimation of a meal. The only indiscretion of the kind I ever saw before was followed by an attack of indigestion which lasted the rash man a week, though he was formally asked to what we thought something extra.[3] Yesterday, I had a pitcher of buttermilk and a grouse both sent me by Mrs Capt. Swords.[4] the Captain was in as they were sitting [*sic*] the table but declined partaking. If it were not for the kindness of some of the ladies I should fare badly. Buttermilk has found great favor in my eyes lately & I often receive a pitcher full which lasts me two days. I am living more indifferently than usual, because it would be a foolish expense for me to buy finery now as I expect to leave here for home before long. Did I expect to remain all the winter I would hire a negress & boy, lay in a winter's supply &c &c. The winter is the worst time for getting a leave but as I calculate on spending it in Va in my particular case it does not matter much. You would hardly believe how nervous &[5] anxious, this waiting, expecting, doubtful situation makes me; should the answer even be unfavorable it will be a great relief.[6] We have fine sport here now hunting grouse & the disposal of my three dogs, gives me no slight uneasiness. Bet, Bill & Tom[7] are each paragons of sense & hunting qualities & each have a striking fancy for monopolizing (which used to be a fruitful source of contention at home), the best part of the fireplace.

I sold Arthur[8] last winter, he being an incorrigible young scamp & have thought of getting a servant in Va. Not a boy for I have had enough of them but some old man of 30 or 40 who might be depended on. The one owned by Mother[,] as she does not use him[,] I have thought of buying (supposing Mother were willing). To answer[,] a man ought to know some little about cooking & to sweep a room & make a bed. At present I employ a Dragoon who costs $10 1/2 per month or about $130 per annum & though very willing is not very expert. He made up my bed the other day with a comfortor between the sheets. on which side of the former he intended me [to] sleep I have no idea. What would be the chance of collecting some of the beauty & fashion of P. Wm[9] at Stony lonesome [at] Christmas & having a regular blow out to a real fiddle. it has occurred to me while writing this & I think it would be glorious? If it were necessary you might intercede with some young lady for a Dragoon & we might enliven the occasion with a wedding but let her not have large hands & feet which I abominate. I intended to take your advice as respects a young lady in Louisville. to state the question mathematically she is plus 4 or 5 negroes & an old uncle who has many more[,] a pretty good education & much reading[,] black eyes & beautiful hands. minus she walks badly[,] once had dirty finger nails (important to know whether by scratching herself or not but did not like to ask)[,] is short & not a belle. She is a pious Catholic & declare[s] she is going into a nunnery, but I suppose that you would put [that] down to her credit though to tell the truth I always thought a[t] church She was too fond of looking at the beaux to be much taken by the service.

Yrs   R.S. Ewell

I hoped before sending this off to write about my leave more definitely but the weekly mail has failed (yesterday) & we have no other untill the 12th. I shall write the 1st information though the leave itself cannot come before the 27th. Write to me here anyhow.

I could hardly suppose you could sell the property for the sums you mention[,] though if so the money would produce a much higher income than is at present derived; More than ten per cent in St Louis. Tell Mammy[10] I tried very hard to get her an Indian pipe when I was in the mtns but as they are valued there as trophies nothing less than a horse would purchase one. Your complaints as to my not writing are groundless. I keep you as well informed of my movements as the War Office of those of the Army but as letters recd at home are made common property of it does not matter much to whom my letters are addressed. You can write to me abusing all your neighbours with perfect safety but there would be no prudence in my doing so. I have received letters from home telling me not to answer certain parts. what a funny tirade that is of yours about the unstable affection of brother and then to speak of Elizabeth's remaining in the Dis[trict] during Tom's visit.[11]

1. George Campbell (1819–1853) was Ewell's first cousin and the brother of his future wife, Lizinka Campbell Brown.

2. French, "just fine."

3. The gist of this sentence seems to be that Ewell invited his guest to a better meal than was common.

4. Thomas Swords of New York had graduated from West Point in 1829 and was promoted to captain in the 1st Dragoons in March 1837.

5. Ewell superfluously added the word "and" after the ampersand.

6. Ewell had an unusually nervous, high-strung temperament.

7. Curiously, Ewell named his dogs after three of his siblings: Elizabeth, William, and Tom.

8. Ewell had purchased the sixteen-year-old boy, named Arthur, in the fall of 1842 for $600. See RSE to RLE, 10 Apr. 1842, LC (letter 13, this volume).

9. Prince William County, Virginia.

10. Fanny Brown, affectionately known by the Ewell children as "Mammy," had been the Ewell family's slave. She tended the family's poultry, cleaned house, cooked meals, fetched water, and did other household chores. When Dick was still a boy, Fanny nursed his father, Thomas Ewell, back to health after a dangerous fever. In gratitude, Thomas granted Fanny her liberty. Although no longer a slave, she remained with the Ewells until her death in 1858.

11. Ewell's sister Elizabeth (1813–1901) was then living in Georgetown, in the District of Columbia, where she later took the vows of a novice in the Order of Visitation. Finding life in the convent more rigorous than expected, she left the order and became the organist of Holy Trinity Church in Georgetown.

Chapter 3

The Mexican War, 1846–1848

During Stephen Kearny's 1845 Oregon Trail expedition, Ewell contracted malaria, a disease that troubled him for the rest of his life. When he returned to Fort Scott, he applied for a leave of absence and returned to Virginia to recover. Shortly thereafter, the United States declared war on Mexico. Ewell signed up new soldiers at various recruiting depots in the Midwest, then joined First Lieutenant Philip Kearny and Company F, 1st Dragoons, at Jefferson Barracks, outside of St. Louis, Missouri. For six weeks Kearny and Ewell drilled the company, preparing it for war. On October 5, 1846, Company F received orders to proceed to Point Isabel, Texas, at the mouth of the Rio Grande.

Initially, Kearny's dragoons performed scouting duty for General Zachary Taylor's army at Saltillo in north-central Mexico. Three months later, however, Company F returned to the mouth of the Rio Grande, where it joined General Winfield Scott's army, which was soon to debark on transports that would take it to the Mexican city of Vera Cruz on the Gulf Coast. Once Scott seized Vera Cruz, he would march 250 miles inland on the National Highway and capture Mexico City. In the coming expedition, Company F would act as General Scott's mounted escort.

Scott invested Vera Cruz in March 1847 and after a four-day bombardment captured the city. His troops then started inland. At a mountain called Cerro Gordo, Mexican forces led by General Antonio Lopez de Santa Anna blocked the way. On April 17, Scott attacked Santa Anna's left flank and carried the hill. Dick Ewell's younger brother Tom was mortally wounded in the attack and died that night with Dick at his side. Dick fashioned a crude coffin from boards and buried his brother the next day.

After a ten-week delay at Puebla, Scott's army continued its advance on Mexico City. Just south of the capital, the general found his progress blocked by an ancient lava field known as the Pedregal. Captain Robert E. Lee, an engineer on Scott's staff, led a reconnaissance, hoping to find a path through the difficult, rocky terrain. Kearny's dragoons and two companies of infantry supported the effort. At the Pedregal, Mexican skirmishers fired on the scouting party. Ewell charged with half his company and drove the Mexicans away.

Lee's reconnaissance uncovered a path that led across the Pedregal to the town of Contreras. Scott sent troops over the path the next day, turning Santa Anna's position. In a running battle, United States forces attacked Santa Anna's army at the town of Churubusco and routed it. Company F pursued the fleeing enemy down a narrow causeway toward the San Antonio Gate. There a Mexican redoubt mounting two cannon blocked its path. When the cannon sprayed grapeshot into the American ranks, Kearny and Ewell leaped from their horses and scrambled by foot over the parapet. Only then did they realize that they had virtually no support. A superior officer had recalled the troops in their rear, leaving them with little more than a dozen men. Kearny wisely ordered a retreat. As the dragoons made their way back down the causeway, musketry and cannon fire thinned their depleted ranks. A grapeshot shattered Kearny's arm, while Ewell lost two horses. The War Department later brevetted Ewell for his gallant conduct in this encounter.

With the victory at Churubusco, Mexico City lay open to capture. Rather than capitalize on his advantage, however, Scott halted his troops outside the city and opened negotiations with Santa Anna. For three weeks the talks dragged on. Santa Anna used the time to improve his position. The key to his defenses was Chapultepec, a fortress just south of the city. United States infantry stormed the fortress on September 13 and captured it. In the assault, Ewell's cousin Levi Gantt was killed. Coming on the heels of Tom's death five months earlier, the blow struck hard.

The assault on Chapultepec sealed Mexico City's fate and effectively ended the war. While diplomats negotiated the terms of Santa Anna's surrender, Scott's army occupied the capital and nearby towns. When he was not leading patrols into the countryside or escorting wagon trains to and from the coast, Ewell enjoyed Mexico City's attractions. In January 1848 his garrison occupied the city of Toluca, forty miles to the west. The Treaty of Guadalupe Hidalgo brought a formal end to the war, and in June the invading army boarded transports that carried it back to the United States. After a year and a half of hardship and sorrow, Dick Ewell was going home.

Of Ewell's Mexican War correspondence just four complete letters survive. Portions of five others are quoted by Mrs. Ewell in subsequent letters to her eldest son, Ben.

24. To Elizabeth Ewell Sr.

We left Jeffn Barracks on tuesday,[1] the day after our orders were recd with 91 men, armed & equipped for years service in the[2] field, & when you take into consideration that our own private affairs had to be attended to, as well as public, & that the men & horses had to be provided for, you will see that Lt. Kearney[3] the commanding Officer of the Comp[an]y, deserves great credit for promp[t]ness & energy. Captain Thompson, the former commanding Officer, has been sent to St. Fe in command of the Mormons, at least that portion of them amounting to about 500 who have been muster'd into the service of the U.S's. Lt. Ky the 1st Lt. of the Comp[an]y of course succeeds him, & very fortunately for me has agreed to take me with him into the field. He could not have confer'd a greater favor upon me, as otherwise I should have been sent to Fort Leavenworth, on very disagreeable duties & have run great risks of being sick, besides the mortification of being at a garrison in time of war. I was in St. Louis nearly all day yesterday & took breakfast with Tasker. Aunt Nancy & all well. . . . Orders arriv'd from Washington, Comp[an]y F, to which I am temporarily attached, should be in readiness to take the field, & to day 5th were officially order'd to proceed to P. Isabel & shall proceed to New Orleans to day enroute for that great Point.

1. This excerpt was taken from a letter written by Ewell to his mother, Elizabeth. That letter no longer survives; however, Elizabeth quoted this portion of it in a letter that she wrote to her son Benjamin on October 27, 1846. At the beginning of the letter she informed Ben that Richard's letter was postmarked October 10, at which time he was en route to Point Isabel, Texas, under the command of First Lieutenant Philip Kearny. Ewell actually wrote his letter on October 5, as indicated in the last sentence of this excerpt.
2. Elizabeth Ewell inadvertently repeated the words "in the" here.
3. Philip Kearny (1814–1862) of New York was then in command of Company F. Promoted to captain in December 1846, he lost an arm at the Battle of Churubusco in the Mexican War. Kearny resigned from the service in 1851 but returned to the army in 1861 as a brigadier general of Union volunteers. He was commanding a division in the Army of the Potomac on September 1, 1862, when he received a mortal wound at Chantilly, Virginia.

25. To Elizabeth Ewell Sr.

Jalapa[1] April 22d 1847

My dear Mother

I wrote you a letter dated the 18th which I hope you have recd.[2] our mails are so irregular that [it] is possible this one may reach you first. I know your firmness & resolution or this painful task would be much more difficult than it is at present. . . . On the 17th a large body under Genl Twiggs[3] including the Rifles commenced the attack on the main works of the enemy. Tom on this day by his gallantry & good conduct excited the admiration of those around him.[4]

The Battle of Cerro Gordo claimed the life of Ewell's younger brother, Tom. General Winfield Scott (shown here) later praised Tom as "the Hero of that fight 'more than anyone else.'" (Library of Congress)

that night they lay on their arms within a few hundred yards of the enemy & ready to resume the attack next morning. . . . When the order was given to charge (after considerable firing) Tom took the head of the regiment, & led [it] to the first line whence the enemy retreated to the 2d. here the order to charge was given a second time, & Tom leaped over the outer work, & rushed into the interior first of all. He told me as follows "I there found about 200 men lying down ready to fire. I found myself on the flank, & passed my sword through the first man. the next was aiming at me. I struck the musket but the fellow fired & struck me"; this was all over by 11 o'clock A.M. After being struck he cut the man down. During this time the Dragoons [were] held in reserve. when the Mexicans were routed, the Dragoons were brought up for the pursuit & near the foot of the hill I found Levi Gantt,[5] who told me of Tom's wound. I went up the hill where I found Tom with several Officer's of his regiment around him & suffering much from his wound. the ball entered on the left side between the navel & point of the hip, about one inch from the navel, & was taken from under the skin just above the extremity of the spine, without depriving him of the use of his limbs. At that time my troop were in pursuit & I joined them leaving Tom with his brother Officers. I returned when the pursuit was over, getting to the hill about 7 o'clock at night. the Dr told me nothing could be done, & that he had told Tom to prepare for the worst. I found him apparently sinking, much easier than when I left him in the morning, & perfectly sensible of his situation—calm as though he were going to prepare for sleep. He said he hoped his great sufferings might be an expiation for his sins, & wished for a prayer book, given to him by Harriet Stoddert,[6] but which with other things about his person, had been taken care of by his friends. Not having a light the book would have been useless then. In the morning of the 18th when I first saw him, he asked me to write home, & mentioned that Major Loring[7] had his watch & purse, & told me that his wound was fatal, saying at the same time that he would rather die than suffer as he did. Between 1 & 2 o'clock of the morning of the 19th he breathed his last with the calmness of a child going to sleep. I was lying by his side at the time & could not tell the exact moment. his breathing became by degrees easier & a slight fluttering of the heart after no breathing could be perceived. the next day by the kindness of some friends I was able to procure a rude coffin & inter him on the scene of his glory. He had expressed a wish to Captain Pope,[8] who was with him the whole time, to be buried where he was. My intercourse with him the whole time that I had been in the field, at the mouth of the Rio Grande, & at Vera Cruz has been more agreeable than ever. he had endeared himself to his regiment all of whom expressed the greatest sympathy for him. Capt. Pope & several men remained with him from the time of his wound to his death & burial. One man Tom told me was the first he had enlisted & had always been very fond of him. this man was by his side the whole night without closing his eyes. An hour or two before his death, he became at times slightly delirious—this word is too strong, I should say confused—but could easily be recalled to the subject of which we had been speaking. A short time before he died, he observed that his legs were becoming numb, a few minutes after, said that leg (placing his hand on it) has opened the ball, alluding to his dissolution. Nothing could be calmer than his deportment. You will see by the papers what credit he acquired & at the same time without breakneck rashness. Genl Scott[9] went up this hill on which he lay to see him—passed through the crowd & knelt by Tom's side, taking his hand & speaking to him in highly complimentary language. "Mr Ewell you are an honor to your name, an honor to the service to which you belong."

This Tom told me. Those around told me that he continued, ["]Sir, you are already a hero, you must not die.["] turning around to the other Officers[:] "Captain Pope he shall not die." When I returned in the evening in the course of it, Tom said to me, "Dick did you hear what Genl Scott told me?" ["]Not his exact words." he then repeated the above & afterwards described his attack to me. Captain Henry Pope of the Rifles, Lt. E. B. Holloway 8th infantry,[10] Lt. N. Coffee[11] attended his funeral, & I took especial pains to point out the exact spot so that it might be known hereafter. The hill was covered with the dead & dying some of whom remain unburied & all that were buried received but the merest apology, a hole scratched a few inches & hardly enough dirt to cover them. I felt myself very fortunate in being able to procure the rough planks & nails & to give Tom a better & more decent resting place. If you subscribe to the Union[12] you will see the reports &c. speaking of him & they should be kept in the family. Consider if you please the subscription mine, but it would be useless to send it, as all papers get lost. He has shown in a military profession the distinguishing talents that marked his course in every path of life. I wish that the history of his last moments might be known, & for fear of accidents from the mails will write again[,] painful as is a recapitulation. It almost seems that Providence were giving this cursed country into our hands so rapid is our conquest. It is peace within a month or two, I think—or not at all.

Yours. R. S. Ewell.

1. This letter was written by Ewell to his mother and copied by her with some omissions, which are noted here by the use of ellipses. Jalapa, also called Xalapa or Xalapa-Enríquez, is the capital of the State of Vera Cruz. Nicknamed the City of Flowers, it lies approximately fifty miles northwest of the City of Vera Cruz.

2. This letter has not been found.

3. David E. Twiggs (1790–1862) was appointed captain of the 8th United States Infantry during the War of 1812 and rose steadily through the ranks to become colonel of the 2nd United States Dragoons. He fought under both Zachary Taylor and Winfield Scott in the Mexican War, emerging from the conflict as a brevet major general.

4. Ewell's younger brother Thomas was a first lieutenant in the 1st Mounted Rifles. He died on April 18, 1847, at the Battle of Cerro Gordo while serving in Twiggs's division, as Ewell relates in this letter.

5. Ewell's cousin Levi Gantt was a first lieutenant in the 7th United States Infantry.

6. This is probably a reference to Ewell's aunt Harriet Stoddert Campbell (1789–1849). Campbell was a younger sister of Ewell's mother, Elizabeth, and the mother of his future wife, Lizinka. Harriet had married George Campbell in 1812 and lived in Nashville, Tennessee.

7. William W. Loring (1818–1886) began the war as a lieutenant of Florida volunteers, but in May 1846 he was appointed to the mounted rifles with the rank of captain. The following February he was promoted to major. During the Civil War, Loring became a major general in the Confederate army. He commanded a corps in the Atlanta Campaign before surrendering with General Joseph Johnston at Bentonville, North Carolina.

8. Henry C. Pope of Kentucky was a captain in the mounted rifles. He resigned from the army on the last day of December 1847 and died in a duel the following May.

9. General Winfield Scott (1786–1866) was America's leading soldier in the first half of the nineteenth century. The hero of Lundy's Lane and the conqueror of Mexico City, "Old Fuss and Feathers" served as a soldier for half a century and ultimately became commanding general of the United States Army. An ambitious and proud man, Scott ran for president of the United States as a Whig in 1852 but was defeated by a fellow general, Democrat Franklin Pierce. Scott retired from the army at the start of the Civil War and died five years later.

10. Edmunds B. Holloway of Kentucky was an 1843 graduate of West Point. He served briefly in the 4th United States Infantry before transferring to the 8th Infantry in 1845. He died early in the Civil War while serving as a colonel in the Missouri State Guard.

11. Unidentified.

12. A Washington, D.C., newspaper.

26. To Benjamin Ewell

Jalapa Mexico
May 3d 1847

My Dear Ben;

I opened yesterday a letter addressed by you to Tom. I should have written to you at first after the battle of Cerro Gordo where he fell but I gave a long account of the event to Mother & the details were too painful to repeat without great exertion. In the short term of service that he was here, by his good conduct, activity & gallantry he gained great reputation. His gallantry, coolness & zeal place him beyond any person (I do not refer to Generals) who has figured in this war. He found the road to the top of Cerro Gordo & led the way. May's famous charge[1] did not equal his in results for the road is open to Mexico & the taking of that hill[,] which he more than contributed his share[,] led to the surrender of 5000 Mexicans & the retreat of more than that number, 40 pieces of cannon & 4 or 5 breastworks. May had to do what he did or be branded a coward & could not have done it worse. Tom did [it] in a style that will not be equalled.

You say in your letter you wrote to me some time since. I never received your[2] letter, though I should have been very glad to have done so.

It is said the last mail goes tomorrow that we may have for months as we go into the interior towards Mexico & it is thought our communications may not be kept up. I have been writing untill 12 o'clock & must be up early tomorrow. Should an opportunity occur I will write again & hope you will write for the chance.

Yrs &
R. S. Ewell

Remember me to Julia & Lizzy.

May 7th To-morrow I start with a train of wagons for Vera Cruz[3] & shall take this letter down there to mail. There is no prospect of a move from here for ten days to come as we require so much transportation though there will be no resistance between this and the city of Mexico provided we move speedily. The inhabitants of the cities will not permit them to [be] defended.[4] They admit that the Army fight well but prefer their fortifying outside, as the cit[i]es we attack are not improved. This country is to all intents & purposes conquered. No Army or anything else. St. Anna[5] is a wanderer & though he may raise 1 or 2 1000's to attack a baggage train cannot raise another formidable Army unless with most extraordinary assistance from our bad management. We have only to send home the volunteers & keep possession for a year or two & extend our laws to make this a part of the United States.

I shall finish this letter when I get to V.C. if I have time to write there, but for fear I may not & you see fit to write to me address to Lieut. R. S. Ewell Co. "F" 1st Dragoons Vera Cruz, Mexico, & they will be sent to me. The chances are slightly in favor of my being a Captain at this time.[6]

1. Charles A. May (1817–1864) of the 2nd United States Dragoons earned three brevets during the Mexican War, including one for a celebrated charge that broke the Mexican line at the Battle of Resaca de la Palma.

2. Ewell repeated the word "your" here.

3. Scott had captured Vera Cruz at the outset of the campaign and was using the city to import supplies for his army.

4. Above the word "defended" Ewell has scribbled the word "fortified."

5. Antonio López de Santa Anna (1794–1876) began his lengthy public career as an officer in the Spanish army only to turn against Spain and help lead Mexico to independence. Elected president of the Mexican Republic in 1833, he later soured on democracy, suspended the Mexican constitution, and declared himself dictator. Over the next twenty-two years he was alternately in and out of power. He left politics for good in 1855, fleeing to exile in Cuba. He returned to Mexico in 1874, just two years before his death.

6. Ewell received a captain's brevet on August 20, 1847, for gallant and meritorious conduct at the battles of Contreras and Churubusco. He did not attain the full rank for two more years.

27. To Elizabeth Ewell Sr.

3 miles from the Halls[1]
Sept. 1st 1847

Dear Mother—

The Army left Puebla[2] on the 7, 8, & 9th of August & reached this vicinity about the 12th & continued in the neighbourhood untill the 19th when the attack commenced on the side opposite to where the Vera Cruz Road entered the city of Mex.

We merely got into position the evening of the 19th & did not attempt anything decisive & the Mex. were so rejoiced at not being immediately whipped that they spent the night in dancing &c.

At ten next morning 6000 men under Valencia were after ten minutes fight utterly dispersed & destroyed beyond redemption leaving 800. dead any number wounded & near 1000. prisoner. This was the ad[v]anced position of the enemy & the army followed up its advantages untill before 4 P.M. the Mex. Forts (very strong) had been taken[,] 25 000 men driven[,] killed or dispersed & 40 cannon & any amount of ammunition &c. Capt. K'y comp'y with another of the 3d Dragoons charged the retreating enemy to the very gates of the city where we were recd by a heavy fire of grape, round shot &c. &c. killing my horse under me & knocking several men & horses over. We had come upon a work at the very gates which fired their artillery upon us & their own fugitives & we had to retire, not being supported.[3] One half of their works being gone

& the town exposed to be taken by assault the Mex. signified their willingness to listen to terms of peace & negotiations have been going on ever since.[4] The opinions regarding peace are as diverse as they would be on the subject of rain next week. In the mean time we are kept waiting around the suburbs of the city in the most disagreeable state imaginable, not permitted to enter & very much an[n]oyed with ennui & fleas.

My Comp[an]y was in another fight (ski[r]mish) on the 18th when we were reconnoitering a road on the very spot where the battle afterwards took place. Some 200 rancheros fired upon [us] from the crevices of the rocks &c. but we dismounted & soon convinced them it was no place for Mexicans.[5] The charge that we made to the city gates was so much exposed to fire that I lost my hor[s]es & had another shot under me. Capt Kearny [lost] his left army [*sic*] & Lt Graham[6] had a pistol-shot through the left arm.

I shall give more particulars in my next. this letter is smuggled off by a friend & I merely write to say I am alive. My health of late has been excellent with the exception of home sickness (for I wish to see Pr Wm again) & is likely to continue so as this rainy season is about coming to a close. Remember me to Mrs Slye[7] & the young ladies. Gantt is well.

Yrs &

R. S. Ewell

1. The "Halls of Montezuma"—i.e., Mexico City.
2. Puebla, a city of eighty thousand inhabitants, is fewer than one hundred miles southeast of Mexico City. The U.S. Army halted at the town for nearly three months in the summer of 1847, recruiting its strength prior to its advance on Mexico City.
3. Gabriel Valencia (1799–1848) commanded the Mexican Army of the North. On August 20, 1847, American forces led by General Gideon Pillow routed Valencia's army near the town of Contreras. Scott then pressed his advantage, attacking the rest of Santa Anna's force along the Churubusco River. In the heavy fighting that followed, he routed the Mexican army and drove it back to the gates of the capital. Ewell and others in Captain Philip Kearny's company chased the fleeing Mexicans down a causeway toward the San Antonio Gate, unaware that a superior had called off the pursuit. Captains Andrew T. McReynolds's and Alphonse M. Duperu's companies of the 3rd Dragoons joined in the charge. A pair of Mexican cannon blasted the dragoons with grapeshot as they approached the gate. Too late Kearny realized that he and his small force were unsupported. He ordered a retreat, but before he could escape, grapeshot struck him in the arm.

4. Following the Mexican defeats at Contreras and Churubusco, Santa Anna requested a truce. Scott, wishing to secure peace without humiliating the Mexican people, agreed. For two weeks the armies suspended hostilities while commissioners met to hammer out a peace. Negotiations stalled, however, and on September 7, 1847, Scott renewed his efforts to take Mexico City.

5. On August 18, 1847, Captain Robert E. Lee of the engineers led a nighttime reconnaissance of the Pedregal, a fifteen-square-mile lava field south of Mexico City, seeking a route that would enable General Scott to bypass the strong Mexican defenses at San Antonio. The 11th Infantry and two companies of dragoons, including Kearny's Company F, accompanied Lee on this mission. Near an eminence called Zacatepac, Lee encountered a Mexican force and in an exchange of gunfire put it to flight. It was Ewell's first time under fire. He described the action more fully in his November 25, 1847, letter to Ben (29).

6. Lorimer Graham of New York received two brevets during the war, the second for gallant and meritorious service at Churubusco, the same battle in which Kearny lost his arm.

7. Perhaps either Marian Slye (b. ca. 1835) or Gwynetta Slye (b. ca. 1857). Both women lived in Fauquier County, Virginia. Marian was a seamstress; Gwynetta a teacher.

28. To Nancy Gantt

The first safe opportunity of sending to Vera Cruz that we have had since the battles now presents itself, & I take advantage of it to write to you & send the enclosed.[1] Gen. Scotts dispatches have been twice taken on the road & I looked upon the within as too important to risk. You will see our position before this City from Levi's letters up to the 22d August. The Army remained quartered in several villages around the western side of the City, during the negotiations until on the 16th Septr when Gen. Scott became satisfied that the Mex[i]c[an]s shamelessly violated the armistise.[2] On that day the Mexcs were inform'd that hostilities would recommence within 24 hours, & accordingly Twiggs' Division 7th Infy Re[giment][3] commenced the attack on one gate, & Worths[4] on another. On the 8th the battle of Molino del Rey[5] was fought & tho' we conquered yet our loss was dreadful, & our situation depended on the next move. Chepultepec[,] a strong castle built on a hill fortified in every possible manner both on the sides & around the base, was cannonaded on the 11th 12th & the morning of the 13th. Gen. Scotts headquarters were at Tucabaya,[6] Genl. Twiggs was 3 miles to our right & Chepultepec 1 mile from Tucabaya toward the City. About sunrise on the 13th in consequence of preceding orders all the Drags were drawn up on the side of Tu. next Che., where the firing of Artillery was pretty heavy. I was much astonished at this place to see Levi come from some Infty to shake hands with me, for the day before I had left him at Gen. Twiggs camp. He told me that he & his men composed part of a storming party to attack Chepultepec, that volunteers had been called for, from his regiment & he had offered his services. Every Corps in the Army was represented in that party. Levi then went on to give me directions about his affairs in case he should fall, told me that he had left a watch in the clerks hands to be minded, & that I should find a note giving further directions. We were not together more than 10 minutes. The Drgs were sent off in another direction to meet the enemies Cavalry, & at the same time the storming party was ordered to advance. As everything was ready for us the[7] loss of course was very severe on our party. Chec was attacked on 3 sides at once & carried in a few minutes. The Drags moved on the side opposite to where the storming party advanced & it was not until 11 o'clock at the City gates that I heard of Levi's fate. We returned to Tu. at sunset, & I found that Levi had been carried off the field by his party & taken back to Twiggs Camp. I had started for this place, when I met the 7th coming round to enter the City by the gate. Not having been engaged the Officers had paid every attention to Levi's remains & at my request the coffin was left with me. I had the grave prepared by my comp. that night & the next morning he was buried in the Church yard at Tucabaya by the Revd Mr McCarty[8] an Episcopal clergyman attached to the Army. I found a no. of letters among Levi's effects[:] 2 to you, 2 to Ann, 2 to Mrs Mason, 2 to B. L. Gantt, 1 to Tasker & 1 to Benj.[9] These I will send as directed. . . . Corporal Kelly of Co. G, 7th Infy[10] was of the storming party & close to Levi when he fell. he told me they had just commenced to get under the enemys fire & were under a shed when 1 of the men asked for an Officer to look & see if a party on the flank were Amercns or Mexcs, that Levi moved to the open side for that purpose when he instantly recd a musket ball in his breast & fell into the Corps arms. The Corpl moved him a few feet into the house directly but he was dead. He did not speak merely waved his hand twice, gently. Levi was 2d in the works at Cerro Gordo & cut down 2 Mexcs. he was for that action recommended to be brevetted. The Officers of the regiment speak in the highest terms of his gallantry in every action during the war. I know no officer whose bravery is so highly spoken of as his, without detraction, & this ever since I have been in the country. Our intercourse had been very intimate whenever we had come together, which was the case at Monterrey,[11] Vera Cruz, Jalapa, Puebla, & more particularly between the battles of Contreras & Chac. His sympathy for the loss of Cerro Gordo[12] was invaluable to me & [served] that day in a great measure to bring us closer than we had ever been before.

1. Ewell wrote this letter to his aunt Nancy Gantt. She received it on November 10, 1847, which suggests that it had been written toward the end of October. The original letter has not been found. Nancy Gantt quoted this part of the letter to Dick's mother, Elizabeth Ewell. She in turn quoted it to her son Benjamin in a letter written on December 5, 1847, but misdated 1848.

2. On August 22, 1847, following the Battle of Churubusco, Scott and Santa Anna agreed to a temporary truce in order to give diplomats time to negotiate a peace. Both sides agreed not to engage in any military activity during the truce. When Scott on September 6 learned that Santa Anna had violated the terms of the treaty by fortifying the town, he cancelled the truce and resumed his attacks on the city.

3. An illegible word follows the abbreviation "Inf" here.

4. William J. Worth (1794–1849) served as an aide to General Winfield Scott in the War of 1812, distinguishing himself in the battles of Chippewa and Lundy's Lane. Later he served as commandant at West Point and commander of the 8th United States Infantry. He emerged from the Second Seminole War as a brigadier general and commanded a division in Scott's army during the Mexican War.

5. Scott's first objective after ending the truce was the capture of Molino del Rey, a collection of stone buildings two miles west of the city walls and just one thousand yards west of Chapultepec. In a series of assaults launched on September 8, 1847, Worth captured the buildings but at a cost of nearly one-quarter of his force.

6. Tacubaya is approximately one mile south of Chapultepec.

7. The word "the" is repeated here.

8. The Reverend John McCarty of New York served as a brigade chaplain in Twiggs's division.

9. Tasker, Ann, and Benjamin were Levi's siblings. Benjamin Ewell was his cousin, and B. L. Gantt may have been an uncle. Mrs. Mason has not been identified.

10. Unidentified.

11. Monterrey was then the largest city in northern Mexico, having between ten thousand and fifteen thousand inhabitants. It lies on the north bank of the Santa Catarina River, in the state of Nuevo León, approximately two hundred miles south of the Rio Grande.

12. A reference to Thomas Ewell's death.

29. To Benjamin Ewell

Vera Cruz Mex.
Novr 25th 1847

My Dear Ben;

I have been wishing for some time to write to you but the breaking off of our communications has chiefly prevented me. Mother has not lately mentioned your whereabouts so that I presume you are still in Lexington.[1]

You of course have read accounts of the battles here untill you are tired of them but you must have patience to hear a little more. I really think one of the most talented men connected with this army is Capt Lee[2] of the Eng's. By his daring reconnois[s]ances pushed up to the cannon's mouth he has enabled Genl Scott to fight his battles almost without leaving his tent. His modest, quiet deportment is perfectly refreshing compared with the folly & bombast of the Genls & Officers made by Mr Polk.

I suppose you have seen some of the strictures upon Genl Pillow but they are nothing to what would be written could an accurate account of his follies & absurdities be got at in the States. There was a court of Inquiry lately (in reference to some howitzers taken at Chepultepec which he tried to appropriate) whose proceedings convict him very plainly of falsehood & other little weaknesses such as trying to throw the responsibility on his Aide Pd Mid. Rogers of the Navy.[3]

You of course know of the death of Levi Gantt. I was with him not 10 minutes before he fell. He formed a portion of one of the storming parties for Chepultepec & the place whence he started being a rather central one, the Cavalry were moved there to be ready for any point. Levi came to me in lower spirits than I have ever seen him & gave me a few directions concerning his watch &c

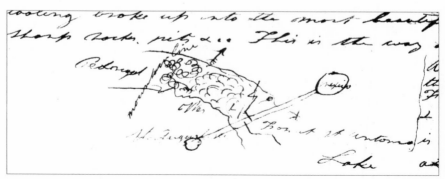

Ewell's sketch of the Pedregal. (Library of Congress)

Captain Philip Kearny led a headlong pursuit of routed Mexican troops at Churubusco. When a canister ball struck Kearny in the arm, Ewell helped him off the field. (Library of Congress)

& just then the Drags were ordered into the saddle & his party advanced to the attack. Within ten minutes he was a corpse being shot by a musket ball in the centre of the chest. *Entre nous*[4] I have been told that he had stepped forward to lead the Marines, who did not on that day get any credit worth having. This comp'y[5] has generally been Gen. Scotts escort & we have had the luck to be in tolerably exciting scenes more than once on that account. One part of our duties was to accompany the Eng[ineer]s on reconnoit[e]ring trips where a small force only was required & on the 18 August we were sent out with Capt Lee to examine the road toward the Pedrigal. This you know is the name given to a stream of lava several miles across, which in times past ran from the mountains almost half across the valley & in cooling broke up into the most beautiful combination of sharp rocks, pits &c. This is the way of it. We were at St

Augustine. the Avenue to the city goes through the Fortification at St Antone & on the left of the road is the Pedrigal & the right a lake.[6] We wished to cross the Pedrigal about the arrow head to[7] turn the other works & as I said before our Drags & several hundred Inty under Col. Graham[8] escorted Capt Lee somewhere towards the Arrow head[9] but not across the Pedrigal. When we got to the edge The Dragoons were a few hundred yards ahead of the Inty. & about 200 Mexicans stuck away in the cracks & behind rocks began firing on us quite to my surprise for it was the first time I had been under fire. It was some time before I could clearly comprehend but presently a horse in ranks tumbled over shot through the heart & I could hear the bullets striking the ground around us & singing over our heads. A path led a short distance into the Ped & Capt. Kearny let me take one half the comp'y that was up & gallop down the path as fast as I could, where I dismounted leaving the horses in a hollow safe with a guard & I had the gentlemen Mex's in rear & flank. They did not fire at me after I started. Capt. K. brought up the remainder & Col Graham's Int'y came up & sent a comp'y on the opposite side but the Mex. had retreated as soon as they found 20 men on fair terms with them leaving 8 or 10 dead & about as many Pris[oner]s. The next day our Army began to take up positions entering the Ped. at the very spot where we had the skirmish. The evening of the 19th we went out with Genl Scott & staff who stood on a hill overlooking the scene of

The assault on the Mexican fortress of Chapultepec led to the capture of Mexico City and effectively ended the war. Ewell's cousin Levi Gantt died in the assault. (Library of Congress)

operations. Nearly all the army was in the lava crossing to the other side by four or 5 different routes while Valencia from his works kept up an incessant fire of heavy artillery upon the different columns now & then blazing away with his 6000 muskets as though our troops were within 50 yds (A Mex. fashion) & then by way of change throwing a shell across at the Genl or at the Cavalry but fortunately without harm, though they sometimes fell among us.

The Mex. were so surprised at not being at once driven off that they thought a great victory was gained & commenced a jubilee that night. among other things their bands would strike up "Hail Columbia" play about half through it & then suddenly stop. Valencia Brevetted some of his Officers & was crazy with joy. St. Anna knew something more of the Yankees & ordered Valencia that night by an Aid to spike his pieces & retire. Pshaw! pshaw! said the latter. tell St. Anna to go to Hell. I have saved the Republic. A fight of ten minutes the next morning as utterly destroyed his army as though each man had been summoned to the other world. Then St Anna abandoned St Antonio & we rushed our heads against Cherebusco & a bloody field it was. Capt. Kearny was ordered at the close of the fight to follow the Mex's down the Avenue along which thousands of them were retreating & we overtook them about 1/7 a mile from the City gates & I rather think they suffered somewhat.[10] The gate was a good deal obstructed & we pushed them so rapidly that they got into the water on each side of the road—began firing upon us & to some effect too. When we approached the gate I saw the crow[d] before us open as if by one movement & then saw a piece of artillery frowning over the works. Capt. K. had given orders to dismount in such a case & car[r]y the works but when I looked around to my horror found the drags retiring some distance in rear. There were 3 companies in all Capt. K's leading.[11] Col Harney[12] had ordered the recall to be sounded in rear[,] & as it took some time for the information to get to the head of the col- umn they not being able to hear it in all the noise & confusion we were engaged while the rear was retreating. Col. Harn[e]y had refused to lead the charge[,] & of course should not have interfered as it was out of his power to control after we passed him. Only a miracle saved Capt. K & myself. he lost his arm by a grape shot after (so great was the confusion) getting in & out of the works & I had two horses shot[,] one by a Musquet[13] from the side of the road[,] the other by a canister shot through the neck. The second was able to bring me back at a walk. Capt K. & myself came back from the presence of the Mexican[s] 4 or 500 yds without molestation to our troops. A Mexican mail was captured the day after but one the battle & the letters being interesting were published. I send Mother a copy & asked her to send them to you should you like to see them. Several of them speak of this charge.

I have sent an account to Jackson D.C.[14] to collect for my horse. If he gets it you are welcome to use it should you wish. If not & you should want funds I would be glad to let you have what you want. Write to me & if you wish I[15] will continue my experiences of the battle. direct to the City of Mex.

I came back to escort a baggage train & will return Monday.

R S Ewell

1. Ben was a professor of mathematics and military science at Washington College from 1846 to 1848.
2. Captain Robert E. Lee was then an engineer on General Winfield Scott's staff.
3. Gideon J. Pillow (1806–1878) of Tennessee was a militia officer and a law partner of James K. Polk, who, as president, appointed Pillow to be a major general of volunteers. Following the fall of Chapultepec, Pillow took two captured Mexican howitzers as personal trophies, one of which ended up at the quarters of Midshipman Robert C. Rogers. When word of Pillow's actions became known, Winfield Scott ordered a court of inquiry. Although the court cleared Pillow of most of the charges, many, including Ewell, continued to believe that Pillow was behind the thefts.
4. French, "between us."
5. Ewell's Company F, 1st Dragoons.
6. Here Ewell added a crude sketch of the terrain (see p. 74).
7. Ewell repeated the word "to" here.
8. Lieutenant Colonel William M. Graham of the 11th United States Infantry died on September 8, 1847, at the Battle of Molino del Rey.
9. The arrowhead appears on a map that Ewell drew of the battlefield (see p. 74).
10. Kearny's dragoons pursued the Mexicans down a causeway toward the San Antonio Gate.
11. Kearny was supported in his charge by Captain Andrew McReynolds's and Captain Alphonse M. Duperu's companies of the 3rd United States Dragoons.
12. Colonel William S. Harney commanded the 1st United States Dragoons during the Mexican War. He became a brigadier general in 1858 and retired from the army five years later.
13. Ewell wrote vertically across the page: "If I have spelt musket with a q correct it."
14. B. Lowndes Jackson (b. ca. 1815) was a Washington, D.C., grocer and a kinsman of Ewell.
15. Ewell repeated the word "I" here.

30. To Elizabeth Ewell Sr.

At present I am encamped out in the neighborhood of Vera Cruz[1] & am tormented by the most abominable Norther[2] you can conceive, shaking the tent as though it would come down any moment, at one moment bringing clouds of sand & dirt, at the next raining as if it were going to flood the land, all of which is not very well calculated as you may imagine, to put me in a very good humour. On the march down the night before getting here as I was sleeping in my tent I was roused by feeling something like a bee sting, & after getting a light found a large scorpion in the leg of my drawers. he had stung me twice below the knee without causing as much discomfort as if it had been a bee, though some Mexns gave me a horrid account of what was to take place in a few hours. I think this shows fairly the exaggeration that exists about this country, that is the proportion. I have been almost equally disappointed in every thing I have seen from this to the City. . . . A more stupid, begotted race cannot easily be imagined. Almost half of every City I have yet seen is in ruins & though there is an immense population of beggars but a small part of the land is under Cultivation. . . . Genl. Scott the day after the battle of Churubusco made very particular enquiries in reference to Tom as to whether he was able to understand what the Genl. said to him on the field &c. & observed to an Officer who was by when he was talking to me that he was the Hero of that fight "more than anyone else." he asked me if I had parents living, & told me he had more concern for my life than for any one else &c.

1. This letter was written by Ewell to his mother from Vera Cruz on November 25, 1847. The original letter has not been found. This excerpt is quoted in Elizabeth Ewell Sr.'s December 5, 1847, letter to her son Benjamin Ewell. She misdated the letter 1848.
2. A northern gale.

31. To Elizabeth Ewell Sr.

Last week[1] the 2 comps 1st Drag. that are with this part of the army were order'd together with about 2000 Infty. & a batty. of Artil. to Toluca[2] about 30 miles from here—contains about 10,000 inha[bitan]ts & is the seat of Govt. of the Dept. of Mex. the people had been expecting troops for some time, & the 2d day after leaving Mex. when we were 11 miles out[,] the City Council met Genl Cadwallader[3] (in command) to signify their submission &c. &c. they had prepared quarters in anticipation, & recd us as long expected guests. Evening

before last I was told to be prepar'd to bring dispatches to Gen. Scott, left Toluca at 2 o'clock yesterday, & reached here to day.[4]

. . . I have been 2 hours running about trying to find something for Lizzy.
Tyler[5] is starting for home on sick leave tomorrow & a large train goes to V.C.
I could see nothing I fancied, & unless in the morning I should buy a Mex.
bolero (cotton shawl)[—]they wear no bonnets here[—]I fear she will have to
do without. Tyler says he will buy his presents in New Orleans, where they are
better & cheaper. . . . I return to-morrow to Toluca. expected to remain here
a week. I send to the U.S. by T. Lewis frock coat, Pistols, sword, watch, ring
&c.[6]

. . . I dined yesterday with Genl Scott, & am not at all prepar'd by it, for
writing.

1. These excerpts, written by Ewell to his mother between January 12 and 14,
   1848, were copied by Mrs. Ewell in a March 5, 1848, letter to her son Ben. The
   first paragraph was written on January 12, the second on January 13, and the
   third on January 14. Ewell's original letter to his mother has not been found.
2. Toluca is sixty-five miles west of Mexico City.
3. George Cadwalader of Pennsylvania had been appointed brigadier general of
   volunteers in March 1847 and was brevetted major general for gallant and
   meritorious conduct in the Battle of Chapultepec in July 1848.
4. Elizabeth Ewell summarized the next part of her son's letter as follows: "He
   could get sick leave, but might be sent recruiting, prefers waiting till spring,
   when he can get a longer leave & have a chance of going to the springs. In a
   military point of view he has advantages by staying there for a month or two
   longer. Drag. Officers are very scarce & he has command above his rank."
5. Second Lieutenant Charles H. Tyler of Virginia had graduated from West Point
   in 1848. Dismissed from the army on June 6, 1861, he offered his services to
   the Confederacy. He attained the rank of colonel and led brigades in Missouri
   and East Tennessee.
6. Unidentified.

32. To Elizabeth Ewell Sr.

To use a common expression here peace stock is very high.[1] Genl Scott told
me that he had very little doubt but that the Mexican Congress would immediately agree to the treaty,[2] particularly as the modifications were agreeable to
all parties. . . .[3]

Two nights ago a Mexican house was broken open & the Chief Clerk murder'd in attempting to defend the premises. the thieves alarm'd, attempted to escape before accomplishing their object, but left one of their number behind, who turned States evidence, & gave up his accomplices, 12 in all, 4 of whom are Officers of the Pennsylvania Volunteers & are now in confinement. it is very much to be hoped that the whole batch will be hung.

1. These excerpts, written by Ewell to his mother between April 2 and April 7, 1848, were copied by Mrs. Ewell in a May 14, 1848, letter to her son Ben. Ewell began the letter in Toluca and finished it in Mexico City, where he had escorted some witnesses to a court of inquiry.
2. In the Treaty of Guadalupe Hidalgo, signed on February 2, 1848, Mexico relinquished all claims to Texas, recognized the Rio Grande as the boundary between the two nations, and ceded 525,000 square miles of territory to the United States. In return, the United States paid the Mexican government $15 million and forgave Mexico's debts to American citizens. The United States Senate ratified the treaty on March 10, 1848, after deleting a provision that guaranteed the security of Mexican land grants. The Mexican government, in turn, ratified the modified treaty on May 19.
3. Paraphrasing her son, Elizabeth Ewell added, "Genl Butler he says is ignorant & partial in the highest degree."

Chapter 4

Back East, 1849–1850

With the Mexican War at an end, United States volunteer regiments disbanded and regular army units returned to their normal duty stations. Dick Ewell reported for duty at Jefferson Barracks, but in August 1848 he left Missouri on a leave of absence occasioned by illness and went home to Virginia. When his leave expired in October, Ewell engaged in recruiting duty at Carlisle Barracks, Pennsylvania; Baltimore, Maryland; and Richmond, Virginia. The duty lasted ten months. During that time he attended numerous social events, including a medieval tilting tournament hosted by the Carroll family at "Doughoregan Manor" near Baltimore.

Promotion occupied Ewell's thoughts a great deal during this period of his life. To recognize his gallantry in Mexico, the army had awarded him the brevet rank of captain. Brevet rank was purely honorary, however, and had no practical bearing on a man's standing relative to his fellow officers. Genuine advancement came slowly and was based on a soldier's seniority within his grade. Ewell therefore felt aggrieved when he learned that First Lieutenant James W. Schaumburgh had applied for reappointment to the regiment. Schaumburgh had resigned from the army in 1836, and his fellow officers did not want him back. Ewell had personal reasons for opposing his return. Since Schaumburgh's appointment to first lieutenant predated Ewell's, his name would precede Ewell's on the promotion list. In March 1849 Ewell traveled to Washington, D.C., on behalf of the regiment's officers to speak with the adjutant general, the secretary of war, and President Zachary Taylor in an effort to block Schaumburgh's reappointment. Apparently he succeeded, for Schaumburgh was not reinstated.

Ewell was not as successful in the case of Lucius B. Northrop. Like Schaumburgh, Northrop had been a first lieutenant in the regiment. Compelled to go on disability in 1843 after accidentally shooting himself in the knee, Northrop pursued a career in medicine, a move that prompted the adjutant general to drop him from the army rolls. Northrop's foray into medicine failed, however, and he applied for reinstatement to the 1st Dragoons at his former rank, a move that would place him ahead of

Ewell on the promotion list. Ewell felt that Northrop had intentionally avoided service in Mexico and tried to thwart his reappointment. His protest failed. Northrop was a close friend of Senator Jefferson Davis, who used his influence on Northrop's behalf. On August 12, 1848, Congress reinstated Northrop as an officer in the 1st Dragoons and promoted him to captain.

Northrop's appointment delayed Ewell's advancement only briefly. On August 4, 1849, he became captain of Company G. Ewell joined his regiment in New Mexico in 1850 after a brief stop at Fort Leavenworth. For the next ten years, the Southwest would be his home.

33. To Benjamin Ewell

Carlisle Brrk M[ar]ch. 13. 49

Dear Ben;

I wrote a letter to Buckland[1] a few days since for you, but have heard since that you had gone to Williamsburg[2] & therefore as it might be of importance I write to you [at] the latter place a repetition of my first letter.

Fifteen years[3] ago a 2nd Lt. Schaumburg resigned as an Officer of the U.S. Army (he at that time belonged to the 1st Dragoons) his resignation being to take effect at some future day say six months. There was an order published in the interval that all such resignations might be recalled provided the Officers reported by a given time at their Regimental head quarters. during this interval also Schaumburg was promoted to 1st Lt. & the Adjutant General published an order accepting his resignation as 1st Lieut. S. did not report as required but claims a right to come back into the service with the rank he would have had had he remained in the service because he reported to the Adjt Genl and because of his being a 1st Lt. when the Resignation [took effect].[4] I understand from Major Kearny[5] that there are three letters of S to the Depts showing that he considered himself at that time as bono fide out of the service & as he resigned as an "Officer of the Army" and for strong reasons given by Major Turner[,][6] in or about 1845 then Adjt[,][7] the Officers of the Regt[8] think that if a trial could be had before a Board of Officers they could show just cause why he should not be re-appointed. On this statement of facts the U.S. Senate, in 1844 or 5 when his name had been placed on the Register[9] by Pres[iden]t Tyler, by a large majority passed resolutions unfavorable to his claims; the result of which was that his name was stricken from the rolls.

It appears from the Ledger[10] of a few days since that on the 2d of March the Senate passed Resolutions rescinding those above mentioned. As those Officers[11] who will suffer by the loss of Rank attendant upon his return had no opportunity of showing a counter statement it is evident that untill they be heard action upon the case may cause injustice.

I would request you, if in your opinion it could do any good, to stop in Washington and through Col. Bliss[12] or by personal application to the Prest.[13] have action upon this matter suspended or a Board of Officers convened to end the matter for ever.

Yrs &—

R S Ewell

1. Buckland, Virginia, was the closest post office to Ewell's Prince William County home, Stony Lonesome.
2. Ben accepted a position as professor of mathematics at the College of William and Mary in August 1848 and took up his duties two months later. He became president of the college in 1854, a position he occupied until 1888.
3. Ewell has inserted the word "about" above the line here.
4. Second Lieutenant James W. Schaumburgh of the 1st Dragoons was under arrest in 1836, when he learned that his father was sick and expected to die shortly. When his commanding officer, Lieutenant Colonel Stephen W. Kearny, refused to release him from arrest, Schaumburgh tendered his resignation, to take effect a few months later, and hurried to Louisiana to be with his father. At that time it was customary that if an officer required leave to attend to an emergency and could not wait to obtain an order granting that leave, he could, at his own risk, tender his resignation, at the same time enclosing a letter explaining the circumstances and requesting that the resignation not be accepted. Schaumburgh did precisely that. Just weeks after he took this action, the War Department issued an order formally abolishing this practice. At about the same time, Schaumburgh received promotion to first lieutenant. Apparently he was a troublemaker, and Kearny used his influence to have the adjutant general accept Schaumburgh's resignation, an action countenanced by General-in-Chief Alexander Macomb. Schaumburgh appealed this ruling, and Secretary of War Lewis Cass promised to reappoint him as a first lieutenant as soon as a vacancy occurred. The appointment had not been made by the time Cass left office, however, and his successor, Joel Poinsett, did not espouse Schaumburgh's cause. The aggrieved officer had political connections, however, and in 1848 the U.S. Senate passed a resolution asking the president to submit papers relative to Schaumburgh's case along with a statement by the adjutant general explaining its merits and demerits. President Zachary Taylor still had not received the statement eight months later when it came time for him to nominate officers for

promotion. With Schaumburgh's case still pending, Taylor appointed Ewell rather than Schaumburgh to fill a captain's vacancy in the regiment. Schaumburgh ultimately won his case, however, and was awarded more than $11,000 in back pay.

5. Although Philip Kearny lost an arm as a result of his wound at Churubusco, he recovered and returned to the army at the rank of major.

6. Henry S. Turner had been brevetted to major in December 1846 for gallant and meritorious conduct at the battles of San Pasqual, San Gabriel, and the Plains of Mesa, California.

7. The words "then Adjt" (adjutant) refer to Turner.

8. Ewell's original letter repeats the words "the Officers" after the word "Regt."

9. The *Army Register* was a biannual publication issued by the government giving the names, places of birth, dates of entry into the service, and dates of promotions and transfers for all officers in the United States Army.

10. Ewell may be referring to the *Philadelphia Public Ledger,* a daily newspaper started in 1836.

11. Ewell mistakenly added the word "of" after "Officers."

12. William W. S. Bliss had graduated from West Point in 1833, was brevetted twice during the Mexican War, and was at this time a brevet lieutenant colonel in the 4th United States Infantry.

13. Zachary Taylor (1784–1850) had been elected president in 1848. He died in July 1850, less than halfway through his term.

34. To Benjamin Ewell

Carlisle Mch 18. [1849]

Dear Ben;

I write to tell you that I have received a letter from Senator Mason[1] in reference to Schaumburg, who says that action in his case can not come from the Senate but from the executive and recommends that the Officers sign a respectful remonstrance addressed to the Secty of War setting forth the facts of the case. I have already made out a request that action be suspended untill we can hear from those who know the facts in the case, Turner and others, and then if no one else will I shall go to Washington myself and lay[2] them before the Secty of War.

Col. May[3] has retd from Washington and says S. is very active in making headway for his claims but without an accident I hope we shall head him [off] yet. There is no wind that does not blow good at some time. this case puts

May one file farther from a Majority than he is at present. Schaumburg is a great blackguard and any one who opposes his unjust claim will be pretty sure to get into a difficulty with him, Though I for one am willing to run the risk if thereby I can have any hopes of accomplishing my end & things certainly look more favorable than they did, for our side. I have received some very droll letters from Graham & Kearny in reference to these claims & they rather give me to suppose that S—g will have a disagreeable time if he gets in. The first rumor we had was that the man had been appointed & then that the Senate had passed resolutions instructing the Prest to appoint him to the 1st vacancy. As it stands now the Prest. has it at his option to do what he pleases, so I infer from Mason's letter. I wish I had known in time that there was to be such an overwhelming quantity of Brevets made out & I certainly should have tried hard for another & might have got it.[4] Many are Brevetted who staid at home the whole time in command of single companies, one man for taking care of Worth's family &c.

I have recd a letter from Ben Gantt[5] but it contains nothing of any interest, does not[6] notice my request to him to lend me a book.

I wish to goodness when You pass through Washtn you would purchase an Army Register and send it to me. An Officer promised to send me one but failed to do so. You have not mentioned my dogs in any of your letters. I hope great things from the Pointer. It might be worth while to try the Setter with a gun. if she shows fear she ought to be shot immediately for she will contaminate the other by the force of example. The people here say that there is fine partridge hunting in the fall. Trout fishing unsurpassed commences the 1st of May. Suppose when you take Mother to Maryland[7] after getting tired there she comes on here. Boarding in town half a mile from the Barracks is only about $4.00 per week & very decent. The society is pleasant enough besides there are several nice girls in town and if I only knew how to choose might get suited to a fraction. There is every prospect that for some time I shall have my hands full here so that I can not look forward to going home very soon. The Barracks are to be repaired which will place more work on my shoulders.

Your[s] & R S Ewell

1. James M. Mason (1798–1871) of Virginia was the grandson of patriot George
   Mason and the son of General John Mason. He served in the United States
   Senate from 1847 to 1861, becoming an outspoken advocate of states' rights
   and a close associate of John C. Calhoun. When the Civil War began, Mason
   sailed to England with John Slidell in an effort to secure Great Britain's support

for the Confederacy. The U.S. Navy seized their ship, the *Trent,* on the high seas, nearly prompting a war between the United States and England. Although briefly imprisoned, Lincoln released Mason and Slidell to avert hostilities. Mason moved to Canada following the Civil War, but he returned to Virginia in 1868 once the threat of arrest had diminished.

2. Ewell mistakenly added the word "then" at this point.

3. Charles A. May (1818–1864) had received three brevets during the Mexican War and at this time was a brevet colonel in the 1st Dragoons. He resigned at the onset of the Civil War and died on Christmas Eve 1864.

4. Brevet rank conferred upon its recipient the honor of a promotion without the substance of one. As in Ewell's case, they were often given to individuals at the conclusion of a war as a reward for faithful service.

5. Benjamin S. Gantt was Ewell's first cousin.

6. In his original letter, Ewell ran the words "does not" together into a single word.

7. Benjamin Ewell was probably taking his mother to visit her sister, Ann Gantt, who lived near Bladensburg, Maryland.

35. To Benjamin Ewell

Carlisle Brrks Pa
April 4th 1849

Dear Ben;

Ten days ago Col May retd from a visit to Washington where he saw Schaumburgh and thought that he stood a good chance to return.

An Officer wrote me that Calhoun had told his son, an Officer of the 2d Dragoons[1] that he thought the result of the Senate's resolutions would be to restore S—g. By May's persuasion & wishing to visit Va I thought it well to go on and started accordingly on the 26th Ult.[2] I went to Old Jones[3] who after keeping me waiting for some hours, said he knew nothing about it but supposed that S would be restored, but finally told me to see the Secty of War;[4] which I did and learned that S's name had not appeared before the new administration. I thought it best however to see the Prest[5] and was told by him that the subject had not been brought before him as yet by Schaumburg and that he considered him out of the service by his own act. I said that the Officers interested only asked for a fair showing before any action in the man's favor should be taken by the executive &c. &c. All of which was duly promised, and I retd last night to this place tired to death. I started Monday at 4 A.M. reached Wtn between 1 & 2 the same night spent the two next days on Schaumburg & visiting Mammy[,]

Ben Gantt[,] & Mr Prout[6] and left by the Stage at two for Stony Lonesome. In Buckland J. H. Carter[7] lent me his pony & walked home himself. They were all well at home. Dr McIlvaine whom I saw in York, in good health told me he intended visiting Va. in a week or ten days and I advised him to write home a few days previous to let them send a carriage to the stage road which he said he would do.

I received one of your letters, sent after me to Willard's[8] & the 2d one last night. I left home Sunday[,] staid Monday in Washtn & reached Carlisle last night. I saw Mrs Reynold[s] in Baltimore at an expense of 50 cts for dressing myself & a plenty of trouble, but after I had been in the house 15 minutes she said she had an engagement & left. I am always unfortunate in my endeavours to see her. the last time before this I promised in the morning to return at 7 in the evening but when I did so found the establishment cleared out for church. I then thought I would not trouble myself about returning but met Mr Reynold[s][9] last Winter in Phila and had to promise him that when I passed through Balt. again I would call to see him, hence my sin, for I had not intended to return. It is a stupid place where one is bored to death either with Presbyterianism or the Mexican war.[10]

I met Benny Roberts[11] in Baltimore who told me that S. . . . . . g would as soon as he found that a Dragoon Officer was in town would, if he could ascertain that his visit was in reference to his claims, try to make a personal affair of the business & advised me to go prepared. I was aware that this was the plan of the gentleman and made up my mind to tell him as quietly as possible the object of my visit to the District and if possible to avoid any difficulty with him particularly after the gross newspaper abuse received by Chilton last Fall. I felt very uneasy from the want of some sensible friend in case I should meet with insult &c from him to assist me in steering between the two dangers of caution on the one and rashness on the other side.

S . . . g is a professed pugilist & his tactics are not to fight a duel but to use his fists & write for the newspapers in the most scurrilous and abusive manner of those he is in contact with.[12] I stopped at Willards where I understood S. to be, both on my way home & back but did not see him. I rather think he was sick. The plan he has adopted is to remain quiet untill the Senate meets again & as he must be aware that Genl Taylor is unfriendly to past matters with the Senate[,] as he thinks[,] they are safe. We shall see what we shall see.

Miss Maria Berry[13] was at Mr Prout's & I staid there untill after 10. O'clk. Miss M. sang & played &c. &c. She looked rather grim I thought. she has improved in her singing & playing very much I thought but forgot to tell her so.

I am glad you think the setter pup is worth anything as I rather feared she was too timid. I remember perfectly well offering her to you but you then declined her. It would be a capital plan to cross her as you propose though the first litter of pups is never so good as the 2d. The last plan would be to fasten her up the 1st time she went in heat & then to put her up with the dog the 2d time; the interval between the times would be the same as though she had gone to the dog and had a litter. If you carry your plan into operation I wish you would save me one of the pups if the slut be fastened up the whole time. It is very important that she have nothing to do with curs, as the 2d Litter is not so good if the slut has had pups by a cur.

Your letter is quite melancholly as regards the young ladies & I am beginning to feel very much interested in Miss Tucker[14] whom I then thought the prettiest girl in Williamsburg & am anxious to learn how Page[15] succeeded. I thought Mr Dennison was on very easy terms with Miss Alice and hope the close of the oyster season will not act unfavorably upon his feelings.[16]

I thought when in Wmburg that there might be many worse things, than a berth in the asylum[17] & you re[me]mber agreed with you in thinking the place not a bad one for the whole family. Write.

Your &c   R S Ewel[l]

Remember me to my acquaintances in Wmburg.

RSE

I gave Mammy some money to take he[r] home. She was sick. I did not know your Buggy was in town or I might have been tempted to take it up. I was too tired to ride.

1. John C. Calhoun (1782–1850) of South Carolina was one of the most important statesmen of the nineteenth century, having served the country as a congressman (1811–17), secretary of war (1817–25), vice president (1825–32), senator (1832–43, 1845–50), and secretary of state (1844–45). His son, Patrick Calhoun, graduated from West Point in 1841, one year after Ewell, and was at this time a first lieutenant in the 2nd Dragoons. He died in 1858.

2. *"Ultimo"*—i.e., of the previous month.

3. Adjutant General Roger Jones of Virginia began his military career in 1809 as a second lieutenant in the Marine Corps. He was a brigadier general at the time this letter was written. He died in 1852.

4. George Washington Crawford served as secretary of war from March 8, 1849, to July 23, 1850.

5. Martin Van Buren.

6. Jonathan Prout (b. ca. 1796) was the husband of Ben Gantt's sister, Ann L. Gantt. Ewell's aunt Nancy Gantt was living with the Prouts by 1850.

7. A man named John Carter lived near the Ewells in Prince William County. He was approximately seventy years old at this time.

8. The Willard was Washington, D.C.'s, most prominent hotel. It stood on Pennsylvania Avenue not far from the White House.

9. William Reynolds (ca. 1799–1873) was a Baltimore lawyer. He was married to Ewell's second cousin, Rosanna Ewell Reynolds.

10. Ewell had a strong prejudice against Presbyterianism. For other instances of this, see RSE to RLE, 12 Nov. 1840 (letter 9, this volume), and 2 Mar. 1844, LC (letter 16). The Reynolds family was Presbyterian. For evidence of this, see RSE to LCB, 29 June 1865, PBE (letter 162, this volume).

11. Captain Benjamin S. Roberts of Vermont had been an officer in the 1st Dragoons before transferring to the mounted rifles in 1846. During the Civil War, he served as chief of cavalry for Major General John Pope's Army of Virginia.

12. In a newspaper advertisement published at this time, Edward H. Fuller described Schaumburgh as "an unprincipled man—a liar, swindler, coward and poltroon . . . a servile cur . . . a despicable and dastardly creature . . . a lying braggart—a backbiting knave." Fuller, a hotel proprietor, claimed that Schaumburgh had run up a large tab at his establishment and refused to pay the bill. Fuller went on to describe his nemesis as "about six feet high—a form well made up by tailors, and always very fancifully dressed, in a style between the Beau Brummell and the B'hoys—large savage gray whiskers—a large burn on his face, caused by falling into a pot of boiling taffy when a child—small gray eyes, deeply set in his head, so small and insignificant, indeed, that they are hardly to be seen—hat set on his head 'h la Mose'—a small cane in his hand, the scarecrow of all the little boys whom he happens to meet; and so he swaggers up and down the Avenue, the ridicule of men and the disgust of women." Outraged by Fuller's announcement, Schaumburgh fell upon Fuller in the streets and deliberately shot him. Schaumburgh escaped prison and fought for the Union during the Civil War. Bunn, *Old England and New England,* 1:201–4.

13. Maria Berry (b. ca. 1833) was the sixteen-year-old daughter of Zachariah and Priscilla Berry of Bladensburg, Maryland. Zachariah Berry was a wealthy planter, owning $96,100 in real estate in 1850.

14. Possibly Virginia S. B. Tucker, an eighteen-year-old girl then residing in York County, Virginia.

15. Possibly a reference to Ewell's West Point classmate, Brevet Major Francis Nelson Page of the 7th United States Infantry. Like Ewell, Page had received a brevet in the Mexican War for gallant and meritorious conduct at Contreras and Churubusco. He died on March 25, 1860, on the eve of the Civil War.

16. Then, as now, oysters were considered an aphrodisiac. Mr. Dennison and Miss Alice have not been identified.

17. Williamsburg was the home of the Public Hospital for Persons of Insane and Disordered Minds, later renamed the Eastern Lunatic Asylum. Authorized in 1770 by an act of the Virginia colonial legislature, it was the first institution in America constructed solely for the treatment of the mentally ill. Although the original building burned in 1885, the facility is still in operation under the name Eastern State Hospital.

36. To Benjamin Ewell

Balt. Md June 7. 49

Dear Ben;

I enclose a receipt for yellowwashing[1] sent me by the Qr Mr Clerk at Carlisle. He is a desperate punster among other failings hence his postscrip[t]. Light is a Soldier that we had in the Office to run errands &c & most remarkable for his stupidity.[2] I wish you would tell me in writing your criticism upon the definition of the quantities entering into the equation of a line. Wood evidently did not understand me.[3] Ochre cost at Carlisle 3 cents a lb.

I just met Cap. Jordan[4] [of the] Army[,] a Class mate[,] & in looking at Penna 5s[5] worth 88 I pointed out what I had done. He in return showed me the Ohio Life Insurance & trust Comp'y in which he bought two months since 77. shares at $74. worth now 88 clearing $1000, & over. He says he paid his expenses in N.Y. by stock purchases. He says he would buy say 40. shares on this. he would re-invest & so on untill a rise would be worth something. I told him I was about investing a few hundreds & he said any of those "State securities" will be profitable provided the investment be made at once as they will all likely rise. How would you like to try the Indiana 5. at 67. but rising. there is something of a speculation. To be sure it may be some years before they will be at par. I am confident that no time ought to be lost in investing.

You did not let me know the result of your Coast survey experiments.

The Italian troupe is making another experiment here by playing to the million & is doing better at 25 cts than at the O.P. They play at the Museum & I believe I will ask cousin Martha to go.[6] The amateurs tell me the part of

Berta in the "Barber" is the most difficult & one of the finest.[7] It was selected & played by Cousin Dona she told me.[8]

Yrs,

R S Ewel[l]

1. While stationed at Carlisle Barracks, Ewell was engaged in the repair of the post buildings. A wash, or coating, made of yellow ochre was frequently used to paint the exterior of military buildings.
2. Unidentified.
3. Possibly Thomas J. Wood of Kentucky. Wood graduated from West Point in 1845 and, after brief service in the topographical engineers, transferred to the 2nd Dragoons. During the Civil War, he fought in the West, attaining the rank of major general.
4. Thomas Jordan of Virginia graduated next to last in Ewell's West Point Class of 1840. An officer in the Regular Army, he resigned his commission in 1861 to fight for the Confederacy, attaining the rank of brigadier general.
5. This and the references that follow refer to state securities.
6. Neither "the Museum" nor the "O.P." have been positively identified.
7. Berta was the housekeeper in Gioachino Rossini's opera *The Barber of Seville*.
8. Cousins Martha and Dona have not been identified.

37. To Benjamin Ewell

June 20. 1849

Dear Ben;

I went to day to see a stone cutter to make inquiries about the mantle pieces and enclose the card of the most respectable establishment in the city. you are so indefinite however, in your letter that I cannot give much information. I saw mantels from $35 to $150. black & Egyptian marble—for $35. I saw a very pretty one, the two side pieces and the front piece (vertical) of Egyptian the rest black. There were some white & colored mantelpieces as low as $17. depending chiefly on the quality of the marble. Black marble for the sides or fronts of the jambs cost 80 cts the running foot. The mantels can be made of any size but the price does not vary in proportion. An inch or two larger or smaller would be the same price.

I had a letter from home a day or two ago with a postscrip[t] from Becca who complains of your taking her money or notes or something without leaving a note or memorandum. I rather think she is afraid of your running away or having the cholera or something. Major Haller started to York this morning to be married to-morrow to a Miss Cox, not Ophelia I believe.[1] He has taken a warm time for it and though the nights are now at the shortest I think he will find them long enough. I fear it will be an unhappy match for of all men he is worse afflicted with an unceasing flow of words. He spent yesterday morning looking at the daguerr[e]otype pictures I suppose for a grand display of himself & bride in costume.

Col. Taylor read me a letter to-day from Genl Smith from California who among other things says he is unable to hire a servant for $200. per month and that the average gain at the mines is ten dollars per diem.[2] He says diggers & traders make the money & that the house he lives in rents for $5000. per annum & is not worth at home $800. I think we had better go.[3]

None of the Stock brokers know anything of the Va. In. &c. Comp'y.[4] I think the investment would be a good one more particularly as the state stocks are all going up so high that they will be out of reach before you will be farther than having your plans laid. It will be receiving 5 per cent & paying 6 I am very much afraid, before long. Rather than lose a month by writing to me after you have the money in hand I would even prefer your placing it in U.S. which bring but 5 per cent for investments.

Since you were here Pa 6. have gone up about 5, and I believe will go up 5 more to fall double before this time next year unless California destroys all reasonable calculations. Some think with reason that Pa will pay her August dividends (there is no doubt of this) and have trouble for some two or three after payments. August would send them sky high to fall in proportion. I think I will sell my 5s & invest in The No. F & Va. I. co if you conclude to invest in that as it will be better than seperating & I will continue to invest in that. It will be better than State except to speculate, and I will not be here for that I hope. As this money is certain to come, why not borrow the amount rather than lose time? I am thinking seriously of borrowing on the strength of my 50 & buying others untill after the 1st of August.

I have just been persuaded to visit another marble yard & enclose the card which I like better than the other. The 2nd is Bevons & Sons. You see they put the Mantles at 20. the Size will make but little difference. I saw very neat ones for $27.00. Mantels do not require altering to suit different sized fire places as the pieces nearest the fire place can be shifted without the same being shown.

Yrs

R. S. Ewell

P.S. I saw a letter advertised for you to day in the N.Y. Herald of June 16. Address. Prof. B. S. Ewell. Should you choose to write for it, the date of advertisement would be necessary. I wish you would give me a receipt[5] for corns if you know any. The pavements make me suffer very much and I wear larger boots than I used last winter.

Col. May passed through town yesterday for Washington to attend his sister (Mrs Macrae's)[6] wedding. He laughed about the last meeting & said we would have had a nice time of it had Magruder[7] not been in the way. He said he looked for us Sunday to dine as he had a splendid table. Tell Lizzy to pick me out a wife in Wmsburg. Yrs &c

R. S. Ewell

P.S. 21.[8] I found a letter from Mother this morning who says nothing in particular except that Becca said nothing to you about receipts but began talking of them after you left before she was out of bed next morning & that Dona was the prettiest girl at Haymarket Church. Mother complains of your not writing and is anxious about the cholera. Miss E. D. is not coming West this summer.[9]

1. Granville O. Haller was a captain in the 4th United States Infantry. "Ophelia" is a reference to the comely daughter of Polonius in William Shakespeare's play *Hamlet*.
2. Lieutenant Colonel Joseph P. Taylor had been appointed assistant commissary general of subsistence in 1841. Persifor F. Smith had been a brigadier general of volunteers during the Mexican War and at this time was serving as colonel of the mounted rifles.
3. The California Gold Rush was then in full swing, sending prices in California through the roof.
4. Virginia Life Insurance & Trust Company.
5. "Receipt"—i.e., remedy.
6. May's sister, Julia (1819–1876), married Powell McRa on April 30, 1839.
7. Brevet Major John B. Magruder (1810–1871) of the 1st United States Artillery later became a major general in the Confederate army. After service in the Peninsula Campaign, he was sent west to command the District of Texas. Refusing to surrender in 1865, he fled to Mexico, where he accepted an appointment as major general under Maximilian.
8. This postscript was written the following day, June 21.
9. Miss E. D. has not been identified.

Ewell's sketch of two love birds. (Courtesy Jerry Wilborn)

38. To John Love

Baltimore Decr. 30 [1849]

Dear John;

If you mean to say in yours of the 18th rec'd to day, that you had written me the last letter I can only assure you that it is a great mistake as a little reflection will show you.

I should have written to congratulate you upon your change of state had I known where to direct in time. Of course it would be mockery to do so now as you have been married long enough to repent & repentance is sure to follow it is said. I can only at present give you good advice & (if you only knew it) the same is worth more than precious stones, viz: Beg, borrow or steal a copy of Rasselas (Johnson's)[1] and read from the XXV to the XXX chapter and if you are particularly busy you can give up the bible the while it takes to read the above. Duly weigh the words of wisdom & I mistake if you do not derive more benefit from them than from anything you have yet seen in the bible.

I tried to draw two doves in a sort of ornament above but did not succeed very well as you may see.[2]

As for Mr. Schaumburg, I have been very busy trying to get my promotion vice Eustis[3] and have expended money as well as time. I have seen & left a favorable impression upon Shields,[4] Mason, Hunter,[5] Barbour,[6] Cass &c &c. I have had extracts from the report of the senate formerly published which I shall take to Washington & give to each one I can get letters to. You will see upon reading the enclosed that S'g bases, in his letter to S[ecretar]y Poinset,[7] his decision to return upon 2 points. There is a 3d one which he urges now with more earnestness than any. The 1st is change of time of accepting the res[ignatio]n from Oct 31. to July 31. but Genl. Scott['s] report [((]see note[)] shows precedent for this & the res[igna]t[io]n is not given on this condition. 2nd Under benefit of Order No 43 but the change of dept[?] of dates removes him from any grounds there for Order 43 says those "that have been accepted" but his was not accepted for two days after orders no (44) & therefore it no more applies to him than you or me. 3d what is the main reliance for the present is his promotion but his letters to Jackson & Bell[8] certainly kills that plea in equity if not in law. Jeff Davis[9] told me that [he] looked upon that as a mere clerical error that did not vitiate the resignation at all. I can tell you though the man has a good chance to return if not now the next vacancy. It is in the hands of the Atty Genl[10] who has already voted in the senate (1849) in his favor. It will not affect you though as much as me because it deprives me of vital rank, promotion to a captaincy & you will lose nothing for S. will not remain long in service. Of course he draws his back pay.

Kearny expects this Winter to proceed to California to join his Comp'y.[11] I have written to him to ask, if I get my promotion, to transfer with me. I want to go to California being tired of living poor. Dont you want to send me some money to speculate with?

Please give my respects to Mrs. Love. George Campbell & his Sister[12] have been East & George staid some time with me in Balt. where he lost his heart. My Mother went to Nashville with them. Nothing in Baltimore, deservedly famous as it is for beautiful & interesting "Heavenly," can compare in my eyes with his sister. Dont you want to confer an everlasting favor on me? If so & I go to the West work in such a way that I can visit Nashville to buy those horses.[13]

Yours &c

R. S. Ewell

Capt. Love

P.S. Ask if a transfer between Kearny & myself or myself & any Captain [in the] West would be approved & if so get the Adj't to send a little Official note to that effect. Gardiner I think will resign.[14] I will for money & I hope to get that in Cal.

1. Dr. Samuel Johnson's novella *The History of Rasselas, Prince of Abissinia* was first published in England in 1759. It chronicles the travels of an Ethiopian prince who sets out to discover the secret of happiness.

2. Ewell, who displayed a distinct lack of talent when it came to drawing, inserted a rough sketch of two doves kissing one another at the top of the page. See p. 96.

3. Captain William Eustis had graduated from West Point in 1830. After serving for three years in the infantry, he transferred to the 1st Dragoons. He became a captain in 1845 and resigned on August 4, 1849. His resignation opened up a vacancy in the regiment that Ewell hoped to fill.

4. James Shields (1810–1879) immigrated to the United States in 1826. He served in the Illinois legislature and later became a jurist on the state's supreme court.

During the Mexican War, he was appointed brigadier general of Illinois volunteers, and in the battles of Cerro Gordo and Churubusco he was brevetted to major general. At the time this letter was written, Shields was a member of the U.S. Senate. Later he would become governor of the Oregon Territory. President Abraham Lincoln appointed Shields brigadier general of volunteers at the start of the Civil War, but he resigned his commission in 1863 after being defeated by Ewell and Jackson in the 1862 Shenandoah Valley Campaign.

5. Robert M. T. Hunter (1809–1887) of Essex County, Virginia, served as speaker of the U.S. House of Representatives but was turned out of office when he became a states' right Democrat and a disciple of John C. Calhoun. Reelected to the House in 1845, he served but two years before accepting a seat in the U.S. Senate, where he was a tireless defender of the South. He withdrew from the Senate following Lincoln's election and committed himself to the Confederacy, serving briefly as its secretary of war and later as a member of the Senate. In February 1865, he joined Alexander Stephens and Judge John A. Campbell in representing the Confederacy in a failed peace conference with President Lincoln at Hampton Roads, Virginia.

6. James Barbour (1775–1842) had a distinguished public career. He served successively as the Republican governor of Virginia (1812–1814), U.S. senator (1815–1825), secretary of war (1825–1828), and minister to Great Britain (1828–1829).

7. Secretary of War Joel R. Poinsett (1779–1851) had been the first United States minister to Mexico. A native of South Carolina, he led Unionist efforts there during the Nullification Crisis. In 1837 President Martin Van Buren appointed Poinsett secretary of war, a position he held during the Seminole War. He retired from public life in 1841.

8. Andrew Jackson had been president of the United States from 1829 to 1837. John Bell (1797–1869) of Tennessee had a long political career in the U.S. House of Representatives and the U.S. Senate and even served for a few weeks as secretary of war in William Henry Harrison's administration. A conservative Southern slaveholder, Bell became head of the Constitutional Union Party. He ran for president as a moderate in 1860 with the slogan, "The Constitution of the country, the Union of the states, and the enforcement of the laws." He garnered few votes, however, outside the border states.

9. Jefferson Davis (1808–1889) graduated from West Point in 1824 and served seven years in the army, where he met and later married Sarah Taylor, the daughter of Colonel (later President) Zachary Taylor. She was the first of his two wives. In the Mexican War, he commanded a regiment known as the

"Mississippi Rifles," helping Taylor gain a victory at the Battle of Buena Vista. After the war Davis resigned from the army and was elected to the U.S. Senate, where he served from 1847 to 1851. Two years later he accepted an appointment as secretary of war under Franklin Pierce, a post that he held for four years. He then returned to the Senate, where he became a leading spokesman for the South. When the South seceded from the Union, Southerners elected Davis as their first president.

10. Reverdy Johnson (1796–1876) of Maryland resigned his seat in the United States Senate in 1849 to accept an appointment as the attorney general of the United States. In 1861 he attended a conference in Washington, D.C., designed to avert civil war. When that failed, Johnson remained loyal to the Union, serving Maryland in the state House of Delegates and again as a U.S. senator.

11. Philip Kearny led an expedition in California against the Rogue River Indians in 1850 before resigning from the army the following year.

12. Elizabeth ("Lizinka") McKay Campbell (1820–1872) was Ewell's first cousin. This is the first recorded reference by Ewell of his affection for Lizinka, whom he later married.

13. Ewell wished to purchase horses cheaply in Nashville and then take them to California, where he could sell them at an enormous profit. A stop in Nashville would also afford him an opportunity to visit Lizinka, who was a resident of the city.

14. John W. T. Gardiner of Maine had been a classmate of Ewell's at West Point, graduating twenty-sixth in his class. Like Ewell, he joined the 1st Dragoons, becoming a captain in October 1851. He retired from the army in 1861.

39. To Rebecca Ewell

Balt. Md
Feb'y 23, 1850

Dear Becca;

I think of going to Va. with you on Monday, but from the nature of things must reach Washington on the last of the month in time to take the evening train for Balt. at 1/2 past 5. My going will depend on this contingency. Should I go I will be in Washtn by the early train which gets there at 1/2 past 8. You can have the carriage somewhere convenient so that I can leave the cars and get directly in the carriage.[1]

I recd the other day a letter from Mother who seems to be quite happy.[2] No particular news.

Should I not go I will most probably telegraph Aunt Rebecca[3] so that you may not be cramped in your time of starting.

Yours &c
R. S. Ewell

1. Apparently Ewell planned to take a train from Baltimore to the District of Columbia on February 25. His sister Rebecca (who seems to have been staying with the Gantts) would meet him there, and then they would ride together in a carriage to Stony Lonesome. Dick had to be back in Washington by 5:30 P.M. on the twenty-eighth in order to catch the last train back to Baltimore. He later canceled the trip.
2. Ewell's mother was then in Nashville, Tennessee, visiting her sister Harriet Campbell.
3. Rebecca Stoddert Hubbard (1798–1872) was the younger sister of Ewell's mother. Rebecca married David Hubbard (ca. 1792–1874), a cousin of Sam Houston. Hubbard fought in the War of 1812. Seriously wounded at the Battle of New Orleans, he was promoted to major. He later moved to Alabama, where he took up law and engaged in business. A strong states' rights advocate and skilled debater, Hubbard served no fewer than nine terms in the Alabama legislature and two terms in the United States Congress. When the Civil War began, he took a seat in the Confederate Congress, serving until 1863, when he accepted an appointment as commissioner of Indian affairs. Financially ruined by the war, he moved to Spring Hill, Tennessee, where he and his wife became neighbors of the Ewells.

40. *Undated Letter Fragment*

. . . we rode over. . . by 7.[1] I staid all night, and having an engagement to ride next day with Miss Pat, started at 8. in the rain reached town at 12 1/2 brushed up and Miss P. rode to a neighbour's 7 miles where by appointment we met young Davies & Miss Morris in a buggy. We knew the Swans were not at home and had the whole house to ourselves. Being hungry I was perfectly rejoiced to see a basket taken out of the buggy and having the keys of. . . .[2]

Col. R. E. Lee is stationed in Balt. you know with his family and a most agreeable set they are. For the last few days there has been a Miss Peters[3] from N.Y. staying with him and I have s[e]ldom seen so agreeable and interesting personage. Her highest praise though is to mention that Col. [Lee] admires her excessively and the Colonel does.

1. A postmark identifies this letter fragment as being sent from Baltimore on February 25, 1850. It appears on the bottom quarter of a sheet of paper, which has writing on both sides. The first paragraph is on one side; the second paragraph on the other. Percy G. Hamlin, in his compilation of Ewell letters, *The Making of a Soldier,* ignores the first paragraph and attaches the last paragraph as a postscript to Ewell's February 25 letter to his sister Rebecca. However, this may have been part of a separate letter written one day earlier.

2. The various individuals Ewell mentions here have not been identified.

3. Mary Lee's cousin, Britannia Peter.

41. To Rebecca Ewell

Balt. Md
Feb'y 25th 1850

Dear Becca—

I have to be in Balt. to attend Military duty that cannot be dispensed with on Thursday the last of the month and the prospect of rain last night with the dislike to make two such long journeys as I would have to do both Monday & Thursday, made me determine not to go to Va. to-day.

If you should still be in[1] Wash. & not [go] to Va before Friday it will be in my power to go then and stay a week. Now I could only remain Tuesday and Wednesday and to leave Thursday early enough to reach Washington to take the train at 1/2 past 5. for Baltimore. This all should have det[erre]d me from making up my mind to go but the advantages & disadvantages were not so plain untill a young lady who was to leave to day told me yesterday that she was not to leave untill Friday.

I expect I have put Aunt Rebecca's patience to the test, but I hope she will remember that man is born to trouble as the sparks fly upwards.[2]

You had better write to me and let me know your plans.

Could you not come on and spend a day with cousin Rosanna[3] pleasantly? I know she would be glad to see you and I will go with you to the Germania musical soiree[4] or anywhere else you may take a fancy to go. You may possibly see you[r] Sister-in-law too as I am perfectly devoted to at least half a dozen. I am to ride with a young lady this evening worth $200,000 and "lovely as the day." I expect I shall not be able to think of anything below the moon for the next 6 days. Tell William to send me one or two of his prospectusses[5] and I will show them where they might do some good. I have Ben Gantt's horse a very fine one. When I go from here I shall likely sell him and at a sacrifice. Would you all like to have him provided he goes cheap. He works well and is handsome and spirited.

Write—

> Yours &c
> R. S. Ewell

1. Ewell repeated the word "in" here.
2. Job 5:7.
3. Rosanna Ewell Reynolds (ca. 1813–ca. 1897) was Ewell's second cousin. They shared a great-grandfather, Charles Ewell. Rosanna's grandfather was James Ewell, and her father was James Ball Ewell. She was married to Baltimore merchant William Reynolds.
4. Founded in 1840 by German immigrants, the Germania Club hosted a variety of literary and musical productions in Baltimore.
5. Advertisements for a school that William was running at Stony Lonesome.

42. To Rebecca Ewell

> Balt Md
> Aprl 24 1850

Dear Becca;

Not having as yet succeeded in collecting from either Ben Ewell or Lowndes Jackson I cannot send you the note.[1] I would advise you though to invest the money in shares of the Corporation of Georgetown when I give you the money & I will do so in case of a lucky speculation. Your interest will be safer & the money under your own control. Mr Reynolds says Va State Stocks would be the proper investment for William to make of Scott's[2] money.

I wish to find out what became of the paper of Tom's. I fear it was left at the Court House. Tell William to attend to it.

Last night I placed before Hough the peculiarities of William's school.[3] of course would not urge him to send his boy there but thereby the matter is before him. It is likely I will go to Richmond, Va after a while.

I pay the postage (enclosed) because this is partly on my business. I have heard from George Campbell but it does not amount to much. Mother well.

I sent some papers for the boys the other day. I have a visitor & must close as there will be no chance to write a long letter. Tell William to send me one or two prospectusses post paid, not however sent 7 days after rec'g this—i.e. if not sent at once dont send at all.

> Yours &c
> R. S. Ewell

1. Jackson and Benjamin Ewell helped Dick invest his money. Since neither man had paid Dick what they owed him, Dick in turn could not pay his debt to Rebecca.
2. Unidentified.
3. William had recently opened a boys' school at Stony Lonesome. He taught sixteen pupils, who, according to his sister Rebecca, were vulgar and ruining the house. Hough has not been identified.

43. To Rebecca Ewell

Rich[mon]d Va May 26. 1850

Dear Becca;

I gave Wm a det[aile]d copy of the statement of the money recd from Ben on acct of you & Wm and as Jackson's[1] amount overpays me I forward a draft for the surplus. I send the draft to Wm because I presume you can trust each other and it makes the matter simpler to have but one set of accounts between him & me without bringing in a third person. The same thing of course applies between you and him. This I understand agrees with his letter proposing to borrow your money to pay me. I now understand myself to be square. I believe I would be entitled to one month's interest on $400.00 but pay it to Mammy.

I have had a letter from Mother since I came here but it contained nothing of any particular importance. It was directed to Elizabeth & myself. I think she would like to come in & to-day wrote to George that if he would bring her half way I would meet her half way & bring her on.[2] Jackson must have been pushed for money as it has been a month since he had the accounts presented to him.

I believe George Campbell has sold his house in Nashville for $30,000.[3]

I believe you & Wm both owe me letters.

Your[s] &c
R. S. Ewell

1. Ewell's cousin Lowndes Jackson had recently given Ewell money.
2. Dick's mother, Elizabeth Ewell, was apparently visiting her sister Harriot Stoddert Campbell in Tennessee. George Campbell Jr. was Harriot's son.
3. Ewell may be mistaken about George Campbell selling his Nashville house, for when Campbell died three years later, he left a large house in the state capital to his sister Lizinka Campbell. For additional information about this structure, see Pfanz, *Richard S. Ewell*, 508.

44. To Benjamin Ewell

Fort Leavenworth Mo
August 10th 1850

Dear Ben,

Your sheet of foolscap came to hand yesterday.

I reached this place about the 6. with Webb in good order though so abominably fat that he could hardly walk for panting.[1]

The 228 recruits expected to be found here were reduced by sickness & desertion to 160. the young gentlemen in charge let the[m] glide like water in a steam boiler. I hope they will not credit me with the mismanagement at Wash. as I am the last in command. No desertions have taken place since I came here. One de[tachmen]t. will probably start the day after to-morrow and mine about the 15.[2] we are waiting for horses, but expect them by the 11. It is as hot as possible here. we are in camp 3 miles from the barrack 2 Drag. Officers besides myself, who lay in bed untill 7 & remain under shelter of their arbor all day. I heard as the de[tachmen]t. was approaching Jeff. Brrk the Officer in charge ordered for the first time, the roll to be called which innovation so disgusted them that they broke into a regular mutiny & without actually beating the Officer in charge gave him a slight choking & hustling about the boat. He had to get Col. Mason to go on board & try to bring them into subjection.[3]

They seem to be tame enough at present.

Webb became so used to travelling that he is not willing now to go on foot. Yesterday when I drove in a little carriage to the Fort he tried all the way to get in it being too warm. Day before yesterday for the first time quite early I took him out hunting but he performed miserably[—]seemed to have very little idea of hunting and when amongst a flock of grouse seemed to take them for chickens without hunting. I was lucky enough to bring one down & let him mouth it but his after performances only brought several whippings on him. He is improving fast as he pointed a sparrow yesterday. Patience & time will answer though both are very scarce with me just now.

At Carlisle I sent Reynolds $150 with a request to sell 800 Md Sixes & buy Illinois 6's but he has not answered my letter. I told him to write to me here. In a few days I will send him $500.00 & wish you to take the acknowledgement for the same. I do not like to have too much in any one's hands. I will probably

[*Third and fourth pages are missing.*]

When the de[tachmen]t. reached Jeff Brrk such was the state of things that Gen. Mason was preparing charges against all the Officers but his death saved them. I would think from what I heard that they deserved trial.

1. Webb was a pointer.
2. Ewell was headed to a new assignment in the New Mexico Territory.
3. Richard B. Mason was the commander of the 1st Dragoons. Born in Virginia, he rose through the ranks of the regiment to become its colonel in 1846. He received a brigadier's brevet in 1848 for meritorious conduct but died on July 25, 1850, just three weeks before this letter was written.

Chapter 5

New Mexico, 1852–1857

Ewell once told a fellow officer that he had spent twenty years serving in the West, where he had learned everything there was to know about commanding a company of dragoons but had forgotten everything else. He spent six of those years in New Mexico, a territory acquired by the United States as part of the Treaty of Guadalupe Hidalgo, which ended the Mexican War.

Throughout that time, he was in command of Company G, 1st Dragoons. Ewell took charge of the company in October 1850. It was then stationed at Rayado, a two-company post located on the Canadian (or Red) River, roughly eighty miles northeast of Santa Fe. Nearby, the eastern branch of the Santa Fe Trail met the road to Bent's Fort. The dragoons' mission was to protect the territory's settlers against hostile Indians, who swept down from the surrounding mountains to plunder unwary travelers and isolated ranches.

Company G remained at Rayado but a short time. In August 1851 the dragoons made a punitive expedition into Navajo territory and established a post there, which they called Fort Defiance. Forage at Fort Defiance was not sufficient for a large mounted force, however, and in December Company G moved to Los Lunas, a town on the Rio Grande, twenty-five miles south of Albuquerque. It remained there for five years, giving chase to marauding bands of Navajos, Utes, and Apaches.

Ewell was frequently the only officer on duty at the post. As such, he had to drill the troops and handle the paperwork involved in feeding, clothing, paying, and supplying them. He maintained discipline and administered justice. At times he sat on court-martial boards. When not engaged in military activities, Ewell grew vegetables in the post garden, harvested grapes at the post vineyard, and supervised the care of the post's chickens and cows. There were days when he was as much a farmer as he was a soldier.

As the post's commanding officer, Ewell had social obligations to fulfill. He hosted travelers at his quarters and met frequently with local inhabitants. Occasionally he commented on women he had known in Virginia, but if he formed a romantic attachment to any of them, there is no record of the fact.

*Money was never far from the young captain's mind. Almost every letter writ-
ten by Ewell during this period contains references to the stock market, the purchase
or sale of land, speculations in livestock, or other financial schemes. He could not
stand to see his money lie dormant. In a letter to his brother Ben, he summed up his
investment philosophy: "Better a bad speculation than none at all." Ewell sometimes
pooled resources with his siblings and frequently loaned or borrowed money from
them. Cousins doubled as financial agents. Through it all he prospered, steadily
building a solid financial base on which he might one day retire.*

45. To Benjamin Ewell

Los Lunas N.M.[1]
July 21 1852

Dear Ben;

Your last letter recd was May 11. You propose therein to purchase a farm
should a chance offer itself. I would like to own someplace where one could
fall back in case of leaving the Army & only fear there is not capital enough to
make return from a farm of much size. I should like very much to buy Brook
Grove[2] if it should come into the market at a reasonable rate. There is every reason too that it should be worth $100. per acre. A plank road to the D.C. would
make it worth that at once. Would it not be well to keep your eye on it for fear
of its going at a sacrifice? It would be the devil to try, without a large capital to
make 10 or 1200 acres of poor land productive.

I am delightfully fixed just now, cows chickens &c & make my own butter
& all that sort of thing as comfortably as any farmer. My garden though late is
coming on finely with a fine prospect of onions & cabbages.[3] I scarcely spend
30 dollars a month on my self & were I on a farm would not lay out more than
half as much. I am very anxious to hear what investment Reynolds has made of
my money. I have about $2000. in his hands that by the latest accounts was not
yet employed. It will be too bad if he leaves it any time unemployed as I hate to
lose the interest. Better a bad speculation than none at all.[4] I have come to the
conclusion in case they make out my land warrant[5] at once, to sell it for what it
will bring. To make it valuable a person ought to be where it can be located.

There has been any amount of travelling up & down the river[6] lately by persons (Officers) going to the States on recruiting service & leave & others taking
their place. I have had several ladies to tea lately & gave them quite a respectable
table. I am only afraid Col. Sumner[7] will find out how luxuriously I am living
& will move me away before I reap the full benefit of my garden & grapes, for

I hired a vineyard which promises to yield finely. I am entirely without Officers & have been so since my return & if they will only keep away, will please me much. My 1st Lt. Wilson[8] from near Leesburg, or at least from that part of the country, is when sober an excellent Officer, but unfortunately is a confirmed Sot & sets such an example to my men that my trouble is doubled when he is present. At the same time he has performed no duty since joining, [being] either drunk or sick. I would like to have an active Officer with the Comp'y so that in due season I might go on leave of absence & attend to my private affairs. I have money enough in Reynolds hands to make it worth my while to look after it. Besides Elizabeth has written so much lately in praise of the metallic & mental charms of a Miss Scolly[9] a sort of cousin that I want to go & try my chance once more. I believe though a man would do better to mar[r]y in this country, provided he never was so imprudent as to return home at unreasonable hrs or when not expected. A Maj. Shepherd,[10] Int'y passed the other day with his wife, a Mexican about 15 yrs old whom he married 6 or 8 m[o]nths since. They stopped here during the heat of the day & the prospect ahead for him made me feel melancholly. He is a fool & coarse brute & neglects this girl very much. There were scoldings &c & disputations when they got into the carriage & temper in the greatest abundance. She, raised among those whose virtue was very easy, young & neglected by her husband, who is crass & not agreeable in his Dep[ortmen]t, has as I can see hardly one chance in fifty of keeping within bounds. The first sproutings looked almost ready to burst forth. I have no doubt when he finds the horns full grown he will make a devil of a fuss just as if they were not entirely owing to his own stupid & brutal course. As we sow so must we reap.

Last night Capt. Buford[11] 1. Drg. staid with me, on his way to the states. He came out with me in 50. without much money, but several fine blooded horses & great skill in cards. He won on one horse race $1800. & by judicious sales of his horses & good luck at cards goes home with 2 yrs pay due & about $8000 in cash. He is on recruiting service. He is a Kentuckian & his Father was one of the most successful racers & stock raisers of his day, the owner of the celebrated Medoc,[12] whose Offspring probably won $20 000 for the old man. One of them was the gainer of this race I mentioned above. Buford as you may suppose is hardly calculated to shine in any ball room except a Mexican fandango, where he seems in his element. Here the natives call him, Hellroaring Buford. He is over 6 feet & out of proportion large in other respects. He married a Sister of Arnold Harris.[13]

You must be mistaken in your idea that you answer every one of my letters. I have written a great many to which I have recd no answer.

Yours &c

R. S. Ewell

P.S.

Remember me to Mrs Ewell & Lizzy.

1. New Mexico Territory.
2. Brook Grove was the Maryland farm owned by Ewell's aunt Ann Gantt who had recently moved to Washington.
3. At Los Lunas, Ewell and his soldiers sowed twenty-five bushels of wheat, twelve bushels of barley, five bushels of oats, and several gallons of clover. In addition, they planted twelve acres of corn and one acre of potatoes, as well as a three-acre vegetable garden.
4. The details of Ewell's investments are unknown; however, information in earlier letters indicates that he invested heavily in stocks and bonds.
5. In accordance with the Military Bounty Land Act of September 28, 1850, Ewell received a bounty of 160 acres for serving in the Mexican War. He claimed his bounty on March 15, 1852, at a court of law in Valencia County, New Mexico Territory. He had the land warrant sent directly to his brother Ben in Williamsburg. Ben, in turn, forwarded it to a relative named Lowndes Jackson, who sold it.
6. The Rio Grande.
7. Sumner was then in command of the Ninth Military Department, which encompassed the New Mexico Territory.
8. Clarendon J. L. Wilson had graduated from West Point in 1846 and became a first lieutenant in 1849. He died just seven months after this letter was written, on February 21, 1853.
9. Unidentified. Elsewhere spelled "Scollay."
10. Brevet Major Oliver L. Shepherd of the 3rd Infantry had been a classmate of Ewell's at West Point, where he had graduated thirty-third in the class. A native of New York, Shepherd commanded the 15th United States Infantry during the Civil War. He was brevetted to brigadier general in March 1865 for gallant and meritorious service at the Battle of Stones River, Tennessee.
11. Abraham Buford (1820–1884), a native of Kentucky and a captain in the 1st Dragoons, was well known for breeding horses and other livestock. After joining the Confederacy late in 1862, he commanded a cavalry division under Nathan Bedford Forrest.
12. Medoc, an excellent racehorse and an important sire, was the offspring of another famous racer, the chestnut colt American Eclipse. Medoc was born in 1829 to Young Maid and was America's leading sire in 1840–41.

13. Arnold Harris of New York had graduated from West Point in 1834, two years after Benjamin Ewell. He remained in the army but a short time, resigning his commission in 1837.

46. *To Rebecca Ewell*

Post Office (Sante Fe N.M)
Albuquerque N.M.
Octr 28th 1852

Dear Becca;

Yours of Sept 3rd has just come to hand. I am here on business & merely write a line as it can go by mail, at once. I do not consider that I owed or borrowed money from you. no one but William Stoddert was engaged in where abouts the money was to come from or was responsible. If I return you the $400. I am just that amt. out of pocket. However I will wait untill you can get Wms note or statement & in the meantime pay you ten per ct on $400.

I write to Mr Reynolds by this mail accordingly. Unless William settles the matter you had better take legal measures.

Yrs in haste
R S Ewell

47. *To Benjamin Ewell*

Los Lunas N M–
Decr 23 1852

Dear Ben;

Your last letter by the last mail announced that you had my Land Warrant. Please forward it to Lowndes Jackson to whom I send authority to sell it. I want to sell it for account of Elizabeth[1] so that it would be as well not to delay in forwarding it to Jackson. There is nothing new out here things going on in the same old style.

I am obliged to you for your offers to select a finer specimen of the genus woman than can be found in New Mex. but as you have not seen these latter I doubt your capability of judging. Yet awhile these are good enough for me. What a pity that you did not profit by the rise in land in your vecinity. it is never a matter of chance, this sort of thing & if you would only reason as clearly as on Newton's Theorem for the Binomial[2] it might put more dollars in your pocket.

I have a most perfect idea of the annoyances of a Tavernkeeper without the prospect of the dinner. I have been entertaining with great want of interruption for the last 6 m[o]nths. Today I have been pestered by a Mexican for several hours[,] a Dutch Jew Merchant[,] & lastly an Irish carpenter. All these things prevent my being able to write a long letter as I had intended.

So you must take the will for the deed & write me a long answer for the promise of better on my part. The mail starts in the morning & I will be writing on business long after bed time.

Yours &c
R S. Ewell

1. Ewell may have been helping to support his older sister, Elizabeth, who was a novice in Washington.
2. Ben, as a mathematics professor, was well versed in the theorems of Sir Isaac Newton.

48. To Rebecca Ewell

Jan'y 28th 1854

Dear Becca;

Your most incomprehensible letter about the darky came to hand by the last mail. I was out on campaign[1] or would have answered it by this m[o]nths mail. I have sent a check to Lowndes Jackson. it is on Maj. A. D. Steuart[2] in St. Louis & written what it is for. I sent $200 for Mr Tyler[3] & also write to him. If you want more I will advance it. You write that I might as well have advanced the $400. The chief reason for my trade with William was ready money. if you loaned him I will return you the money with interest if you will have the Farm called Thornberry's[4] sold to me at a fair proportional estimate, say at the current price for land at the time I sold out with 6 per cent from that time added on. It would be a hard case for me to sacrifice my property & then receive no return.[5]

I dont know from your letter whether you refer to one or two negresses nor can I extract without making it too long. I would infer though that there are two, one of whom is bo[ugh]t & the other cannot be. Why dont you buy Horace too?[6] I will probably enter shortly into some speculations that will make me much better off or lose what I have. But in either case a few months hence will make it entirely in my power to advance the needful.[7] I think of buying sheep to take them to California obtaining a leave for the necessary time. They are said to be worth a good deal there.[8] There has been a failure of the mails this month as all that came to me was one letter from Aunt Rebecca from Nashville. She says Cousin L's[9] property is estimated at $500.000 & Aunt Stoddert's at $100.000. There does not seem to be any thing that can drive such things from the heads of some people. The best thing about L's property is that the management of it will occupy her so much that her mind will not be able to contemplate her misfortunes. I believe from what I have seen of her that in the end she will be a happier person than ever before, not of course because she has the property but because the duties it will entail, will keep her mind employed. I have not written to her since hearing of George's death, partly because her residence was constantly changing & partly because her pain I thought, must be so great that sympathy would appear like mockery.[10]

Since the 16th of Dec. I have been leading a very active life, marching several hundred miles through the mountains & travelling on horseback at more than the usual rates. To day I returned from Sante Fe 66 miles making it in about 8 travelling hours. Within three days I start for Fort Union 200 miles off to be absent untill nearly the end of the month, very probably to start on a Campaign half way to California on my return.[11] I like this way of doing business very much as it keeps me in better health, & keeps one from thinking. Let me know if more money be required. If I only had an honest & active agent whom I could employ[,] this time next year would see me clear of dependance upon the Army.

Yrs &—

R. S. Ewell

1. Ewell departed on a scouting expedition to the White Mountains on December 16, 1853, and did not return to Los Lunas until January 15, 1854.

2. Adam D. Steuart of Virginia was a paymaster in the United States Army, a position that he continued to hold throughout the Civil War.

3. Unidentified.

4. Both John Thornberry and William Thornberry owned farms near Stony Lonesome. Ewell did not purchase a farm from either man.

5. Ewell may be referring here to the sale of his interest in Stony Lonesome. He had inherited a one-sixth interest in the estate after the death of his father in 1826. He had sold his share in the property to his brother William on May 16, 1850, for $1,200.

6. Another slave.

7. "Needful"—i.e., funds.

8. Ewell did, in fact, put money into sheep, an investment that yielded him a handsome return.

9. Lizinka Campbell Brown, Ewell's future wife.

10. Lizinka was one of the wealthiest women in Tennessee, having inherited almost eighteen thousand acres of land in Tennessee and Mississippi from her husband, James Percy Brown, who had died in 1844; from her father, George

Washington Campbell, who had died in 1848; from her mother, who had died in 1849; and from her brother, George Campbell Jr., who had died in 1853. It was Lizinka's inheritance from her brother, who died unmarried and intestate in Rochfort, France, that prompted Ewell's comments here. For a breakdown of Lizinka's landholdings, see Pfanz, *Ewell*, 508–11.

11. Post records indicate that Ewell remained at Los Lunas throughout February and March. He was absent on detached service for much of the next four months.

49. *To Benjamin Ewell*

Feb'y 25. 54

Dear Ben;

Kit Carson[1] & a number of returned men from Cal. make the following report—*Large heavy dray* horses in good order are worth from 800 to $1200 in San. Fran. The danger of stampeding is the drawback. what can such horses[,] the coarser the better, be bot. for in the States? By taking ambulances which double their cost, Corn for the whole journey Via N.M. can be taken leaving in Sept. wintering here & reaching San. F. in April.

Suppose you go into it. I will go from here with you. We would want 30 to 40 horses 10 men & 5 ambulances. I wrote to Sherman[2] a Class mate some time since asking if what I had been told were true i.e. that he would take money from Officers at a heavy interest. He is in a Banking house with Turner & Lucas of St. Louis. I would like to put in $8000 have but 6000. could you put in the two either on my security & a fair interest or at your own risk & profit. Answer by return of mail.

(Over)   Yrs in haste—

R S Ewell

I see that there is a very strong probability of an increase of the Army.[3] If you will go to Washington & lobby a little for me I will come down very handsomely, paying all expenses if you fail & say $1000. One thousand dollars for the grade of Major. Wonders are sometimes done by spending a little money judiciously among the proper agents—Ver Cum Sap.[4] One thing I will swear & that is that you will theorise beautifully whether you do anything or not. Remember me to Lizzy.

R S Ewell

1. Christopher "Kit" Carson (1809–1868), a resident of Taos, New Mexico, was a renowned trapper, guide, and army scout. In 1853 he was appointed United

States Indian agent of the Utes. When the Civil War began, he helped organize the 1st New Mexico Volunteer Infantry and became its colonel. Brevetted to brigadier general at the end of the war, he was commander of Fort Garland until his resignation from the army in 1867.

2. William T. Sherman (1820–1891) graduated sixth in the U.S. Military Academy's Class of 1840, seven places ahead of Ewell. He resigned from the army in September 1853 and moved to San Francisco to pursue a career in banking. During the Civil War he became the Union's second most famous general, after Ulysses S. Grant. From 1869 to 1883, Sherman served as commander-in-chief of the United States Army.

3. In 1855 Congress added two regiments of infantry and two regiments of cavalry to the army. Ewell enlisted Ben's help to secure himself a major's commission in one of the two cavalry regiments. For details of Ben's unsuccessful efforts lobbying for his brother's promotion, see George W. Lay to BSE, 15 Jan. 1855, LC; and J. F. Lee to BSE, 8 Mar. 1855, folder 14, WM.

4. An obscure Latin phrase possibly meaning, "Wisdom before youth."

50. To Rebecca Ewell

July 1st 1855

Dear Becca;

Yours of April 30th was received this afternoon & I have only time to write a few lines. I am much obliged to you for what you write of Cousin's [*sic*] Lizinka's offer,[1] but wish you had been more explicit. My letter to her had you understood it, was neither "obsequious or submissive," but this makes no difference. Any disposition that I might have to accept Cousin's L's offer would spring more from the admiration that I have always had for her than from any idea of getting rich & philosophically speaking this very admiration would be the best reason for not accepting.

I never met any one who had not an uncertain temper except those that were uniformly bad. This makes no difference however. I have business in the States sufficient to warrant my going in for a short time, & I dont think there is any likelihood that I shall resign. Uncertainty of temper would be an objection to Stony Lonesome also.[2]

I am glad that you found out your mistake about the $400 loan, though I am surprised you ever made it.

In the last three yrs had I been in business in this Territory with the Capital I possess I would now have been independent. Some little money that I used in the way I speak of i.e. carrying sheep to California, more than doubled itself

Lizinka Campbell Brown was Ewell's widowed first cousin. When she asked him to leave the army and manage her farm in Tennessee, Ewell declined, despite his admiration for her. (Courtesy Dace Brown Farrer)

every time I tried it. Could I have gone into it myself I would now have been rich.

Money is to be made with capital & labor but it is not the one thing needful.[3]

You are mistaken in supposing that any position I may have held in society has been due to my office. It might afford easier access possibly, but all Army Officers are not in what I call good society & at the same time many are in the best.

I merely write to answer your letter. please answer me as quickly as you can, as I may be going East & explicitly.

Yours &c

R. S. Ewell

P.S.

I will engage when your school gets under way to furnish for a certain period, one scholar.[4]

RSE

1. Lizinka needed a manager for her plantation near Spring Hill, Tennessee. In 1855 she wrote to Ewell, offering him the position. Ewell visited Spring Hill during a leave of absence late that year, but he declined the offer.

2. Rebecca apparently accused her brother of having an "uncertain temper" and chided him for answering Lizinka in an "obsequious and submissive" manner. In a letter to Lizinka, Dick's cousin Tasker Gantt likewise accused him of "vacillation and indecision," claiming that "If it became necessary to decide

between a certain sacrifice and a possible or probable great recompense, he would be paralyzed. . . . One's respect is necessarily impaired by such weakness and want of poise." TTG to LCB, 26 Dec. 1855, TN.

3. Ewell seems to be referring to Luke 10:41–42, in which Jesus tells his hostess: "Martha, Martha, you are worried and upset about many things, but only one thing is needed" (New International Version).

4. While living at Stony Lonesome, Rebecca earned extra money by teaching. Here Dick offers to sponsor one of her students.

51. Undated Letter Fragment

Side View—Front—dimensions and in fine a complete drawing of the whole affair.[1] I shall get one made that will contain 50 oz. of silver, or at least what is necessary for the expenses of making will more than complete that part of the $50. that is deficient. There is nothing new out here. The Mexicans across the line are getting up proclamations &c. &c. about fillebusteros who exist only in imagination, but the Governor ends his proclamation by calling on them to contribute liberally towards the expense of getting up a force to repel these outlaws as by that they will save the government the necessity of forcing the contribution. So it is only an excuse to take money from them.[2]

I have not time to write more except to say not to forget about the tea pot. I have just received a supply of very fine black & green tea from San Francisco.

Remember me to all. I expect my next will be addressed to Nashville.

Yrs &c
R S. Ewell

1. The date and the correspondent to whom Ewell wrote this letter are unknown. The reference to Nashville suggests that it was written in the summer of 1855.

2. Perhaps a reference to Sonoran president Ignacio Pesqueira. At that time Sonora was the target of American adventurers, known as filibusterers, who were attempting to foment insurrection against Mexico's central government.

52. To Elizabeth Ewell Jr.

Williamsburg
Va.
Jan'y 15. 1856

Dear Elizabeth;

Please procure & forward the following seed[1] for which I enclose five dollars & credit me with the balance.

Cabbages

Early York	1/2 pint
Large late Drumhead—3/4 of pint	
Cauliflower—12 Papers	
2 table spoonsful	
Nutmeg melons—	one Gill
Spinach	Do[2]
Turnip—Ruta baga	1/2 pint
flat dutch—	One pint
Best watermelons	1/2 pint

Please send by mail pre paid to (quickly)

Commanding Officer—
Company "G" 1st Dragoons
Sante Fe
New Mexico

& send me the acct. yrs in hast[e]—
see you soon.

R. S. Ewell

1. Ewell may have wished to use this seed in the post garden at Los Lunas, or he may have had a private garden of his own. For more information on the post garden, see Pfanz, *Ewell*, 70–71.
2. Ditto.

53. To Elizabeth Ewell Jr.

March 5. 56.

Dear Elizabeth;

I called twice to see you in Georgetown but without success.[1] I wanted to say to you that my fiscal affairs being somewhat more straitened than I had expected prevented my making the bargain we were speaking of. I have to spend a good deal of money & prefer letting our affairs remain in statu[s] quo. You gain by this as you have your One hundred doll[ar]s & land besides.

You will never have any difficulty in raising $1500. with your prospects, as you could sell the annuity for nearly that. Besides its not being pecuniarily convenient for me to pay you the $140. there would be no time to make the papers. Land offers greater inducements here to purchase than anywhere I have seen but lack of mon[e]y cramps my genius.

Yrs &c R. S. Ewell

1. After visiting Lizinka in Tennessee in the fall of 1855, Ewell continued east to Virginia. After visiting with his mother, Rebecca, and William at Stony Lonesome, he stayed for three months in Williamsburg with Ben and Lizzie. While at Stony Lonesome, he made two trips to Georgetown to see his sister Elizabeth, but in each case he was unsuccessful.

54. To Elizabeth Ewell Jr.

Planters House[1] St. Louis
March 21. 1856

Dear Elizabeth;

I wrote you on the road but my finger being badly inflamed I br[ough]t. the letter to an abrupt conclusion. I have heard news here that has made me regret writing that letter—so, if it be not too late, please dont take any steps— writing &c in consequence thereof.[2] I am busy here preparing to get away and cannot write at length, but from what I hear think it very likely Miss Scollay is to be married & if she be not, it is the same thing. Should you write to her, let it be because you owe a letter & say nothing in regard to your humble servant but the pleasure received by the visit. I am trying to make an investment here that may keep you out of your $40. for a month or so, but will make me rich if I succeed. write to me at Fort Leavenworth by return of mail. Should I not receive it, it will follow me to New Mexico. remembrances to Cousins Francis & Angeletta.[3] I enclose the dollar.

Yrs &c
R S. Ewell

1. Planters House was a prominent hotel in St. Louis, where Ewell stopped for several days on his way back to New Mexico at the conclusion of his trip to Tennessee and Virginia.
2. See RSE to ESE, 5 March 1856, LC (letter 53, this volume).
3. Francis and Angeletta Lowndes (Loundes) were Ewell's distant cousins. Francis was born in 1793 in England, while his sister was born around 1810 in Virginia. At this time they lived in Georgetown in the District of Columbia.

55. To Benjamin Ewell

St. Louis Mrch 26. 56

Dear Ben;

I have been delayed here longer than I expected. I think you have given up the Hog Island farm[1] from what you write of the terms. Much better business can be done in speculations here. I spoke to Majr Turner on the subject of investments in California but though he tells me that money can be secured there at 3 per cent per month yet his firm wont do it for Officers or any one else, so that chance is gone. William[2] made a proposal to go there and invest for me, supporting himself by keeping school. Maj. Turner says that there is no trouble investing there at that rate & seems to think it would be a good plan for Wm to try. I have not mon[e]y enough tho to make it worth while, but I really believe an independence might be had in that way. Would you add $2000. to mine in case anything of the kind should be attempted? Turner is going to write to his partner in California & let me know his views. I say that I suppose you have given up Hog Island, because 1700 acres are in the Island instead of 800 as you thought & it would be impossible to pay $17,000 with our means, and ever buy negroes.

The speculation I spoke of to you is over, but others are always turning up and Tasker has consented to invest for me. The great point is to begin & if you could assist me with some funds say from $500 to $1000, Tasker would then be interested & no doubt a good business could be done. I would lose were I to realize before the 1st of July, and I want to get back to N.M. before I do anything. If that Sutler's post[3] should offer, I will take it & will want my capital, as also if William goes to Califor[nia].

Write to me at Sante Fe on the prospect of things in general & if you can advance a sum & we operate through Tasker, both of us may profit. I would prefer to get the money from you on interest. After a few m[o]nths I will have a thousand dollars. If you could borrow 2 or 3,000 at 6 per cent we would do a good business, Even Mortgaging Stony Lonesome.

There is an Academy going to begin here & they want a Pro[fessor]. Salary $2000, but a house would cost from 6 to 800. & a person could not live on less than from 3 to 4000 even plainly & besides the first Pro. will be expected to work miracles. It would be much better to come in on the second heat. Write quickly to me & remember me to all the family. I shall ow[e] Mr Reynolds about $150 the 1st of July after he draws my semi annual interest. I wish you would write to him or tell him when you see him (if you are willing) that you will pay him and I will remit to you; i.e I dont want him to sell out my stock yet. I will write to him if he wants the mon[e]y to write to you before selling out.

Yrs &—

R. S. Ewell

1. Hog Island lies in the James River, nearly opposite Jamestown.

2. William accompanied his older brother from Virginia to St. Louis and continued with him all the way to Los Lunas. Tasker Gantt, a cousin whom Ewell and Stoddert visited frequently while in St. Louis, wrote that Stoddert was "one of the most unbalanced men I ever saw," being both paranoid and childish. At different times of his life, William was a preacher, farmer, and teacher. TTG to LCB, 2 June 1856, TSLA.

3. Sutlers operated stores on military posts under contract with the army. Because they often held a monopoly on local trade, they generally prospered.

56. To Lizzie Ewell

June 29—[1]

Dear Lizzy;[2]

It is 1/2 past two in the morning, the mail leaves at 1/2 past 3, & for 24 hrs I have been writing & travelling—very little sleep. You are to take care of your teeth yourself. I dont encourage laziness or trusting to a dentist. Tell your daddy to let me know how much money on all accounts I have received from him [&] Mother. An Officer (Capt Easton)[3] wants me to get a box of tea for us both, so he must not let it all go.

Buy some Cologne with the enclosed doll[ar].[4] More another time.

Yrs [&]c R S. Ewell

PS.

Kiss some of the young ladies for me, any that are pretty Miss Sally[5] for example

Your Uncle Dick

1. Ewell's comment that he had just returned from twenty-four hours of travel suggests that this letter was written in 1856. In that year, he returned to Los Lunas on June 28, 1856, after three weeks of detached service. By contrast, post returns indicate that he was engaged on mounted expeditions on that date in 1857 and 1860. In 1858 and 1859 he was at his post on June 29, but there is nothing to indicate that he had traveled immediately before those dates.

2. Ewell's niece, Elizabeth Stoddert Ewell Jr. (1841–1911), was Benjamin's teenage daughter. At different times, Dick referred to her as Lizzy, Lizzie, Elizabeth, or Betty. Dick and Lizzie maintained a frequent and playful correspondence throughout her youth.

3. Langdon C. Easton of Missouri graduated from West Point in 1838 and served as a lieutenant in the 6th United States Infantry until 1847, when he was promoted to captain and transferred to the Quartermaster Department. Easton remained loyal to the Union during the Civil War and in 1865 received a major general's brevet. He died in 1884.

4. Ewell often enclosed some spending money for Lizzie, who was his only niece.

5. Unidentified.

57. To Benjamin Ewell

July 28. Since writing the former part of this letter,[1] orders have arrived moving my Regt from this Territory to California & Tuzon.[2] The latter is a town about half way between this & Cala in the country acquired by the Gadsden or Gadsen treaty.[3] Four Companies go to the latter, my own among the number. I prefer this to Cala as the latter is in some parts sickly & as much isolated. Being entirely new it is doubtful how letters are to be directed, but untill more is known you had better write to the care of Assistant Adjutant General, U.S. Army Sante Fe. N.M. As soon as I know how the Regular Mail route will go, I will let you know. I dont care much about the move, except that my garden is just beginning to yield & I dont like to lose its benefit. It is more however for the sake of testing different products, than for my own use. I am anxious to know how my sweet potatoes[,] artichokes &c will turn out. We may not move for a month yet & in that case I will be able to save many seeds &c for another year. One of the Lieuts of my Comp'y the other day was asked why he did not make a fuss about the orders changing our stations &c but, he said that all he cared about was seeing how the sweet potatoes would turn out. This looks silly but is in reality a key to Army life. Unless one drinks or gambles it is necessary to keep from absolute stagnation that interest should be taken in something. Promotion & the profession dont answer & I have not time to explain why & hence it is necessary to get up some outside humbug to take interest in & not to let yourself know that it is humbug.

I recommended Mrs Fry,[4] a belle of Louisville, who complained of the want of anything to amuse her, that she should imagine it to be the most important thing in life to raise chickens. I believe she acted on my advice untill her Husband, by his frolicking gave her employpint [*sic*].

I did not receive a letter from you by the July mail as I expected. Why didnt you tell me about Miss Scollay's wedding or is all your interest gone in that lady? I regret very much that I did not go to see her when I first went East.

Remember me to your family.

Yours &c

R. S. Ewell

1. Internal evidence indicates that Ewell wrote this letter to his brother Benjamin in 1856. The first part of the letter has never been found.
2. Tucson.
3. The Gadsden Treaty was signed on December 30, 1853. In it, Mexico ceded 29,670 square miles of land to the United States for $10 million. The treaty firmly established the boundary between Mexico and the United States and made possible the construction of a southern rail line to California.
4. Unidentified.

58. To Lizzie Ewell

Camp near Tusson[1] N. M

Decr 27. 1856

Miss Lizzie Ewell
Wmsburg, Va

Dear Lizzie;

The mail of Sept. reached me a few days since, bringing your letter of the 8th of Augst (myself & William)[2] & yours from York postmarked Sept 13th marked inside Augst 31st. I dont know whether to write in the witty, satirical, paternal or negligent vein, but rather incline to scolding as I cant find some papers I want & the tent is generally uncomfortable. In your future correspondence you will find that people who "have nothing to say" (meaning ["]*to write*" I suppose) dont *want* to say & it is better to leave that much blank as yr. correspondent may think you had not time, or give any other reason dictated by vanity (which is always ready) whereas, if you write you have nothing to say there is no loophole but the individual is obliged to think you have no interest. Your letter of Augst went to some place in Mo. the "Missouri" being larger than anything else on it. I enclose the proper direction which please show to any of my correspondents you may happen to be with. I am afraid you are getting very lazy. Judging from the beginning & your assertions I expected quite a crowd of letters from you but the result has not borne out my hopes. Happy to hear the wine is safe in your Father's Storeroom & will be still happier if it stays there. If Miss V.[3] chooses to write poetry you ought not to let your feelings of rivalship

Benjamin Ewell served as president of the College of William and Mary and as chief of staff to General Joseph E. Johnston. His daughter, Lizzie, became Dick Ewell's favorite correspondent. (Courtesy Stan Aylor)

carry you away so. There is room for both. Which of yr. Williamsburg ladies wrote such an ++++++++++————+++++[4] as yr. Father would say about my being engaged to Miss S.B.E.[5] to Miss L. Scollay & thereby cause that lady to marry & blast my prospects for ever?

I am destined (Elizabeth Ewell writes me) to live a bachelor, owing to my admiring too ma[n]y at a time. They say however the Mormons are going to convert the world & then I shall begin to marry.[6] As it is I cant think of making but one happy.

Can you tell me what fish a bird always finds at night & what other sometimes finds the bird.[7] These are original & when you guess them & make as good I will do better.

> Direction—(In six lines)
> ⸻ Captain R S. Ewell
> Tusson
> Comp'y "G" 1st Dragoons U.S. Army
> Care of Maj. Nichols
> Santa Fe
> New Mexico

Tusson is the proper spelling.

I intend to enclose a gold dollar under the seal & you can use it as well as one that I will send every month untill there be enough, in buying a set of wine glasses for the Governor.[8] 24 sherry & 12 Champaigne. I expect yet to hear of some one being poisoned.

Now I have a plenty more to *write*[9] but duties of the highest importance that wont admit of delay, imperatively bring this to a close. So much pleasure do I derive from a correspondence with my dear Niece, that nothing but want of time & infrequency of mails prevent longer & more frequent letters on my part.

Allow me to recommend the "model letter writer" to you. It gives letters for all cases & you have only to fill up the blanks.

Yours &
R. S. Ewell

1. Tucson.
2. Lizzie had addressed the letter to both Dick and his brother William Stoddert, who had accompanied him to New Mexico.
3. Possibly a reference to Martha Vest (b. ca. 1840), the daughter of merchant William Vest of Williamsburg, who was about Lizzie's age.
4 Ewell apparently used these symbols to express outrage or profanity.
5. Unidentified.
6. The Mormons were polygamists.
7. The answers are "perch" and "catfish."
8. Ewell's nickname for Lizzie's father, Benjamin Ewell.
9. Ewell underlined the word "write" here to tease Lizzie, whom he had earlier chided for using the word "say" when she meant "write."

59. To Lizzie Ewell

Feb'y 3d 1857

Dear Lizzie;

Pressed as I am for time nothing can prevent the pleasure of writing to tell you that I am well[,] have a great deal to say & much that is interesting to write of, but unfortunately ten Mexicans hired at 50 cts per diem are waiting for work, Dragoons are tending their horses & want orders[,] besides many things of great importance. I will write again with mor[e] time but for ten days I have been up at light or a little after.

I enclose the 3d installment on the wine glasses.[1]

Yrs &c
R. S. Ewell

1. In earlier letters, Ewell had placed under the seal a gold dollar that Lizzie was to use to purchase a set of wine glasses for her father. See RSE to LE, 27 Dec. 1856 (letter 58, this volume).

60. To Elizabeth Ewell Sr.

Gila River N.M.
June 10th 1857

Dear Mother;

If you feel disposed to criticize my writing, you can try what sort of a fist any one else will make of it whom you can persuade to sit cross legged & write on a board held on the lap.

I have been scouting since the 3d of May chiefly among the mountains around the middle of the course of the Gila & on the Gila itself. I managed to find a herd of Indian horses which I appropriated & which made the Indians attempt to stampede mine in the night. They whooped and yelled and fired at a foolish distance until they tired and then went off. My horses were securely tied to trees.[1]

I have not heard from Lizzy since the fall, probably she is busy studying.

Cousin Lizinka used to write regularly but I have not heard from her for some time when I started & as it may be a month before I receive a mail, she may think I have the bad taste to neglect the correspondence. When you write to her please mention that I am on a scout that may possibly last six months & it is not improbable that in that time I may not see a letter.

I hardly expect to eat any vegetables except what are found in the woods, including wild cherries & some sour currants but which serve to keep off the scurvy.

I have not heard from William but believe he is well & much pleased with Fort Union.[2] There are 13 families there & as if that were not enough they are quarrelling & scolding like so many sitting hens. He has given up the idea of going to Tuzon.[3] It is a pity he is not married. I have heard something in reference to a Miss Green, many years his senior; much poorer than Job's turkey and not much smarter. What Solomons you all made of yourselves about that Miss Balch![4] I think the object of neuralgia & other aches is to keep people from meddling with the business of others.

A great part of my scout has been in a country without inhabitants but with the ruins of what must once have been large towns abandoned centuries ago. These same ruins can be traced through many parts of the U.S. particularly Ohio & all show the existence of war. It would seem to be a semi civilized people, migratory & followed by another race at war, as the shoals of herring are followed by the dolphin & shark.

Why did not Mrs Vest[5] send the letter you spoke of and which you said she was going to enclose in yours? I suppose before you receive this you will have been to Prince William & back to Wmsburg & possibly the cold weather will have set in again. I am very tired of chasing a parcel of Indians about at the orders of men who dont know what to do or how to do it if they knew what they wanted.[6] I would prefer the less romantic but hardly less inhuman business of raising potatoes & cabbages. I say hardly less inhuman because going as we now are about starting in a "Solumn" (Solid) Column of 600 men, we will not be apt to see Indians[,] & mules & horses will be the only sufferers.

I am too busy to write a letter. I will take every opportunity of writing back. Remember me to enquiring friends.

Yrs &c

R. S. Ewell

1. In May and June 1857 Ewell took part in a large mounted expedition against Apache tribes that had been raiding settlements along the Rio Grande. These tribes, residing in the mountains overlooking the Gila River, were known collectively as the Gila Apaches. For a discussion of the campaign, see Utley, *Frontiersmen in Blue,* 155–57.
2. After several months of residing with Dick at Los Lunas, New Mexico, William moved to Fort Union.
3. Tucson.
4. Presbyterian minister Thomas B. Balch lived just down the road from Stony Lonesome. He had four daughters who lived to maturity: Ann (b. 1821), Elizabeth (b. 1824), Julia (b. 1837), and Mary (b. 1842).
5. Eliza A. Vest, aged forty-eight, lived with her family in Williamsburg, Virginia. Her husband, William, was the town's leading merchant, owning $12,350 in real estate and $112,000 in personal property.
6. Ewell is probably referring to either the expedition's commander, Colonel Benjamin L. E. Bonneville, or Bonneville's wing commander, Lieutenant Colonel Dixon Miles of the 3rd United States Infantry.

61. To Lizzie Ewell

Santa Fe N.M.
October 31. 57

Dear Lizzy;

The last letter I have had the felicity of seeing of yours was dated the 7. July & as no names are mentioned in it, I am in a state of great doubt for whom it is intended. As it was enclosed to William[,] my own private opinion is that it is an artful dodge to make one letter answer for two persons[,] you thinking as it will do for either him or me that both will claim it. You deal in generalities that will do equally well for him or me. However, as it is the last of the month & I believe the last letter has been received by me (I wont say that I owe you as you cant pretend to strike a balance with one in "high official position["]) I will condescend to pass over the apparent attempt to humbug your two respectable Uncles. Two months ago I was sent to try to get some money for our post but have been kept waiting here partly to attend a Court Martial and partly to await the arrival of money from the States. At present I expect to start back before very long. A week since, in order to relieve myself from the tedium of nothing to do I went down the river on a hunting excursion & was quite successful obtaining something like one hundred birds—including Snipe, ducks, Geese & crane, All of which I have been distributing among the Officers families here. The greatest acquisition I made was of a lot of potatoes, an article in great demand in N.M. and which are more welcome to the ladies here than compliments even would be. The mail closes in an hour or two & I have only time to write a short letter. You must say to Mother[1] that I wrote on the 15th and have not time to write another besides this. I have received no letters except one or two from your Uncle William since August & of course cannot be taken to task for delinquency. My mail has probably gone to my post.

There is nothing new just now except a report that the Indians have run off some 25 or 30 cows that I had near Tuson.

I place a dollar under the seal.

Yours with remembrances to all the family.

R. S. Ewell

P.S.

Criticisms on your last with more time. There is plenty of room.

---

1. Dick's mother was then living with Benjamin and Lizzie in Williamsburg.

Chapter 6

Arizona, 1858–1861

As a result of the Mexican War, the border of the United States for the first time stretched from the Atlantic to the Pacific. Manifest Destiny was no longer simply a national aspiration, it was a reality. Settling the West would be more difficult than conquering it, however. Two thousand miles of prairie, mountain, and desert stretched westward from the Mississippi River to the Pacific. Travel to California took weeks by sea and months by land. Travel by ship was expensive and subjected passengers to the fury of storms in the southern latitudes. Those traveling overland suffered physical hardship and risked illness, starvation, and attack by hostile Indians. Clearly a better way was needed.

The railroad provided a ready solution. Locomotives had been part of American life for thirty years. They were fast, convenient, and relatively inexpensive. Moreover, they could haul large amounts of goods over vast distances at a reasonable cost. A transcontinental line was an important step toward the permanent settlement of the West.

The Rocky Mountains posed the greatest obstacle to that goal. The U.S. government had identified three potential routes across the mountains: a northern route, which ran through Montana and Oregon; a central route, which followed the Platte River to South Pass; and a southern route, which ran through the recently acquired New Mexico Territory. A small portion of the southern line ran through Mexico. In the 1853 Gadsden Treaty, the United States acquired from Mexico 29,670 square miles of land in southern Arizona and New Mexico to accommodate the projected line. To establish U.S. authority in the new land and to protect Mexican settlers there from Apache attacks, the government in 1856 ordered four companies of the 1st Dragoons to establish a military post near Tucson.

Major Isaac Steen commanded the dragoon detachment. Finding Tucson incapable of supporting a large military post, Steen settled his troops at Calabasas Ranch, sixty miles farther south, in the Santa Cruz Valley. Steen's superior, Colonel Benjamin L. E. Bonneville, objected to the site as being too far from Tucson, however, and in 1857 Steen moved his command to Ojos Calientes on the Sonoita

River. He named the post Fort Buchanan in honor of America's new president. From this new post Ewell gave chase to Apache bands that swept down from the mountains to plunder Mexican ranches. Among those with whom he had to deal was a young warrior named Cochise, soon to gain fame as a great Apache leader.

Twice during this period, Ewell's duties took him across the border into Mexico, once in pursuit of deserters and once on a diplomatic mission to Governor Ignacio Pesqueira of Sonora. Pesqueira had recently expelled representatives of an American company that had gone to Sonora to map its public lands. The expulsion violated an agreement between the United States and the Mexican government, and the War Department sent Ewell to the port town of Guaymas to demand that Pesqueira comply with the agreement. Ewell accomplished his mission with the help of Captain William D. Porter, whose armed sloop, St. Mary's, had gone to Guaymas on the same mission.

While posted in Arizona, Ewell continued his quest for financial independence, investing in a local silver mine. If he could salt away $10,000, he planned to leave the army and buy a farm. He never came close to achieving that goal. Although the mine offered an abundance of ore, Ewell's partners mismanaged the enterprise, prompting the unlucky captain to sell his interest at only a marginal profit.

Illness meanwhile was making inroads on the captain's constitution. Fort Buchanan was situated on an unhealthy site, and at certain times of the year fever ravaged the post. Three successive commanders fell ill and had to take extended leaves of absence. Eventually, Ewell also succumbed. In January 1861 he left Arizona and returned to Virginia to recover his health. By the time he was well enough to return to duty, Confederate forces had fired on Fort Sumter. The country was at war.

62. To Lizzie Ewell

Fort Buchanan N.M.[1]
March 8th 1858

Miss Lizzie Ewell

Dear Lizzie;

That letter of mine on the subject of nothing to write must have been a "powerful drawing one."[2] You seem to have no trouble in filling a very respectable letter now & I have quite a feeling of self complacency whenever I receive a letter from you at the effect produced. You would probably give right smart for the pleasure of writing 2000 miles that you have nothing to write about. I hope you have that production of mine as it must be a remarkable specimen.

I have been turning my attention lately to minerals. This country is full of silver mines— Almost every hill, but the most would break the Rothschilds. My room is completely filled with chemical machinery & my table boasts of Several crucibles & books; blow pipe, scales, charcoal, supports & at least 6 different kinds of minerals.[3] Maj. Steen[4] left a piece of mineral with me which he thought was rich but appeared ordinary to me. He begged me for a long time to try it & at last thinking of "fool for luck" did so & found it very rich[—]then reduced some & found it worth at the rate of two dollars the pound of ore. ten cents is considered good from the same amt of ore. You can point out to your Pa. how I reduced the ore when he could not or would not although he had every advantage.

I am very much in want of crucibles. the Hessian[s][5] I brought are broken & some I had made here are useless. The reason this paper is not very nice on the other side is because the ores having been laying on it have left a mark.[6]

I am very much puzzled by some that are brought. one in particular is very black, shining, soft, & twice as heavy as graphite. The men tried to bring it in their handkerchiefs but it escaped through them. Pulverized it floats[,] as it were[,] in the air. Maybe the Governor can tell.

Probably before this reaches you I shall be en route to California whither they say we are bound. A matter of indifference to me.

Does the Algebra still present as many "pontes arinarum"[7] as ever? Why dont you try if Miss Leslie's cookery[8] be not more congenial & present more satisfactory results?

I was up late last night & have been on my feet all day & have written several letters & it is late & I am getting sleepy. A longer letter would be a task instead of pleasure & I must conclude. I would like to know how much wine your Daddy has for me. Tell your Aunt Becca I have recd her letter & will answer it next mail. As for buying Stony Lonesome it would be useless if the rest would not sell, but we will see about it.[9] Remembrances to all.

Yrs &c
R S Ewell

1. The U.S. Army established Fort Buchanan in 1857 to protect Mexican settlers in the Santa Cruz Valley from attack by hostile Apaches. The post stood forty-five miles southeast of Tucson on Sonoita Creek in the shadow of the Santa Rita Mountains, just west of the modern town of Sonoita. The army abandoned it on July 21, 1861. Six years later, it built Fort Crittenden on virtually the same site. For an excellent article on Fort Buchanan and Fort Crittenden, see Serven, "The Military Posts on Sonoita Creek."

2. RSE to LE, 27 Dec. 1856, LC (58).

3. Instruments necessary for testing, or assaying, the quality of silver ore. At West Point, Ewell ranked eighth in his class in chemistry and tenth in mineralogy.

4. Enoch Steen had been a dragoon since 1833 and a major since 1853. At the beginning of the Civil War, he was the lieutenant colonel of the 2nd United States Cavalry. Steen was in command at Fort Buchanan until April 1858, when ill health compelled him to return to the states on an extended leave of absence. He would not go back to the New Mexico Territory. Major Samuel P. Heintzelman, later a general in the Union army, wrote that Steen did "not bear a good reputation—in fact [was] a disgrace to the army," an opinion shared by Ewell. North, *Samuel Peter Heintzelman,* 75.

5. A type of crucible.

6. The back of the page exhibits several smudges.

7. The meaning of this foreign phrase is unknown.

8. A reference to Eliza Leslie's book, *Miss Leslie's Directions for Cookery.* Published in 1851, this was one of the nineteenth-century America's most influential cookbooks.

9. When Ewell's father died in 1826, his will divided Stony Lonesome equally between his six children. Dick had sold his share in the estate to his brother William for $1,200 in May 1850. Rebecca Ewell wished to sell her share of the farm to Dick and suggested that he also buy out Ben, Elizabeth, and William.

63. To Lizzie Ewell

May 16. 1858
Fort Buchanan N.M.

Miss Lizzie Ewell

Dear Lizzie;

I have the happiness to acknowledge your letter of "March" sent with one of Mother's of March 30th thereby cheating the Post Office out of 3 cents.[1]

You write with your face you say covered with starch & of 3 colors.[2] As variety is charming you ought certainly to have made your appearance. Your letter is chiefly taken up with anticipatory descriptions of the farm which I have no doubt will be an excellent place, for sweet potatoes at least, as it is said to be sandy. What a pleasant place it must be in comparison with this, where it is all dust & flies. Maj. Steen who commanded for two years is the greatest liar &

scamp in the world, & a miserable old setting hen & his successor[3] is too much of an invalid to attend[,] as he ought, to his duties.

Your suggestions about the two sisters would be more valuable if I were not of your Aunt Elizabeth's opinion i.e. that marriage is a purgatory upon earth— at least in some cases.[4] You are not likely to have an aunt very soon as far as I am concerned.

What will make up for the loss of the student's society at the new place?[5] They would leave a void hard to fill. I suppose they are making undying love just as they did fifty years ago, and forming engagements to last several days after graduating.

I enclose an advertisement for glass ware which I hope will suit the table of the President.[6] Two dozen can be bot. for a sum that ought to be in reach of almost any one.

Tell "Pop"[7] I am about taking an interest in a silver mine[8] which promises to rival any that can be mentioned. We propose to take out a fortune in silver & another in stocks to be sold when all the silver is extracted. You might create a sensation by proclaiming yourself the niece of a bachelor who owns a part of a silver mine.

The Indians are around us robbing all the time, but without any prospect of rousing the Fabius[9] who commands us. so as Mars is out of fashion we will worship Plutus.[10] I have sold my ranch[11] so the prospect for wealth depends altogether upon the mine. I may enclose a small piece of the ore.

This place is dull beyond anything I ever imagined. Nothing going on. I try to work myself tired in the company garden so as to sleep away some of the time but it wont do. I suppose if I make myself a millionaire from the silver mine "Pop" will say it was because he gave me those chemicals whereas the ore was analyzed by a simple method pointed out in a little pamphlet that cost 6 1/4 cents. I am puzzled to know what I shall do with so much mon[e]y: whether to make the Pacific rail road, buy New York City or what. May be you can give some useful hints. What is the secret you are so anxious to tell me & would concern you so much were it to get out? Have you taken the skin from your tongue with frosty iron or has Miss Anna Hough a luvyier?[12] Much more important secrets might get out here without creating excitement & you may always have the greatest confidence in my discretion—so at least said the President when he gave me my commission.

I wont have time to write to any other member of the family by this mail. Such an effort as this is exhausting. Tell Mother I sent by the last mail an order on Mr Reynolds for some mon[e]y to pay & stop the "Spirit of the Times" &

to pay up the laborers on the Home Journal,[13] And I want to know when it is done. I received two letters from Mrs B. neé Campbell (Cousin Lizinka)[14] last mail, which for want of instructions I answered, directed to Washington.

Remember me to all.

Yrs &–

R. S. Ewell

1. Ewell's mother was then living with Ben and Lizzie in Williamsburg, Virginia.
2. A reference to cosmetics.
3. Brevet Major Edward H. Fitzgerald assumed command of Fort Buchanan when Enoch Steen left Arizona in the spring of 1858 on an extended leave of absence. Fitzgerald suffered from hemorrhaging of the lungs, and after just four months he too left the region. He died of tuberculosis two years later.
4. Lizzie was apparently attempting to play matchmaker for her bachelor uncle— most likely in jest. Ewell's sister Elizabeth became a novice in the Catholic Church and never took a husband. Ewell added above this line: "She says she will take hers in the next world. Has she had an offer lately?"
5. When Ben accepted a professorship at the College of William and Mary, he also agreed to serve as the college's interim president. He took up residence in the President's House on campus but later built his own house outside of town.
6. A reference to Lizzie's father, Benjamin Ewell, who had become president of the College of William and Mary in 1854.
7. Another reference to Lizzie's father.
8. Ewell and five other men purchased Patagonia Mine, near the Mexican border, for a modest sum in 1858. The group proceeded to hire workers, sink shafts, and construct furnaces for smelting the ore. Mismanagement eventually compelled the owners to sell the mine, which in 1860 was purchased by Sylvester Mowry and renamed the Mowry Mine. Under Mowry's administration the mine flourished, producing more than eighty dollars per ton of ore. For additional information on the mine, see Mowry, *Arizona and Sonora,* 27, 61–62, 73–76.
9. Probably a reference to Ewell's commanding officer, Major Edward H. Fitzgerald, although it may refer to the departmental commander instead. Quintus Fabius Maximus was a Roman general who defeated Hannibal in the Second Punic War by avoiding decisive contests with his foe.
10. Mars was the Roman god of war, whereas Plutus was the Greek god of the underworld. As combat (Mars) was out of fashion, Ewell could devote himself to his silver mine (Plutus).

11. Ewell raised sheep on a ranch a few miles outside the post.

12. "Luvyier" is probably Ewell's way of mimicking the way Lizzie or her friend pronounced "lover." Anna Hough has not been identified.

13. *Spirit of the Times* may refer to a Cincinnati newspaper that began publication in 1840. It changed names several times before closing its doors in 1958 as the *Cincinnati Times Star.* New York also had a nineteenth-century newspaper called the *Spirit of the Times,* which was first published in 1831. A weekly sporting journal, that paper eschewed politics and catered to an elite readership. The *Home Journal* may be a reference to the *California Home Journal,* a San Francisco periodical first published in 1858.

14. Lizinka had married a Mississippi planter named James Percy Brown, who died in 1844.

64. To Lizzie Ewell

Fort Buchanan N.M
August 10th 58—

Dear Lizzie;

Your letter of May 9th came by the last mail. You ought to remember as regards, what you are please[d] to call satire that it is alw[a]ys best to know the worst but you know the truth is sometimes the severest criticism and at all events it is better to know the worst. Probably many of your "sweet" correspondents among the young ladies are severe in spite of their pretended admiration.

I am now keeping or about to keep bachelors hall. One of my subalterns, Lt. Moore[1] is about going on rec[rui]t[in]g service & the other is married,[2] so that I will have to live by myself. I would give a good price for a trusty housekeeper so that if your talents for cooking &c justify your undertaking so a responsible a position you can have the refusal. You would have to give security not to marry some young, poverty stricken, conceited Lieutenant who would expect my best cow & probably old Hester[3] to cook and then grumble if he could not borrow chairs, tables, spoons, plates, Towels napkins &c. &c. as well as pestering me with your quarrels. I thought when I commenced this that it was a double sheet, but since the commencement it has turned out only a half, which my dear niece, is a subject of great regret as there is nothing that delights me so much as writing you a letter. But as the Methodists say, it looks like the finger of providence. I am very much occupied just now as I am settling private accts that have accumulated during the last 3 years & which cover several classes of money operations. I wrote a long time since to "Pop" but have not received the pleasure of an an[s]wer. Possibly he holds back on the privileges of age.

Ewell pinned his hopes for financial independence on the Patagonia Mine, "the darkest, gloomiest looking, cavern you can imagine." Mismanagement by his partners forced Ewell to sell his interest in the enterprise at but little profit. (Taken from J. Ross Browne, *Adventures in the Apache Country: A Tour through Arizona and Sonora, with Notes on the Silver Regions of Nevada.* New York: Harper & Brothers, 1869)

The Pa[t]agonia mine (—so they call the one in which I am interested) is fast sinking towards the centre of the earth. It is the darkest, gloomiest looking, cavern you can imagine—about 50 feet deep with prospects looking quite bright. I have been offered $1000, for my interest, having at that time expended about $100, so if we fail, the croakers cant say it was an absurd speculation.

You may rest assured that your Uncle is living very economically not to be obliged to give it up for want of funds. If the college regulations are altered so that the Govr[4] resigns you can tell him that there are five openings here. The Chaplaincy is vacant & no questions asked of the applicant—pay $1200. with house & fuel & provisions at eastern prices. We want a scientific manager for the mine—good wages with a chance for outside speculations. Bill of fare dried (jerked) beef and beans.

If I can clear by the mine $10,000. I shall take up my line of march for the states & settle down. It sometimes almost gives me the chills for fear that it may turn out a failure—more from the wise "I thought so" of friends than the loss of the money.

Yours &–
R. S. Ewell

1. Isaiah N. Moore of Pennsylvania had graduated from West Point in 1851. Before leaving Fort Buchanan on August 15, 1858, he was Ewell's right-hand man. He died on January 16, 1862, while serving as a captain in the 1st United States Cavalry.
2. Possibly Second Lieutenant Alfred B. Chapman.
3. A slave.
4. "The Governor" was another nickname for Lizzie's father, Benjamin Ewell.

65. To Lizzie Ewell

Fort Buchanan N.M
Novr 14. 1858—

Dear Lizzie;

I have received two letters from you since writing but one did not require answering & I have been campaig[n]ing (peacefully) for the last two weeks & therefore have not had time to write. There is nothing stirring out here of particular interest—the Indians scaring one man last week & stealing a beef the week before.

How does your country residence come on & what does the Governor intend to do with the surplus income from the farm?[1] Balt & Ohio rail road stcok [*sic*] is a good speculative investment if he be at a loss.

What was your objection to the joint occupancy of the pew? In the Catholic churches one may see the "princess & beggar" side by side. Though in your case neither character was represented yet the principle holds good. You ought to pay attention to your cooking & housekeeping, for although there is no rail road running to this country as yet; there is a bi-weekly line of mail coaches[2] & there is no telling how soon the other may come off. It is only about 15 days at present from Memphis & on a pinch one might trust that mode. If I find the book I will enclose a picture for you which rather struck my fancy.

I wrote to your Uncle William to have one of those puzzle rings[3] made for you in Santa Fee [*sic*] but it is doubtful if he [will] attend to it. The Silver mine has not been doing much of late owing to the want of hands or rather managers. There are any number of suitable persons in the States who would be glad to receive $50 per month. here we cannot find one at four times that amount. Labor commands out here from $40. to $75 per month & hard to get even at

While at Fort Buchanan, Ewell had frequent dealings with the Pima Indians, whom he described as "compounds of children & foxes." (Library of Congress)

those prices. My interest in the mine would if attended to make me independent but at present the Debtor side of the balance sheet is the greater. If the abominable Indians would only stop stealing, one might give a little attention to the mine but at present the Mexican expression of doubt suits better than any other—that is, pero. quizas. Quien sabe.[4]

On my return from a visit to the Apaches I found a delegation of Pimo Indians[5] who wanted arms & ammunition, provisions & blankets &. &c. I took pains to explain to the chief by himself that I had no authority to give clothing, but made him a present of some Cotton for himself. This morning he came back with the same string of wants, winding up with the information that he had given away the cotton & wanted some more. Not taking any notice, he walked off in high dudgeon looking as though he felt himself very much outraged.

It is the most provoking thing in the world to have business with these people who are compounds of children & foxes. I have some business to attend to, before the mail goes & so must close.

Yrs &—

R S Ewell

1. In addition to the President's House at the College of William and Mary, Ben owned a farm on the outskirts of Williamsburg. The large three-story frame

house, located at 130 King William Drive, is currently the administrative office of Williamsburg Memorial Park.

2. The Butterfield Overland Mail route ran 2,800 miles from St. Louis, Missouri, to San Francisco, California. Although designed principally to carry mail from the states to California, passengers could secure passage on the coach at a price of between $100 and $200. The one-way trip took less than a month. Started in 1857, the stage line operated for just four years before the Civil War caused it to close.

3. Puzzle rings are worn as jewelry on the fingers. They are composed of multiple interlocking rings, the assembly of which takes the form of a puzzle.

4. Below this, Ewell has written a translation: "But perhaps, Dont know."

5. The Pimas were a peaceful tribe that resided in villages along the Gila River. An agricultural people, they grew wheat, melons, pumpkins, and beans, some of which they sold to the Butterfield Overland Mail Company, to miners and traders, and to the U.S. government.

66. To Lizzie Ewell

Fort Buchanan N.M
Novr 28th 1858—

Dear Bettie;

I have been earnestly racking my brains since the receipt of your letter asking for a prescription against, or rather for obesity with which you are threatened. I saw a few days since that it was fashionable and maybe your anxiety was all pretended & nothing more than a modest way of letting it be known how elegant[,] fashionable, & plump you had become. The article stated that young ladies were eschewing pickles &c and eating such things as are know[n] to have the contrary effect. If you really desire to grow thin you will have to use a great deal of forbearance & self-denial in the winter. In the summer if you should happen to have a dislike to any dish—fat meat for instance—a hearty meal in the warmest part of the day will keep you from increasing in weight for at least one week. Swallowing a fly is also good. Probably you would give it up in despair if you were to see desc[r]ibed the rigid course went through, by[1] Byron,[2] who was very much inclined to grow fat. If you dont eat you cannot fat[t]en & after all[,] this & exercise are the only panaceas. I find the ownership of an interest in a rich mine, which the people are too lazy to work has a good effect. Walking with small gravel in your shoes, having a pin sticking in your flesh, making yourself ridiculous at a party & see the people laughing, get into another row in church & have it published, as the description of the last, that I enclosed to Mother—In short anything to keep you fretting are valuable helps.

You made some remarks about a half sheet I wrote on being like another to Mother but that is nothing strange as I purchase by the quire & not by the half sheet and one half sheet in the same quire, out here, is generally like another from the same lot. But my remark was applied to finding two half sheets together. These were not torn apart.

We are very much in want of horses out here for though the Co's are nominally full there are many unfit for service. If the Govr were to go to Washington he could easily get a contract to bring out 40 or 50 & make $60 each. You might come on one. There are two bachelors here now, one an Irishman Doctor U.S.A.[3] red head & hot tempered as possible and the other a Lieut. from Ohio[4] who, on a march we made together, some time since, when he catered, provided, to my dismay, nothing but a big hog which we were to eat fresh. I suppose in honor of his native state. It is needless to say that I did not fatten on that trip. They would not be very good catches.

When you move to the farm you need not be under so many apprehensions of plumpness. At a distance from market, with no students I have an idea the table will not be apt to produce gout. Probably none of you are good providers and when one bolts his food like Papa[5] he cares not a fig whether he is eating fish, flesh, or fowl. Does not know in fact.

I had a treat coming home the other day from a short trip. I lent one of the Soldiers some fishing lines & very soon he made his appearance with a fine string of fish which I duly admired. He walked off with them & just as I had worked myself in a fury at his impudence he came back with one nicely cooked & hot in the frying pan. I have thought better of soldiers ever since. During this short trip I gave my coffee to the men who brought me my allowance & as they pitched my tent made my fire &c. &c. I did all the rest of the cooking for myself, consisting chiefly in broiling venison on the coals (I had two quarters) an occasional partridge. It is needless to say they were remarkably well cooked.

Is there any more wine for sale in Williamsburg of the kind bought for me—Sher[r]y & madeira.[6] I want some more.

You[r]s in haste

RSE—

P.S.

I have not heard from Mr Reynolds since last winter. What is the matter?

RSE

1. Here Ewell had written the word "with" and then later added the word "by."
2. English poet Lord George Gordon Byron (1788–1824).

3. Irishman Bernard J. D. Irwin (1830–1917) was Fort Buchanan's assistant surgeon. A career officer, he retired from the Army in 1894 with the rank of colonel.

4. Second Lieutenant Richard S. C. Lord, a graduate of West Point's Class of 1856, served briefly in both the artillery and the infantry before transferring to the 1st Dragoons in June 1857. As an officer in the 1st United States Cavalry, he was brevetted twice during the Civil War, attaining the rank of brevet lieutenant colonel. He died in 1866.

5. Benjamin Ewell, Lizzie's father.

6. Ewell was fond of wine, particularly Madeira.

67. To Lizzie Ewell

Decr 21. 1858—

Dear Bettie;

Preparing to indite you an epistle I could find nothing but the half sheets I tear from Official letters & it is too late to get more. Your last letter was from York[,] Pa[.,] written I suppose, to show the improvement that had followed "fine" writing lessons. Five more in the same proportion will leave your writing as formal & inexpressive as that of any other young lady. There are very few of those with whom I correspond whose writing does not look exactly as if it had all been formed[1] in the same moulds like so many lambs or pea blossoms or any thing else that is sweet & silly. It seems to me a little irregularity is better than such sameness.

Your letters lately have been filled with anxious expressions on this same subject & I am at a loss to guess at your reasons unless you expect to be addressed[2] in a letter and want to give a model answer. It may be taken as a rule though that such (I mean proposals) are never the result of deliberations & that its not coming at once may be taken as a bad sign. I rather guess when the victim has sufficient presence of mind to deliberate there is but little prospect of committal.

I should think you would like very much to accept Cousin Lizinka's invitation to Nashville. It must be worse than the penitentiary to spend one's life in Williamsburg with no higher prospect than dancing with students who forget as soon as they go.

Wmsburg is a sleepy kind of place & the Vests seem the only people who are at all awake. The only thing to eat there are oysters & it is more trouble to get them than they are worth.

Cousin Lizinka's house is very pleasant and so is she. It is to be hoped you have common sense enough to know how to get along with anybody. Masterly in-activity, never in the way. Never to seem as if you wanted to be amused. When I was there she was expecting a visit from Cousin Ann[3] & I remember the delight with which she spoke of taking her to the Hermitage,[4] Not as it seemed to me on account of the pleasure of the trip but the killing one of the days of the visit. That is she expected to find it difficult to entertain her &c. Now if a person did not force this exertion to please, their visit would be more agreeable. Rich people dont like trouble; almost all like Company in an easy sort of way. I dont know whether you take my meaning or not, but acting on the idea that I have tried imperfectly[5] to explain I flatter myself my visit was not such an awful bore to the hostess as it might have been. I am satisfied you will pass your time pleasantly. All merits are included in rules, all defects in the contrary. You will meet Aunt Rebecca (Mrs Hubbard) whose sole idea is that people should marry rich & whom you need not believe when Cousin L. or her affairs are the subject of discussion. On other points she may be believed for all I know, but she believes in Cousin Lizinka.

I have been entertaining for the last week a French Priest and would rather have the 7 year itch than see him come around again. The fact is my house is a sort of tavern & I am annoyed to death at the impudent & unblushing pushing of these people.

I was looking the other day at a receipt book to mend China &c. and saw directions for "popping the question" how the lady ought to reply &c and intended to copy to send it to you but have not time. I may do so some other time.

I could not find a receipt that would answer to mend my tea pot and am going to have one made of silver. I wish you would send me as soon as possible a drawing of that old one of Mothers: Handle, Spout &c &c

P.S. I hear from Tasker that Cousin Lizinka is in very bad health which I regret very much. they are both going to Europe, Tasker next year. If my affairs here were closed I would try to go with one or the other.[6] Maj. Hubbard is left in charge of the property.

If your Aunt Rebecca[7] conclude[s] to settle [the] farm sale without more stipulations or fuss, you had better lend her your assistance & judgement in managing the affairs. I shall keep five horses there and as soon as things are regulated will improve, regardless of expense.

I don't want to resign unless my income is sufficient to support me without depending on the farm and I hope that will be the case next year. If this be not arranged I will purchase land on the bay of San Francisco [some]where within 20 miles of the city & regular daily steamboat communication. the soil & climate are said to be all that can be wished. Probably that would be a better spot to revive the former glories of the Ewells than the worn out lands of Prince William. It requires more mon[e]y however. You can tell Becca that the potatoes thrown away there as not worth taking away are larger than what they can raise in Prince William. You would likely be able to marry a Captain there but washing costs so much that likely you would still have to do it yourself.

RSE—

1. Ewell initially wrote "moulded" in the text and then wrote "formed" above it, so as not to use the word "mould" twice in the same sentence.
2. The word "addressed" here refers to a proposal of marriage.
3. Probably a reference to Ann Gantt, the daughter of Dick and Lizinka's aunt Nancy Gantt. The reference may be to Ann Ewell (b. ca. 1815), the daughter of Thomas Ewell's younger brother, Alfred Ewell, and his wife, Sarah Strother, but this is unlikely.
4. The home of President Andrew Jackson, just outside of Nashville.
5. Ewell wrote "imperfectly tried" then changed the word order to read "tried imperfectly" by placing the words in parentheses and numbering them "2" and "1" respectively.
6. Lizinka took her children to London and Paris in 1860. The family returned to the United States the following year.
7. A reference to Ewell's sister, Rebecca Ewell, not to be confused with his aunt Rebecca Hubbard mentioned earlier in the letter.

68. To Lizzie Ewell

Fort Buchanan N.M.
May 19th 1859

Dear Bettie;

The only excuse I have for not writing to you before, in answer to your letter written after Mothers death, is the great disinclination I have had to writing except when absolutely necessary on business.[1]

I received ten days since a letter from William Stoddert son of Benj. Stoddert, Mother's oldest brother.[2] I heard but little of Uncle Ben & probably you less, but still I was very glad to receive his son's letter and have answered it as warmly as I could. The letter is well & correctly written and to the point and, as far as that goes, speaks well of him. He has two subjects of inquiry, the 2nd in reference to an estate that he says, he has always heard spoken of, in his

family, left by Grandfather Stoddert.[3] "Not for any great desire of realizing anything therefrom, but the mere satisfaction of knowing." I answered this by telling him that I always heard that Grandfather died insolvent & that had such a
thing existed, Aunt Rebecca would have mentioned it. His other inquiry is in
reference to this country, as he says he has saved something & wants to seek a
new field for investment. I answered this part by advising him to visit the country and inviting him to my house. He writes from Downieville[,] Cal[iforni]a.
He speaks of an elder brother Benjn who is with him. He is 26 yrs old, has a
sister younger. Benj. is 40, both Bachelors & he says he is likely to remain so.

Your concern at the loss of your Grandmother has good reason, for in all
her letters she showed constant interest in your welfare. One advantage about
youth is that these losses do not make a lasting impression compared with the
grief of greater age & it is a law of nature that at your time of life the usual
gayety is soon resumed. As for myself I endeavor to occupy my mind as much
possible in my usual business, as it hardly shows any very sensible course to
neglect one's duty for no good.

We were commencing the work of reducing lead ore to silver very profit-
ably when some cut th[r]oat Americans compounded of murderers & highway
robbers made an uncalled for attack on the Mexicans of this section, killing
some and driving off others, declaring that none should live in the country &c.
&c. and in consequence the Mexicans, who are the laborers, all left the country
and every thing was brought to a stand still. However the better class of citizens
turned out in the business & four of the worst of those concerned are now in
the guard house here, in irons.[4] There is no civil authority in the Territory &
the military have assisted the law & order portion in preserving order. I think
one part of these murderers were induced by the hope of driving off all Mexican
labor & forcing the people to hire Americans at their own price. Americans
here ask $40. per month for common field labor. Two or three of these men
have shed so much blood at different times that they seem to be urged on like
the tiger to murder without cause. There is a large portion of this population
who were driven out of Cal[iforni]a & came here for a refuge.

I have tried to sell my interest in the mine, or in default of this, have offered
to buy out the other owners. As yet I dont know the result.[5]

Please remember me to the family. Do you know when Mary Jane
Stoddert[6] is to be married?

Yours &c
R. S. Ewell

Miss Bettie Ewell

1. Ewell's mother, Elizabeth Stoddert Ewell, died on January 18, 1859, in Williamsburg, Virginia. She is buried in an unmarked grave in the College Cemetery on the grounds of the College of William and Mary. General Ewell's will set aside funds to erect a marker over his mother's grave, but the provision apparently was never carried out.

2. Benjamin Stoddert Jr. was born in 1782 and died in 1834.

3. Benjamin Stoddert Sr. (1751–1813) of Maryland served as secretary to the Board of War during the American Revolution. A successful merchant, he was appointed the United States' first secretary of the navy by President John Adams. Among Stoddert's nine children was a daughter, Elizabeth, who became the mother of General Ewell.

4. For more on these murderers, see Isaac V. Reeve to John Wilkins, 20 May 1859, M1120, R10, F404–07, NA. Reeve wrote that five men were apprehended.

5. After a promising start, the Patagonia Mine fell on hard times. The mine was originally purchased by Ewell and five other individuals: Col. James W. Douglass, Richard M. Doss, and Lieutenants Richard S. C. Lord, Isaiah N. Moore, and Horace Randal. In 1858–59 Lord and Doss sold their interest in the mine to Elias Brevoort, giving Brevoort a controlling interest in the mine. Brevoort's mismanagement and abrasive personality offended the remaining four owners, who ultimately sold their interest in the mine to Brevoort, thus making him the mine's sole owner. Brevoort in turn sold the mine to Henry T. Titus for $25,000, but Titus subsequently was unable to make the required payments. In 1860 Lieutenant Sylvanus Mowry purchased the mine from Titus and the others for $25,000 dollars. Under Mowry's management, the enterprise (now called Mowry Mine) flourished, producing rich profits for its owner. For additional evidence of Ewell's disgust with Brevoort's management of the mine, see North, *Heintzelman,* 134.

6. Mary Jane Stoddert (b. ca. 1835) was Ewell's first cousin and the daughter of William Stoddert of Jackson, Tennessee. She married lawyer William Caruthers.

69. To Lizzie Ewell

August 1st 1859

Dear Bettie;

I have been intending to write to you for some time, but without doing any thing. I have been busy & considerably worried.

I have been expecting a man from the east during the last month in order to make some arrangements here about business, After which I shall be more independent. The prevalent feeling here seems to be dread of the chills & fevers which were very bad last summer & seem to be promising worse now. We have had one regular case of cholera, fatal[,] & several touches of it in a less degree. These were intemperate persons.[1] This is the nutting season of this country. the Acorns are just getting ripe & Mexicans, Indians & Americans (owing to bad example) are gathering acorns & cracking them like so many pigs. The oaks here are green all the winter, rather a handsome tree and at this time are full of acorns, which are about as large as a hazlenut and not quite so bitter as ours. They would not be noticed in a decent country, but here where all fruits are so scarce & so much in demand they bear a high price. These Acorns a short distance from here in Sonora are said to be worth four doll[ar]s the bushel. It would be the best place for some of the families in the states blessed with an overplus of children, that I ever saw. The first rain that falls on these after they fall, ruins them for eating.

It has been raining here for the last month with remarkable persistence untill the last day or two.

I promised you a ring some time ago of a purely Mexican type but though I wrote to William to attend to it, he failed to do so. There is a man at work here now & I will try to have it made.[2] I write this while preparing to trail up some Indians who killed a white man a day or two since.[3] As I may be off a week or two I scratch a few lines that you may not think you are neglected. The fact is that I have been postponing a letter from day to day for some weeks.

Yours
R. S. Ewell

P.S.

I have received two letters from you since New Years.

RSE

1. In an extensive report written in February 1859, Fort Buchanan's assistant surgeon, Dr. Bernard Irwin described the diseases that plagued the post: "Since the occupation of the place, the troops have suffered continually from malarial disease, which has attacked every person at the post during the last year. . . . In the spring, catarrhal affections prevail extensively. During the autumnal months diarrhoea and dysentery of a very aggravated type are of frequent occurrence. . . . Throughout the whole year intermittent fever of a very severe form prevails extensively, especially during the autumn and winter months." Quoted in Serven, "The Military Posts on Sonoita Creek," 33.
2. For this earlier reference to the puzzle ring, see RSE to LE, 14 Nov. 1858, LC (letter 65, this volume).

3. On July 31, 1859, a band of Tonto or Pinal Apaches attacked the Patagonia Mine. One white man and one Indian were killed. Ewell set out to intercept the murderers. For a full explanation of this episode, see Isaac V. D. Reeve to John Wilkins, 3 Aug. 1859, M1120, R10, F441–460, NA.

70. To Lizzie Ewell

Fort Buchanan N.M.[1]
Aug. 16, 1859.

Miss Elizabeth Ewell

Dear Bettie,

I have mislaid somehow your last letter (I placed it away to answer) and can not take time, in the number and amount of rubbish about the house, to look it up. I mean to say only that it is stuck away in the rubbish as it was a very creditable production and I took unusual pains with it. I remember you asked me about the silver mine and I will let you know the present status of that property. A man disagreeable to me in every respect, managed to become interested to such an extent in the mine as to influence the management.[2] I wrote to an officer in the States interested with me, that I did not want to be concerned and gave him authority to sell.[3] I explained at length and repeatedly that I would sell for $4000 and would have no business relations with the man here. They were offered $25,000 in cash for the mine which would have given me considerably over what I asked, but they refused this offer and now I am trying in vain to sell for a much less rate the interest I hold. What makes it worse this very officer has been unable to pay his proportion of the expenses of the mine which I have had to advance. He has asked me to sell his interest or any part of it to pay his assessment, but others here are like myself, they wont enter into business relations with Mr. Brevoort. Strange to say this officer is a man of talent and sense as well as a business man. He has the foible so common to our family, that is, of placing unbounded confidence in some person to be fooled and then with equal stupidity fasten to another. The above-mentioned objectionable person is or was Lt. Moore's (I. N.) favorite. Lt. Moore is from P[ennsylvani]a. Now we are waiting with great anxiety to know what to do next. Some trials I have made at the mine demonstrate it to be one of the most valuable in the country. There would have been no trouble had I been able to place some one there in whom I had confidence. It is astonishing among the number of beggarly acquaintances and relations one possesses how impossible it is to get hold of one to do any thing. I wrote your Uncle William to come and he would have made a fortune, but his health would not permit his travelling. He sent, some time ago an application to be made Chaplain here, but at the same time wrote me a long letter explaining how his health would suffer and that he would lose a large sum, etc., and so of course I put the whole in the fire. I have not heard from him for some time though I have written several letters. When he does write he postpones it to the last moment and never answers ones letters though on business. Like Elizabeth he guesses at your meaning and when one wants a fish he gives a scorpion. I have paid you the compliment to write about business. if I find you have copied to any one so that some one will write an answer to my letter to you I shall be very cautious in any thing I write in future besides giving you credit for much less sense than at present. I regretted very much to learn that Mrs. Caruthers, née Stoddert, had been to Old Point[4] without going to Williamsburg. They treated your Uncle Tom in time of need with more kindness and forbearance than would have been shown, I fear by any of us to any one in the world particularly as he was a little dissipated[,] and such a marked slight would seem to indicate some feeling. No Mother or Sister could have been more kind and forbearing than they were towards Tom. The house seemed at his disposal even after smashing[,] in a frolic, their carriage and this is a sore trial to ladies.[5] I have been living so far in fear and trembling on account of the intermittent fever. So far I have escaped although nearly half of the command is on the sick report. I have come to the conclusion that one half of the sickness is caused by over-stuffing and though I am fond of good eating have reduced my fare considerably. My usual breakfast during the excessive heat is either lettuce, or cucumbers, or cabbages (cold slaw) with the same dressing, that is, a table spoon of vinegar with pepper and salt at discretion poured in your plate and then two or three table spoons of the best oil added, the whole beaten up a little together with a spoon or fork the lettuce, etc., added. This dressing is easily made and is very wholesome. This salad with a cup of coffee and a biscuit forms my breakfast—soup is added for dinner. Spite of the apparent and generally considered indigestibility of cucumbers or raw cabbages I am never troubled, although I can not eat boiled cabbages and was made sick the other day by toast and coffee. You may be sure you eat too much particularly if your food comes up. Being hungry is no sign as the stomach is a muscle which is stronger from exercise and demands its habitual allowance of[6] exercise although the rest of the system be well enough with less. The stomach is not provided with brains to know what is sufficient for the health of the other parts.[7]

Please remember me to the family. It is necessary to remark that here we only eat in the summer, early York cabbages and these are headed and perfectly white.

Yours,

R. S. Ewell—

P.S. What were the distressing circumstances you refer to connected with the death of Cousin Sallie Gantt?[8]

1. This letter was copied from a typescript found at the Library of Congress. The original has not been found.
2. The "disagreeable" man was Elias Brevoort. For details about the Patagonia Mine and Ewell's conflict with Brevoort, see note 5 to letter 68, this volume.
3. The unnamed officer was probably Second Lieutenant Horace Randal, who was then on a four-month leave of absence from Fort Buchanan.
4. Old Point Comfort lies at the mouth of the James River, twenty miles southeast of Williamsburg, Virginia. Fort Monroe was built on the site between 1819 and 1834.
5. In 1837 Ewell's mother sent her son Tom to Jackson, Tennessee, where he studied law with Mary Jane's father, William Stoddert.
6. This word appeared as "or" in the original typescript. As this was obviously an error, it has been changed.
7. Ewell complained of dyspepsia (digestive problems) throughout his life. As a result, he often ate bland foods.
8. A daughter of Ewell's aunt Nancy Stoddert Gantt.

71. To Lizzie Ewell

Fort Buchanan N.M[1]

Dear Lizzie;

Yours of July 14. came duly to hand. I am glad to learn from you that you have profited or rather remembered my council about the students, Though there ought to be no necessity with so many warnings as are scattered along the path of life in Wmbg. I fear something besides amiability dictated the remark about a young lady aged 22 with an admirer younger than herself. May be when 22 you will be glad of one of any age. I have been studying Lavater[2] who says the indulgence of feelings on thought produces their impress on the countenance. So if you want to be good looking which, in the highest sense, is the expression of goodness, you must not only be amiable before folks but in private & in the innermost recesses of the mind. I am not positive however that good looks are the strongest motives of action with a young lady. There is a heap of good sense in a copy of Chesterfield[3] I gave the governor. You would not lose time to read it, and it is a remarkable instance of patience, long-suffering & forgiveness in one not a professed Christian. You misunderstood me on the subject of filling a sheet. I said nothing about that, merely the repetition of "nothing to write about" was criticized. Stop in the first six lines if you choose—your reader may think it was for want of time and commend your industry. Dont suppose I want to insinuate that your letters are too long. They are, if you labor at them. Your hand, that you complain of, is remarkably like that illustrious Saint your Aunt Elizabeth & is an excellent one for a foundation. A strong glass of brandy toddy might impart, temporarily, more flexibility to it. As the Spaniards say "No esto Malo".[4] We are about 100 miles from a Mex'n town (Madelina).[5] Several of our Officers not myself have been entertained very well at the house of a Mr Padres.[6] I see many notices in the papers of young ladies running off with foreigners. A political refugee from Sonora was here for some time—Dark eyes & hair, splendid moustache and very distinguished looking—talks English. He bored every one to such a degree that it was signified that his room was better than his comp'y & he left. "Doctor," says he, "where can I get a tooth brush? that of Lt. Chapman's[7] is so large." He had been using the nail brush & yet in bearing & manners &c untill you found him out he was equal to the heroes of romances & would have created a furor in Wash. N.Y. or Boston. To return to Padres. After being invited by the officers he paid us a visit with four girls[,] nieces & stepdaughters, partly to see the fort & partly to get medical attendance for one who was sick. I heard of them while out on a march & staid longer, not to be bored, but found them at the house of a Lieut. on my return. My house was stripped of table furniture &c for them & old Hester reported in high dudgeon that they had had her on her feet over there from morning to night & she was sick & had left &c. Finally owing to sickness of servants I had to bring them here to eat. I was never so annoyed in my life. All their manners different from ours & without a particle of refinement or education. They take every thing on the table not having sense to see, even after several days, that we take only what we want. They eat in the most vulgar way, the mouth open & talk with it full to the great detriment of a delicate stomach. In short it was proved to my satisfaction that these specimens of elegant foreigners are very vulgar. But they bow & scrape & say their house is yours & use a set [of] parrot phrases that take wonderfully with the verdant.

If you want to go to Europe you ought to study French, Italian, German & Spanish. I read French at leisure moments with great success.[8] What remarks did I make about the "loves of the students" that you ask if it was meant for you? Dont trouble yourself about the copy of that "beautiful poem of James Barron

Hope."[9] I have not read all of Shakespear[e] yet. There will be time enough. I like your idea of going to school but would not put it off for two years were I you. I will pay expenses and the sooner the better. Go this fall & I will pay & give you some pin money besides, but if it is put off it will be too late. If the mine makes me rich I cant delay my visit[10] untill "session after next when I study a year under Papa & then go to Mr Lefebre[11] for a year". I shall want whoever goes with me to be accomplished[,] elegant[,] easy in manner & with good teeth and a knowledge of the languages. Take care in your cooking that you dont make the hands too large. Who knows with so many accomplishments but you may captivate a beggarly French or Italian Count. If the mine fail the accomplishments may be shown off to advantage at a post where the ladies spend their leisure playing cards and quarrelling.

Yours &c
R S. Ewell

"Pa" owes me half a dozen letters.

1. A postmark on the envelope identifies this letter as being sent in September 1859.
2. Johann Kaspar Lavater (1741–1801), a German theologian.
3. Philip Dormer Stanhope (1694–1773), the fourth Earl of Chesterfield, was a British statesman whose published letters to his son received wide circulation.
4. Translation: "It couldn't hurt."
5. The town of Magdalena is in Sonora. It lies approximately 65 miles south of the Arizona border and 130 miles south of Tucson.
6. Unidentified.
7. First Lieutenant Alfred B. Chapman of Alabama was an 1854 graduate of West Point. During the Civil War, he served the Confederacy as a captain of artillery.
8. Ewell had studied French during his first two years at West Point.
9. James Barron Hope (1829–1887), the grandson of Commodore James Barron, was among the South's most illustrious poets. Hope served as the commonwealth's attorney in Virginia in 1856. The following year he published his first volume, *Leoni di Monota and Other Poems,* which won him instant acclaim. During the Civil War, Hope was an assistant quartermaster with the rank of captain. After the war, he resumed his literary career and in 1881 was selected by Congress to be the official poet of the Yorktown Centennial.
10. Ewell planned to retire from the army and travel to Europe if his silver mine prospered.
11. Hubert P. Lefebre (b. ca. 1820) was a private tutor living in Richmond, Virginia.

72. To Rebecca Ewell

Sept. 27th 1859

Miss R. L. Ewell

Dear Becca—

I cannot lay my hands just now on your last letter, recd about ten days since.[1] I wrote a few lines then in answer & said I would write again soon, but my house has been full of visitors ever since & I have had no time. You dont say where I am to direct. I saw the death of Mr Moxl[e]y[2] some time ago in the papers but it was never mentioned in any of your letters untill your last. I hope Lizzy was able to pass her time with some pleasure at Stony Lonesome. There was a Mexican silver smith here at work and I tried to have one of those puzzle rings made for her according to promise but the man was not skillful and failed to make a good one. Such as it is I will enclose it to her in my next letter.

You mention the mine in your last letter. It was so miserably, if not fraudulently managed, that I sold for much less than its value. I was reduced to losing all I was worth by the way in which it was carried on or to buy or sell. Buying, would have left me without capital to carry it on & so I sold for a sum that would clear me for my expenditures, but much less than what it was worth. $25000 in cash were offered for it last summer in the States & owing to the bad judgment of those in whose hands it was placed for sale, the offer was declined. As a specimen of the manner in which it was conducted, it is in a dense forest and with every thing ready to work, furnaces in order and ore ready to be smelted, hands waiting a[t] high wages. they would be sometimes a fortnight waiting for coal to smelt with. Sheer laziness or rascality. I was anxious for William to come & take charge of it, in which case I should have secured the controlling interest at any sacrifice & if after a few months trial, it continued as it had begun, I should have resigned & it could have been easily sold for $100.000. It is immensely valuable both for amount of ore, richness in lead & silver & locality.

I should have tried it myself with a few thousand doll[ar]s of means more than I possessed. William's health however did not permit his travelling without suffering as he wrote to me and I was unable to manage it myself and so urged the others to sell with the result mentioned above.[3] I had been in hopes that William Stoddert[4] (our cousin) might come, but he had engaged in a quartz gold vein & could not leave.

I have had no ague this summer, a fact I attribute in great measure to having been around the furnace a great deal in June & occasionally getting a puff of the vapor which is loaded with arsenic & lead. There is a good deal of fever (intermittent) here but not as severe in its attacks as it was last year.

An industrious, hard working, sober & faithful Irishman will be discharged from my Company this Winter. He would be invaluable to any one wanting such on a farm. If you choose I will send him to your farm when his time is up. An inducement to him would be a chance of buying for himself after a while or having an interest in the produce. He has starved himself in every possible way during ten years & has amassed some $2500 or $3000. which he will stick to. Of course he is a perfect miser, but honest. It is not very certain that he would go either, as he may have a fancy for New York. I keep him at work in my Co. garden where he does remarkably well, but wont re-enlist. During the winter he stays about the house and looks after things in general.[5]

I dont know whether this is properly directed. I am at a loss as regards William's movements, not having heard from him since early in the Spring.

Yrs &–
R S. Ewell

1. Ewell adds here "dated Aug. 24."
2. Numerous members of the Moxley family lived in Prince William County. In his 1917 book, *Recollections of a Confederate Staff Officer* (p. 56), General Moxley Sorrel mentioned that he was a distant cousin of Ewell's.
3. The nature of William's illness is not known. Four years later he resigned as chaplain in the 58th Virginia Infantry because of bronchitis.
4. William Stoddert (not to be confused with Ewell's brother of the same name) was the son of Ewell's mother's eldest brother, Benjamin Stoddert. He lived in California, where gold had been discovered ten years earlier.
5. Ewell apparently hired the man to keep house for him.

73. To Lizzie Ewell

Octr 26th 1859—

Miss Betty Ewell

Dear Betty;

I believe you owe me a letter, or two or three of them, but as it is sometime since I wrote I have concluded to inform you that there is nothing stirring. I am just recovering from the effects of a very hard ride I took a few days since. Every now & then the soldiers seem to be taken with a fit for deserting and last Friday week[1] a Corporal & private of Dragoons took it into their heads to leave, with two of my best horses. I returned from a short absence, the day after and started with one man in pursuit, the deserters being about 36 hours in advance. I rode, without stopping, that night & next day, arriving within 15 miles of them about sun set. Sunday night, about 4 in the morning I started back with the Corporal, the post being 128 miles off & riding all Monday & Monday Night reached it at 8 in the morning, making in about 60 hrs 250 miles, the longest stop being from sunset untill 4 oclock Sunday night. The horses were changed of course on the road. After overtaking the deserters the reasons for the speedy return were, untill leaving the Mexican Side of the line, where I overtook them, the danger of interference by Mexican authorities & also from robbers. After that, as there was no one to watch the Prisoner while I slept, I thought it best to keep on to the post. The Corporal & private had employed some Mexicans to guide them & the guides, when the whole party were walking, at a concerted signal, one knocked the Private down & the other jerked the Corporal's pistol from his belt & fired at his head, the ball passing through his hat. The Corpl rode back at speed for help & a party of Mexicans returned to the place with him. They found the other deserter hung by his handkerchiefs to a tree supposed to have committed suicide. This was the reason that I only brough[t] back the corporal. We thought the other committed suicide because a Mexican would not have thrown away his handkerchief but would have stabbed or shot him. They murder, each the other (Americans & Mexicans) on this and the other side of the line[2] without the slightest remorse and as if they wanted to see which was the most atrocious.[3]

Since my return I heard they[4] had collected a party to follow me but when they were ready to start, I was then across the line. The most of the people there of any standing, are very friendly disposed towards me and though they might go through forms would be very far from showing ill will.

After a journey of 12 months my 2d Lt. and his wife[5] arrived a fortnight since, without a servant & she perfectly helpless, having almost lost her sight.

It is very fortunate for them that I have a good servant woman[6] & a comfortable house.

The lady is of course very miserable & wishes herself back in Connecticut. I think it must require a great deal of affection to make a man willing to degrade a lady, almost to a cook or washerwoman. As for any love standing such trials, it is absurd to think of it. The woman can justly complain of the selfishness & neglect of the man, while her natural fretting & complaining, under the circumstances, will disgust him, notwithstanding her sufferings may have been great. As you[7]

There was a Mexican silver smith employed here & I asked him to make me a puzzle ring. The one I enclose is the best he could accomplish. It is a very poor one but I have had no opportunity to get one from Santa Fee [sic] though I wrote, but without success.

Remember me to the family.

Yours &–

R. S. Ewell

1. October 14, 1859.
2. "Line"—i.e., border.
3. The *Tucson Weekly Arizonian* published the following account of this episode in its October 27, 1859, edition:

> On the 14th inst, Corporal Gorman, and Private Caulfield, of G's Company, 1st Dragoons, deserted from Fort Buchanan, while out in charge of the Fort herd; taking with them three horses, arms and accoutrements, and fled into the State of Sonora; where they met with a reception very different from that which they expected. Some thirty-six hours after their flight they were pursued by the indefatigable Arizonian "VICDOCQ," James Graydon of Casa Blanco, and overtaken after a hard chase, at Barajito, Sonora. It appears that these misguided men, employed some Mexicans to guide them down towards Guaymas, who, in a lonely part of the highway, fell upon and robbed them. One of the robbers snatched Gorman's pistol and discharged its contents at his head, the ball passing through his hat, which sent him to the "right about in double quick time," leaving his companion, who was less fortunate, in the hands of the highwaymen. When Caulfield was again discovered, he was found hanging to a mesquoite [*sic*] tree, suspended by means of his own pocket-kerchief, and it is supposed, HE may have been driven, by his forlorn and desperate condition, to self-destruction, as the thieves had plundered him of his horse and everything about him. Gorman and his horse were recovered and brought back to the Fort by his pursurers [*sic*], after a hard ride of near THREE hundred miles, performed in SIXTY hours. This is another sad illustration of the kind of sympathy, which Americans WILL receive in Mexico, as long as barbarous retaliation, is the "order of the day," on both sides of the Boundary Line. Much praise is due to Capt. Ewell, for the unceasing energy and persevering manner in which these men were pursued.

4. The people living in Sonora, south of the Mexican border.
5. Second Lieutenant Horace Randal returned to the post on October 11, 1859, having been absent from the company for nearly two years.

6. Ewell's elderly slave, Hester.

7. Ewell left this sentence incomplete.

74. To Rebecca Ewell

Fort Buchanan N.M
Jan'y 10th 1860

Miss R. L. Ewell

Dear Becca;

Yours of Decr 7. 59 came to hand a few days since and I take the first lei-sure moment to reply. You offer, as I understand, to sell me the land "South of the Brentsville road for so much" money or interest ($3000. and or $180. per annum) & certain rights kept back by you & William. This differs somewhat, chiefly in being more advantageous to me, from your former offer & supports my theory that each one is different from the former. William can get ten per cent for his money & therefore I should prefer paying the $3000 down, & the same to you, as I dont want to pledge or bind anything left by Mother. As I wrote, it is insuperable that legal titles should be made, as I dont want to pay twice for the same thing and a relinquishment on [the] part of Ben or Elizabeth without the legal forms would not be considered by me as I have had enough of wrangling out of the family without running the risk of the same thing in it. Untill then I shall take no steps on the subject.[1]

Since early in November I have been away from here almost the whole time on one or other sort of duty and have had very little time for correspondence during the short interval of being here. One portion of my absence was taken up in a visit to Sonora where I went to call on the Governor by direction of the Sect'y of War and had to go as far as Guaymas.[2] Since then I have been on Indian campaign suffering from cold and fatigue and heartily anxious to be somewhere else.[3]

During the last few months I have had to prepare for some heavy payments of mon[e]y left in my hands by soldiers and whose term of service is about expiring. Yesterday I paid $800 & have to meet between one & two thousand more before the end of the winter, but I have been preparing for some time and will be able to fix it all without trouble. I mention this because I would other-wise wish to make you a remittance which could not be done just now without more inconvenience than I like. You can however make any improvements you see proper on credit as well as purchase the "12 or 15 acres of woodland" that you say ought to be joined to the farm. I drew some mon[e]y from Mr Reynolds to pay some debts incurred in my mining operations. A portion has been returned to me and the balance is due within two months. I have quite a drove of cattle here that I have bought reasonably & which I think will yield me a respectable profit, before the end of the year. You see that I am full of the spirit of speculation and if the Indians did not come down occasionally I would be well off in herds at least.

The Irishman I thought of sending to Va.[4] has been for ten years about me and puts up with anything, sleeps anywhere and works without knowing what fatigue is, provided he can make money. You seem to think that he has pretentions to style or luxuries. I shall try to keep him about me for a time at least. I received notice by the last mail that a sale had been effected of a mine out here, in which I am interested in so far that the sale will prevent any loss.

Yours in hast[e]—

R. S. Ewell

P.S. Not knowing your whereabouts I have sent one or two letters, I think, to you directed to Williamsburg.

RSE—

1. This paragraph deals with the sale of land at Stony Lonesome, bequeathed by Elizabeth Ewell Sr. to her children.
2. On October 10, 1859, the War Department directed Ewell to call on Ignacio Pesqueira, the governor of Sonora, to protest the expulsion of Captain Charles P. Stone from that Mexican state. Stone and his party had gone to Sonora in March 1858 to survey and map the public lands there in accordance with a treaty made between the U.S. government and Mexico, but Pesqueira had expelled them. The governor's high-handed actions increased tensions between Mexico and the United States and prompted some members of Congress to recommend Sonora's annexation. Ewell met with Pesqueira at the port town of Guaymas in November 1859 in the company of Captain William D. Porter of the United States Navy. He returned to Fort Buchanan at the end of the month.
3. Two weeks after returning from Sonora, Ewell took part in a mounted expedition against the Pinal Apaches. On December 14, 1859, the United States troops attacked a Pinal Apache village, killing eight men and taking twenty-three prisoners. Ewell was the only soldier injured in the attack, suffering a slight wound to the hand. The dragoons returned to Fort Buchanan on January 3, 1860, having traveled 350 miles in twenty-one days.

4. For additional information about this unnamed Irish soldier, see RSE to RLE, 27 Sept. 1859, LC (letter 72, this volume).

75. To Lizzie Ewell

Fort Buchanan
N.M. May 2d 1860

Miss Eliz. Ewell Junior

Dear Bettie;

The last mail brought your note, enclosed with one of Becca's in which you take me to task for not writing oftener. Since November I have written several times to you probably fully as often as I have received letters. During this time I have been on several detached duties three of which required an absence of over 20 days each, besides constant minor duties of ten to 15 days at a time.[1] Adding to these the time required for preparation & the many things to be attended to at once on my return you will eas[il]y see without much calculation [that my position] has kept me pretty much occupied during that time. In March I was absent for three weeks the Indians having taken off two captives, An American woman & a girl of nine or ten. The woman was left for dead & managed to crawl back to her people; the child was taken to their country & finally exchanged again for some Indian prisoners that were here.[2]

The people made a great fuss about the child and not knowing how to thank Providence for the safe recovery, vented their gratitude in making a fuss over me. I was marched into the convention,[3] had a county called after me,[4] and a public hall, all of which under a different description, would appear very ridiculous. The fact is, they had not time to think over the matter being taken as it were, by surprize.

We are in the midst of all sorts of trouble here now, the locality of the post being changed and all the annoyances of moving coming at the worst time.[5]

We are to have a large post and grand military etiquette. I suppose coats will have to be buttoned and minutia of equal importance as if the safety of the world depended upon the amount of useless annoyance they can give.

My military duties have been of a more active nature and I have great horror of those details. We have but one lady at the post at present but when the new troops arrive probably there will be a greater surplus.[6] If your possible fate in the way of single-blessedness does not show some brighter spots, you will only have to come out here. I take your own statement as to your prospects, and suppose you are like all other young ladies & consider such a state of things as unfortunate. At a post of six companies there are always a number of young Lieutenants who are to be had for trying. Their wives often have to take a large share in the cooking and washing, so that the establishment goes on comfortably. More so now as government furnishes bad whiskey at eastern prices, making frolics quite reasonable. To write this letter I have been part of the time talking to visitors & to soldiers partly while waiting for breakfast and there has been an interval of two days detached service, so excuse the effort if it should tire you.

Remember me to the family.

Yours &-

R. S. Ewell

May 5th 1860—

1. Ewell ran together the words "a" and "time."
2. Pinal Apaches seized Larcena Pennington Page and eleven-year-old Mercedes Sias Quiroz from a lumber camp in the Santa Rita Mountains in March 1860. Page managed to escape. To secure Quiroz's safe return, Ewell had to release two dozen Pinal Apache women and children then being held as hostages at Fort Buchanan. The exchange took place at Aravaipa Canyon, northeast of Tucson.
3. Arizona's constitutional convention was in session at that time.
4. Ewell County encompassed land now in Pima and Santa Cruz counties. Its name was changed in 1864 after Ewell threw his allegiance to the Confederacy.
5. As a result of repeated Indian depredations, the U.S. Army decided to create a large six-company post at the junction of the San Pedro and Aravaipa rivers. By locating the new post in the heart of Apache territory, the army hoped to intimidate the hostile tribes and to protect the Butterfield Overland Mail Line. Ewell christened the new post Fort Aravaipa, but his superiors changed the name to Fort Breckinridge in honor of Vice President John C. Breckinridge.
6. The August 1860 census showed 107 white males and 12 white females at Fort Buchanan.

76. To Lizzie Ewell

Fort Buchanan
N.M. July 27. 1860

Miss Bettie Ewell

Dear Bettie;

Yours of the 10th of June arrived day before yesterday. What a place Wmsburg must be. it takes as long for a letter to come from there here as to go from here to Washington & back—less two days. I would not insinuate anything for the world against your veracity but when you say that you have sent me letters 3 times[1] in the last 11 months, you err greatly. None of your letters have missed coming as can be seen from the text and they have not come that often.

You can tell if this error were entirely unintentional on your part by the way in which you take the correction of your statement. If you get angry you may be pretty sure that your conscience is hurt.

In driving out the other day I met a man taking some goods to a mine they have just opened on the San Pedro.[2] Next morning about sunrise as I was dressing he rode up to my window & I saw something bad had happened.

He said he had arrived at the mine about midnight and no one answering struck a light and saw his cousin stretched lifeless with his head split open. They did not wait to see more but returned & I sent out a party, who have just returned with the news that the Mexican employees had risen[,] murdered the Americans & robbed the place and ran off to Sonora. The Americans were Messrs. Bronkow, Moss of St. Louis & James Williams of d[itt]o.[3] Such is life out here. This is much worse than would have been done by Indians, who dont betray confidence in this manner.

I see nothing particular about either your stamped paper or hand writing. may be the latter is a little better. In answer to queries.

You say a young gentleman went 1400 miles to see you. may be he had some other business. Did he think the sight paid for the journey? I am glad to hear Miss Page Saunders has grown up so pretty. You say she & Miss Douglass are the belles.[4] I dont think much of the position seeing the beaux are young boys that would be much better employed studying their grammar & geography than running about to get something extra to eat and keeping young ladies that ought to know better from attending to their duties at home. I admire your distaste for housekeeping. If that chap should be disinclined for another 1400 miles trip have you another string or do you propose qualifying for a professorship? I might give good wages at Stony lon[e]some but it must be for great skill in directing the culinary dept. as I am partial to good eating. If your Aunt Rebecca be there please say to her that I have written to her directed to Bristoe's,[5] offering $4000. cash, or $300 per annum, which is all I[']ll give. The letter is in detail and next week I'll send a copy to her directed to Williamsburg.[6]

My going east depends upon fiscal arrangements. I cant go this year anyhow. Remember me to the family and excuse haste.

Yours &–

R. S. Ewell

When I write again I will try to do better. RSE—

1. Ewell repeated the words "3 times."
2. The Brunckow Mine was located in the San Pedro Valley, approximately ten miles south of Fairbank, Arizona.
3. Prussian mining engineer Frederick Brunckow (ca. 1820–1860) established a silver mine near the later town of Tombstone, Arizona, in 1857. He hired W. M. Williams to superintend the mine, James Williams to be its machinist, and John C. Moss to assay the ore. Mexican mine workers murdered Brunckow, Moss, and James Williams in 1860. The murderers were never brought to justice.
4. The Douglass (or Douglas) family lived in Prince William County. On Reid Lane, just west of the Kettle Run Bridge, is a wooded knoll on which stands a tombstone to Benjamin Douglas (1743–1827). On the reverse side of this headstone is an inscription for Sophia Douglas Euell [*sic*]. Page Saunders has not been identified.
5. Bristoe Station, a stop on the Orange and Alexandria Railroad, became the scene of fighting between Union and Confederate forces on October 14, 1863. The station was approximately four miles east of the Ewells' farm, Stony Lonesome.
6. Ewell's offer pertains to his sister Rebecca's proposal to sell him land from the family's Stony Lonesome estate.

77. To Lizzie Ewell

Albuquerque, N.M., Jan. 22, 1861.[1]

Miss Bettie Ewell

Dear Bettie,

I believe I wrote last to you from El Paso (Fort Bliss.) Since then I have been very ill with vertigo, nausea, etc., and now am excessively debilitated having occasional attacks of the ague. Chills and fevers were not the form taken by my disease but violent pain in the head with sick stomach.

I am here on a continuation of the same Court Martial which took me to El Paso and which only now seems to be coming to a close. When it is through there seems to be some prospect that I will be allowed to go east, but all is doubtful with our present commanding officer.[2] Coming from the same neighborhood as himself, one might think he would be at least as liberal towards me as the other officers but this has been far from being the case. In fact he has been unusually harsh, whether that he may force me out of the service and thereby raise his son-in-law a file or whether he dislikes me because I know how small he was when he entered service, I can not tell.

Possibly I may get away when the Court closes. I have the recommendation of two army surgeons to leave this Dept. as soon as possible.

It is not likely that I could stand another season in Arizona as I would be much more debilitated than before and the last one nearly did the business.

I presume you are enjoying the usual number of parties, etc. For my part I would rather have a dozen good oysters on the shell with a glass of wine than attend the grandest collection of beauty and youth that will unite this winter.

Of all miserable places this is the worst. Whiskey is abundant every where and scarcely anything else. The Post Office does not afford a stamp nor is one to be had in town. I have a few stamped envelopes but am afraid to use them for fear of getting out altogether.

The last mail brought me a letter from Aunt Rebecca who writes uneasily about Cousin Lizinka. I would visit Alabama if possible.[3]

Every one here is on the tenter hooks of impatience to know what the Southern States will do.[4] Officers generally are very much averse to any thing like civil war, though some of the younger ones are a little warlike. The truth is in the army there are no sectional feelings and many from extreme ends of the Union are the most intimate friends. I look to the business with particular dread because every cent I have in the world may be lost in distress and trouble of civil war and disunion as the same, for from this point of view no one doubts but that the one will turn into the other. They say here that war can not be postponed for 60 days. In Kansas it may be said to have commenced already.[5]

The Tax Department here is without funds as likewise the other disbursing departments of the army and to-night the Mexicans are holding a meeting not to trust the government any longer. The miserable brutes are only kept alive by the troops and if these were removed they would become as before, herders for the Navajoed Apache Indians. They are in fact more depraved and cowardly than the Indians. More Americans have been killed by them in cold blood than by the latter.

I expect you will wonder why I have written such a dry uninteresting letter, but you will be able to see how one may be spun out even when there is nothing of common interest and besides I may be if in remarkable good luck on the road shortly and then it will be impossible to write.

If my health were good I would rather remain here until public matters are quiet, but this is out of the question. I fear that there is a possibility of being left without a cent in case of great troubles. Remember me to your father.

Yours,

R. S. Ewell

30th. I have received yours of the 17th ult.[6] I start to-morrow in a wagon for San Antonio, Texas en route for the States.[7]

R. S. E.

1. This is a copy of a typescript found in the Library of Congress. The original has not been found.
2. Colonel Thomas T. Fauntleroy (1795–1883) of Winchester, Virginia, commanded the 1st United States Dragoon Regiment. Sixty-five years of age in 1861, he was too old for active service. When the Civil War began later that year, Fauntleroy volunteered his services to the Confederacy, but the government declined his offer.
3. Ewell's aunt Rebecca Hubbard lived in Lawrence County, Alabama. She had received several letters from her niece Lizinka Campbell Brown, who had been on a European tour with her daughter and son. Hubbard may have expressed anxiety about Lizinka's health.
4. In response to Abraham Lincoln's election, South Carolina seceded from the Union on December 20, 1860. Within six weeks, six other states from the Deep South—Mississippi, Florida, Alabama, Georgia, Louisiana, and Texas—had left the Union. Delegates from those states met in Montgomery, Alabama, in February to form a new government. Virginia, Arkansas, North Carolina, and Tennessee joined the Confederacy only after the bombardment of Fort Sumter in April.
5. Passage of the Kansas-Nebraska Act in 1854 had overturned the ban on slavery in territories north of the 36°30' latitude established by the Missouri Compromise twenty-four years earlier and left the issue of slavery to be decided by each individual territory. At the same time, the act authorized the creation of two new states, Kansas and Nebraska. Nebraska was unsuited to slavery and would obviously enter the Union as a free state. Kansas could go either way. For the next six years, free-soil "Jayhawkers" battled proslavery "Border Ruffians" for control of the state. The killing and lawlessness that characterized the conflict fueled tensions between North and South and earned the state the name "Bleeding Kansas."

6. "Ult."—i.e., *ultimo,* or "in the last month."

7. On January 26, 1861, Fauntleroy granted Ewell a two-month leave of absence with permission to apply for a ten-month extension. Ewell's leave was "to take effect after the adjournment of the General Court Martial, convened by 'Special Order No. 155' War Dept. Series of 1860." Ewell applied for the ten-month extension in a letter received by the Adjutant General's Office on March 21, 1861.

Chapter 7

The War Begins, 1861–1862

Although Ewell was a Virginian and had owned or rented more than one slave in his life, he was hardly a fire-eater when it came to secession. Like most career military officers, he had many friends in the North and felt a strong allegiance to the United States. Ewell's ties to his adopted state were stronger than his loyalty to the national government, however, and when Virginia voted itself out of the Union on April 17, 1861, he resigned from the United States Army and accepted a lieutenant colonel's commission from the State of Virginia.

Five weeks later Ewell found himself on outpost duty at Fairfax Court House in northern Virginia. In one of the earliest military actions of the war, a company of U.S. cavalry charged through the town, scattering two of the three Confederate companies he had in his command. Dressed only in a nightshirt, Ewell put himself at the head of the remaining company. When the Federal horsemen returned, the Southerners drove them away with a couple of short-range volleys. Ewell received a minor wound in the fray, making him perhaps the first field officer on either side to be wounded in the war.

The skirmish at Fairfax Court House made Ewell famous in Virginia, and on June 17 he was promoted to brigadier general and placed in charge of an infantry brigade. At the First Battle of Manassas, or Bull Run, fought on July 21, Ewell occupied a position at Union Mills on the extreme right flank of the Confederate line. General P. G. T. Beauregard, who commanded the Confederate army in that battle, intended for Ewell to spearhead an assault on the Union army's left flank. Beauregard's orders to Ewell miscarried, however, and the commanding general found his own flank turned instead. Although the Confederates rallied from this misfortune and ultimately triumphed, Ewell's reputation suffered.

The army's new commander, General Joseph E. Johnston, had faith in Ewell's ability, however, and when he reorganized the army in February 1862, Johnston promoted Ewell to major general and placed him in command of the Reserve Division, formerly belonging to E. Kirby Smith.

Ewell had hardly settled into his new position before the army abandoned its winter camp near Centreville, Virginia, and fell back to the Rappahannock River.

The Army of the Potomac's commander, Major General George B. McClellan, did not seriously pursue. Instead, he placed his army upon transports and sailed to Fort Monroe in an effort to capture Richmond from the southeast. Johnston marched to the Peninsula to confront McClellan, leaving Ewell's division to hold the upper Rappahannock line. Ewell was a fighter and chafed at being left at what appeared to be an inactive front. Nevertheless he did his duty, all the while looking for an opportunity to strike.

If Ewell's military career seemed to be temporarily on hold, his personal life was not. On December 1, 1861, he proposed marriage to his first cousin Lizinka Campbell Brown, whom he had admired since his youth. She accepted his offer. For the prospective groom it was a good match. At age forty-one, Lizinka was perhaps the wealthiest women in Tennessee. She had inherited some fifteen thousand acres of land in the state from her father and brother, as well as another twenty-seven hundred acres of land in Mississippi from her deceased husband, James Percy Brown, plus lots in Nashville, St. Louis, and Washington, D.C.

Lizinka had two children from her first marriage, a son named Campbell and a daughter named Harriot, familiarly called Hattie. A third child, Percy, had died eight years earlier. At Lizinka's request, Ewell accepted Campbell onto his staff in 1861. The young man proved valuable as Ewell's aide-de-camp and later as his assistant adjutant general. Ewell became the father that Brown never knew, and Brown became the son that Ewell never had.

78. Undated Account of Fairfax Court House

[R]eforming his men, Col. Ewell awaited the return of the enemy.[1] As they re-appeared, being the third appearance in the town, some of our men refused to fire, saying &c Challenged them. Who goes there? Ans. Cavalry. What Cavalry. Answer was given from the pistol of the leader. Our men fired. Several saddles were emptied, Several horses killed, 5 or 6 prisoners were taken & arms & accoutrements.[2]

There were two comps. of Confederate Cavalry at Fairfax Ct. House. The "Rap[p]ahannock" under Capt. Shack Green & the Prince William Capt. Thor[n]ton. The former had been there for some weeks unsupported, its pickets constantly driven in by the enemy. Occasionally a member of the Co. was shot by them untill this collection of inexperienced men were thoroughly demoralized. The Prince Wm Cav'y having been there but a few days were in better spirits.[3] When the alarm was first given, "the Yankees are coming[,]" Col. Ewell sent for Capt. Thornton but before any instructions could be given the enemy made their appearance. Capt. Thornton went to join his Co. & Col. Ewell to

Ewell became perhaps the first field-grade officer wounded in the Civil War when a bullet clipped him near the base of the neck during a skirmish at Fairfax Court House on June 1, 1861. (Library of Congress)

get out the Warrenton Rifles. Capt Thornton's Co.[,] served badly[4] with a few shot guns[,] were kept always saddled at night. The[y] formed in a small stable yard by the road, but with no room on account of fencing &c to charge, no ammunition to fire they fell back perfectly self possessed before the enemy. Capt. T. was too late to join but fired his revolver from the lot at close range, drawing some shots from the Yankees. The Rap[p]ahannock Cavalry were dispersed—a small number formed near the Warrenton Rifles but then scattered when the Yankees came back again the first time without any order. A year after a[t] Front Royall these same men charged the Yankee Int'y with great courage losing many of thei[r] number but helping to capture a whole Regt.[5]

1. Ewell probably scribbled this account of the skirmish after the war. Unfortunately, only this fragment of the manuscript remains.

2. After charging through Fairfax Court House, the Union cavalrymen re-formed and returned to the town, this time approaching from the west. Ewell had meanwhile formed a company of infantry—the Warrenton Rifles—into a line of battle across the road. As the horsemen approached, Ewell ordered the men to fire, but they hesitated for fear that the approaching troops might be their own cavalry. To settle the matter, Ewell stepped forward and demanded the approaching horsemen to identify themselves, at which point their leader,

Lieutenant Charles H. Tompkins, drew his revolver and shot Ewell in the shoulder, not far from the neck. Ewell's men replied with a volley that scattered the Northerners.

3. The Rappahannock Cavalry later became Company B of the 6th Virginia Cavalry. The Prince William Cavalry became Company A, 4th Virginia Cavalry. Captains John Shackleford Green and William W. Thornton commanded the units.

4. "Served badly"—i.e., armed poorly.

5. On May 23, 1862, Confederate infantry routed the 1st Maryland Regiment (U.S.A.) at Front Royal, Virginia, in the Shenandoah Valley. The Rappahannock Cavalry and three other companies of the 6th Virginia Cavalry spearheaded the pursuit. As the Confederate horsemen closed on their quarry, the 1st Maryland formed a line of battle to meet them. The 6th Virginia Cavalry slammed into the much larger Federal force, shattering its formation and capturing all but one hundred of its members. Ewell witnessed the charge and the next day told the 6th Virginia's commander, Lieutenant Colonel Thomas T. Flournoy, that his regiment had made "a glorious charge." Ewell dubbed the regiment "the Bloody Sixth."

79. To Lizinka Brown

I was ordered from Ashland to Culpepper Ct. House[1] to assist in instruction of Cavalry.[2] Immediately on my arrival at Cul. news came of the occupation of Alex[andria] & the forces there joined the camp at Manassas junction.[3] In a few days I was ordered in advance & came here[4] where was a force of 2 companies Cavalry & one of Infantry.[5] On the morning of June 1st the pickets came in with reports that the enemy were advancing. A few moments afterwards I saw their Cavalry[6] coming up the streets firing right & left. The Cavalry that I had were without firearms & confined in narrow streets.[7] I went to the Rifle company of Infantry as fast as I could & marched about 30 men to the street up which the Cavalry of the enemy had passed through the town. I soon saw the horsemen forming & firing took place when they fell back. Presently the enemy tried a second time to get back & were again beaten back & this time made their escape through the fields losing about ten men killed & wounded[,] 3 Prisoners and quite a number of horses & arms &c.[8] Capt Marr commanding the Rifles was killed before reaching the ground.[9] I received a bullet through the neck or rather shoulder (a slight flesh wound[10]) & they picked up five stragglers. I give you the history because there are so many false statements. The enemy passed through on the turnpike & it was in trying to get back that they were repulsed.

They had 80 men.[11] I have been expecting an attack ever since & have not had 2 nights sleep as I keep dressed all night & have to be up at 3 o'clock A.M. I have 700 men here & there are 1000 & 7 pieces of Artillery at Centreville. My cavalry, the few I succeeded in forming, disappeared at the first fire. An advantage over Inf. in being mounted . . . It seems to me with the excessive worry & fatigue having no officer of experience to answer all complaints & to whom all apply &c that I would give anything for a few days rest of mind & body.

I believe we are in the right. I trust so. Our soil is invaded with the most barbarous threats too often carried into execution & there is nothing to be done but what we do. I don't blame Tasker as I believe he is conscientious, but he is governed by his friends.[12]

Genl. Lee's[13] family have just passed through, refugees from their home & every day the people are flying from Alex[andria].[14]

Beauregard,[15] a host in himself[,] is at Manassas Junction.

1. This undated letter was written by Ewell to his cousin and future wife around June 10, 1861. The original letter has been lost; however, Lizinka's daughter, Harriot, quoted this portion of it in a letter she wrote to an aunt on June 16, 1861.

2. Ewell took command of a camp of instruction for cavalry at Ashland, Virginia, late in April 1861. On May 19, he received orders to report to Culpeper Court House, seventy-five miles to the northwest, to take charge of a camp of instruction there.

3. The Orange and Alexandria Railroad and the Manassas Gap Railroad met at Manassas Junction, twenty-five miles southwest of Washington, D.C. The South concentrated forces there in the summer of 1861 following Virginia's secession.

4. Fairfax Court House, Virginia.

5. Ewell's small force consisted of the Rappahannock Cavalry, the Prince William Cavalry, and the Warrenton Rifles. The Warrenton Rifles later became Company K, 17th Virginia Infantry.

6. The attacking force was Company B, 2nd United States Cavalry.

7. A few members of the Rappahannock Cavalry were armed with double-barreled shotguns, but they may not have had any ammunition.

8. Ewell overestimated the number of Union casualties. Lieutenant Charles H. Tompkins of Company B, Second United States Cavalry, who led the charge through Fairfax Court House, reported that his command lost four horses wounded and nine missing. He did not state the casualties among the troops of

his command except to say that one man was shot in the foot. A postwar source quoted Tompkins as saying that he had three men wounded, three missing, and six horses killed in the fight. On June 5, 1861, Union Brigadier General Irvin McDowell noted that Tompkins had two horses shot from under him, one of which fell on his foot, giving Tompkins a contusion. Confederate Brigadier General Milledge Bonham on June 2 reported one Union soldier killed, several wounded, and three captured "each of whom I saw and examined." In his report of the skirmish, Ewell cited a *New York Times* article dated June 4, 1861, which listed the Union loss as six killed and wounded. *OR* 2:60–61, 64.

9. John Quincy Marr (1825–1861) was the first Confederate officer to die in combat. He perished in the early stages of the battle when a spent musket ball struck him in the chest, just above his heart.

10. Ewell's wound kept him out of the saddle for several days.

11. Tompkins reported having fifty men under his command. Four officers from other commands also accompanied the expedition, giving Tompkins a total of fifty-four men.

12. Ewell's first cousin Thomas Tasker Gantt was serving in the Union army as judge advocate on Major General George B. McClellan's staff.

13. General Robert E. Lee's wife and daughters had left their home in Arlington, Virginia, in mid-May and moved to "Ravensworth" in Fairfax County.

14. Judith W. McGuire was staying at Fairfax Court House at this time. In her diary, under the date May 29, 1861, she wrote: "Several of our friends from Alexandria have passed to-day. Many families who attempted to stay at home are escaping as best they may." McGuire, *Diary*, 22.

15. General Pierre G. T. Beauregard (1818–1893), the "Hero of Sumter," took command of Confederate troops in northern Virginia in June 1861. One month later he led them at Bull Run, or Manassas, the war's first land battle.

80. To Milledge Bonham

June 21. 1861

Genl Bonham[1]

My Dear Sir;

I wonder if you were as much astonished as I was at my promotion?[2] I assure you it is a matter that gives me no rejoicing as the responsibility is painful, particularly in my present state of health.[3] I dont know how things stand here, but I hope if I am kept at this place that you will continue to have the direction.

I dont think it necessary to tell you how much pleasure it will give me to carry out your views.

I believe my suspicions against Mr King[4] were unfounded. He was searched by the pickets & a strict surveillance has been kept over him. Govr Smith[5] confirms the statements Mr King makes of his being driven from Washington.

Yours &c

R S. Ewell

1. Milledge L. Bonham (ca. 1814–1890) of South Carolina had received his commission as a brigadier general on April 23, 1861. He resigned from the Confederate Army early in 1862 over a dispute in seniority and spent much of the war serving in the Confederate House of Representatives.

2. Ewell had been promoted to brigadier general on June 17, 1861, and took command of a brigade consisting of the 5th Alabama, 6th Alabama, and 6th Louisiana infantry regiments. The Confederate Congress confirmed his appointment on August 29, 1861.

3. Ewell's shoulder was still smarting from the wound he received at Fairfax Court House on June 1; however, the reference here appears to be to a different illness, possibly malaria or neuralgia.

4. A man known only as Mr. King fled his home in northern Virginia in June and came to Fairfax Court House. There he met Ewell, whom he described as "an old friend that I had known for some time in New Mexico." Ewell sent King to Bonham at Manassas, where Bonham assigned King a place in the engineers and sent him back to Ewell. King served as Ewell's aide during the June 1, 1861, skirmish at Fairfax Court House and later made use of his familiarity with the region to conduct reconnaissances and make maps. He transferred back to Bonham's staff that summer. "Letters Received by the Confederate Secretary of War, 1861–65," M437, R25, Item 10,676, NA.

5. William "Extra Billy" Smith (1796–1887) served as Virginia's governor from 1846 to 1849 and again from 1864 to 1865. Although appointed to the Confederate States Congress in 1861, Smith continued to fight in the Confederate army as colonel of the 49th Virginia Infantry and later as a brigadier general in the Second Corps.

81. Ewell Memorandum on First Manassas

A false statement having been published in the Columbus daily Sun of July 29th 1861[1] signed, "Upson" and dated "Manassa[2] July 23.["] relative to my

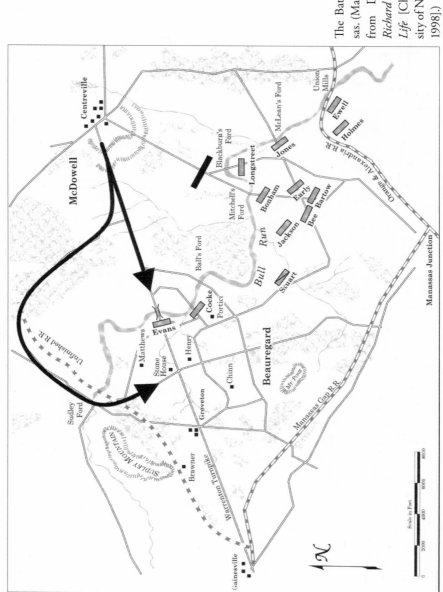

The Battle of First Manassas. (Map by Ed P. Coleman, from Donald C. Pfanz, *Richard S. Ewell: A Soldier's Life* [Chapel Hill: University of North Carolina Press, 1998].)

movements on the day of the battle of Manassa, I give the following copies of orders received during the day & extracts from Genl Beauregard's written statements. The originals of these are in my possession.[3]

Before Sunrise[4] I was ordered to hold the Brigade in readiness to advance at a moments warning.[5]

The next communication from Head Quarters was a visit from an Aide of Genl Beauregard's who knew of nothing besides the above.

I heard nothing further untill about ten when Genl Jones wrote me that Genl Beauregard had written to him that I had been ordered to advance. I at once acted on this order untill I was recalled by the following: "10 1/2 A.M." "On acct of the difficulties in our front it is thought advisable to fall back to our former positions. (Sd) G. T. B.—[6]

Genl Ewell"

I next, in the afternoon, received a verbal order through Col. Terry[7] to advance to attack a battery. After proceeding about 1 1/2 miles in obedience to this order, I was directed to Stone Bridge.

Hearing various reports in reference to these movements I wrote to Genl Beauregard who answered by stating that orders for me were sent to Genl Holmes[8] & that the latter had told him they were never received. Furthermore Genl Beauregard[9] writes that, "the order sent you in the Afternoon to recross the Bull run to march towards the Stone Bridge—it was sent you by Genl J. E. Johnston,[10] as I am informed by him, for the purpose of supporting our left if necessary.

A short statement of the above is, that orders were sent Genl Holmes for him & myself to advance which were not received by Genl Holmes but notice of which coming an hour later through Genl Jones, were at once acted [upon] untill rescinded in writing by Genl Beauregard, while in execution. Another verbal order in the afternoon again countermanded on the march by orders to fall back to Stone Bridge.

The morning order lost less than an hour in coming through Genl Jones instead of Holmes.

1. Written in Ewell's hand, this undated memorandum responding to the *Sun* article appears to have been composed around August 1861.
2. The rail line that ran west from Bull Run to White Plains, Virginia, was called Manassa's Gap Railroad, after a man who lived at Thoroughfare Gap. Over time, the railroad and its junction with the Orange and Alexandria Railroad

were shortened to "Manassas." However, Ewell and many other northern Virginia residents referred to the junction as "Manassa."

3. It is hard to understand Ewell's irritation over this article, which clearly attributed his failure to promptly cross Bull Run to the miscarriage of Beauregard's order. Ewell may have been angered over the author's statement that "had the orders to Gen. Ewell been received and carried out, and our entire force brought upon the field, we would have destroyed the enemy's army almost literally."

4. July 21, 1861.

5. Beauregard's order read:

> Manassas Junction, Va., July 21, 1861.
>
> General:
>
> You will hold yourself in readiness to take the offensive on Centreville at a moment's notice, to make a diversion against the enemy's intended attack on Mitchell's Ford, and probably Stone Bridge. You will protect well your right flank against any attack from the eastward. General Holmes' brigade will support your movement. If the enemy be prepared to attack in front of your left, leave it (said brigade) in proper position, with orders to take the offensive when it hears your engagement on the other side of the Run.
>
> I intend to take the offensive throughout my front as soon as possible.
>
> Resp'ly your Obd't Sev't,
> G. T. Beauregard,
> Brig.-Gen. Comdg.

A copy of the post-battle correspondence between Ewell and Beauregard appears in Beauregard, *A Commentary,* 115–18.

6. Signed by Gustave Toutant Beauregard, the Confederate army commander.

7. Elsewhere Ewell refers to this staff officer as Colonel Lucy. There is no record of either a Colonel Lucy or a Colonel Terry as having served on Beauregard's staff; however, a Colonel B. F. Terry of Texas served as a volunteer on Brigadier General James Longstreet's staff. Brigadier General David R. Jones mentions a "Mr. Terry" in his report of the battle.

8. At Manassas, Brigadier General Theophilus H. Holmes (1804–1880) commanded a brigade that supported Ewell's men at Union Mills.

9. Ewell inadvertently repeated the name "Beauregard" here.

10. Joseph E. Johnston (1807–1891) held the position of quartermaster of the United States Army in 1861, when he resigned his commission to accept a

position as a general in the Confederate States Army. Assigned to command Southern troops at Harpers Ferry, Johnston joined Beauregard in July 1861 in time to participate in the Battle of First Manassas. After the battle, he took command of their combined forces, which later became known the Army of Northern Virginia. Johnston was wounded at the Battle of Seven Pines on May 31, 1862. Upon returning to duty in November, he was assigned of the Department of the West. He continued to command Confederate forces in the Western Theater for the rest of the war, surrendering the Army of Tennessee to William T. Sherman on April 26, 1865, at Bentonville, North Carolina.

82. To Lizzie Ewell

July 31, 1861.

Miss Lizzie Ewell[1]

Dear Lizzie,

I received your note with the envelope a few days since. I am very sorry that I can not gratify your taste for blood and your ambition by any account of glory that I was to have reaped on the 18th or 21st.[2] When we fell back from Fairfax Court-house Station my post had been assigned, in advance, at Union Mills on the extreme right flank of our position. I was, when directed to do so, at the critical moment, to take the road to Centreville to attack the enemy in flank, and the various other brigades, between this and the point of attack of the enemy, were also to cross the run and do likewise. On the 17th[3] we all remained in position as the enemy did not make a decided attack. On the 21st we were roused before daylight with orders to hold ourselves in readiness at a moments warning, and very soon we could hear the booming[4] of artillery and the faint discharge of musketry far up the run towards the turnpike.[5] About nine A.M. the next General above me[6] sent word he had crossed and was advancing, sending me a copy of his orders which looked to my doing so, although nothing had come to me.[7] I also moved forward, but we were all arrested by an order to fall back to our old positions. The reason I had not received the order was that it had not been sent,[8] but the time lost was so short that it made no difference—less than an hour.[9] The reason of our recall was that our hands were full up the run, and the scales were doubtful.[10]

At three P.M. I again received orders to cross,[11] and went about 1 1/2 miles when I was directed to march my brigade to the stone bridge over Bull Run. My feelings then were terrible, as such an order could only mean that we were defeated and I was to cover the retreat. I reached [there] in time to find we had won, and marched back to Union Mills (Rail-road crossing of Bull Run.) Our line of battle from extreme left to right was nearly five miles. The battle took place on the left—across Bull Run—on open ground, the enemy having turned our flank. We should feel deeply our gratitude for the victory, for the march of the enemy was as a swarm of locusts, burning and destroying. They drove peoples stock into their pens merely to butcher them, leaving farmers without a live animal on their farms. The private memoranda found on the field speak of their depredations on the route.

On the 17th, the day we fell back from Fairfax, owing to the hurry of affairs, the troops at the Court-house fell back without warning me at the station, and the result was that Col. R. E. Rodes of my command (formerly of Lexington) was engaged with the enemy, and my flanks were about being turned before we knew that General Bonham had orders to retire.[12] Either the Yankees lost their way or were over cautious for we extricated ourselves without loss of baggage or life. We were very near being surrounded by 10 or 15000 while we were less than 2000 without artillery. In the hurry of movements they forgot the most important orders sometimes. Col. Rodes is an old acquaintance of Benjamins, an excellent officer, behaved very gallantly, but in the blaze of more recent events his little skirmish will be overlooked.[13] He killed and wounded some 40 of the enemy, including one captain, and drove them back to wait for their artillery. In the meantime we retired. All is doubtful as to future movements.

Remember me to the family. There is talk of an advance.

Yours,

R. S. Ewell.

1. This letter was copied from a typescript at the Library of Congress. The original letter has been lost.
2. The Battle of Blackburn's Ford and the subsequent Battle of First Manassas.
3. Ewell meant to write "18th" here, the date of the fighting at Blackburn's Ford.
4. The typescript has this word as "looming," an obvious typographical error.
5. The Warrenton Turnpike crossed Bull Run at the stone bridge. Beginning at 5:30 A.M., Union artillery opened fire at the stone bridge while infantry crossed the run at Sudley Springs Ford, two miles upstream, to turn the Confederate left flank.
6. Brigadier General David R. Jones commanded a brigade at McLean's Ford, one and one-half miles upstream from Ewell's position at Union Mills.
7. Jones's orders, marked 7:00 A.M., read as follows:

General:

    General Ewell has been ordered to take the offensive upon Centreville. You will follow the movement at once by attacking the enemy in your front.

Resp'ly

G. T. Beauregard

Quoted in Beauregard, *A Commentary,* 114.

8. Beauregard claimed that he had sent the order by a courier but that it was not delivered.

9. Ewell greatly underestimated the time lost. Jones received his copy of the order shortly after 7:00 A.M. Ewell did not receive the copy of Jones's order until 10:00 A.M., nearly three hours later.

10. The 10:30 A.M. order recalling Ewell, Jones, and Longstreet to the west side of the stream was delivered to Ewell by Colonel A. R. Chisolm. According to Beauregard's later testimony, the order read: "On account of the difficulties of the ground in our front it is thought advisable to fall back to our former positions." Campbell Brown, then serving as Ewell's aide-de-camp, later wrote: "We afterwards understood that [the order] was written in consequence of Gen. D. R. Jones' having been repulsed in an attack injudiciously executed on the battery & supports in front of Mitchell's Ford." Beauregard, *A Commentary,* 115; RSE to Joseph Johnston, 15 Aug. 1866, PBE; CB, "From Fairfax C.H. to Richmond," PBE.

11. According to a later account by Ewell, the purpose of this second advance was "to attack a battery at McLean's Ford." RSE to Joseph Johnston, 15 Aug. 1866, PBE (178).

12. For Rodes's report of this action, see *OR* 2, 459–61.

13. Robert E. Rodes (1829–1864) was a civil engineer and taught at the Virginia Military Institute before the Civil War. As colonel of the 5th Alabama Infantry, he had fought well under Ewell at First Manassas, and Ewell later enthusiastically supported his promotion to brigadier general. Rodes was in command of a division when he died in action at Third Winchester on September 19, 1864. For additional evidence of Ewell's high opinion of Rodes, see CB to "My dear Aunt," 20 Aug. 1861, folder 8, PBE.

83. To Lizinka Brown

P.S.[1] A letter from Lizzie Ewell to day mentions one written to Hattie.[2] Your letter of the 2nd arriving to day, caused the destruction of several pages of stuff

Ewell and his cousin Lizinka (left) became engaged in December 1861. Lizinka's son, Campbell (below, left), supported the marriage. Five years later, Campbell married Susan Polk (below, right), the daughter of Brig. Gen. Lucius Polk. (Courtesy Donald Pfanz and Tennessee State Library and Archives)

I had written to you. You judge me incorrectly if you think any step, that would estrange the affections of your children from you, or cause their unhappiness would not be as repugnant to me as to yourself.[3] I am more than satisfied by what you write; indeed in spite of the clouds gathering over our country I am almost happy. You must forgive the anxiety I have felt, as the amount showed how deeply I have been involved.

Events are fast thickening and I hardly know if every letter may not be the last, for a long time at least, and but that I cannot express myself more strongly than I have or more openly, I would weary you with my protestations.

My prayer is that I may prove worthy of the great happiness you have conferred on me & which to my wildest fancies seemed hopeless. I trust that in any way possible you will remove any shadow or worry or anxiety from your child. I should a thousand times prefer to a moments estrangement between you &

her that I should confine myself to the recollection of the 1st of Decr[4] and the almost intoxicating thought of being of interest to you. I say this because I can see no brightness in the future, if accompanied with a cloud to you or her. To this time I feel as though all human calculations were overthrown and I have hope & faith in the future. At all events it seems to me that the future has more to look forward to than I ever thought possible. Do you realize however that disaster and disgrace & calumny may attach themselves to my name by those who by doing so try to screen themselves?[5] I have a great appreciation of envy & malice. No one knows himself but I earnestly pray for Divine assistance, as has been given to me hitherto.[6] Of late this has seemed to me more apparent, as my need has become greater.

Yours, R S. Ewell

How glad I am that I postponed my answer untill hearing from you again, as I misunderstood some parts of your letter, thinking you would ignore the conditional promise of a former letter[7] & which is all I now ask and is given in the letter to which this is an answer.

11th I have been re-reading & burning your letters this morning, with less regret as I have them by heart. I persuaded you in Phila to take your daguer[r]eotype, but I found the original was present & it would have been like looking at a mirror when you were by in person.

1. This undated postscript appears to have been completed on January 11, 1862.
2. Lizinka's seventeen-year-old daughter, Harriot Brown.
3. A short time earlier, Ewell had asked for Lizinka's hand in marriage, and she had accepted. At first, Hattie seems to have opposed the betrothal, placing the marriage in jeopardy.
4. This may have been the day that Lizinka expressed her love for the general or consented to their marriage.
5. This is probably a reference to Beauregard, who, at First Manassas, had sent a courier to Ewell with orders to cross Bull Run and attack the Union army's left flank. The courier failed to deliver the order, however, and Ewell failed to make the attack. When Ewell later learned that Beauregard had criticized him for disobeying orders, he wrote Beauregard a letter reviewing the facts of the case and demanding the name of the courier who had delivered the order. Beauregard did not know the courier's name and in the end sent Ewell a letter of apology. But, as Campbell Brown in his memoirs recalled:

Genl Beauregard gave Genl Ewell full permission to publish his (Genl B.'s) letter in his own defence—but presently wrote to him, begging him to wait for the publication of his (Beauregard's) official report, which would fully & satisfactorily explain the matter. Genl Ewell did so wait—but when the report came out its way of stating the affair was so vague & unsatisfactory that he was greatly disgusted, seeing the probability that nine out of ten who read it would still impute blame to him when in fact it belonged to Beauregard. (Jones, *Campbell Brown's Civil War,* 28–29.)

6. Although Ewell had not been particularly religious as a young man, his faith grew stronger when he returned to the States in 1861, thanks in part, perhaps, to Lizinka's influence. Later contact with "Stonewall" Jackson and his staff stirred Ewell's faith still more. The Right Reverend John Johns confirmed Ewell at St. Paul's Church in Richmond on October 2, 1864.

7. Lizinka's acceptance of Ewell's proposal of marriage may have been contingent on the approval of her children.

84. To Lizinka Brown

Centreville
Jany 30th 1862

Mrs Lizinka C. Brown
Nashville Ten.

Dear Cousin;

I am glad to be able to introdu[c]e to you Capt. D. B. Harris,[1] Engineer Corps, who accompanies Genl Beauregard to the West.[2]

Capt. Harris's services have been of the most valuable kind to our cause, both at the battle of Manassa & in those operations more particularly pertaining to his branch of the Military Profession.

I hope Capt. Harris will be in charge of the works about Nashville and I feel confident that the interests of your town cannot be in better hands.

Yours &–
R. S. Ewell

1. David B. Harris (1814–1864) attended West Point and served briefly in the United States Army before leaving the service to become a tobacco farmer in

Goochland County, Virginia. When the Civil War began, he became an engineering officer. He held the rank of colonel when he died of yellow fever in
October 1864.

2. In late January 1862, Beauregard transferred to the Department of Kentucky
and Tennessee, commanded by General Albert Sidney Johnston. He departed
for his new assignment on February 2.

85. *To Lizinka Brown*

Feb'y 10. 1862

Dear Lizinka;

Last night I wrote a very long letter to you, but as it is rendered old news
by your[s] of the 2d, I have concluded to write it over.

C.[1] & myself paid a short visit to Wm Stoddert the other day. he had been
very sick, is better and was revived by our visit.[2] We called by Doctor Macrae's[3]
where we saw some young ladies[,] daughters of Col. R. B Lee of St Louis.[4] He
has just recd a letter from T. T. Gantt—amt'g to nothing—mentions something
about paying taxes on L's[5] property. Mrs G. sends her affectionate regards to Mrs
L & daughters. they write from Washington. The hand recalled many reminiscences from 34. to this time[6]—all the long associations broken beyond all human possibility of repair. He will probably join the army of invasion. Yesterday
we heard Fort Henry was taken. I think from all I can see that Donelson must
follow & Nashville is the next point.[7] You may go to Ala[bama] if the Yankees
dont show more than their usual energy.[8] C. is very unhappy about you[—]does
not know whether to apply for a leave or whether there may not be greater emer-
gencies. You would relieve him & myself very much by a promise to telegraph if
he can help you. Your letters show as much absence of fears for yourself as if the
Yankees were no where. An exodus from Nashville would show selfishness that
would amaze you. Should you have to go & decide to leave your house you could
leave some whites in it. Buell, Grant & Sherman[9] are all acquaintances of mine
and would respect if possibly [*sic*] a letter stating that I had advised you to apply
to them. Sherman (Wm Tecumseh) is in every sense a gentleman generous &
high toned. You may prefer to destroy. But one alone cannot do much by that. I
wrote several pages of stuff that you may think yourself fortunate to miss.

You are surprized it would seem from your letters at my want of any desire
for rank,[10] but I have very little confidence in the style of our troops[,] the manner they are disciplined &c. &c. and one hazards more than life with them.[11]
Want of success of course is laid to the fault of the leaders.

C. is now the only Officer on my personal staff & is acting as Adjt Genl.[12] He is the only Officer that I can get who is always ready, intelligent and satisfied. Why dont I make him Asst. Adjt Gen? because the pay is of little consequence, because of his relationship and his youth. He is too good natured in dealings with me and as I told him the other day, if we were going anywhere & he knew I was on the wrong road yet he would not insist upon it. The fact is I find myself so identified with him that I hesitate to make him prominent as I do for myself. The more I feel personally attached to him the more anxious I am that his merits should be in advance of his position. It seems to me that a mistake on his part would be a thousand times more annoying to me than if he were an indifferent acquaintance. My apologetic letter about the wines at Washington's sale was unnecessary. He and Green[13] went up to buy, but seem to have been so taken up by the ladies at Mr Turner's (Miss Lee & Miss Turner)[14] that the sale was neglected & C. bo[ugh]t only or at least secured only a few gallons of Madeira and some whiskey. C. bot. more but did not secure it in time & others took it off at cost for the purpose of speculating. I laugh at him about it and he retaliates by laughing at my going to meet him & Miss L. at the rail road.

His bed is the most surprizing affair—a long narrow frame, the bottom of narrow strips of plank several inches apart, just as if intended for a penance. a curve in the frame answers for the pillow, replacing a log of wood that was used before the last bedstead. His cot went back to Stony Lonesome when the order for sending off heavy baggage was promulgated. You ought to feel very happy in the affection which he shows for you. You seem to be peculiarly blessed in the love of your children, apparently made stronger by your unvarying kindness.

The great point of interest here now is the re-enlistment of volunteers. As many as can go on furlough re-enlist very readily, but there it seems to hang and the Virginia Legislature have shown a shameful neglect in not preparing some bill.[15]

I think your friend Maj. Reese[16] was too fast in the compliments he quoted as paid to the 3rd Regt. of Ten.[17] I remember going to see the Review but the impression seemed to be that there was more room for improvement than almost anywhere else. But I believe there was a marked improvement spoken of in comparison to what had been at Harper's Ferry. I feel always more interest about the Tennessee troops because their Officers dont seem generally well informed as in other states. The neglect or ignorance of the Officers tells terribly on the men who are left helpless.

I shall take the first opportunity to call on Maj. Reese when I hear he is in the camp.

Love to Hattie. Yours, R. S. Ewell

1. Campbell Brown, Lizinka's son.
2. Ewell's younger brother, William, was appointed chaplain of the 18th Virginia Infantry Regiment on October 2, 1861.
3. Dr. James W. F. Macrae (b. ca. 1798) lived near Gainesville, Virginia, and was one of the wealthiest men in the county, having $30,000 in real estate and $14,200 in personal property in 1860.
4. Richard Bland Lee of Virginia, an 1817 graduate of West Point, had served as a commissary officer in the United States Army, where Ewell had first met him. At the time of this letter, he was serving in the Commissary Department of the Confederacy with the rank of colonel. He died in 1875.
5. Lee's.
6. Ewell may have first met his cousin "Tasker" during an 1834 visit to Brook Grove, the Gantts' farm near Bladensburg, Maryland.
7. Forts Henry and Donelson blocked the incursion of Union gunboats up the Tennessee and Cumberland rivers respectively. Capture of the forts on February 6 and February 16 opened central Tennessee to invasion by Union forces. The Confederate army evacuated Nashville less than two weeks later.
8. Lizinka's principal residence was in Nashville, adjacent to the state capitol. As Union forces approached the city, she apparently wrote to Ewell asking his advice about a course of action to pursue. In the end, she took Ewell's advice and fled to Alabama to stay with the Hubbards, leaving her Nashville house in the care of two Unionist friends. Lizinka left behind a note addressed to Generals Grant and Buell asking them, in Ewell's name, to respect her property. The generals never got the letter, and the house was confiscated by Union authorities. It was later used as a residence by Tennessee's Unionist governors, Andrew Johnson and William G. Brownlow.
9. Generals Don Carlos Buell (1818–1898), Ulysses Simpson Grant (1822–1885), and William Tecumseh Sherman (1820–1891) held high positions in the Western army of the Union. Ewell knew each of them from West Point.
10. For other evidence of Ewell's ambivalent attitude toward promotion at this stage of the war, see RSE to Milledge Bonham, 21 June 1861, Bonham Papers, the South Caroliniana Library, University of South Carolina, Columbia (letter 80, this volume).

11. "More than life"—i.e., honor.

12. Brown was on Ewell's staff throughout the war, first as an aide-de-camp, then as an assistant adjutant general, and finally as assistant adjutant and inspector general. He emerged from the war as a major.

13. Major Benjamin H. Green (1826–1890), an engineer from Mississippi, initially served Ewell as a volunteer aide-de-camp. He became the chief commissary officer of Ewell's brigade on September 2, 1861, and later held a like position in Ewell's division.

14. Miss Lee may possibly refer to Mildred Lee, the youngest daughter of General Robert E. Lee, to whom Brown later became warmly attached. The identity of Miss Turner is unknown.

15. Many Confederate soldiers had enlisted in the spring of 1861 for a period of one year. With the expiration of their terms of service approaching, the Confederacy faced a crisis. On April 16, 1862, the Confederate Congress passed the nation's first Conscription Act, requiring the enlistment of all nonexempt white males between the ages of eighteen and thirty-five.

16. Unidentified.

17. Lizinka had paid to outfit one company of this regiment earlier in the war, and her son Campbell had briefly served as a lieutenant in the unit before joining Ewell's staff.

86. To Lizinka Brown

Centreville
Feby 18. 1862

Dear Lizinka;

All is in doubt and anxiety here yet although the symptoms seem very unfortunate. I hope C. has arrived before the necessity for leaving Nashville shall arise.[1] Should you leave N. and come east you will probably be safer in Richmond or some intermediate point, between this & there.

Fear of my letter being intercepted prevents my writing as I would, but you must not stop in the Country in case of awaiting their advance.[2] The towns are the only safe places. They cannot keep their soldiers from plunder if they would. Here they destroy every thing and impoverish helpless females by killing their stock & running off their negroes.[3] I hardly know whether to wish you to stop in N. or not. I mean for your material interests.

It seems to be the general impression here that you had better leave it, but you know best. Your negroes ought to be moved anyhow.[4]

In your troubles & afflictions you can give one thought to the sympathy and pain felt by me for your situation. Not the least being the inability at every sacrifice consistent with duty & honor, to go where I could aid your movements.

I hastily write this to try if it can happen to find you.

Yours—

P.S. Dont let C. leave as long as he can assist you. I am utterly unable to advise you as to leaving. Many regret leaving Alexandria as their houses have been turned into barracks or hospitals. I am afraid to cou[n]sel because my wishes would bias my Judg[me]nt.

1. On February 14, 1862, following news of Fort Henry's capitulation, Ewell granted Campbell Brown a twenty-day leave of absence to assist his mother and sister in evacuating their Nashville home. "But by the time I got to Knoxville," Brown recalled, "Fort Donelson had fallen, & on reaching Murfreesboro I found the Army there & Nashville abandoned. I bought a horse & crossed the country to Spring hill, where I learned that Mother & Sister were already in Alabama at Maj. D. Hubbard's." Hearing that the Federals already occupied Nashville, Brown paid two men $100 in Confederate money to go to his mother's house, adjacent to the state capitol, and secure his sister's harp. The men returned with the instrument and with tidings that Union troops had not yet entered the city. Brown took the harp to his mother and sister in Alabama before returning to Virginia. Today the instrument is in the collection of the Museum of the Confederacy in Richmond, Virginia. Jones, *Campbell Brown's Civil War,* 56.
2. Union troops under Brigadier General Don Carlos Buell were advancing steadily toward Nashville, prompting Lizinka and Hattie to flee their home. Buell's men entered the Tennessee capital on February 25, 1862.
3. See also RSE to LE, 31 July 1861, LC (letter 82, this volume).
4. The 1860 census records show Lizinka as having 90 slaves at her Maury County, Tennessee, plantation. She claimed to have owned 120 slaves in 1861, all but 10 of whom she had inherited from her deceased brother's estate.

87. To Lizinka Brown

Feby 20. 1862

Dear Lizinka;

I merely write to get rid as far as possible of my dismal thoughts & forebodings. I have been probably far more anxious about you than you are yourself, as

In February 1862, Lizinka had to abandon her house in Nashville, Tennessee (top). At the same time, Ewell was visiting with Major General Gustavus W. Smith at his boyhood home in Centreville, Virginia (bottom). (*Harper's Monthly Magazine* and Library of Congress)

we are entirely in the dark here. But if the worst happen that may[,] as long as we are all alive there is hope & love and devotion. Your children are grown[1] so that the want of education, the most irreparable of all, will not be felt by them. I am afraid to write anything but generalities as this may never reach you.

The telegrams give no clear or possible version of the terrible calamities in Ten.[2]

I received a letter from you dated the 12th.

It is perfectly inexplicable that you should have been left in Ten. with two rivers perfectly open leading to the heart of the country. The President's infatuation for Johnson (A.S.) seems to be of the blindest and most unaccountable nature.[3]

How earnestly I long to hear from you & what a pleasure if I could see you for only a few moments. I hope C. will remain with you as long as he can assist. He must not dream of leaving in less than 30 days unless you come east, and he must stay longer if necessary or proper.[4] Such is the advantage of being Aid & this is partly why I kept him in that position.[5]

Genl G. W. Smith is quite sick.[6]

Yours—

You know I presume that large sums were appropriated by the last Congress to the defence of the Ten. & Cum. Rivers. Yet look at the neglect.

My views of your character & disposition are such that I would attach no importance on your account, to the loss or temporary deprivation of wealth, Except so far as it may affect Hattie. As for C. my views always have been since knowing him that he would have a better chance for distinction if forced to exert his mind even as his Grandfather did.[7]

I was a long time yesterday in our old house in Centreville[8] where is G. W. Smith and thought much over old times, when I went often to bed on a piece of corn bread & of your tears at Mother's being obliged to keep school. Yet those were probably as happy as any days Mother had passed to that time. Since then with money for every want I have passed no happier.

Yours truly[9]

1. Campbell was then twenty-one years of age. His sister, Hattie, was seventeen.
2. The fall of Forts Henry and Donelson in February 1862 opened the Tennessee and Cumberland rivers to Union navigation and prompted the Confederate army to abandon Tennessee and fall back to Corinth, Mississippi.
3. General Albert Sidney Johnston (1803–1862) commanded the Confederacy's Western Department, which included the State of Tennessee.
4. Once Brown reached Tennessee, he telegraphed Ewell to request a ten-day extension of his leave, which the general readily granted.
5. As an aide-de-camp, Brown was solely accountable to Ewell.
6. Major General Gustavus W. Smith (1822–1896) commanded a division in Beauregard's army.

7. Ewell's and Lizinka's grandfather, George Washington Campbell (1769–1848), was a native of Scotland. He came to the United States with his family at the age of three, graduated from Princeton University, became a member of the Knoxville Bar, and was elected to the U.S. House of Representatives. He later served as a judge on the Tennessee Supreme Court of Errors and Appeals, as a U.S. senator, as secretary of the treasury, and as ambassador to Russia.

8. In addition to their Prince William County farm, Stony Lonesome, the Ewells had owned a house and four lots in Centreville, Virginia. The Centreville property was sold to Andrew Grigsby in 1846.

9. Ewell left the letter unsigned for fear that it might fall into enemy hands.

88. *To Lizinka Brown*

Feby 21. 1862

Dear Lizinka;

You must excuse the storm of notes I am sending to you, but the eyes of the Confederacy are turned towards Nashville at this time and mine more than any. We understand that they are preparing to defend the city. I hope not from the immediate vicinity for we all know the fate of a town taken by assault and I had rather trust wolves than the Volunteers of the North, roused by the excitement of success. It is very evident that Johnson (A. S.) has been badly outgeneraled.

I feel relieved at the evident probability that C. has joined you. I feared he might not[1] in time. Dont let him leave you before he has done every thing to enable [you to] make your arrangements. He must stay his 30 days at all events & longer if necessary. I enclose a paper for him which you can give or not as you see fit. When matters were reported at their worst—Nashville taken &c. &c.[—]some of us here were forming a plan to emigrate to Brazil when all resistance in the South should be over. But we can & will vindicate our country if the people will it. Bad appointments have been made and the President is obstinate and the administration interfere[s] shamefully with the Army here & I presume elsewhere, but of the final result if the South hold together, there is no question. There will be wrecks of fortunes and there is misery. I believe that the rule is general, that where females remain on their property within the enemy's lines, it is respected except slaves. Where property is left, it is taken as evidence of disaffection on [the] part of the owners & abused. You can judge best what to do on the spot, but there are fears for Richmond. Probably the west of N. Car. may be safest. Negroes seem to be lost whether the owner stays with them among the Yankees or not. Mrs Commodore Jones[,][2] widow[,] had all her property taken[,] negroes and all[,] & is now in Prince Wm County destitute.

The people urged her to bring her slave[s] away but she said the Yankees would respect her. Negroes will not be let alone by them.

If you leave Nashville I hope I shall see you although in the long past I have been accustomed [to] being by myself. Lately I have been spoiled by being with friends and felt ridiculously lonesome for a day or two after C. left.

There are four letters here for him from you.

Yesterday the owner of the boy,[3] one of 3 brothers C. spoke of buying, sent here to know the decision. I requested them to wait, that I heard you wished to purchase but the news from N[ashville] was so conflicting and your movements doubtful that there could be nothing done untill you had written.

I hope you will inform me of your decision as soon as possible.

Love to your Children

Yours—

R. S. Ewell

at Molino del Rey we lost between 25 and 30 per cent.[4]

R.S.E—

I may not see your friend Reese but the symptoms now are that I would like him in some Capacity[—]Aid (Extra) or Asst. Adjt Genl.[5]

1. Ewell repeated the word "not" here.
2. Thomas Ap Catesby Jones (1790–1858) was born in Westmoreland County, Virginia. As an officer in the U.S. Navy, he fought with gallantry in the War of 1812. Jones later commanded the navy's Pacific Squadron. In 1823 he married Mary Walker Carter, the daughter of Charles B. Carter of "Richmond Hill," Virginia.
3. A slave.
4. The American army suffered 800 casualties of 3,400 engaged at Molino del Rey, a battle fought on the outskirts of Mexico City. Mexican forces, by contrast, incurred some 2,700 losses.
5. Assistant adjutants general performed administrative duties at a headquarters. Aides held lower rank and performed unspecified duties. Reese did not serve on Ewell's staff.

89. To Lizinka Brown

Feby 23. 1862

Dear Lizinka;

Yesterday I was riding all day & did not write. In fact not having a letter from you for some time (the latest dated the 12th) I almost despair of my letter reaching you. However to day, being kept from going to Church as I wished, by the Officers of the Brigade coming to tell me goodbye,[1] I do what seems to me next in its influences & feelings and scribble you a few lines, hoping they may possibly reach you. There are four letters here for C. from you. The latest, of the 14. I opened, because, aside from my great anxiety I had a visit from the owner of the negroes on the subject of purchasing & I thought possibly you might mention them. This was the reason I took the liberty. William received th[r]ee letters for C. from you & being sick at S. L.[2] and in great anxiety, he opened one, that speaking of the visit & breakfast of B's Staff.[3]

It will interest C. to know that I am to take the "Reserve Division."[4] I went there yesterday and Mrs XXX[5] and her sister set out lunch—Cold tongue, beef, & pickles &c. There were no plates or knives and as the ladies cut up the viands with fingers & no forks and as it was reasonable to conclude as there were no napkins they would wipe their fingers by licking them. I took some bread & meat, as bound in gallantry to do, but from some cause I cannot understand the compound gave me the dyspepsia.[6] I thought as their hands were enormous in size the enjoyment of the viands ought to be greater. Why they expect one to pull a slice of beef to pieces with the teeth when it would be so little trouble to give a knife I cant imagine. I felt tempted to take out my pocket knife.

Tell C. Maj. Green has applied for a leave. his getting it is doubtful. C. got his without difficulty because he was on my personal Staff. It is considered the Genl can do as he sees fit with those. I hope you will keep C. as long as he is important to you.

The new Division has every thing arranged like clock work & there is no necessity for any great trouble just now. Except from extracts from Northern papers we are perfectly in the dark with respect to the disasters at Donelson. I see that they state Buckner[7] is held for treason. With the vast preponderance of prisoners they have,[8] there is much greater probability of their severity than before the late disasters. You easily imagine the gloom these events cast over us. Statements are made of Pillow & Floyd in reference to their falling back that are anything but complimentary. That whole states should be made miserable by the misconduct of one or two men is a terrible trial.[9] The letter to C. from you, that I opened showed great anxiety at the prospect, but self command and a spirit that I wish could animate our people. I feel more sorrow in this struggle for your sex that see your interests and relations exposed to danger without being able to share their perils or contribute to the cause except by the most painful labors of hospitals &c.[10] What torture it must be to see home & comfort passing off by the weakness or neglect or incompetency of those whom favoritism has placed at the head of military operations? Howeve[r] I will not add to your troubles.

Wm is here—nearly well. Genl G. W. Smith has been sick but is recovering. Garland[11] takes this Brigade untill a Brigadier is appointed. You mentioned a rumor in your letter that E. K. Smith goes to East Tennessee. It is said that Wise[12] is to come here. When McClelland[13] will [move] depends, I expect pretty much on the roads, which would seem to preclude anything of the kind at present.

This letter may fall into the hands of the Yankees, who published some found at Port Royal not calculated to please the writer at seeing it in print. Love to your children.

Yours[14]

P.S. After living all winter in a tent I am now to go in a very nice house with some furniture—six rooms &c—The one you were to take last fall when you spoke of coming near the lines. Should you come this way as seems to be possible, there is a place near, for us & you could still have it.

My chief reason for writing, outside of general principles, was to say that I cant find Cs keys (key) anywhere. He told me they would be with Turner,[15] but T. says he has not [seen] them. John[16] says C. told him to tell T. that I had them & would turn them over. I have searched everywhere in vain.

1. In November 1862, Ewell assumed command of James Longstreet's former brigade, consisting of the 1st, 7th, 11th, and 17th Virginia infantry regiments. Three months later, he was promoted to major general, his commission dating from January 25, 1862, and placed in charge of the "Reserve Division," formerly commanded by Major General E. Kirby Smith.
2. Ewell's younger brother William Stoddert was then sick and recuperating at the Ewells' farm, Stony Lonesome, which was located approximately ten miles southwest of Centreville.
3. General P. G. T. Beauregard was transferred to the West in January 1862. When Albert Sidney Johnston died at the Battle of Shiloh, Beauregard took command of the Army of Tennessee.
4. The Reserve Division consisted of three brigades commanded by Brigadier Generals Arnold Elzey, Richard Taylor, and Isaac R. Trimble.
5. Ewell deleted the woman's name, perhaps fearing that the letter might be captured.
6. Ewell suffered from dyspepsia (probably a chronic ulcer) throughout his life.

7. Brigadier General Simon B. Buckner (1823–1914) surrendered Fort Donelson to Major General Ulysses S. Grant. Exchanged in August 1862, Buckner fought in the Western Theater and eventually attained the rank of lieutenant general.

8. Grant captured approximately fifteen thousand Confederates at Forts Henry and Donelson.

9. Buckner surrendered Fort Donelson to Grant after his two superior officers, Brigadier Generals John B. Floyd (1806–1863) and Gideon J. Pillow (1806–1878), fled the doomed post to escape capture. Buckner was imprisoned at Fort Warren until his exchange in August 1862. He was promoted to major general later that year and served the Confederacy with honor throughout the war. Floyd died in 1863. Pillow continued to serve the Confederacy, but he was never again trusted with an important command.

10. Lizinka was a member of the Ladies Hospital Association of Nashville and by 1862 was the superintendent of one of the city's military hospitals.

11. Colonel Samuel Garland Jr. (1830–1862), 11th Virginia Infantry, was promoted to brigadier general on May 23, 1862. He died leading his brigade at South Mountain four months later. Brigadier General A. P. Hill succeeded Ewell in command of Longstreet's brigade.

12. Henry A. Wise (1806–1876), a congressman and outspoken defender of slavery, served as governor of Virginia from 1856 to 1860. He served without distinction as a brigadier general in Virginia, North Carolina, and South Carolina, surrendering at Appomattox Court House in April 1865.

13. Major General George B. McClellan (1826–1885) commanded the Army of the Potomac. Slow to move and prone to exaggerate the enemy's strength, McClellan was relieved of command by Lincoln in November 1862. Nominated by the Democratic Party as its presidential nominee in 1864, McClellan ran against Lincoln but was soundly defeated.

14. Ewell did not sign the letter, fearing that it might fall into enemy hands.

15. Thomas T. Turner (1842–1897) of Missouri was a volunteer aide-de-camp on Ewell's staff. In April 1862, after Turner turned twenty-one, Ewell appointed him aide-de-camp with the rank of first lieutenant. Turner became a captain in 1864 and continued to serve on Ewell's staff until the end of the war. In October 1865 he married Ewell's stepdaughter, Harriot Brown.

16. Either John Taliaferro, an aide-de-camp on Ewell's staff, or John Frame, the general's black valet.

90. To Lizinka Brown

Manassa
Mrch 5. 1862

Dear Lizinka;

Yours of 21st Ult.[1] the first I have recd from you since that of the 12th has just arrived. You cannot imagine my anxiety and suspense during these 2 weeks of silence. The same mail brought C's of 25th and his telegraphic despatch asking for 10 days extension came at same time. I told him before starting to take the extension—wrote to him also. I shall telegram him at same time that I send this to stay as much over the ten days as requisite.

You & your all have been at the service of the cause[2] and I consider that I am assisting that in aiding any of our people to secure their means. *That* duty has intense pleasure when at the same time you have the happiness of being with your son. I cannot write of Military affairs, but I think Maj. Hubbard[3] is unnecessarily alarmed for Richmond at this time. Of course the gross blunders of Johnson (A. S.) will cause changes of positions. Wise has been equally unfortunate & his command disgraced at Roanoke.[4]

I wrote daily for 8 or ten days after C. left untill [I] saw that the mails were stopped & Nashville yielded. I could not dream of what had become of you in this long silence. I wrote so that if the mail were inter[r]upted mine were not calculated to throw any light on matters. I merely write a few hurried lines now to try to send them by the morning mail. I am sorry to see you so depressed. If our people are true to the cause they have made there is no fear of the result. But they have not yet begun in earnest—mean demagogism & truculent legislation have marked the course of things. May be we will wake up and the true man will appear. Richmond in the Martial law & other signs seems to show evidence of the right spirit. The cheering news you pray for is shown a little in the safe arrival of the steam ship Nashville.[5]

I judge from the general opinion with some exceptions, that you were right in leaving Nashville. You would have been conspicuous and to some extent possibly might have been insulted. Your property is safer removed. I could not advise you as I was not a disinterested counsellor. It is hard to say what will be the course of events here, but it seems to be the intention to make Richmond as strong as possible. It would be a source of great gratification if you find it in your power, or advisable, to spend part of your time east. Please remember me to Aunt Rebecca & Hattie & C.

I dont write of Army matters lest the letter fall into Yankee hands. But remember that the Country is not safe, in case of occupation by the enemy. Any town is so, comparatively, but in the Country you are subjected to insults from small marauding bands of the enemy and even our own lowest class would take advantage of such times. In a city the enemy always are in organized bodies, commanded by Officers of rank who wish to conciliate. Remember how Stony lonesome was exposed last summer to our own people. Nashville would probably for a day or two be the scene of disorder. Or if a battle had been fought near it might have been sacked.

Remember to leave the country if the enemy advance, even if you were to go back to Nashville. The more out of the way a place, the more exposed to outrage as there is less restraint over the parties who spread around.

I will write again in a few days.

Yours
R. S. Ewell

P.S. When Dr Hancock[6] heard Nashville was abandoned he wrote to me to ask you to his house where you would have a "Virginia Welcome." In case of a crowded state of things in R. such an arrangement might be pleasant for a short time. He urged it orally, since his return.
RSE

1. February 21.
2. In addition to giving her son to the service of the Confederacy, Lizinka had labored at a Confederate hospital and had paid to outfit Company G, 1st Tennessee Infantry, a unit commanded by a relative. The company was called the "Brown Guards" in her honor.
3. Upon fleeing her home in Nashville, Lizinka had taken refuge with Major David Hubbard and his wife, Rebecca, at their home, "Kinloch," in Lawrence County, Alabama. Rebecca Hubbard was a sister to both Lizinka's and Ewell's mothers.
4. On February 8, 1862, Union Major General Ambrose E. Burnside defeated Brigadier General Henry Wise on Roanoke Island, North Carolina, capturing 2,500 prisoners.
5. The C.S.S. *Nashville* eluded the Union blockade and entered Beaufort, North Carolina, on February 28, 1862. Union warships tried to bottle it up there, but the ship slipped past the blockading fleet on the night on March 17 and headed for the open seas, an incident that Assistant Secretary of the Navy Gustavus V. Fox called "a terrible blow to our national prestige." *Official Records of the Union and Confederate Navies* 1:332–35, 7:136–39.

6. Dr. Francis W. Hancock served Ewell first as medical director of his brigade and later his division. Hancock had a residence on Main Street, between Third and Fourth streets, in Richmond. On February 10, 1862, he had returned home on a twenty-day leave of absence due to sickness. Ewell later stayed at Hancock's house while recuperating from the injury he sustained at Groveton.

91. To Lizinka Brown

12 at night—
Manassa
March 7. 1862

Dear Lizinka;

I write with but little hope that my letter will reach you. The confusion attending a move of the magnitude we are making[,] i.e. drawing back all our Army, stores &c. &c.[,] extends of course to the mails. Our wagons start back to-morrow, the men in the afternoon. The move has been going on in the way of send[ing] back stores &c for several days and the enemy, hearing of the move are threatening our front, Or rather what will be our rear. A retreat is said to be impossible without a disaster, so that this requires very careful management and safety consists in keeping the exact moment concealed.

Of course the move is consequent upon the terrible disasters caused by Johnson's bad generalship in Tennessee, our whole position being untenable. We will be stronger, being more concentrated, but much of the state of Va. will be given up to the Yankees and great consternation prevails among the people. Rumor places our new lines on the Raprahannoc [*sic*].[1]

I have received one letter from you and one from Campbell, Yours dated the 21st Ult. I wrote suggesting to C. that it might be economical to bring on a servant and so save $20. a month that he pays for hire.[2] I think Maj. Hubbard was needlessly alarmed about the Yankees as they have not advanced sufficiently to send marauding parties as far as his house & they are not prepared quite yet for hanging for treason. they must conquer some more territory & then confiscation &c will begin in earnest. My only fear is that our people are not sufficiently aroused—that they may only be in a transient state and cool down, before the enticements of peace. You know best what is going on with your people. Here there is much determination being shown and some energy on the part of government. If the people will it[,] the cause is safe. I saw Genl Toombs[3] to-day for the first time. He looks like an able man. I could not talk with him. Love to the family.

Yrs &c[4]

I erase my name for fear this may not get into the right hands.   RSE

P.S.[5]

You may easily imagine Dear Lizinka what anxiety I have felt in the last five weeks on your account and how much I should have liked to have rendered you assistance in your need. I know well that you would think none the better for me if I were to abandon these duties where I am placed. I assure myself often that you are carried away in regard to myself by your anxiety for the safety of myself & C. and that your love for your son is reflected on me. Still in spite of this I cannot help hoping that the future has happiness in store for me. Your expression "in life or death we shall be united" is to me fraught with promise.[6] It has seemed that were our union limited to this world that it would be comparatively valueless. During my life I have looked to knowing you & loving you in another world & your letter supports the thought. You may think I am in my dotage but I cannot weigh my words. We are falling back and it is doubtful when I can write to you again. You are suffering from the acts of fanatics and politicians over which you could not exert any influence and in that are typical of many of our people. where the end of this will be no one can tell. I, who was equally helpless with you have even now been so highly compensated by the past that I sometimes feel fearful of some calamity in the future.[7]

When I invited C. to come on my staff the feeling was, that he being more highly educated & more intelligent than any around me, that I could not do better, and would at the same time, oblige you. After he had been with me for some time I found myself becoming very much attached to him, which had not occurred to me as likely to happen, and then for the first time, the thought flashed over me that possibly what had ever seemed out of the reach of earthly contingencies, might happen and that I might have more interest with you than I could ever have hoped. I dont know that I would so unhesitatingly have asked him to join me, had I looked for such a result, Because I would have had on my conscience the acting from interested motives.

I write all this because I feel nervously anxious to lay every[thing] open to you & I believe were there a thought or act of my life that would cause you to discard me with contempt, I would unhesitatingly disclose it to you. I want to conceal nothing from you. not that I pretend to have lived without great errors, but if I were to conceal my thoughts from you or anything you may *wish* to know, the discovery, *sure to come, sooner* or *later* would bring on me your contempt—worse than death. Hence what you may ask in the past will always be truthfully told you—or the present.[8]

1. On March 8–9, 1862, the Confederate army abandoned its position around Centreville, Virginia, and took up a new line behind the Rappahannock River. The retreat was prompted less by events in Tennessee than strategic considerations in Virginia. The Confederate army, overextended and outnumbered, could not adequately cover Richmond from its Centreville position.

2. Brown returned with a slave named Willis.

3. Robert A. Toombs (1810–1885) was a wealthy Georgia planter. Prior to the Civil War, he had served in both houses of the United States Congress. When the South seceded from the Union, he became secretary of state for the new Confederate States government but resigned from that position in July 1861 to accept command of a Georgia brigade then fighting in Virginia. He left the army in March 1863 after being denied promotion and held no other posts of high responsibility during the war.

4. Ewell's name is blacked out in the original.

5. This postscript is undated and unattached to its original letter. Ewell's reference to five weeks of anxiety on Lizinka's account and to a Confederate withdrawal suggests that the message was written on March 8, 1862, as a postscript to this letter.

6. Lizinka apparently used this expression in her February 21, 1862, letter to Ewell, a document that no longer survives.

7. This obscure passage may refer to Ewell's successful courtship of Lizinka, his military advancement, or both. For a similar expression of caution, see RSE to LE, 10 Aug. 1858, LC (letter 64, this volume).

8. For the second time in this letter, Ewell signed his name and then scratched it out.

92. To Lizinka Ewell

Rappahannock Rail
Road (O&A. R.R.) Crossing.[1]
March 16. 1862

Dear Lizinka;

I have heard once from C. and have received yrs. of the 21st. This is all I have had. I have written innumerable letters which I presume are consigned to the flames ere this. However they were generally written with a view to this chance. We are falling back to Gordonsville,[2] a military necessity after the casualities [*sic*] in Ten[nessee]. Do you expect to remain long at Aunt Rebecca's? I hope not, because you are not as safe as in Nashville. You must not dream of remaining in the country, either in the immediate vicinity of our Army or

Ewell's youngest brother, William, became a Presbyterian minister. "His life was a pure and unselfish one," remembered a relative, his goal being "to do all he could for others." Ewell's sister Elizabeth also devoted her life to God, becoming a novice in the Order of Visitation at Georgetown, District of Columbia, and later serving as the organist at Holy Trinity Catholic Church in Georgetown. (Courtesy of the estate of Lizinka Ewell Crawford Ramsey of Gretna, Virginia, and Stan Aylor)

in the enemy's lines. In a town, however small[,] you are comparatively safe as there are always Officers & more or less discipline & order. But the houses in the country cannot have a guard at each one and they are the prey of any marauding party of 4 or 5 men of either side who choose to plunder. The depredations & outrages committed by this army from Manassa are as bad as though they had been in an enemy's country. Every bad soldier is trying to get off from his company to pillage & maraud[e]. But at Kinloch[3] you are exposed to the marauding expeditions of the Yankees, always worse than where they occupy permanently. Really I would prefer in your case, if you are in the enemy's lines, if I were you, to being in Nashville than where you are. This move is greatly to be deplored. It is one of the worst consequences of the Donalson [*sic*] disasters. Va & Ten. are the wealthiest portions of the South and in losing them we are incurring great losses. When the legislature of Va adjourns 20 days in the most important part of the session to enjoy the xmas holliday & up to this time has enacted no efficient law nor any that is not contradictory towards the laws of the Confederate Congress, When those who hold the power refuse to act, what can be done by the Generals? Should the Secty of war's orders & permits been carried out by Genl Johnston as regards forming Arty & Cavalry this whole Army would have been broken up, except those two branches.[4] You would be surprised to see the amt. of weakness, favoring & time serving exhibited to-wards favorites to the injury of any part of the service. However I did not begin to write to find fault, but to say how much I would like to know where & how you are and how much I sympathize with you in your troubles.[5]

I have William Stoddert with me, whom I brought along to assist me in staff duties, writing &c, but he broke down the first day and has been laid up ever since.

Maj. Green fell from his horse and is laid up with a sprained ancle [*sic*] so I have his services for all the writing I require. Turner is with me & although I am getting along very well I miss C. very much indeed. Large amounts of Stores were destroyed at Manassa as the Rail Road was defective and the delay in the movements of the Army were continued as it was beyond what was prudent, a retreat being always very hazardous.[6]

The Yankees, contrary to our expectations[,] have allowed us to fall back so far without any demonstration although they might have inflicted great injury on us. Volunteers are always undisciplined & hard to manage and offer great advantages to an enemy of enterprise. The first night out Genl Johnston staid at Stony Lonesome having two of his Staff with him. Wm gave him a bottle of fine Madeira wine that he seemed to admire very much. It seemed a pity to leave the old place to be destroyed by the Yankees and to leave old furniture &c hallowed by the recollections of the past to be profaned by their presence. It would be a relief it seems to me, to hear that they had burned the old house down. Wm was very much tempted to do so & I believe it would have been better. He tried to get some white people to go there but failed. If the Yankees continue possession[7]

1. The Orange and Alexandria Railroad crossed the Rappahannock River at Rappahannock Station, now Remington, Virginia.

2. One week after crossing the Rappahannock River, General Joseph E. Johnston withdrew forty miles farther to Gordonsville, where the Orange and Alexandria Railroad joined the Virginia Central Railroad. From there, he was in position to move his army quickly by rail to Richmond. When the army fell back, Ewell's division remained at Brandy Station to hold the Rappahannock River line.

3. Kinloch was the Hubbards' home in Lawrence County, Alabama. Lizinka and Hattie briefly took refuge there after fleeing Nashville.

4. The Furlough and Bounty Act, passed by the Confederate Congress in December 1861, granted a bounty and a sixty-day furlough to all noncommissioned officers and privates who reenlisted for the war. In addition, the act permitted soldiers who reenlisted to form new companies, elect new officers, and even

transfer to other branches of service. Two months later, in February 1862, Virginia ratified a conscription law requiring all men between the ages of eighteen and forty-five not in military service to register for service. Many Virginians in the Confederate army were nearing the end of their one-year term of enlistment. Once they received their discharge, they would be liable to conscription. Rather than wait to be drafted, many soldiers reenlisted under the generous terms of the Furlough and Bounty Act. Infantrymen, in particular, took advantage of the act's provisions to transfer to the cavalry or artillery, which they viewed as preferable to serving in the infantry.

5. Ewell crossed out several lines here.

6. In its retreat from Centreville, the Confederate army left behind a million pounds of food that the Commissary Department had stockpiled at Manassas Junction.

7. The last page of this letter is missing.

93. To Rebecca Ewell

Culpepper Co. Va
May [*sic:* March] 23d 1862—

Miss R. L. Ewell

Dear Becca;

Yours of March 5. just received. I shall copy for Cousin Lizinka Mrs Wright's[1] remarks which may be peculiarly applicable for all I know pro or con. It is highly possible that Lizinka's affairs may be in confusion for a time but if any one survive the shock it ought to be she as her property is in many different shapes.[2] I am sorry that I can only offer sympathy to her, as my means were all lost in the crash. In offering my sympathy I have a very vivid recollection of the kindness shown by Aunt C.[3] on many occasions, more particularly when Paul[4] was a Medical student.

If our people will it, our cause will in all human probability prosper, as any other solution would seem impossible. It is doubtful if you [will] have a fight on the Peninsula.[5] the appearance would seem to be that the Yanks intend turning by water.

I wrote a letter to Ben some time since but received no answer.[6] Does Lizzie still have her great ideas about the "Chivalry"?[7] Here they seem pretty generally to be played out. Very few re-enlisting, none to all intents & purposes and having the best of every thing. Our men are more afraid of them on picket than of the Yanks, As they are always shooting at whatever they see, friend or foe[,] cows or pigs. Please tell Ben that Genl Johnston stayed one night at Stony Lonesome en route here & Wm gave him a bottle of the Madeira which he enjoyed exceedingly, saying it was the best he had almost ever drank. I am now staying at the house of a Mr Cunningham. Very wealthy—splendid estate.[8] He has left his house & most of his furniture with orders to his overseer to apply the torch when the Yanks come. He has left some dozens of wine—Old Madeira that has been kept untill the corks are completely decayed. I tried a bottle of it, but it does not compare with Ben's; Now that it has settled. Old Genl Trimble[9] told me the other day he was pining for a glass of Ma[diera] & I told him to dine with me & I opened the last bottle to his delight. He tried to criticize it, but when I gave its history at which he discovered new qualities. Tell B. not to send me any more unless I call for it. It ought to be buried—If the Yanks come. Love to the family.

R. S. Ewell[10]

Address to me at the Rappahannock.

1. Possibly Jane Wright (b. ca. 1832) of Brentsville, Virginia, the wife of Charles Wright, Prince William County's jailor.
2. In addition to her extensive landholdings, Lizinka had a considerable amount of money invested in gold, stocks, bonds, and personal loans.
3. Harriet Stoddert Campbell, Ewell's aunt and Lizinka's mother.
4. Paul Hamilton Ewell (1812–1831) was Ewell's older brother. Like his father, he pursued a career in medicine. As a boy, Paul was an apprentice to a local physician. He later studied medicine at Columbia College. According to family tradition, he died of typhoid fever after walking from his home in Prince William County, Virginia, to Washington, D.C., and back, a forty-mile round trip that he made by foot in order to save his family money.
5. Rebecca appears to have been staying at Williamsburg, Virginia, at this time. Williamsburg was on "the Peninsula," the extension of land between the James and York rivers.
6. At this time, Benjamin was on the Peninsula serving as colonel of the 32nd Virginia Infantry.
7. A miscreant clipped Ewell's signature from this letter, taking with it the words "great ideas about the." I have relied on Percy Gatling Hamlin, *The Making of a Soldier,* 109, to supply the missing words.
8. Richard H. Cunningham (b. ca. 1799) owned a farm near Brandy Station, Virginia. According to the 1860 census, he owned $75,000 in real estate and $68,000 dollars in personal estate.

9. Isaac R. Trimble (1802–1888), a West Point graduate and a railroad executive, was appointed brigadier general in August 1861. He commanded a brigade in Ewell's division in 1862 until he received a severe wound at Second Manassas. He returned to action as a major general in April 1863 and took command of Major General William D. Pender's division on the second day at Gettysburg. Wounded in Pickett's Charge, Trimble lost a leg and was taken prisoner. He was exchanged in February 1865 but saw no further action.

10. The last letters of the word "family" and Ewell's signature are missing in the original letter, having been cut out by a thief. They have been supplied by the editor.

94. To Joseph Johnston

April 8. 62

Dear General;

There is a rumor that the President has avowed his intention of going to Ten[nes]see since the death of Genl A. S. Johnson.[1] If so he will undoubtedly take Taylor & the La. Brigade. If so I will have too many or too few, here & if events make it possible for me to be of use in the Peninsula, I hope you will not forget me.

All the streams are overflowing & I should take the opportunity to run up to Rapidan[2] to find out more definite information as to the forces &c at Fredericksburg, the officer in command & how far my jurisdiction extends.

Ewell served under Joseph E. Johnston early in the war. Later, Ewell told his brother that if he thought Johnston wanted his services, he "would have gone in spite of every thing. I would be a Captain under him if he were Col. of a Regt." (Library of Congress)

Stuart started his cavalry to day though I did not understand that he was to hurry off any but the one Company to relieve the one at Rapidan, as you mentioned that that Company was to start at once.[3]

Some of the Companies re-enlisted of the 13. Va. claim the right at end of 12 months time to go where they please, to serve in any branch of service. I should like to know of this as the Secty of War Benjamin has so decided & this would break up a Regiment.[4]

Respectfully &–

R S. Ewell—

1. General Albert Sidney Johnston (1803–1862) had been killed on April 6, 1862, at the Battle of Shiloh.
2. The Rapidan River joined the Rappahannock River just above United States Ford. The Rapidan appears to have been the line that divided Ewell's jurisdiction from that of Brigadier General Charles Field at Fredericksburg.
3. General James Ewell Brown "Jeb" Stuart commanded a cavalry brigade in the Confederate army. Johnston had left Ewell and Stuart behind to guard the upper Rappahannock River line in April when he marched for the Peninsula. Within days Johnston ordered Stuart to join him, leaving Ewell with only a token force of cavalry.
4. A reference to the Furlough and Bounty Act. For information on this act, see note 4 to letter 92, this volume.

95. To Lizinka Brown

April 13th 1862

Dear Lizinka;

I write after three days of intense suspense. Contradictory reports have been in circulation in regard to our affairs out west. But a mulatto spy sent into the enemy's lines has just reported that he has been in Washington and that it is reported there among them that Beauregard has been defeated with a loss of 17000 prisoners, his own arm shot off &c. &c.[1] I have not yet told this to C.[2] nor will I do so untill there is some confirmation or better news over the wires. My first care in this is for our country, but who in the country will suffer more than you & in whose suffering will I feel more sympathy than in yours. I do not feel for myself for all of my cares are absorbed in others. While I write I have to be annoyed by staring stupid bores, who are satisfied to be in the room with an Officer of high rank, although he may be a mere ephemeral production of the Prest and who do not care if they bore him or not, so they are not turned out of the room. 14th No news yet. C. went to-day on business to Rapidan & Orange Ct. House. He improves in his duties and is one of the finest, most patient[,] willing, youngsters I ever knew—Brave & cool. It is a shame that I ever came near—even by accident—placing a young man as Asst. Adjt. Genl, but Ferguson[3] has failed to come when he should have been present & though I may & probably will place an older & more mature person in the place I will not risk any younger Officer.

Wm is going to join his regt. He is sick & I am anxious that he shall return with me, as it is somewhat a relief to have him here.

C. wrote yesterday—left his letter open & told me to write & place the strip of paper in his letter. I left it folded around the letter but he did not observe it & sent the letter off leaving my note behind. Hence I inflict this on you, so soon after his, as he gives you all the news. The Yankees say McClelland is going to Richmond from the East, Banks from the West & when they get there, then this R. Road[4] will be repaired & they will have a clear road from Washington to Richmond.

I have not heard from Ben[,] Lizzie or Becca for some time. It is reported that preliminary skirmishing has already begun there.[5]

I wrote with my horse waiting merely to take advantage of William's going to a post office, there being none around here. My last letter from you was dated the (12)? of March.

With love to Hattie & Aunt Rebecca

Yours
R. S. Ewell

1. On April 6–7, 1862, Union Generals Ulysses S. Grant and Don Carlos Buell battled Confederate General Albert S. Johnston's Confederate Army of Mississippi at Shiloh Methodist Church, near Pittsburg Landing, Tennessee. In what was the bloodiest battle of the war up to that point, Grant and Buell defeated the Confederate army and forced it to evacuate Tennessee. The Confederates lost approximately eleven thousand men; Union losses topped thirteen thousand. Johnston was among those killed in the fighting. Beauregard, who took command of the army after Johnston's demise, was not injured.

2. Having seen his mother and sister to safety, Campbell Brown returned to the army in March 1862.

3. Ewell may be referring to Samuel Wragg Ferguson (1834–1917), a twenty-seven-year-old former officer of the 2nd Dragoons who was then serving on

Beauregard's staff. Ferguson accompanied Beauregard to the West and briefly commanded a brigade at Shiloh. By the end of the war he was a brigadier general.

4. The Orange and Alexandria Railroad.

5. At Williamsburg, Virginia.

Chapter 8

Fighting under Stonewall, 1862–1863

For Dick Ewell the first twelve months of the Civil War had been decidedly un-
eventful. Except for the skirmish at Fairfax Court House and his undistinguished
role at Bull Run, he had had little contact with the enemy. That changed on
April 30, 1862, when he led his division across Swift Run Gap into the Shenandoah
Valley. There he came under the authority of Major General Thomas J. "Stonewall"
Jackson. Over the next six weeks Jackson and Ewell engaged Union forces on five
separate occasions. In each instance they emerged victorious.

Jackson, as commander of the Confederate forces in the Shenandoah Valley,
quite properly received credit for the campaign's success. However, Ewell also deserves much credit. His division battled the Federals without material assistance
from Jackson's troops in three of the five battles (Front Royal, Harrisonburg, and
Cross Keys) and played a prominent role in the other two (First Winchester and Port
Republic). In each contest, Ewell was in the thick of the fighting. His courage, good
judgment, and prompt obedience to orders gained him the trust of his men and the
approval of his commander.

In June, Jackson and Ewell left the Shenandoah Valley and joined General
Robert E. Lee's army outside of Richmond. There, in a week-long series of battles
known collectively as the Seven Days, the Confederates succeeded in driving the
Army of the Potomac away from Richmond and saving the capital. The campaign
again showcased Ewell's zest for battle. At Gaines's Mill, the Virginian held his
ground under trying circumstances for several hours while Lee struggled to orches-
trate a coordinated attack. A few days later, at Malvern Hill, Ewell rallied defeated
Confederate troops and led a charge against massed Union batteries.

With the Army of the Potomac at bay, Lee turned his attention to Major General John Pope's Army of Virginia, a hodgepodge force cobbled together from commands defeated by Jackson in the Valley. In July, Pope's army edged south toward
Gordonsville, an important railroad junction near the headwaters of the Rapidan
River. Lee sent Jackson north to block Pope's advance. When the Union general
foolishly divided his forces, Jackson lunged across the Rapidan River, striking Pope's
leading corps at Cedar Mountain. Ewell led Jackson's advance but had only a minor

role in the engagement itself. As he himself admitted, the battle was Jackson's and he alone deserved credit for the victory.

A few days after Cedar Mountain, Lee arrived at the Rapidan with heavy reinforcements. When an attempt to trap Pope between the Rapidan and Rappahannock rivers failed, Lee sent Jackson on a wide turning movement behind Union lines. While Ewell's division screened the movement at Bristoe Station, Jackson captured Pope's supply base at Manassas Junction. Pope belatedly realized that Lee had split his army and hurried northward to crush the Confederates menacing his rear. Jackson pounced on a portion of Pope's passing army at Groveton. In the ensuing battle Ewell was shot in the left knee, an injury that required the amputation of his lower leg and nearly resulted in his death.

For nine months he was out of action. He convalesced first at Millborough Springs, a village in the Allegheny Mountains, and then at Richmond. In May 1863 news reached the capital that a battle had been fought at Chancellorsville. The Confederates had won the battle but had lost Jackson, who died after being mistakenly shot by his own men. Lee took the opportunity to reorganize his army into three corps. James Longstreet continued to command the First Corps; Lee appointed Ewell to lead Jackson's Second Corps; and A. P. Hill headed the newly minted Third Corps. Ewell reported to the army on May 29. Before doing so, he transacted a piece of business that was a quarter-century in the making. On May 26 he married his first cousin, Lizinka Campbell Brown. The love of his youth had finally become his bride.

96. To Lizzie Ewell

Valley of Va
May 13. 1862

Miss Lizzie Ewell

Dear Lizzie;

I have just received your letter with your mournful account of the journey from Richmond. It is useless to cry over spilled milk is I believe an old proverb. You omitted to say where you were staying in Richmond, but I take it for granted you are with the Revd Mr Hoge.[1] I have spent two weeks of the most unhappy I ever remember. I was ordered here to support Genl Jackson pressed by Banks.[2] But the former immediately on my arrival started in a long chase after a body of the enemy; far above Staunton & I have been keeping one eye on Banks & one on Jackson & all the time jogged up from Richmond untill I am sick & worn down. Jackson wants me to watch Banks[,] at Richmond they want me elsewhere & call me off[,] when at the same time I am compelled to remain untill that enthusiastic fanatic[3] comes to some conclusion. Now I ought to be en route for Gordonsville, at this place & going to Jackson at the same time. That is there are reasons for all these movements and whi[c]hev[er] one is taken makes it bad for the others. The fact is there seems no head here although there is room for one or two.[4]

I have a bad head ache, What with the bother & folly of things. I never suffered as much from dyspepsia in my life, and as an Irishman would say[,] I am kilt intirely.

Hate away at the Yankees[:] it will tend to relieve you from your troubles. We seem to be making pretty good head way against them considering we commenced the spring campaign with our army almost broken up[5] and the Yankee forces at the greatest state of perfection they can hope to attain.

I send you above a check for some money. I suppose there is not much to buy in Richmond. The check is for ninety dollars. You had better get it out without delay & I have 150 more there. if Richmond is taken you had better try to get it out. Mr Hoge may help you to do so. Otherwise it may be lost.

Yrs &–
R S. Ewell

1. The Reverend Moses Drury Hoge (1819–1899), a graduate of Union Theological Seminary, was the first pastor of the Second Presbyterian Church of Richmond, which under his influence became the largest church in the Synod of Virginia. He remained pastor there until his death more than fifty years later. During the Civil War, Hoge ran the Union blockade to acquire Bibles and other religious literature for the Confederate army. Lizzie Ewell was a close friend of Hoge's daughters, Mary and Bessie, and often stayed with them in Richmond during the Civil War.

2. Nathaniel P. Banks (1816–1894) had been governor of Massachusetts and a member of the U.S. Congress prior to the war. At the time this letter was written, he commanded a force of nineteen thousand men in the Shenandoah Valley.

3. Jackson, a devout Presbyterian, was zealous in his religious beliefs.

4. On April 30, 1862, Ewell's division crossed the Blue Ridge at Swift Run Gap and marched to Conrad's Store (modern Elkton), Virginia, where he was in position to check the advance of Major General Nathaniel P. Banks's corps up the Shenandoah Valley. Jackson meanwhile disappeared into the Allegheny Mountains to confront another Union force advancing on Staunton, Virginia, from the west. Jackson ordered Ewell to remain in the Valley until he returned.

In Richmond, authorities feared that Banks would detach a portion of his army to augment Major General Irvin McDowell's corps at Fredericksburg. Thus reinforced, McDowell could then march south, join forces with Major General George B. McClellan on the Peninsula, and capture Richmond. To forestall such an occurrence, President Jefferson Davis's military advisor in Richmond, General Robert E. Lee, urged Ewell to unite with other Confederate forces at Gordonsville and intercept any troops that Banks might send to Fredericksburg.

The Eastern Theater of the Civil War. (Courtesy Civil War Trust, www.civilwar.org.)

Ewell would have liked nothing better, but he felt constrained by Jackson's orders to remain in the Valley until Jackson returned.

5. From the effects of the Furlough and Bounty Act.

97. To J. E. B. Stuart

May 14, 1862

Genl J. E. B. Stuart

Dear General;

I have [been] wishing to answer your note but except [by] the tender mercies of the mail which takes from two days to as many weeks to [reach] Richmond there has been no chance. Your Corp[oral] who seems to be a sort of Inspector General of pickets gives me a safe opportunity.[1] Genl Jackson is off possibly "Somewhere" and leaves me standing gaping at the gap[2] while he is after the Yankees. Tell Genl Johnston that this was not in the programme that he gave me when he left. Banks is fortifying at Strasburg and by Genl Jacksons orders I am to proceed down the valley. The Yankees have kept themselves so well posted in the mountains that we have not had many chances. One Reg. of the La Brigade was in a skirmish the other day & killed (left on the ground 13) and brought off 24 prisoners (2 of them wounded[)].[3]

One of my scouting parties came near catching Shields[4] the other day.

Please remember me to Genl Johnston & tell him that I wish he would give me an order to do something or anything.[5] We expected to get Longstreet up here.[6] One of my cavalry companies, Capt. Dulaney's,[7] went to the Manassa Rail Road without seeing a Federal Soldier the day before yesterday & w[o]uld have destroyed two trains but thought it best to wait as one was empty & the other only had wood. he thinks to get one with army stores. Genl Jackson made a great mistake in coming here from Kernstown in not holding the New Market pass over the Massanutta Mtn. He would have kept Banks far down then.[8]

Green is a Captain of Cavalry, so you may depend there is one Caval[r]y Regt. much neutralized.[9] Genl Jackson seems thoroughly convinced that the world is centered in this valley & would keep me here if Richmond & all the Confederacy were at stake.

The best way to communicate through the pickets is to start a letter daily & let the chief of each line receipt on it the hour of acceptance. Remember me to all friends.

Yrs &
R. S. Ewell

1. In April 1862 General Joseph E. Johnston led his army to the Virginia Peninsula, between the James and York rivers, to block the Army of the Potomac's advance on Richmond from Fort Monroe, Virginia. When he did so, he left Ewell's division behind to guard the upper Rappahannock River and to provide a link between Jackson's army in the Shenandoah Valley and Confederate forces at Fredericksburg. Brigadier General J. E. B. Stuart's cavalry remained with Ewell until April 8 and then rode to join Johnston on the Peninsula, leaving Ewell with just two mounted regiments to patrol the river, the 2nd and 6th Virginia Cavalry.

2. New Market Gap.

3. Shortly after leaving for Richmond, Johnston ordered Ewell to support Jackson in the Valley if called upon to do so. Jackson ordered Ewell to cross the Blue Ridge on April 30, 1862, and take up a position at Conrad's Store, where he could check the advance of Major General Nathaniel Banks's corps up the Shenandoah Valley. No sooner did Ewell arrive than Jackson promptly disappeared to fight a Union force in the Allegheny Mountains. Prevented by Ewell from proceeding farther up the Valley, Banks withdrew to Strasburg. He entrenched around the town and sent Brigadier General James Shields's division to reinforce Union troops at Fredericksburg. At Jackson's orders, Ewell cautiously pursued Banks down the Valley. On May 7, the Louisiana Tigers and the 7th Louisiana Infantry fought a small seesaw battle with the 13th Indiana Volunteers and Company B, 1st Vermont Cavalry, near the town of Somerville on the South Fork of the Shenandoah River. The Federals reported losing three killed, five wounded, and twenty-one missing in the action.

4. James Shields (1806–1879), an Irish immigrant and career politician, had been a brigadier general of volunteers during the Mexican War. Wounded at Cerro Gordo, he was brevetted to major general. As a brigadier general in the Civil War, he commanded one of the two divisions in Banks's Department of the Shenandoah.

5. Johnston was Ewell's commanding officer, but after Ewell moved to the Valley they had little communication.

6. According to Captain David F. Boyd of the 9th Louisiana Infantry, Ewell was so disgusted by Jackson's secrecy that he sent Brigadier General Richard Taylor to Richmond to urge President Jefferson Davis to either send an officer to replace Jackson as commander of the Valley District or to appoint a superior officer to oversee his movements. As Taylor was Davis's son-in-law, Ewell hoped that Davis might heed Taylor's advice. Boyd claimed that Taylor persuaded the president to send Major General James Longstreet to take command of

Confederate troops in the Valley, but before the secretary of war could issue the necessary orders Jackson returned to the Valley and began his offensive against Banks.

7. Captain Richard H. Dulaney led Company A, 6th Virginia Cavalry, also known as the Loudoun Dragoons. He later became colonel of the 7th Virginia Cavalry regiment.

8. The Massanutten divide the Shenandoah Valley and can be crossed at just one point, New Market Gap, which lies about halfway down the mountain range's fifty-mile length. After his defeat at Kernstown on March 23, 1862, Jackson fell back to Rude's Hill, where he reorganized his small army. When Banks moved against him there in April, Jackson withdrew beyond New Market Gap to Conrad's Store at the southern end of the Massanutten. Banks promptly seized New Market Gap and pushed the vanguard of his army forward to Harrisonburg.

9. Captain John Shackleford Green commanded Company B, 6th Virginia Cavalry, nicknamed the Rappahannock Cavalry or the Old Guard Cavalry. Ewell had been Green's superior at Fairfax Court House in 1861.

After chasing Union troops through the Allegheny Mountains, Jackson returned to the Shenandoah Valley in mid-May. He intended to unite with Ewell's division and overpower Banks's troops, who were then digging in at Strasburg. On the eve of this enterprise, Ewell learned that Shields's division, comprising fully half of Banks's command, had crossed the Blue Ridge and was marching toward Fredericksburg. Earlier orders from Johnston dictated that if Banks's army crossed the mountains, Ewell was to follow. Ewell was reluctant to obey those orders, however, for he recognized that he and Jackson could accomplish more for the Confederacy by defeating Banks in the Valley than they could by reinforcing Johnston at Richmond. Ewell prepared to obey the distasteful orders, but before doing so he rode to Jackson's camp at Mount Solon, a dozen miles southwest of Harrisonburg. Jackson urged Ewell to remain in the Valley until he could communicate with Johnston. Ewell agreed, thus keeping the campaign alive.

On May 21 Jackson's troops crossed the Massanutten at New Market Gap and united with Ewell's forces near Luray. Their combined army, now numbering seventeen thousand men and fifty guns, proceeded down the Page Valley and on May 23 surprised and overwhelmed a one-thousand-man Union garrison at Front Royal. The Union force (which consisted of the 1st Maryland Infantry, U.S.A., and a small number of other troops) retreated across both forks of the Shenandoah River and attempted to burn the Manassas Gap Railroad bridge behind them. Colonel

Henry B. Kelly saved the bridge by gallantly dashing into the river with his 8th Louisiana Regiment and extinguishing the flames. Lieutenant Colonel Thomas T. Flournoy's 6th Virginia Cavalry then pursued the Federals across the smoldering span and brought them to bay at Cedarville, two miles to the north. In a classic cavalry charge, Flournoy shattered the Union line, hauling in nearly seven hundred prisoners.

The Confederates pushed toward Winchester the following day in an effort to cut Banks's line of communications. Ewell led the Confederate march via the Front Royal Road, while Jackson turned west at Cedarville and headed for Middletown on the Valley Pike. He took with him Taylor's brigade of Ewell's division and the three brigades of his own division. Later in the day Jackson summoned Elzey as well, leaving Ewell with just Trimble's brigade and the 1st Maryland Infantry Regiment. Unsure of Banks's location or intentions, Jackson ordered Ewell to halt at Nineveh and await orders. When Ewell heard fighting on the Valley Pike, he took it upon himself to continue the advance on Winchester.

Ewell reached the outskirts of the town that evening. At first dawn, he sent Colonel William W. Kirkland's 21st North Carolina forward on the Front Royal Road. Union troops, posted behind stone walls, surprised the Tarheels and drove them back, wounding Kirkland. At that point, a heavy fog settled over the battlefield. When it lifted about an hour later, Ewell resumed his attack, sending the 21st North Carolina down the road once again, supported by Colonel John T. Mercer's 21st Georgia on the right and by Colonel Bradley Johnson's 1st Maryland on the left. At the same time, over on the Valley Pike, Jackson sent the Louisiana Brigade against Banks's right flank. The Union line collapsed. Banks rallied his army north of town and led it toward the Potomac River. Fatigued by weeks of fighting and marching, the Confederates did not pursue.

Instead, Jackson directed his army toward Harpers Ferry. For two days he skirmished with Union troops outside the town, but with Federal forces closing in on his rear, Jackson ordered a retreat. On June 1, while Ewell's division held off Major General John C. Frémont's army on the Wardensville Road (Moorefield Pike), the rest of Jackson's army slipped through Strasburg, escaping the Union snare.

98. Undated Account of the 1862 Valley Campaign

. . . as from the War Dept. to move my command to Richmond as the enemy were moving up the Valley[1] & some of my command was on the march for Gordonsville when I received conflicting orders from Genl Jackson & halting those troops already in motion rode all night to Mt. Solon & was directed to retake my position on[2] Luray & be ready to follow the enemy.

On the [twenty-second of May][3] we moved by Luray down the east bank of the Shenandoah & reached Front Royall on the [following day], my Division in advance, Taylor's[,] Elzey's & Trimble's being the order of Brigades, the Md. Regt a detached command leading the whole.[4] Front Royall was occupied by the enemy as an outpost & was attacked & rapidly carried by the advance, supported by Wheat's Tigers.[5] The enemy fell back to some high ground west of both branches of the stream where they posted a battery of Art'y & tried to burn the R.R. bridges. Their efforts were frustrated by the rapid attack of Kelly with the 8th La who wading the stream under a brisk musketry fire dislodged the enemy & secured the crossing.[6]

The enemy was pursued & captured by Brig Genl George H. Steuart with the 2nd & 6th Va. Cavalry[7] & the Md Regt (Inty)[,] Col. Kenley the Com'g Officer having been wounded & taken prisoner. It proved to be the Md Regt of the Northern Army & chance directed that the only Southern Regt from the same state should be instrumental in its discomfiture.[8] Genl Banks was at this time falling back down the Valley via Mt Jackson & Strasburg.[9]

From Front Royall the direct road to Winchester is about 23 miles while there is another route via Strasburg, somewhat longer, there being several roads communicating between the two routes. Our forces started on the direct route next day for Winchester but Jackson's Division was very soon moved across towards Strasburg & a short time after the Genl went by another crossroad in person taking Taylor's Brig. to be soon followed by Elzey leaving me halted ten miles from F.R. with Trimble & the Md Regt, Genl G. H. Steuart taking the Cavalry by still another route & attacking the enemy with boldness & efficiency.[10] By 12 M.[11] there were indications that the troops then near Strasburg were engaging the enemy & pressing them towards Winchester. Without instructions my situation became embarrassing, but I decided after consultation with Genl Trimble & Maj. Brown of my staff, to move on to Winchester. I was soon overtaken by a courier with the usual laconic style of orders from Genl Jackson to move on to[12] Winchester. It was getting late & to move fast I had already commenced Col. Kirkland's 21st N.C. placing his field musicians[13] at the head of his Regt & marching at quick time we reached the enemy's picket post near Winchester about dusk.[14] The Brigade was placed into position & Kirkland & his gallant Regt were thrown forward to press the enemy & develop his position. They were soon engaged & continued to skirmish with the enemy untill day light. I received several messages from Genl Jackson during the night, but as circumstances had in every case changed the condition of things before their arrival, I was forced to follow my own judgement as to Genl Jackson's intentions.

As day dawned I pushed forward Col Mercer & the 21st Ga. to support of Kirkland with[15] Courteny [*sic*] Battery of Art'y com[mande]d on that day by Lt. Latimer.[16] All doubts as to Jackson's intentions were dispelled soon after day break by hearing his Art'y on the Valley pike nearly opposite to my position & I at once pressed my attack with vigor.

Lt. Latimer handled his Art'y with great skill giving the first proof of the skill & ability that marked that young Officer up to the time of his mortal wound at Gettysburg. Kirkland & Mercer pressing the enemy into the town[,] Kirkland's regt suffered severely from the enemy posted behind some stone walls in superior numbers & that Officer being badly wounded the Regt was withdrawn in good order ready to re-engage. Mercer finding the enemy flanking his position also moved back to prevent capture.

A dense fog for a few moments suspended operations but the day cleared off beautifully in a few moments & I prepared to renew my attack with the advantages of better knowledge of his position & forces. Artillery & skirmishers were engaged when we could see that the enemy were being driven through the town from the Valley pike. Jackson had ordered Taylor to charge them with his superb La. Brigade which attack was entirely successfull & the enemy was in rapid retreat. The pursuit was kept up for several miles with the Int'y towards Harper's Ferry some accident preventing the early advance of our Cavalry.[17] Next day we marched near Harper's Ferry where we confined ourselves to a simple reconnaissance.[18] On the [last day of May][19] I moved back to Winchester meeting on my arrival a courier from Col Conner Com'g the 12th Ga. on duty at Front Royal announcing that he had been driven out & urging re-enforcements. The 12th Ga. won on many a bloody field their name for bravery[,] second to none in our Army[,] & I had no suspicion of the personal courage of the Colonel. I attributed his misfortunes to the nervousness from a new & responsible position & without experience in very difficult circumstances.[20] The next day I was moved up the pike towards Strasburg, Winder[21] with the Stonewall Brigade being still at Harper's Ferry. I encamped near Strasburg & was ordered next morning to move on the Moorefield pike where a few miles out[22]

Here Ewell's narrative abruptly ends, the last pages of the manuscript, like the first, having been lost. Jackson's army continued its retreat up the Valley to Harrisonburg, where it turned east and headed toward Port Republic. Between June 6 and 9, it inflicted defeats on its pursuers at Harrisonburg, Cross Keys, and Port Republic. Ewell played a major role in each of the three battles, gaining for himself a reputation as a reliable and resourceful officer. By the time the Valley Campaign concluded, he had indeed become, as General D. H. Hill later wrote, "the right arm of Stonewall Jackson."[23]

1. This is a fragment of a heavily edited draft of a memoir Ewell wrote on the 1862 Valley Campaign. It is unknown when he drafted it. The beginning and end of the document are missing.
2. Here Ewell wrote the word "near" above the line.
3. Ewell left the two dates in this sentence blank.
4. Brigadier Generals Richard Taylor, Arnold Elzey, and Isaac R. Trimble led the three brigades of Ewell's division. In addition, Ewell had command of the Maryland Line, an independent unit led by Brigadier General George H. Steuart and comprising the 1st Maryland Infantry Regiment and the Baltimore Light Artillery.
5. Major Chatham Roberdeau Wheat (1826–1862), a former filibusterer and lawyer, commanded a notorious battalion known as the Louisiana Tigers. Officially designated the 1st Special Battalion Louisiana Troops, the unit included thieves, cutthroats, and other unsavory characters culled from the New Orleans waterfront district. Defending Front Royal were nine companies of the 1st Maryland Infantry (Union), two companies of the 29th Pennsylvania Infantry, two guns of Captain Joseph Knapp's Pennsylvania battery, and a body of pioneers, a force altogether numbering approximately 900 men.
6. Retreating Union soldiers attempted to burn the bridge over the North Fork of the Shenandoah River in an effort to hinder Confederate pursuit. Colonel Henry B. Kelly and the 8th Louisiana Infantry thwarted their plans. The regiment splashed across the river and drove away Union troops on the other side, allowing Jackson to extinguish the flames and save the bridge.
7. Ewell wrote the names of the regiments' commanders, "Flournoy & Munford," above the line here.
8. Ewell pursued the Federal force with Brigadier General George H. Steuart's 1st Maryland Infantry Regiment (C.S.A.), Colonel Thomas Munford's 2nd Virginia Cavalry Regiment, and Lieutenant Colonel Thomas T. Flournoy's 6th Virginia Cavalry Regiment. Flournoy caught up with Colonel John R. Kenly's 1st Maryland Infantry (U.S.A.) at Cedarville, four miles north of Front Royal, and shattered it in a charge that wounded Kenly and resulted in the capture of most of his regiment.
9. Major General Nathaniel P. Banks (1816–1904) commanded a Union force of seven thousand men at Strasburg. The capture of Front Royal by Jackson's

army forced Banks to evacuate his entrenched position at Strasburg and retreat to Winchester so as to maintain his lines of communication and supply.

10. When Banks learned of Jackson's attack on Front Royal, he immediately ordered a retreat to Winchester. Unaware of Banks's intentions, Jackson sent Ashby's cavalry toward Strasburg on the morning of May 24, while Jackson himself led Taylor's brigade of Ewell's division toward Middletown, a few miles farther to the north. He hoped to cut off Banks if the Union general remained in Strasburg or to strike the Union column on the march if he found it was retreating toward Winchester. Meanwhile, Steuart, who that very day had been assigned to command Ewell's cavalry, harassed the enemy at Newtown, north of Middletown. At Jackson's orders, the rest of Ewell's division remained in reserve at Nineveh to await developments.

11. "12 M." stands for 12 o'clock meridian—i.e., noon.

12. Ewell repeated the word "to" here.

13. This word is unclear.

14. Colonel William W. Kirkland (1833–1915) and his 21st North Carolina Infantry marched at the head of Ewell's column. Promoted to brigadier general in August 1863, Kirkland survived three wounds and lived for fifty years after the war.

15. Ewell wrote "Latimer's" here and forgot to cross it out when he later substituted the word "Courteny."

16. Colonel John T. Mercer (1830–1864) led the 21st Georgia Infantry, while eighteen-year-old Lieutenant Joseph W. Latimer (1843–1863) commanded the Courtney Artillery. Latimer had grown up in Prince William County, Virginia, not far from Stony Lonesome.

17. The delay in the Confederate pursuit resulted from stubbornness rather than chance. When the Union line gave way, Jackson sent staff officer Sandie Pendleton to Steuart with orders to give chase. Incredibly, Steuart refused to obey the order because it had not come through Ewell, his immediate superior. By the time Pendleton found Ewell and transmitted the order through him to Steuart, Banks was well on the way to Harpers Ferry.

18. After driving Banks from Winchester, Jackson's weary troops remained at the town for two days, resting and recruiting their strength. On May 27 they continued northward as far as Halltown, a village on the outskirts of Harpers Ferry.

19. Ewell left the date blank here.

20. Jackson had left Colonel Zephanier T. Conner and the 12th Georgia Volunteers at Front Royal when he advanced to Winchester. Conner had orders to secure Union stores captured in Front Royal and to hold the town, thereby protecting

the Valley army's lines of retreat. But when Union troops suddenly appeared at Front Royal on May 30, Conner panicked and fled, leaving a subordinate to extricate the regiment. Jackson promptly cashiered him for his conduct.

21. Brigadier General Charles S. Winder (1829–1862) commanded the Stonewall Brigade. Left back at Harpers Ferry to cover the Confederate retreat, Winder's men marched thirty-five miles in a single day, rejoining Jackson's army at Strasburg on June 1.

22. In an effort to trap Jackson in the lower Valley, President Abraham Lincoln ordered Frémont and McDowell to converge on the Confederates at Strasburg and cut off their retreat. On June 1, 1862, Ewell confronted Frémont on the Moorefield Pike, west of Strasburg, and held him at bay until the rest of Jackson's army had passed safely through the town.

23. *Southern Home* (Charlotte, N.C.), 5 Feb. 1872. John William Jones also used this phrase to describe Ewell. See Jones, "Career," 84.

99. To Lizzie Ewell

July 20. 62
Gordonsville

Miss Lizzie Ewell

Dear Lizzie;

I received a letter from you yesterday in which you speak of your sympathy unnecessarily thrown away on my wound, of writing me several letters &c. I have received two[:] this & one your Father gave me in Richmond. He spoke of coming this way when I left R[ichmond] last Monday.[1] I went to Mr Hoge's while there but he was out. The young lady is not in town I believe.[2]

You write with great satisfaction at my having been in a battle. Are you not aware that I was in all of those in the valley? They were not on as grand scale as those in the Peninsula but were tolerably bloody. It may be all very well to wish young heroes to be in a fight, but for my part I would be satisfied never to see another field. What pleasure can there be in seeing thousands of dead & dying in every horrible agony, torn to pieces by artillery &c. many times the wounded being[3] left on the field for 24 hours before they can be cared for? I wish this war could be brought to a close, but except by the hands of providence I can see no way of its coming to an end. Ben & Wm were both in Richmond when I left there a few days ago—spoke of coming this way. Wm has been transferred to one of the Regts. in my Division[—]58th Va.[—]but he is sick just now.[4] I direct my letters to Cousin Lizink[a] at Littleville[,] Lawrence County[,] Alabama[,] care of Maj. David Hubbard, Via Montgomery[,] Columbus[,] & Tuscaloosa. It is barely possible, but not probable that she & her daughter will come east. she spoke of it in one of her last letters.[5]

I am glad you are out of Richmond.[6] It is not the place just now for refugees there being so many sick & wounded Soldiers and every thing being at such extravagant prices. Of course the fewer there the better. I was sorry to see how frequent the hearses were [rolling] through the streets.[7]

I have been sick with the exposure & malaria of the Chickahominie swamps, as has been a great part of our Army.[8] I hope the Yankees are worse off still. When you & others were doing your best to bring this state of things about, you little thought of these consequences. However I believe the worst portion of the war has fallen on the females. They have nobly borne their portion[,] helping to carry the burden. If I should happen to go in your vicinity you may be sure I will do all I can to see you. I am not taking much pains with this letter because I fear it may not reach you. Your letter did not give your direction, but as it was marked on the outside H & S. Post Office[9] I direct accordingly. I think I shall keep this a few days untill I see your Father or can learn your direction otherwise. Since March I have been almost constantly within hearing of skirmishing, cannon &c. &c. and I would give almost anything to get away for a time so as to have a little rest. I dont know that I ever lived so hardly & so much exposed to every thing disagreeable as during the last few weeks. It is impossible for 20 miles below Richmond to get out of the sight & smell of dead horses. The dead people were pretty much removed, but the Artillery & Cavalry horses killed in the battles lined the roads. The Yankees are now in Culpepper & I learn are systemmatically destroying all the growing crops and every thing else the people have to live on. Sometimes they ride into the fields & use their sabres to cut down the growing corn. They seem bent on starving out the women & children left by the war.[10]

It is astonishing to me that our people do not pass laws to form Regiments of blacks. The Yankees are fighting low foreignors against the best of our people, whereas were we to fight our negroes they would be a fair offset & we would not as now be fighting kings against men to use a comparison from Chequers.[11]

Yrs   RSE—

1. July 14.
2. Probably a reference to either Mary or Bessie Hoge, both of whom were Lizzie's friends.

3. Ewell repeated the word "being" here.

4. William became chaplain of the 58th Virginia in August 1862. He no sooner joined the regiment than he asked for a leave of absence, both to take care of his failing health and to take care of Dick, who was without a staff in the months following his amputation. On April 7, 1863, William resigned from the army because of bronchitis. He took the oath of allegiance later that year.

5. At this time, Lizinka and her daughter continued to reside at the Alabama home of David and Rebecca Hubbard.

6. Lizzie appears to have evacuated Richmond during the Peninsula Campaign and gone to live with friends at Hampden-Sydney, Virginia, where her father earlier had been a college professor.

7. Ewell had visited Richmond after the Seven Days' Campaign.

8. Ewell and many others became sick during the Seven Days' Campaign while fighting in the swampy lowlands bordering the Chickahominy River.

9. Probably Hampden-Sydney, Virginia.

10. Pope's Army of Virginia had been pieced together in the summer of 1862 from the discomfited commands of Banks, McDowell, and Frémont. Pope's bombastic proclamations and his notorious treatment of civilians made him odious to the South. In July he began creeping south toward the vital railroad junction at Gordonsville, Virginia, prompting Lee to dispatch Jackson and Ewell to stop him.

11. According to his cousin Tasker Gantt, Ewell proposed to President Jefferson Davis as early as July 1861 that the South arm its slaves. Davis denied that Ewell ever spoke with him of the matter. The truth may never be known, but this letter makes it clear that Ewell favored arming the slaves at least a year and a half before Major General Patrick Cleburne proposed the same controversial measure.

100. To W. D. Meriwether, Esq.

August 7th, 1862.[1]

W. D. Meriwether, Esq.[2]

Dear Sir,

I could not have believed it possible to be so grieved at the death of one, a short time since a stranger, as I am at the afflicting blow that has removed Major Hugh M. Nelson.[3] His devotion to the cause of his country, his bravery, sense, in short his eminent qualities as a soldier and gentleman, have impressed deeply myself, as well as all those brought in contact with him.

These are mere facts, and the more important as in this war, more than anywhere else, the people stand on their own merit.

His life, under Providence, was sacrificed, I fear, to his too great anxiety to take the field while still under the influence of disease. Major Nelson was at the affair of Strasburg in June, the battle of Cross Keys, Port Republic, and the terrible conflicts below Richmond. It is useless to say that on those days he showed the bravery and devotion to which his descent entitle him; all who knew him need not be informed of this, but I take pleasure in offering a feeble tribute to modesty, worth and patriotism. He received a contusion at Cold Harbor, June 27th, but, except this, escaped uninjured the exposure of the other battles.

Be so kind as to communicate to his family my grief as well for them as for the loss to the country. I make no idle compliments to his memory; my expressions seem to me feeble in conveying my sense of either the official or social loss.

Should my duties permit, I will attend the funeral. My staff will be present.

Yours,

R. S. Ewell

1. This letter was taken from a published source. The original has not been found. I have made some minor editorial changes to bring the style of the letter into conformity with Ewell's other letters.
2. Unidentified.
3. Hugh M. Nelson (1811–1862), a grandson of the Revolutionary War general Thomas Nelson Jr., was a native of Hanover County and a graduate of the University of Virginia. He commanded Company D, 6th Virginia Cavalry, early in the war, but failed reelection in the spring of 1862. In May he joined Ewell's staff as an aide-de-camp with the rank of lieutenant. He served with Ewell throughout the 1862 Valley Campaign and the Seven Days. Nelson contracted typhoid at Gordonsville and died on August 6, 1862, at the home of an Albemarle County relative. Amazingly, he was the only one of Ewell's staff officers to die during the war. A fine sketch of Nelson appears in Johnson, *The University Memorial*, 206–17, from which this letter is taken.

101. To Bradley Johnson

August 13. 62

Col.[1]

It strikes me that you would make a first rate Provost Marshall & would give you a recommendation to Genl Jackson. I am much in want of an Officer in that capacity but you ought to have higher rank than I could get you and I will *warmly* help you with Longstreet, Jackson, or anyone else.

I have no Inspector Genl[,] Lt. Col. J. M. Jones being in such bad health as to be incapable of performing the active duties of the field.[2] Can you help Randolph[3] in getting up his Comp'y? What will be done with your mounted men? I am extremely in want of Cavalry. I can write a stronger letter to the Sec'y of war if you wish. Yrs &[c] R. S. Ewell

M G.

1. Bradley T. Johnson (1829–1903) led the 1st Maryland Infantry in both the Shenandoah Valley and the Seven Days campaigns. When the regiment disbanded on August 17, 1862, Johnson found himself without a command. Ewell wrote to Secretary of War Judah Benjamin seeking Johnson's promotion to brigadier general. Jackson endorsed Ewell's letter. In the meantime, Ewell offered to appoint Johnson provost marshal of his division or to seek a similar position for him on either Jackson's or Longstreet's staff, either of which would come with a higher grade than Ewell could offer. Johnson thanked Ewell for his offer but replied that a staff position would not suit him, asserting, "He had left his home to fight." Johnson later reconsidered. "I concluded to disband the Regiment at once," he explained, "and serve with Ewell in the approaching Battle; then go to Richmond and see the authorities. This dulls the edge of going out of the field on the eve of Battle & I'll get the credit for it." Just before the Battle of Second Manassas, Jackson placed Johnson in command of a brigade in William B. Taliaferro's division. Johnson memoirs, box 5, Miscellany, p. 163, Duke University.
2. John M. Jones (1820–1864) came to Ewell's staff as assistant adjutant general in April 1862 and by June was the division's acting inspector general. Despite Jones's ongoing battle with alcoholism, Lee gave him the command of a brigade early in 1863. Jones led his brigade gallantly throughout the coming months, suffering wounds at both Gettysburg and Mine Run. He died in battle on May 5, 1864, in the Wilderness.
3. Captain William F. Randolph (1831–1914), an officer in the 6th Virginia Cavalry, had been detailed to special service under Ewell. At the time of this letter, he was raising his own company, a unit that became Company B of the 39th Battalion Virginia Cavalry. Randolph was its captain. After the Civil War Randolph worked for Ewell, managing a Mississippi cotton plantation called "Tarpley."

102. To Lizzie Ewell

Augst 14. 1862—

Miss E. Ewell

Dear Lizzie;

Yours of Augst 3 just Recd. I happen to have a leisure moment & hasten to answer it. Your letter is a commentary on fame if one were after that. I was in every battle in the Valley, commanded at one[1] & inflicted the severest blow on the Feds they had & yet you say you were aware I was in some &c. As for risk[,] I was in fully as much if not more than in the Peninsula. The paper you wrote on could hardly[,] as you say, been captured by your Pa, at Malvern Hills.[2] It resembles this very much which was taken near Charlestown in the Valley. You ask for a trophy from the Peninsula. Some of our men took some writing cases and in one was the enclosed needle case which is more appropriate than covering oneself with coarse brass buttons. Since your letter was written we have had a fight near Culpepper Ct House as you will doubtless see by the papers.[3]

I fully condole with you over the gloomy prospects in regard to the war. Some 100 000 human beings have been massacred in every conceivable form of horror with three times as many wounded, all because of a set of fanatical abolitionists & unp[r]inciple politicians, backed by women in petticoats & pants[4] and children. The chivalry that you were running after in such frantic style in Richmond have played themselves out pretty completely, refusing in some instances to get out of the State to fight. Such horrors as war brings about are not to be stopped when people want to get home. It opens a series of events that no one can see to the end. I had a letter from your Aunt Becca in Balt. She has been very kindly treated but says she would prefer living South. She complains that Martha became insupportable & that she was forced to leave the place. There is no doubt that she will be a much warmer Southern person than she was while down South. She evidently writes under constraint—says Mr Reynolds is a "Government Man".[5] Your Uncle Wm has not made his appearance as yet nor do I expect to see him as long as he is coming every day. The worst is he has my bathing tub which puts me to a great deal of inconvenience.

Give my remembrances to all friends[,] Miss Hoge included.[6]

Yours—

R. S. Ewell

1. The Battle of Cross Keys on June 8, 1862.

2. Benjamin Ewell served as the 32nd Virginia's colonel until May 1862, when he was dropped from the regimental rolls. It is unknown whether he saw action at Malvern Hill, a battle fought outside of Richmond on July 1, 1862.
3. The Battle of Cedar Mountain was fought on August 9, 1862, at a point six miles south of Culpeper Court House.
4. "Women in . . . pants,"—i.e., cowardly men.
5. Ewell's oldest sister, Rebecca (1808–1867), was living in Williamsburg when the Civil War began. She left Virginia's colonial capital in 1862 and moved to Baltimore, where she apparently took up residence for a time with the Reynolds family. William Reynolds, Dick's friend and financial agent prior to the war, supported the Union. Martha has not been identified.
6. Bessie Hoge (ca. 1845–?), the seventeen-year-old daughter of the Reverend Moses D. Hoge, was Lizzie's close friend.

103. To Lizinka Brown

Sunday
Near Orange Ct. House
Augst 17. 1862

Dear Lizinka,

We moved this way yesterday as the papers will tell all about it before this reaches you. I will merely mention the movement. Our march yesterday was longer than necessary and made more laborious by our being forced to follow a long wagon train which was alternately stopping & going on untill although we had but 12 miles to march it was sometime after dark before we got into camp. My wagons were far behind & suffering from a cold caught at Cedar Mtn. fight &c I sent to a house near by for accommodations, which was cheerfully granted. I laid down on a bed with but one blanket & after a while C.[1] woke me up to come to supper which I declined. I was very cold at night and woke up several times wondering where C. was & thinking of looking for him. When morning came there was C. shivering under another blanket about two feet off. He had come in so quietly as not to wake me and thinking I was comfortably fixed had remained the reverse himself. We are laying by to day as it is Sunday.[2] I am not well enough to care about going to Church. I asked C. if there were anything in his sister's letter to answer but he said nothing except to acknowledge the receipt of it.

date (July 26th). For a few days we have had weather sufficiently cold to make fires agreeable. I find that my long sojourn in N.M[3] has made me very fastidious in regard to climate. There a diary of the weather for one yr would answer for 1 out of 20. with few variations. Though there is a great variation between day & night they are respectively the same at same season.

I am sick & stupid & you wonder doubtless why at such a time I write such foreign matter but the possibility or probability is that in a day or two we shall be engaged on a grand scale & the God of Battles alone knows the result. I hope & pray that your child may be spared. If God sees fit that it be otherwise, you should remember his virtues, his religion, his merits as reasons which besides Revelation ought to make you hope it is for the best, should he be selected.

I had a paper[4] from which I proposed cutting some extracts describing our late fights but some one has borrowed it. possibly I may find it yet. It gives a pretty fair acct of the fight except that they sent a flag of truce to ask permission to bury their dead & they lost about 2000 in killed & wounded & us less than 1000.[5] Where the printed account speaks of Ewell[,] Jackson ought to be substituted. My Division[,] being in advance[,] movements &c were attributed to me that in effect were Jackson's. Early,[6] Trimble & the 8th La. (Hays) were in my Division. Early acted separately. The 8th La Brigade is to be commanded by Brig Genl Hays but he is absent wounded.[7]

Accident has caused these details to go to you but in fact, I have not had any more or as much to do with this as the other battles that have come off lately. I thought as chance th[r]ew the sketch[8] in my way it might interest you and Hattie. I wish I could send you one of Cross Keys.[9] However we will probably have such shining events before long that this will be forgotten.

I dont know why but I am much better since commencing this letter and had I time would inflict you with a letter of tremendous proportions. We have been waiting so anxiously for Bragg's movements to clear your way to Nashville & give us to the Ohio River.[10] Johnston said his Army is inferior in discipline to any and poorly shod. It is not true that Johnston has reported for duty & been assured a command by the President. He is still sick from his wound but when well will probably have an important command in Va.[11] Lee is gradually assuming the highest portion with us. He has no newspaper puffers & therefore his fame is on more solid foundation.

I hope Buckner will come out with a true statement of Fort Donelson and either acquit or expose Pillow & Floyd. However they both seem to be forgotten.[12]

The Maj. Alford Moss mentioned as a Prisoner and an Aid of mine was an agent of the Commissary Dept. & held no commission at all.[13] They make a point of arresting every one they can lay their hands on, whether they are mistaken or not. General Early is an excellent Officer[—]ought to be Maj. Genl.

He is dissatisfied as well he may be and talks sometimes of going out to join Bragg. He is very able & very brave & would be an acquisition to your part of the world.[14] The statement that we fired chains & railroad iron & that our cannon exploded is all fabrication. Genl Prince[15] U.S.A. was taken prisoner but was not wounded. Bayard's[16] miraculous escape from Madison Ct House is an entire romance founded on Yankee fears. we sent no forces in that direction at all & he might have stayed untill now.

Yours RSE

1. Campbell.
2. An ardent Christian, Ewell's superior, Stonewall Jackson, refused to march on Sundays unless required to do so by military exigency.
3. New Mexico, where Ewell had served in the regular army prior to the Civil War.
4. He added the words "Balt. Amer." above the line here—i.e., the *Baltimore American.*
5. At the Battle of Cedar Mountain, Federal casualties, including those captured, numbered nearly 2,400. Confederate killed and wounded totaled just short of 1,300. The number of captured and missing Confederates was not reported.
6. Brigadier General Jubal A. Early (1816–1894) had taken command of Elzey's brigade following the latter's wounding at Gaines's Mill. At Cedar Mountain, Early found himself separated from the rest of Ewell's division by Cedar Run. He skillfully repulsed several heavy Union attacks against his line. Early inherited Ewell's division six weeks later at the Battle of Antietam and in May 1864 succeeded Ewell in command of the Second Corps.
7. Brigadier General Harry T. Hays (1820–1876) began the war as colonel of the 7th Louisiana Infantry and was promoted to brigadier general on July 25, 1862. Seriously wounded at Port Republic, he did not take command of the Louisiana Brigade until September. In the interim Colonel Henry Forno led the unit.
8. "Sketch"—i.e., newspaper article.
9. The Battle of Cross Keys, fought on June 8, 1862, was one of several engagements in Jackson's Shenandoah Valley Campaign.
10. In August 1862 General Braxton Bragg invaded Kentucky in an effort to draw Union troops out of Tennessee. The campaign ended unsuccessfully on October 8, 1862, when Major General Don Carlos Buell fought Bragg to a standstill at the Battle of Perryville.

11. General Joseph E. Johnston had been wounded twice at Seven Pines on May 31, 1862. He returned to active duty in November as commander of the Department of the West.

12. Simon B. Buckner surrendered Fort Donelson to Union forces in February 1862, opening the Cumberland River to Union gunboats. Prior to the surrender, Buckner's superiors, Brigadier Generals John B. Floyd and Gideon J. Pillow, fled with some two thousand defenders, leaving Buckner to hand over the fort. The Federals exchanged Buckner shortly before Ewell wrote this letter, and he was promoted to major general on August 16, 1862.

13. Alfred Moss (ca. 1816–1862) was clerk of the Fairfax County Court at the outset of the war. A member of the Virginia legislature, he sat as a delegate in the state's Secession Convention. With Virginia's entry into the war, Moss became a volunteer aide-de-camp, first to Brigadier General Milledge Bonham and later to Ewell. Moss was captured in the summer of 1862 and contracted a fatal case of jaundice while in prison.

14. Ewell had a high opinion of Early and lobbied for his promotion to major general while convalescing in Richmond during the winter of 1862–63. Early finally received the promotion on April 23, 1863.

15. Brigadier General Henry Prince (1811–1892) commanded a Union division at the Battle of Cedar Mountain, where he was captured. Released from captivity in December 1862, he went on to command troops in North Carolina, Virginia, and Tennessee.

16. Brigadier General George D. Bayard (1835–1862) commanded a cavalry brigade in Pope's Army of Virginia. An officer of promise, Bayard was mortally wounded by an artillery shell on December 13, 1862, during the Battle of Fredericksburg.

Less than three weeks after his victory at Cedar Mountain, Jackson engaged the Federals at Manassas, the same ground where Confederate forces had defeated the Army of the Potomac one year earlier. In the opening engagement of the 1862 battle, a bullet crashed into Ewell's left knee, shattering the joint and necessitating amputation. For several days it appeared the general might not survive. But Ewell doggedly held on to life and by late September was well enough to travel to Millborough Springs in the Allegheny Mountains. The cool mountain air aided his recovery, and in November, with winter coming on, he was moved to a house in Richmond. Lizinka joined him there and nursed him to health. The love between them grew, and when Ewell returned to the Army of Northern Virginia in

May 1863 he brought Lizinka with him as his bride, quaintly introducing her to amused acquaintances as "my wife, Mrs. Brown."

104. To Jubal Early

Jany 7. 1863

Genl Jubal Early

Dear Genl;

I received your two letters one directed to Millwood & the other to this place written a few days of each other.[1] I was more pleased than surprised at the gallant conduct of your Division in the battle of Fredericksburg as well as Sharpsburg. The letters only arrived a few days since & a very severe accident I met with on Christmas day prevented my answering them sooner.[2] The injustice you & Col. Walker[3] have suffered has been a source of constant anxiety to me & I should already have made efforts to have it repaired but the absence of the President & the injury I have suffered have prevented me. I intend to go to work to have it corrected as soon as I am able with strong hopes of success, but what ought to be most gratifying to you is that the injustice in your case is almost universally recognized. An Officer of high rank in your Division told me the other day they had just discovered they had a trump & the Country is fast arriving at the same Conclusion.[4] I heard some Tennesseans wish you had been in command in E. Tenn. when the Yankees made their raid to Jonesboro as they might not then have found it so easy to get there nor so easy to get away.[5]

As to Adj. Generals I have heard nothing of Barbour[6] since August & think by proper representations you could easily have him dropped. You have a perfect right to recommend your own Adj. Genl & if you recommend Col. Jno. E. Johnson,[7] John Allen[8] or J. Gratten Cabble[9] either of them would suit me very well, but if you choose some of your own particular favorites, you must not expect to saddle me with your bad bargains hereafter.[10] If you have a copy of your report of Cedar Run Mountain I wish you would send it to me.[11] I cannot find a copy of my own report & fear it has been taken West by mistake,[12] A matter of little consequence however as they say Jackson never hands in any reports.[13] You grumble, verbally by Turner and also by letter, at not being Maj. Genl as everybody says you ought to be & you have command of a Division & are likely to retain it for some time as I am still on my back. From the best data [it] is thought Bragg has given the enemy a severe check in the West,[14] but persons who expect impossibilities are disappointed & disposed to disparage the advantage acquired. I am more anxious about Vicksburg & the Miss. River and other military operations at this time.[15]

I would be glad to hear from you when you have time to write.

Yrs. &c

R. S. Ewell

1. After being wounded at Groveton on August 28, 1862, Ewell recovered at Millborough Springs in the Allegheny Mountains, a resort that he mistakenly refers to here as Millwood. In November he moved to Richmond and continued his convalescence at the home of Dr. Francis Hancock, the former medical director of his division.

2. According to Dr. Hunter McGuire, Ewell "was so unlucky as to let his crutches slip from under him, and falling upon an icy pavement, he re-opened the wound and knocked off another piece of bone." *Medical and Surgical History,* 2:242.

3. Colonel James A. Walker (1832–1901) of the 13th Virginia took command of Early's brigade in September 1862 and had led it successfully at the Battle of Fredericksburg. Early and Ewell thought highly of Walker and recommended his promotion.

4. Walker and Early had been passed over for promotion despite stellar performances on the battlefield. For Ewell's high opinion of Early, see RSE to LCB, 17 Aug. 1862, LC (letter 103, this volume).

5. As the new year dawned, Union cavalry had made a raid into western Virginia and North Carolina, burning bridges on the East Tennessee and Virginia Railroad between Jonesboro, North Carolina, and Bristol, Virginia.

6. Major James Barbour of Culpeper County, Virginia, had been a member of the Virginia state legislature prior to joining Ewell's staff as assistant adjutant general on April 29, 1862. He served with Ewell until the general's wounding at Groveton, after which he returned to the political arena to run for senator.

7. John E. Johnson had been colonel of the 9th Virginia Cavalry. When Johnson failed reelection in April 1862, Ewell requested that Adjutant General Samuel Cooper appoint Johnson as his senior assistant adjutant general. Meanwhile, he joined Ewell's staff as a volunteer aide-de-camp. When his appointment to AAG fell through, Johnson left the army.

8. Unidentified.

9. John Grattan Cabell (1817–1896) had been lieutenant colonel of the 4th Virginia Cavalry. Trained in medicine, he served as superintendent of Jackson Hospital in Richmond from 1862 to 1865.

10. On March 24, 1863, Early appointed Major John Warwick Daniel to be his assistant adjutant general.

11. Early's report of the Battle of Cedar Mountain appears in *OR* 12(2):228–33.

12. By Campbell Brown, who temporarily joined General Joseph E. Johnston's staff during Ewell's convalescence.

13. Active campaigning prevented Jackson from writing reports for most of his 1862 campaigns until the army went into winter camp. Lieutenant Colonel Charles J. Faulkner drafted reports for each of the battles, and Jackson then edited them for accuracy. Jackson submitted most of his reports by the start of the spring 1863 campaign.

14. Between December 31, 1862, and January 2, 1863, Bragg's Army of Tennessee unsuccessfully attacked Major General William S. Rosecrans's Army of the Cumberland near Murfreesboro, Tennessee. The battle, sometimes known as Stones River, resulted in thirteen thousand Union and ten thousand Confederate casualties. Unable to defeat Rosecrans, Bragg withdrew toward Shelbyville.

15. Confederate control of Vicksburg, Mississippi, was the primary obstacle preventing the Union navy from gaining full control of the Mississippi River. In December 1862 Major Generals Ulysses S. Grant and William T. Sherman moved against Vicksburg. Sherman suffered defeat at Chickasaw Bluffs, and Grant had to withdraw when Confederate horsemen severed his line of supply. The two men renewed their campaign against Vicksburg the following year and captured it on July 4, 1863.

105. To Jubal Early

R[ichmon]d Va
Jan 26th 63

General Early[1]

Dear Sir

I received your letter with the enclosed report. I have not been able to do anything with them yet on account of circumstance[s] over which neither I nor the Doctors had any control. And I write rather to congratulate you on your long-merited and long delayed promotion.[2] My only regret is that I had nothing to do with it except talking.

Your name went up with Trimbles and Wheelers[3]—no others I believe. And I hope that the Senate has before this acted upon them. I saw General Kirby Smith some days ago. He went to take command of West La & Texas, a sort of head over Magruder & Taylor.[4] But it is reported that he was telegraph[ed]

Fellow Virginian Jubal A. Early was Ewell's close friend early in the war. Early's appointment to command the Second Corps in 1864, however, created a rift between the two men that never healed. (Library of Congress)

while "en route" to return with the object of stationing him in N.C. There is no certainty about this however.[5] G. W. Smith looks better than he has done since the beginning of the War. He is still in N.C.[6] You see from the papers how the Horse Marines are distinguishing themselves in the West.[7] I cannot help hoping, that Rosencranz is getting on short commms[8] and that he will have to fall back.[9] But I know nothing except what I see in the papers.

I have been on my back ever since Christmas.[10] I hope in two weeks at most to be able to get up. On dit,[11] that Gen Harris, has written to his Congressmen here imploring them to get 30,000 additional men and——a general.[12] Bragg seems to be filling the place of scapegoat just now.[13] There is a Col Brewer from Kentucky[14] who comes here every day who is anxious to get a Kentucky Cavalry Regt into service for one year. He says that if they are received, a large number will join us from that State. He has brought the men out with him but as yet has not been able to get them accepted for a less time than the War or 3 yrs.

> I am sincerely
> R. S. Ewell

1. This and Ewell's January 30, 1862, letter to Early are not in his handwriting. They appear to have been transcribed at Ewell's dictation by his brother William Stoddert.
2. Early was promoted to major general on April 23, 1863, to rank from January 17, 1863.

3. Joseph Wheeler (1836–1906) commanded the 19th Alabama Infantry Regiment early in the war and later led a brigade at Stone's River. His promotion to major general dated to January 20, 1863.

4. After a lackluster performance on the Peninsula, Major General John B. Magruder was sent to command the District of Texas. In July 1862, Richard Taylor had been promoted to major general and sent to Louisiana, where, as a lieutenant general, he commanded the Department of East Louisiana, Mississippi, and Alabama.

5. Kirby Smith went west in January 1863 to take command of the Trans-Mississippi Department.

6. Major General Gustavus Woodson Smith (1822–1896) had fought with, and briefly led, the Confederate army in Virginia. After Robert E. Lee took command of the army in June 1862, Smith became commander of the Department of Richmond and later the Department of North Carolina and Southern Virginia. He resigned his commission in February 1863.

7. A "Horse Marine" describes either a marine serving in the cavalry or a horseman on a ship. The term dates from 1836 when a party of Texas Rangers used subterfuge to capture a Mexican supply vessel. The expression was later used to describe someone who was out of place in his surroundings.

8. This scribbled word is possibly an abbreviation for commissary stores.

9. William S. Rosecrans (1819–1898) commanded the Union Army of the Cumberland, then located near Murfreesboro, Tennessee.

10. Ewell had suffered a bad fall on Christmas Day, injuring the stump of his amputated leg.

11. The meaning of this expression is unclear.

12. Perhaps a reference to Colonel David B. Harris (1814–1864), a Confederate officer who served for much of the war under General Beauregard, often as his chief engineer. Harris died of yellow fever on October 10, 1864, at Summerville, South Carolina.

13. Following the Battle of Stones River, or Murfreesboro, Bragg's officers sought to remove him from command. But Jefferson Davis had a high regard for Bragg and stood by him. After Bragg suffered defeated at Chattanooga, however, Davis realized that his friend could not remain in command and transferred him to a desk job in Richmond.

14. Lieutenant Colonel James F. Brewer served as a volunteer aide-de-camp to Major General John C. Breckinridge.

106. To Jubal Early

R[ichmon]d Va Jan 30th 63

General

Will you forward this letter to Chilton[1] at the same time that you send up Greens application for a longer leave.[2] As you see it is a request for a favorable consideration of the application, and I hope that you will feel inclined to assist it.

I wrote a strong letter about Walker and also got one from Elzey.[3] These papers are now in the hands of Staples & Baldwin[4] who are interesting themselves very much in the matter. . . . This is all that I can do as my health has not sufficiently recovered to enable me to get about.

As soon as you find out about Greens leave please let me know as I want to telegraph him.

I am Respectfully
R. S. Ewell

Major Genl Early. (By W. Stoddert)[5]

P.S. If you can help Green in this matter, I will be very much obliged to you, as I feel under obligations to him in more ways than one.

1. Robert H. Chilton (1816–1879) was then serving as General Robert E. Lee's chief of staff.

2. Benjamin H. Green of Mississippi (1826–1890) had been Ewell's chief commissary officer. He continued in that position when Jubal Early took command of Ewell's division. Green had taken a leave of absence on January 9, 1863, and was granted a fifteen-day extension on February 25, 1863.

3. Arnold Elzey (1816–1871) had commanded a brigade in Ewell's division prior to his wounding at Gaines' Mill. After a lengthy convalescence, he was promoted to major general and placed in command of the Department of Richmond. At Ewell's request, Elzey wrote a letter to the War Department supporting Colonel James A. Walker's promotion to brigadier general. Walker, who was colonel of the 13th Virginia Infantry Regiment, had commanded brigades at both Antietam and Fredericksburg. He received the promotion on May 15, 1863.

4. Waller R. Staples and John B. Baldwin both served as Virginia delegates in the Confederate Congress. Earlier in the war, Baldwin had been colonel of the 52nd Virginia Infantry Regiment.

5. Stoddert penned this letter for his brother, who dictated it to him.

107. To Jubal Early

March 8. 63

Genl Early

Dear General;

I have been wishing to write to you but put it off, first because I could not sit up & since because I have had some little to do.

I was much obliged to you for your offer to take Brown on your staff, but before that he had a chance to go with Genl Johnston to his native hog & hominy in Ten. and took advantage of it. His Mother rather wanted him to stay in Richmond but he declared he would go to Fredericksburg & apply to you rather than stay here.[1] My leg is nearly healed over but I am unable to use a wooden leg yet or to keep it long in a vertical position. When I am fit for duty they may do what they please with me, but I think your claims to the Division, whether length of time or hard service be considered are fully equal, if not superior to mine. I dont presume they will interfere with you. What is very certain is that I wont ask for any particular duty or station but let them do as they see proper with me.

I have heard nothing more of Walker's case.[2] the President is sick, but if I get a chance I will talk to him in person.

A great deal of fault is found with Western Va. management, & Johnston wants some one in Eastern Ten. I don't feel up to an [*sic*] separate command, but if you get tired where you are, either of them, I should think would off[er] more greater room for exertion than where you are.

Efforts have been made by some of the politicians to have A. P. Hill[3] sent out West. A good move if they send troops with him as a Majr Genl, but I doubt if [*sic:* it] would answer to supersede Bragg & the rest "to the Manner born."

I commenced this to send by Lieut. Smith[4] of Jackson's staff but since commencing it Majr Green made his appearance & I have concluded to send it by him. I send the report of Cedar Run Mtn by Smith. it is hastily drawn up and is very barren, merely giving the shortest possible notice of events. You may find it worth your time to read over my report & make any correction you may see fit.

Should Genl Jackson or Lee in your presence make any inquiries as regards my health, you will oblige me if you will say that my leg is not yet healed. I am not allowed to ride on horseback yet but drive out a little. I am sitting up to write though it is not pleasant & I have [to] lay down occasionally to rest. Now if they want such[5] services as can be got out of one in that fix I would be most happy to render them untill able to do better.

I was in hopes that the war might be brought to a close before the end of the spring but I have lost all hopes of that. I don't want to see the carnage & shocking sights of another field of battle though I prefer being in the field to any where else as long as the war is going on. Capt. Brown was here with Dispatches from Genl Johnston a few days since. He speaks in very encouraging terms of the improvement in Bragg's Army. Pillow[6] is acting as General of the Conscript Catchers and is doing remarkably well sen[d]ing in crowds every day. It is well they can find something for him to do besides mischief.

I suppose you know my Brother B.S.E. is on Johnston's Staff.[7] I was very glad when he went back to military duty again. The main point of interest here now is the interest people take in getting the refugees out of town. The high price of provisions (Turkeys $15, chick 5, &c) is the chief reason of the endeavors on the part of the citizens & I must say that I cannot blame them. There are enough Quarter Masters, commissaries & their clerks here to form a Regt and it would puzzle a wiser man than myself to say what good one half of them do.[8] Their Depts. are very poorly conducted as far as I can judge from what I hear & they all seem to have two or three clerks.

I am writing about as much at my ease as you can imagine any person would if their foot was being pinched & twisted and cramped occasionally.[9] This must be my excuse for writing nothing worth reading, only to show that my intention is good. Please let me hear the Army news from where you are.

Yours &

R S. Ewell

P.S. I told Green if any ructions are cut up about his being absent to hand in his resignation & I will re-appoint him when I am [fit] for duty.

R.S.E.

1. Campbell Brown accompanied Ewell to western Virginia in September 1862 following the general's wounding at Groveton. In November he traveled to Tennessee to retrieve some items from the family farm, returning to Richmond the next month. As Ewell was still in no condition to return to active duty, Brown in March 1863 accepted a position on the staff of General Joseph E. Johnston, who had recently taken command of the Western Department. Early's offer to take Brown onto his staff arrived just after the young man started to Tennessee to join Johnston.

2. Both Ewell and Early were actively lobbying for the promotion of Colonel James A. Walker at this time.

3. Major General Ambrose Powell Hill (1825–1865) led a division in Jackson's Second Corps.

4. James Power Smith (1837–1923) served on Stonewall Jackson's staff as an aide-de-camp, a position that he retained under Ewell. On December 7, 1863, Smith left Ewell to become inspector of Brigadier General Cullen Battle's brigade.

5. Ewell repeated the word "such" here.

6. Following his censurable conduct in abandoning his troops at Fort Donelson, Brigadier General Gideon Pillow was never again given a position of trust by the Confederate government. At this stage of the war, he was serving the South as a conscription officer in his home state of Tennessee.

7. Benjamin Ewell had been appointed colonel and assistant adjutant general to General Joseph E. Johnson on November 24, 1862.

8. Food shortages in the capital would soon lead to a riot by Richmond's women. For a discussion of this episode, see McPherson, *Battle Cry of Freedom*, 617–18.

9. Ewell may have been experiencing phantom pains from his amputated limb.

108. To P. G. T. Beauregard

Richmond Va.
May 9th 1863

Genl G. T. Beauregard

Dear General;

I have heard from every one such strong expressions of feelings in regard to yourself & hopes that some thing may be done to bring you to this scene of operations that I cannot help thinking you would be gratified at the knowledge of such wishes. R. E. Rodes of Ala whose promotion to Brigr Genl was much owing to your efforts has greatly distinguished himself & been made Maj. Genl, thus vindicating your recommendation. He seems after Jackson to be the hero of the fight.[1]

After the glorious results at Charleston[,][2] hardly less important than Fredericksburg[,][3] it seems to be hoped that you will again be in the field. I dont know what is the plan for the future but troops are going on to Genl Lee & some speak of a forward movement. Your name with the army would be a tower of strength & it seems to be felt that your mission at Charleston is completed.[4]

I know that powerful efforts are being made to remove Pemberton & that you are looked to as the one to succeed him in the West.[5] Probably you know more of all this than I do, but you cannot know the warmth of feeling & confidence of all classes concerning yourself as well as I do. Jackson's life is despaired of by two of his physicians while one has some hope. Pneumonia set in after he was wounded.[6]

Between the need for you here and in the West it is more than likely you will again be under canvass before long.

Jackson's Corps numbering nearly 40 000 is at present under command of A. P. Hill.

I have been in the saddle several times since my leg has healed and find that I have so little trouble in keeping my seat that I have offered my services to resume duty in the field professing my willingness to take a small division in view of my short comings in the way of legs. Except a Court of Inquiry I have been leading an idle life for some time.

We had several reports in town yesterday that you were actually ordered up here. Coming events may cast their shadows before.[7] The grand point of anxiety now however is the South West. Our loss in the late battles will fall short of 10 000. we have not captured much artillery—probably 15 pieces. The enemy lost a great many in killed & wounded. Altogether I doubt if 40 000 under all heads will cover their losses.[8]

Hoping that I dont weary you with this desultory letter.

I remain &–

R S. Ewell.

1. Rodes had spearheaded Stonewall Jackson's May 2, 1863, flank attack at Chancellorsville. In recognition of his distinguished conduct on that battlefield, he was promoted to major general on May 7, 1863.
2. On April 7, 1863, Beauregard's Confederates had decisively beaten back a naval assault on Fort Sumter.
3. The Battle of Chancellorsville had been fought the previous week near Fredericksburg, Virginia.
4. Within a month, the Army of Northern Virginia would start north to Pennsylvania. General Lee proposed bringing Beauregard to Virginia and putting him in command of a force to threaten Washington, thereby holding at bay troops in the nation's capital that might otherwise be sent against Lee. Nothing came of the proposal, however.
5. As commander of the Department of Mississippi, Tennessee, and East Louisiana, Lieutenant General John C. Pemberton (1814–1881) led Confederate forces in the unsuccessful defense of Vicksburg, Mississippi.

6. Stonewall Jackson was wounded by the mistaken fire of his own men on May 2, 1863, during the Battle of Chancellorsville. Surgeons removed the wounded general's left arm, after which he was transported by ambulance to Guinea Station, a stop on the Richmond, Fredericksburg, and Potomac Railroad. After his arrival there, pneumonia set in. Jackson died on May 10. Before his death, he expressed the wish that Ewell succeed him in command of the Second Corps.

7. Ewell is suggesting that the reports of Beauregard's arrival in Richmond, though unfounded, might presage the actual event.

8. By "the late battles," Ewell may be referring to the various actions associated with the Chancellorsville Campaign. If so, he highly exaggerated the North's losses while minimizing the South's. At Chancellorsville, the Army of the Potomac lost approximately seventeen thousand men, while Lee's casualties numbered roughly thirteen thousand.

109. To James Lyons

Richmond Va. May 25. 63

Hon[ora]ble James Lyons[1]

Dear Sir:

Failing to find you disengaged I send you a short statement of the matter of which I spoke to you the other day.[2] I am the Officer and you will at once see the necessity of caution as it might lead to confiscation if I were known at the North to be in any manner connected with the interests. I should therefore prefer that the matter do not go further than yourself. It requires, I believe a marriage contract. this & whatever other papers that may be necessary together with such legal opinion as you may think advisable, I will be glad to have at your earliest convenience.

Resp'y,
R S. Ewell

Attached to this letter was the following scrawled note laying out the chief points of the case.

Money invested in St. Louis on bond & mortgage. Also some real estate.[3]
A part is due to two children minors—notes in Mothers name.
Mother guardian to children.

Property in Tennessee & Mississippi consists of real estate & personal
property notes, stocks &c &c

The Mother is a Citizen of Tennessee.

The Mother wishes in case of marrying a Confederate Officer to avoid
risk of confiscation in Missouri

To retain the control of all the property & to relieve the gentleman
from liability for the debts due the children.

When would the papers for the above be drawn up?

1. Judge James Lyons was a brother-in-law of Brigadier General Henry Wise. Lyons lived with his wife, Imogene, at their home, "Laburnum," outside of Richmond.

2. Before returning to the army, Ewell took Lizinka as his wife. The marriage took place on May 26, 1863, at St. Paul's Episcopal Church in Richmond. Fearing that Federal authorities would use the marriage as a pretext for seizing Lizinka's property, Ewell asked Lyons to execute a prenuptial agreement that excluded Ewell from all rights and claims to it.

3. For a synopsis of Lizinka's landholdings, see Pfanz, *Ewell*, 508–11.

110. To Benjamin Ewell

. . . charges against them for it.[1]

I have made diligent inquiries & find that all deny the accusation. Harriot Brown has been urging her to come up to the Army but it is very dull & I expect she has had enough of the Soldiers since her visit at Orange. However she says if a suitable escort go for her in two or three weeks she will come up.[2]

What became of Parson Stoddert?[3] we have heard nothing of him since May. I expect he has been travelling over the U S. His life would be a rich affair.

Any more weddings your way? I am sorry I was not sent to East Tennessee. My health was plenty good enough.[4]

Please give my respects to General Johnston.

Yours &c.

R S. Ewell

P.S.

As I expected Campbell was anxious to get back to his Corps but not being at the head of Staff thinks the west is the centre of the world—swears by Joe Johnston & I expect would give any thing to get back.[5] I wish he could be kept from the coming fights which I expect will be the most desperate we have had yet. He has been in his share.

RSE—

1. The date of this letter fragment is uncertain. Internal evidence suggests that it was written around the first week of June 1863.
2. This is a reference to Ewell's niece, Lizzie.
3. Ewell's brother William.
4. In the spring of 1863 Johnston put forward Ewell's name as a candidate for the command of Confederate forces in East Tennessee, but President Jefferson Davis apparently disapproved of the idea.
5. In March 1863 Brown traveled to Mississippi to join Johnston, who had recently been appointed to command the Department of the West. He served on Johnston's staff until May, when Ewell returned to duty.

Chapter 9

Corps Command, 1863–1864

Nine months passed before Ewell had recovered sufficiently from his amputation to return to duty. During his lengthy convalescence, the Army of Northern Virginia clashed with the Federals at Antietam, Fredericksburg, and Chancellorsville. Jackson was among Chancellorsville's casualties. Mistakenly shot by his own men in the confusion of the battle, the general died eight days later at Guinea Station, Virginia.

Jackson's death prompted Lee to reorganize the army into three infantry corps of three divisions apiece. James Longstreet continued to command the First Corps; Ewell received Jackson's Second Corps; and Lee appointed A. P. Hill to lead the newly created Third Corps.

Ewell accepted the promotion without recorded comment. On May 29, 1863, he rejoined the army, then near Fredericksburg, and formally took up his duties as a lieutenant general. Six days later his corps broke camp and started north. In a bold gambit for victory, Lee determined to invade Pennsylvania and fight the enemy on his own ground.

The natural route for invasion was through the Shenandoah Valley. A strong Union garrison at Winchester blocked the Confederates' path, but in two days of brilliant fighting and maneuver, Ewell defeated the garrison and cleared the Valley of Union troops. On June 15 his corps crossed the Potomac River and entered Maryland. Pennsylvania lay just ahead.

Ewell led the Confederate march into the Keystone State, gathering much-needed supplies for the army as he went. By the end of June he had reached the Susquehanna River and was poised to take Harrisburg. He never got the chance. With the city just days from capture, Ewell received a note from General Lee informing him that the Union army had crossed the Potomac River and entered Maryland. Lee ordered Ewell to cross South Mountain and unite with Hill and Longstreet near Chambersburg, Pennsylvania.

Hill meanwhile sent troops to Gettysburg, a college town in the south-central part of the state, where he hoped to find shoes for his ill-shod troops. Instead, he found advance elements of the Army of the Potomac, now commanded by Major

General George G. Meade. Fighting erupted as Confederates tried to force their way into the town. Ewell heard the distant cannon fire and turned his corps toward the fighting. Arriving at Gettysburg that afternoon, he fell like an avalanche on the right flank of Federals, routing two corps and capturing four thousand prisoners. The enemy fell back through Gettysburg and rallied at Cemetery Hill beyond. Confronted by massed Union artillery, unsupported by Longstreet or Hill, and shackled by orders from Lee that prohibited him from engaging the enemy in general combat, Ewell refrained from attacking the hill. He has been unfairly criticized for that decision ever since.

For the next two days, the Confederates fought stubbornly in an effort to drive the Army of the Potomac off Cemetery Ridge. When efforts to turn Meade's flanks failed, Lee sent Major General George Pickett's division and other troops against the center of the Union line. Pickett's men briefly gained the crest of Cemetery Ridge but were unable to hold it. The Confederates returned to Virginia. Lee's invasion of the North had ended in failure.

Ewell's reputation declined steadily from that point. Defeats at Bristoe Station and Rappahannock Station in the fall seemed to confirm what many suspected: the army, in the post-Jackson era, lacked strong leadership. Ewell and Hill simply were not fit for corps command. Ewell added to that impression by hosting Lizinka and her daughter at his headquarters between campaigns. More concerned with entertaining his new wife than running his corps, he neglected his duties and made himself look foolish in the eyes of his men. Whatever leadership there was that fall was provided by the meddlesome Lizinka, who managed affairs around her husband's headquarters with an iron hand. "Petticoat government" one officer called it.

Lee was aware of this, and it lowered Ewell in his esteem. In November, Ewell had to leave the army for a few days to be fitted for a new prosthesis. While he was away, the Army of the Potomac crossed the Rapidan River and engaged Lee's forces at Mine Run. Ewell rushed back to take part in the battle, but Lee refused to place him back in command of his corps until the fighting was over. To Ewell it was painfully obvious that he had lost Lee's confidence.

Only success would restore his standing in Lee's eyes. In May 1864 the Army of the Potomac, now accompanied by Lieutenant General Ulysses S. Grant, crossed the Rapidan River and engaged the Confederates in a dark, tangled forest known as the Wilderness. Ewell fought the Federals along a crushed gravel road known as the Orange Turnpike. For two days he skillfully parried the blows of three different corps, inflicting heavy casualties upon his attackers. On the final day of the battle, he attacked the enemy's right flank, routing two brigades and capturing eight hundred prisoners. It was one of his finest performances of the war.

The battle that followed, by contrast, was one of his worst. For two weeks, Union and Confederate forces grappled with one another near Spotsylvania Court House. The Second Corps, holding an advanced position in the center of the Confederate line known as the Muleshoe Salient, came under heavy attack. An assault against the western face of the Muleshoe on May 10 netted nearly one thousand Confederate prisoners. Two days later, Union troops overwhelmed the Salient's defenders in a dawn attack, this time annihilating an entire division. By the end of the campaign, Ewell had just six thousand men capable of bearing arms.

The grueling day-to-day combat took its toll on the general as well. On May 26, with the armies deadlocked on the North Anna River, Ewell fell ill with diarrhea and applied for a brief leave of absence. Lee used the incident to deprive him of his command. Claiming that Ewell would injure his health if he returned to the field, Lee had him transferred to Richmond to superintend the city's defenses. It seemed as though Ewell's fighting days were over. Like a farm horse no longer able to pull the plough, the old soldier had been put out to pasture.

111. To Lizzie Ewell

Chambersburg Pa
June 24. 63—

Dear Lizzie;

I was reminded of you & your letter by Campbell's going out to day to try & make some purchases for Lizinka & my wondering if you were in the list. But C. tells me since that you were included in the purchases he made, or would be.[1] I was in hopes you would have gone to Charlottesville, but I suppose the attractions of Franklin street[2] are too great to be given up.

It is like a renewal of Mexican times[3] to enter a captured town. The people look as sour as vinegar & I have no doubt would gladly send us all to kingdom come if they could. I dont know if we will go to York, yet, anyhow we will be tolerably close to it. I will let your relations off tolerably easy, on your account— probably not taking more than a few forks & spoons & trifles of that sort. No houseburning or anything of that sort.[4] It is wonderful how well our hungry, foot sore, ragged men behave in this land of plenty—better than at home—but I try to have furnished by impressment what it is possible to get for our men.

The worst behaved men I have are the Marylanders who seem wild with the excitement of getting near home. One of them just returned from a scout told me the ladies all send me word that if I go where they are, they will give me no quarter in their delight at meeting me. What a pity a Bachelor could not have such an offer.

Yours with love to Dr Hoge's family.

R. S. Ewell

1. Goods of every description were in short supply in the Confederacy due to the Union Navy's blockade of the Southern coastline. When the Army of Northern Virginia invaded Pennsylvania, Southern officers took advantage of the opportunity to purchase goods both for themselves and for loved ones back home. Campbell Brown purchased five dresses, a pair of stockings, "several gross of small china buttons, a half-dozen calico dress-patterns, some soaps, flavoring essences (peppermint &c) & a few other miscellaneous articles" for his mother and sister. In addition to making purchases for his own family, Brown carried a list of items to buy for Generals James Longstreet and Robert H. Chilton. He was not alone among Ewell's staff in making large purchases in Pennsylvania. Sandie Pendleton, Jed Hotchkiss, and John E. Johnson each made similar purchases for family and friends in Virginia. Jones, *Campbell Brown's Civil War*, 198, 228–29.
2. Lizinka and Hattie had rented a house in Charlottesville, while Lizzie was staying with Dr. Moses Hoge's family on Franklin Street in Richmond.
3. Ewell had been a member of an invading army once before, in the Mexican War.
4. Lizzie's mother, Julia McIlvaine Ewell, lived with her family in York, Pennsylvania. She had separated from Lizzie's father, Benjamin Ewell, when Lizzie was a little girl.

In October 1863 Lee crossed the Rappahannock River and moved north, hoping to slip between the Army of the Potomac and Washington. Meade got timely notice of the movement, however, and hurried toward Centreville. Lee caught up with the Union army at Bristoe Station on October 14 but suffered a sharp repulse when A. P. Hill impetuously attacked Major General Gouverneur K. Warren's Second Corps, which was strongly posted behind an embankment of the Orange and Alexandria Railroad. Warren continued toward Centreville after dark. Lee buried his dead and fell back across the Rappahannock on October 19, tearing up the railroad tracks as he went. The following day, Lee and Ewell rode downriver inspecting their new position. In the following memorandum, Ewell describes the conversation that he had with his commander while on that excursion.

112. Private Memorandum

Oct 20th Private Memorandum

Rode with Genl Lee to Kelly's ford.[1] We talked of the campaign in the Peninsula, in 1862 under Genl J. E. Johnston. Genl L. said there were two occasions

when he thought J. might have crushed[2] McClellan. First when he fell back &
McC. pursued with vigor on which occasion had J. occupied the forts the pur-
suing Column's might have been checked with great damage but the forts were
unoccupied.[3] Afterwards at Seven Pines,[4] that when J. was wounded & G. W.
Smith came into command that S. wished to fall back (retreat) but was urged
by Genl Lee to renew the attack, which was done feebly, that no interference
was made with Smith by Genl Lee except to urge him to renew the attack, that
the report I mentioned that S. had made his arrangements to prosecute the engagement with vigor but was prevented by higher authority was unfounded as
nothing like interference to prevent him was made but rather the contrary, that
it was entirely a mistake to suppose that any check was given, that S. in going
on leave wished to make it a condition that his Staff should remain intact untill
his return & failing to get the promise hesitated for a time to take his leave.
I had heard that Smith wanted to attack but was prevented.[5] 21st Rode with
Genl Lee to Dr Wellford's. The Genl said it was called Farley[—]was formerly
occupied by Champ[e] Carter where he Lee had spent many happy days in
his boyhood.[6] Mrs Carter was a Miss Walker. they had one daughter married
to Maj. Storrer, once an Officer of the U.S. Army. Many of their descendents
live in Va.[7] Genl Lee's Mother used to spend much time there. Mrs Lee was a
Miss Carter of Shirley.[8] We spoke of Jackson's march here in Augs[u]t 62 to
Beverley Ford of the Rapidan when Longstreet went to the Rail Road crossing.[9]
I spoke of Jackson's turning the head of the column up the river after Artillery
firing had commenced, & I was so close to the crossing having already passed
Cunningham's mill on Ruffin run, that the leading regt had been deployed
into the line of skirmishers & were moving forward under the Gallant Colonel
Douglass, 13. Ga. afterwards killed at Sharpsburg.[10] Genl Lee told me that he
saw the difficulty of crossing & the certain loss we must sustain & ordered Genl
Jackson to move higher up the river.[11] This was the beginning of the move which
went on to the 2d battle of Manassa &c. &c.

1. Kelly's Ford was a shallow point on the Rappahannock River, five miles east of
   Brandy Station. Because it was one of the few points along the river where the
   left bank dominated the right, it was a favorite crossing point for Union troops
   wishing to reach the south side of the river.
2. Above the line here Ewell has written "(or worse)." Here Campbell Brown
   added the following note:

   > on reading the statement under "Private Movements" [sic] re-
   > specting Genl Johnston's opportunity to have given McClellan a
   > blow at Williamsburg to Col Ewell who had command there the

1st year of the war, Col Ewell stated that the line of fortifications was very badly chosen, being 5 miles long when a stronger line only 2 1/4 miles or at most 2 1/2 miles might have been selected with open ground in front that Genl Lee had directed him, Col Ewell, to construct this line but had sent Engineer Officers before he could do it, that he Col Ewell had written to Genl Lee when the line was adopted asking to be relieved from all responsibility as the line was not good, that he had remonstrated with Genl Magruder & Col, now Genl[,] McLaws[,] who thought the line of Engineers a bad one[,] on the subject but in vain[,] that our losses at the Battle of Williamsburg were due principally to the unsuitable location of the redoubts & that a great disaster was escaped by but a little, that Genl Magruder told him emphatically just before the evacuation of the Peninsula that a mistake had been made & that the line was badly established & that he wished Col Ewell's remonstrances had been attended to.

3. Ewell is referring to a line of forts that ran between Cub Creek and College Creek, just east of Williamsburg, Virginia, where a battle had been fought on May 5, 1862. Here Campbell Brown added the following remarks:

   Col. B. S. Ewell says that had the forts been properly located they would have been occupied & that had Genl Lee interfered when he should [have] they would have been properly located & that he B. S. Ewell wrote to L. that they were not properly placed & that he, E, would have nothing to do with them. Magruder told E. when they left that the forts were improperly located & that the line was five miles long when it should have been 2 1/2.

4. In the Battle of Seven Pines, or Fair Oaks, fought on May 31 and June 1, 1862, Johnston attempted to crush the left wing of the Union army, which was separated from the right wing by the flooded Chickahominy River. In the first day of the battle Johnston was wounded, and General Gustavus W. Smith took command of the army. At Lee's urging, Smith renewed the attack the following day but did so in such a lackluster fashion that the Federals readily held their ground. The battle ended in stalemate.

5. Here Campbell Brown added the following footnote:

   In conversation with Maj. Hamilton, he tells me that on Sunday Morning at Seven Pines, he asked one of Gen. G. W. Smith's staff (he thinks his Adjt. Genl.) whether Genl S. intended to renew the fight & was told by him that Gen. S. was not certain &

in fact had not made up his mind. Further that he heard from excellent authority that Longstreet on Saturday night visited Genl
Smith asking him to send him 10.000 men and only to hold his
own position, and that he (Longstreet) would drive the enemy in
to the Chickahominy, to which Genl Smith replied, that he was
not certain he could hold his position with his present force.

The Hamilton referred to here is Major Samuel P. Hamilton (1826–1897), who
served as chief of artillery in Major General Lafayette McLaws's division in 1862.
Hamilton briefly acted as judge advocate before returning to the artillery in 1863.

6. "Farley" had been built by William Champe Carter around 1801. Three thousand acres surrounded the house. The Carter family sold the property to
   William N. Wellford in 1843. Wellford in turn sold the house to Franklin P.
   Stearns in 1863. Major General John Sedgwick, commander of the Union
   army's Sixth Corps, used the house as his headquarters in 1863.

7. Carter's wife was Maria Byrd Farley. Francis B. Heitman, in his definitive work
   Historical Register and Dictionary of the United States Army, lists just one officer
   named Storer who served in the army prior to the Civil War: 1st Lieutenant
   William H. Storer of the 1st United States Infantry. He resigned from the service in 1837. Heitman, *Historical Register,* 930.

8. Ann Carter Lee had grown up at "Shirley," the home of her father, Charles Carter.

9. Beverly Ford was a crossing of the Rappahannock River northeast of Brandy
   Station. The railroad crossing mentioned here was at Rappahannock Station,
   now Remington, Virginia.

10. Marcellus Douglass (1820–1862) became colonel of the 13th Georgia Infantry
    on February 1, 1862.

11. On August 21, 1862, Jackson tried to cross the Rappahannock River at Bever-
    ly's Ford, two miles upriver from Rappahannock Station. Confederate cavalry
    drove back the small Union force guarding the ford but fell back to the south
    side of the river when Union reinforcements appeared.

113. *To the Reverend Moses Hoge*

Charlottesville
Novr 27. 1863

Revd Moses D. Hoge D.D.[1]

My Dear Sir;

I have received your kind letter sending me a copy of the Bible. Please add to
the value of the gift by joining in my prayers that I may be assisted in following

the precepts therein laid down & that I may be guided by its wisdom. I am daily more convinced of its importance & more sensible of my dependence.

I am about starting for the Army having been absent because of an injury to my leg.[2] Please remember me to your family. Mrs Ewell & Harriot are well & desire to be remembered.

Yours &c
R. S. Ewell

1. Hoge had recently run the Union blockade to acquire Bibles and other religious literature for Southern soldiers. The Bible he presented to Ewell was undoubtedly one of them. His gift to the general was not unique. Generals J. E. B. Stuart, Robert Rodes, Robert E. Lee, Joseph Johnston, and James Longstreet also received Bibles from Hoge. Letters of thanks from these individuals are in M.C.-3, folder 491A, Museum of the Confederacy, Richmond, Virginia.
2. An ill-fitting prosthesis ulcerated the stump of Ewell's amputated leg. At Lee's insistence, he relinquished command of his corps on November 15, 1863, and the following day started for Charlottesville in the company of his wife and stepdaughter. During his absence, the Army of the Potomac crossed the Rapidan River and engaged the Confederates near Mine Run. Ewell rushed back to the army, arriving on November 29 while the battle was still in progress. He need not have hurried. Lee refused to restore him to command until the campaign was over.

114. To Lizinka Ewell

Sunday
Morton's Hall[1]
Decr 19th 63

Mrs R. S. Ewell

My Dear Lizinka;

Campbell wont go to Charlottesville tho the Doctor urges him; he says he would go into a room in the hospital & keep there untill cured.[2] He has been in a room in this house, but speaks of keeping his tent, like the hermit crab. Such is the amount of Sulphur in the atmosphere that though I am but little in the room yet my clothes smell as strong of Sulphur when I go near the fire, as if I were the one rubbing with the ointment. As the weather is warm it wont inconvenience C. to take a tent with a fire place, which he will have made.

There is no Military news. Genl Lee has not returned.[3] The enemy are between Culpepper Ct. House & the Rappahannock. We have papers (Yankee) of the 5th. They acknowledge a loss of 1000 in the affair with Johnson's Division. We took 800 prisoners, so they did not profit much by that move.[4] Yesterday's papers spoke of Grant's falling back—a rumor. He may be going to our salt works & lead mines in Western Va, or some think possibly to come towards Richmond.[5] Today I received notice that several thousand of the enemy, Cavalry & Int'y[,] were at Front Royall threatening the valley.[6] But I dont think anything is to be apprehended at your place.[7] I have come into possession of a pair of mules, swapping horses & in the course of the changes Prince my pony came into Capt. Turner's hands. He was slightly ornamental & in no way useful to me. I offered him to C. for his mare, but he says he wants her for breeding. These mules have the advantage over those I had before in being larger & quicker & besides belong, in part, to me.

I have been riding Rifle principally who is the only tolerable horse I have.[8]

It seems like a positive loss of this fine weather, not being able to drive you about. I ride a good deal but dont use the buggy much when you are not present.

I was told by Carroll[9] this evening that his wife & her Sister went as far as Harper's Ferry but the Yankee Officer there stopped them said nothing about oath &c but that the orders were imperative from Washtn to allow no one whatever to pass either way. It is a satisfaction when one is doubtful about duty as you are, to know that the action is determined by circumstances over which you have no control.

This was the cause of my writing at this time that your mind might be at rest.

I sent two Officers to examine the country about the Va. Central as to its capabilities for encampments & they have just returned with information that about Tolersville is fine ground with every advantage for encampments of Intfantry [*sic*]. There is an hotel at Tolersville where rooms can be had, as well as houses in the vicinity. The place is in the vicinity of Frederick Hall also.[10] Your letter of the 11th came when I had written so far. C. concludes to go up. Why in the world (I forgot the letter Hill burnt) I was going to say did you put off writing from the 5th to the 11th. I assure you it has been a serious injury to me not to hear from you as I was imagining all sorts of terrible reasons & C. has been as usual the sufferer from my anxiety. I am delighted that the shirts have come. I wanted them very much, as I did not like to wear white & have but one Checked.

You must look out for your confederate candle.[11] If you go out of the room leaving it burning there is great danger of its setting the house on fire.

Hattie's bad luck is well known. We are starting the darkies to making soap & candles. I dont know whether they will or not. I have had a head ache all day, but your letter has relieved me. The linen sheet is here. I told Harry[12] to get my large tin tub—you dont mention it. I send by C. several silver spoons & forks. There are two or three large silver forks & spoons here. You know the silver is like gold—worth its weight in Confederate paper. What a pity you did not buy Carr's place![13] With silver & gold together you have over $1200.

It may be some weeks before we go into Winter quarters, depending upon information Genl Lee may bring. Should we spend x mas here I want to get a visit from you or go to see you, if circumstances permit. But at any rate dont take the labor of writing a long letter after a week or ten days. Drop me a line to say there is no news. A box came from Richmond. It has some letters I would like to have kept. They take but little room & many trifles[,] or as you say "trash[,]" to be thrown away. There are many schemes for the currency, but one thing is needful. by due economy the expenses can be reduced one half. The lavish waste of the Govt first depreciated the currency. There are twice as many Officers as there ought to be. It seems better to hang onto Lydia.[14] You cann[o]t afford to want a servant. I found some U S. postage currency in my trunk & told C. to give them to Miss McP.[15] if she gets angry you can tell he[r] to bring back some stamps.

Genl Early's lecture on laws[,] though familiar to you who are half a lawyer[,] was new to me. I only tried one other business transaction—to sell a land warrant & it was 6 m[o]nths before I could sell though the instructions were printed.[16] I left this matter to you supposing you could fix it. I though[t] Mr Fogg[17] was the trustee. More important matters drove it out of my head. I want C. to make arrangement about the horses.

Enquire about Rode's brother. I think of making him my Aide. All speak highly of his sense—higher than of the General.[18]

C. has a book, "Blackstone's Commentaries" of Morton's of which he gave no direction. Send C. after your Wilmington box. Turner is acting A.A.G. & in quiet times I would prefer a Clerk to him or C. or Pen.[19] My tub ought to be mended with white paint.[20] I want some sodder or white paint for mine here which leaks. If C. will go to Wilmington he can write the order & there is no objection.[21] I will write again to-morrow or as soon as the Mortons go.

I was riding all yesterday & very cold & my head aches.

R S. E.

I will not stop untill I make arrangements for your coming. RSE

The impression is that J. E. Johnston succeeds Bragg. Have you seen an account of the latter in the Dispatch? It shows many cases of unjust censure. I dont like his successor. C. does, but I offer to Bet that he will fail & the Prest be the cause given. If he is to fail we dont want him.[22]

Yours, R S. Ewell

1. "Morton's Hall" was the home of Jeremiah Morton. It was located south of the Rapidan River, two miles due south of Raccoon Ford.

2. Brown was suffering from a skin disease identified only as "Morbi Cutis," possibly ringworm or scabies. Doctors tried to cure it by the application of sulfur.

3. Jefferson Davis summoned Lee to Richmond on December 9, 1863, to discuss various military concerns, including who should replace General Braxton Bragg in command of the Army of Tennessee. Lee remained away from the army for twelve days. In his absence, Ewell commanded the Army of Northern Virginia.

4. On November 27 Major General Edward Johnson's Confederate division successfully battled Major General William H. French's Third Corps at Payne's Farm. This confusing clash constituted the only major fighting in the Mine Run Campaign.

5. In the last week of November 1863, Grant routed Bragg's army at Chattanooga, Tennessee. The Union army remained at Chattanooga until the following spring. It made no effort to capture the Confederate lead mines or salt works in West Virginia.

6. In December, Brigadier General William W. Averell led Union cavalry on a raid up the South Fork of the Shenandoah River, breaking the Virginia and Tennessee Railroad at Salem, Virginia, and destroying three depots bulging with food and other supplies for the Confederate army. In conjunction with Averell's advance, two infantry regiments and a body of Union cavalry under the overall command of Brigadier General Jeremiah C. Sullivan moved up the Shenandoah Valley toward Staunton, Virginia. Lee, monitoring the situation from Richmond, ordered his nephew, Brigadier General Fitzhugh Lee, to Staunton with two brigades of cavalry and sent two infantry brigades from A. P. Hill's corps to reinforce him. Jubal Early took overall command of Confederate forces in the Valley, but he arrived too late to prevent Averell from returning safely to Union lines.

7. Lizinka and Hattie were then residing in Charlottesville.

8. Ewell purchased Rifle from Dr. Francis W. Hancock on November 27, 1861, for $230. Although the general described Rifle as "one fine grey horse," others

were not so complimentary. Lieutenant Robert Stiles described the mare as "a flea-bitten gray" that was singularly like the general "so far as a horse could be like a man." Stiles, *Four Years,* 244.

9. Robert Harper Goodloe Carroll of Maryland served as a private and possibly as a scout in the Confederate cavalry. By November 1863 he held a position on Ewell's staff with the unofficial rank of captain. He formally joined Ewell's staff as an aide-de-camp in July 1864 with the rank of first lieutenant, taking the place of Thomas T. Turner, who had been seriously wounded at Spotsylvania Court House.

10. Tolersville—modern-day Mineral, Virginia—stood on the Virginia Central Railroad halfway between Fredericks Hall and Louisa Court House.

11. Confederate candles consisted of wicks dipped in solutions of beeswax and resin. The wicks were then wrapped around corncobs, narrow bottles, or other objects. They came into widespread use in the South during the Union blockade.

12. Possibly a black camp servant. Ewell seems to have sent him to Charlottesville to get his tin bathtub.

13. Unidentified.

14. This is the only known reference to this servant.

15. Unidentified.

16. For information on Ewell's land bounty, see note 5 to letter 45, this volume.

17. Unidentified.

18. Virginius Hudson Rodes (ca. 1824–1879) graduated from the Virginia Military Institute in 1843. He served on the staff of his brother Major General Robert E. Rodes, holding the rank of captain.

19. "Pen"—i.e., Sandie Pendleton, Ewell's assistant adjutant general.

20. For another reference to this bathtub, see Howard, *Recollections,* 235.

21. Brown's pass permitted him to go to Charlottesville but not to Wilmington. Here Ewell suggests that Brown write himself a pass authorizing him to go to Wilmington, North Carolina, to fetch a box of goods that had been sent to Lizinka and made it through the Union blockade.

22. Joseph Johnston succeeded Braxton Bragg in command of the Army of Tennessee on December 27, 1863. Ewell's footnote suggests that he felt that Bragg had been criticized unjustly and that he had little confidence Johnston would succeed where Bragg had failed. Johnston was on bad terms with President Jefferson Davis. Ewell predicted that if Johnston failed, he would blame his reverses on Davis.

Ewell spent the winter of 1863–64 with Lizinka and her family at Morton's Hall in Orange County. "There was as little exterior charm about Morton's Hall to attract as possible," he later reflected, "yet I was as contented there, except the war, as I could be." (Courtesy Donald Pfanz)

115. To Lizinka Ewell

Morton's Hall
Decr 20. 1863

Mrs R. S. Ewell

My Dear Lizinka;

Yours of the 18th came last night. The series commencing the 16th came to hand on the 18th. In your last you say you are consulting what people will say for the "first time in your life or can remember" &c. Please remember that your doing so is not in connection with what I have said or written. If you take the opinions of Campbell or Turner on matters [on which] they are not so well acquainted as yourself, you may expect annoyance. In one of your recent letters you speak of Pendleton's going off, as leaving the setting sun &c & unless you are mistaken in my strength of character, he is destroying his chance for promotion &c.

Do you think I would recommend or not because a man liked or disliked me ir-respective of his merits? The connection I cannot see. If he is likely to make a good Brig. Genl & to whip the Yankees I would recommend him if he were my worst enemy. I directed on Saturday Campbell & Turner to reconnoitre the country in a certain direction. They would be ready Monday. Monday they would be ready Tuesday because they had found on Monday they had no money & I didnt send them. Pendleton was sent as far, on more troublesome duty, was ready at once & returned promptly doing his duty well. Which is the best friend?[1]

I am sending off the Morton's who are going to Richmond, but want to keep all the other end of the house that Mrs Halsey may take it, in case the Yankees advance. I cant stand this. Col. Morton tells me there is a place for sale 175 acres—poor land— good house—$15.000 of Mr Bocock's in Appomattox Co. 2 miles from South Side R.R. 25 miles from Lynchburg.[2] He may buy or may go to Farmville. Will let me know how it will suit you. He is now going to look at it & though I told him I was anxious to bring you he seems to think I will take our old room again & sleep without fire, because Mrs Halsey may want two rooms for herself & two boys. I am waiting on their movements & in the interim will look for some other place.[3] I told C. to go to Mr Hancock's (D. E.)[4] to see the horses & make arrangements for wintering them or at least his own. The usual price is $150 the winter. I dont choose to impose those horses on Hancock for nothing & C. promised to attend to it which he does not mention. Dr McGuire[5] expressed surprize at his coming back before he was well. C. has no right to put others to the risk of catching a disgusting disease. It is not the question whether he thinks there is danger or not—the Dr says there is & was anxious about himself. I was quite uneasy & there is no isolating himself here as the servants may get it. Your reasons for being annoyed at his going were that you & Harriot had been talking of other people, but that would not satisfy any of the Staff if they were the victims.[6] Col. Morton hopes to get a place for his & Capt. Halsey's family & it is [in] this interim that he wishes to keep the house. I will telegraph you when to come. Had you not better bring your silver? I dont know its bulk, but the Banks neglected to move it from Fredericksburg & the Y[ankee]s took a great deal.[7] At all events I will want my cup.

I regret you did not send my letter to Mrs Hoof.[8] The worst trouble & annoyance you anticipated would not have equalled the present case & I would have been saved much vexation.

You know there is no furniture here, or rather what there is. The mail is waiting & I write in a hurry.

Yours &c—

R S. Ewell

---

1. Since Gettysburg, Sandie Pendleton had been increasingly critical of Ewell's conduct. His criticism seems to have stemmed largely from his dislike of

Lizinka, whose interference at army headquarters in the fall of 1863 he keenly resented. Ewell thought highly of Pendleton, however, and recommended him for promotion to brigadier general in December 1863. In a letter to her husband, Lizinka suggested that Pendleton had forfeited his right to promotion by temporarily leaving Ewell to accompany Early to the Shenandoah Valley in mid-December to combat General William W. Averell's cavalry raid.

2. Several wealthy members of the Bocock family lived in Appomattox County. The Honorable W. P. Bocock (b. ca. 1807), a lawyer and farmer, owned $106,140 of real estate and $254,141 in personal estate in 1860. Thomas S. Bocock (b. ca. 1815), also a lawyer and farmer, had $10,000 of real estate and $20,000 in personal estate. Henry F. Bocock (b. ca. 1818), the county clerk of court, owned $5,500 in real estate and $15,000 in personal estate.

3. Colonel Jeremiah Morton (1799–1878) owned four properties in Orange County, Virginia: "The Hall," "Moreland," "Lessland," and "Stillmore." Ewell made his headquarters in the fall and winter of 1863 at "The Hall." Morton left the Orange County house in December with the intention of either buying a farm in Appomattox County or taking up residence in Farmville, Virginia. Ewell hoped that Morton's departure would free up at least two rooms for the use of himself, Lizinka, and Hattie. He was therefore chagrined when Morton insisted that two of the rooms be kept vacant for the future use of his daughter and her children. If that happened, Ewell and his wife would be limited to a single room with no fireplace.

4. Hancock's identity is unknown. He may have been a relative of Dr. Francis Hancock, the former medical director of Ewell's division.

5. Hunter McGuire (1835–1900), a physician, served as medical director for the Stonewall Brigade and subsequently became medical director of the Second Corps under both Jackson and Ewell. In 1864 he served as medical director for Jubal Early in the Shenandoah Valley. After the war McGuire became a professor of surgery at Virginia Medical College and later at the University College of Medicine. He served as president of the American Medical Association from 1893 to 1894.

6. For Brown's affliction, see RSE to LCB, 19 Dec. 1863, folder 10, PBE (letter 114, this volume).

7. In December 1862 Union troops had ransacked the town of Fredericksburg, Virginia. In the course of their rampage, soldiers broke into the safes of the town banks.

8. Unidentified.

116. To Mrs. Captain Halsey

Morton Hall

Decr 21st 1863—

Mrs Captain Halsey[1]

Dear Madam;

I write with some hesitation lest I annoy you. I am anxious to bring Mrs Ewell to the army and understanding you do not intend occupying this house unless the enemy advance, and in that case as Mrs Ewell would leave at once I would like to occupy the west end.

· Mrs Ewell would have her own furniture & I would lock yours in the small rooms over the Hall.

Such furniture as you would prefer leaving in the rooms would be religiously respected & the apartments would be turned over to you at an hour's notice. If in the afternoon Mrs Ewell would remain in one of the east rooms & you would have the others at your disposition. In the morning Mrs Ewell would go at once for Or. Ct H.[2] You would have your rooms warm & comfortable. Your furniture could soon be re-placed & if you could share our plain fare we would be happy to have yourself & family at our table as long as we might be together.

Should you wish to send your boys to stay here at any time they would be made comfortable in the room now used by the Revd Mr Lacy[3] & myself. My Step daughter would occupy the upper room & if you should wish to come with a view to return to your place, you could use that room, she staying with her Mother or not as might be most agreeable to you. Arrangements will be made to meet all these contingencies in case you assent to this plan. Our table would always be at your or your family's service. It has occurred to me since commencing this that you might not wish to have anything to say about Mr Stearne's house, but Mrs E. received a letter from the owner expressing gratification at her being here &c. &c.[4]

Your furniture would undoubtedly be safer upstairs as the room below might be entered from the windows & robberies are of daily occurrence.

Please command my services at any time. I send to day's paper as you may find it interesting.

I would be obliged for an answer by bearer.

Respectfully &c

R. S. Ewell

P.S.

One contingency I forgot to mention. you may wish to come even if the enemy dont advance. In that case the rooms would at once be vacated & I would turn out the Staff, which I dont wish to do now as they have not arranged their tents for the Winter.

R.S.E.

1. Mildred Jackson Morton, the daughter of Colonel Jeremiah Morton, married Joseph Jackson Halsey, a graduate of the College of New Jersey and owner of Fredericksburg's "Classical and Scientific Athenaeum." In 1847 the couple moved to "Lessland," where Halsey practiced law. While there, they had five children who survived infancy: two girls and three boys. At the beginning of the Civil War, Halsey was appointed captain of the Orange Rangers, subsequently Company I, 6th Virginia Cavalry. For this and other information about the Morton family, the author is indebted to Mildred Tyner of Culpeper, Virginia.

2. Ewell wished to bring Lizinka and Hattie to "The Hall" for the winter; however, Colonel Morton made it clear that his daughter and her children were to have possession of the rooms if an advance by Union troops forced them to leave Lessland. Ewell assured Mrs. Halsey that his wife and stepdaughter would evacuate their rooms in The Hall if Mrs. Halsey and her family needed them. If compelled to evacuate their rooms in the afternoon, Lizinka and Hattie would spend the night in one of the east rooms. If compelled to leave in the morning, they would go immediately to Orange Court House.

3. The Reverend Beverley Tucker Lacy (1819–1900), an ordained minister in the Presbyterian Church, had served as Stonewall Jackson's headquarters chaplain. He continued in that capacity under Ewell.

4. Colonel Morton had recently sold The Hall to Franklin P. Stearns of Richmond to raise money for the Confederacy. Stearns, one of the wealthiest men in Virginia, was a director of the James River and Kanawha Canal Company, not to mention several railroads and banks. He was also a member of the Richmond City Council and the Virginia General Assembly.

117. To Lizzie Ewell

Jany 8th 1864

Miss E. Ewell

Dear Lizzie;

Your tempting bill of fare for the returned prisoners has made me quite hungry.[1] In fact visions of pound & sponge cake with white sugar (we are glad to get brown with our tea when [we] have any tea) and such like delicacies are too much for our equanimity in the presence of musty flour[,] bread & tough beef. However the worst thing about the latter is the fact that our poor soldiers have but a scanty supply—less than a lb.[2] I feel very anxious about the poor families on this side of the Rapidan whose houses were in the lines of the enemy's late advance. The Yankees stripped them of every mouthful & left them, in some cases without a[3] grain or morsel of meat. They do the same in Culpepper & Fauquier but in places where their lines still hold they issue rations, not to let the people absolutely starve. Cannot your Young Men's Christian associa-

The Reverend Moses D. Hoge was minister of Richmond's Second Presbyterian Church. Lizzie Ewell resided with the Hoge family for much of the war. In the group picture, Lizzie (top row, left) appears standing with Mary Hoge. Fanny Wood, Bessie Hoge, and Ellen Wood are seated in the front row. (Courtesy of the estate of Lizinka Ewell Crawford Ramsey of Gretna, Virginia, and Stan Aylor)

tion help these poor people? I am sure there are many in Richmond not more worthy of charity but who receive vital help. I heard yesterday that two boxes of clothing for Hay's Brigade had been collected by the efforts of Mrs Brown[4] & are in Gordonsville where Genl Hays sent for them.

A poor creature came to me day before yesterday about her husband who is under guard. She was evidently from the Emirald Isle & cried & "darlinged" & made a fuss generally, but I fear her Patrick is in a bad way. Charged with desertion & a request from the authorities in Mobile, that he may be tried for highway robbery unless shot for desertion. So I fear she will be left a lone widow without being able to boast of the deceased. You were wise in not coming up here as it is quite dull—hardly a beau in a week. Harriot seems to regret your not coming, very much. Should it become more lively here, or less so in Richmond[,] you had better re-consider your determination. The excitement would not be likely to injure your nerves, at this time at least.

We are most excited at this time on the subject of eating, having two cooks, newly purchased, who fully carry out the old adage about spoiling the broth.[5] However we have butter & tea & tolerable bread.

I was riding the grey mare I bot from your [?][6] a day or two ago when the ground was slippery with snow, when down she went rolling over & leaving me pretty well bruised on the ground. I dont think however she was to blame.

Maj. Greene[7] went to the Metropolis[8] a few days since & will doubtless see you & give the history of matters up here. I dont write because there is anything new or interesting but simply to do my duty as an affectionate & devoted Uncle. I think, but am not quite sure, that you owe me a letter—or vice versa. Tell miss Bessie Hoge that as the year has rolled around & more besides since that eventful sojourn at Dr Hancock's[9] & I am impatient for another "indulgence".[10] She might forward it by Maj. Green or would she prefer that I should send Capt. Turner as my proxy?[11] If no one on the Staff will do, I suppose I will have to go myself.

Ask Miss Mary[12] if she cannot retire for a time from the gay scenes of the Metropolis & pay us a visit up here. She shall have a horse whenever she wishes to ride & can take daily lessons in cooking rice. The latter dish has become an object of the ambition of Harriot & her Mother & they have it brought into the sitting room to be cooked every day. The object is to have it dry & each grain separate, but as yet these requisites have been wanting & the hopeless task is resumed from day to day with mournful & hopeless perseverance.

Captain Smith arrived looking very nice in his new coat & very much pleased with Richmond & the five young ladies all in a row knitting socks. He says when he goes again he will get Mrs Hoge to lock up four of them. Respects to the Dr & Mrs Hoge & family.

Yours &—

R S. Ewell

P.S. I wrote a long letter to your Father some months since. Please ask him if he has received it.

RSE—

1. Lizzie appears to have been involved in providing food for exchanged prisoners of war. The primary points of exchange in the East were at City Point, near Petersburg, and Aiken's Landing, below Richmond.
2. A member of Brigadier General George Steuart's staff wrote of this period: "The physical condition of the men I do not, and did not then, consider good. Their rations had been systematically reduced to the smallest possible quantity and there was almost no variety." In Brigadier General Stephen Dodson Ramseur's brigade, soldiers that winter subsisted on a daily ration of as little as one-eighth to one-quarter pound of meat and one and one-eighth pounds of flour. Men supplemented their rations by hunting for and digging up wild onions. Howard, *Recollections,* 252.
3. Here Ewell mistakenly repeated the word "a."
4. Unidentified.
5. Nothing is known about these cooks, apparently both slaves.
6. Ewell omitted a word here, possibly "Pa."
7. At this time, Benjamin Green was the acting assistant adjutant and inspector general of the Second Corps.
8. Richmond.
9. Ewell is referring to his lengthy convalescence at the home of Dr. Francis W. Hancock early in 1863.
10. "Indulgence"—i.e., letter.
11. Bessie Hoge, then aged nineteen, may have been fond of Ewell's aide-de-camp Thomas Turner. If so, she loved in vain. A few weeks later Turner announced his engagement to Ewell's stepdaughter, Hattie Brown.
12. Mary Hoge, Bessie's sister, was then seventeen years of age.

118. To John Esten Cooke

Camp near Orange C.H. Va[1]

10th Feb'y 1864

Capt. John Esten Cooke[2]

Dear Sir,

The skirmish in which Gen. Ashby was killed took place June 6th 1862.[3] My Division, acting as rear-guard, had encamped on the evening of the 5th, two and a half miles from Harrisonburg on the road to Port Republic, and Ashby's Cav. as I understood, had stopped just below the town. Next morning Gen. Geo. H. Steuart's Brigade[4] was my rear-guard, & the roads being bad, had hardly left camp by noon. Gen. Ashby became engaged with the enemy's Cav. during the morning & about 3 or 4 P.M. had a very successful affair, with a superior force, capturing Sir Percy Wyndham, Col. 1st New Jersey Cav. & thirty five or forty others & driving their Cav. from the field.[5]

About half an hour afterwards (i.e. about 4 1/2 P.M.) Gen. Ashby sent to request Gen. Steuart (who had instructions to give him any support he might require) to furnish him two or three Infantry Regts., as he thought he could strike a blow to advantage at some Infantry the enemy had brought up. The 58th Va. & 1st Md. Regts. were at once started back, & I returned with them. Gen. Ashby pointed out the position of the enemy who were along a fence at the edge of a wood, with a field in their rear. The 58th Va., a small Regt., was formed and advanced through the woods until checked by a very heavy fire from the enemy, advantageously posted. Finding that this small force was making no impression on the enemy, I hurried up the Maryland Reg't. & directed it to charge them in flank. The move was gallantly executed, & they were driven in confusion across the field in their rear, exposed to a most deadly fire from our men. The enemy turned out to be the "Buck Tail Rifles," a large & crack Pennsylvania Reg't. of sharpshooters. Lt. Col. Kane,[6] Com'g. them, was wounded & taken; his Adjutant & several[7] others were also taken. The fight lasted about fifteen (15) minutes, in which time our two Regts. lost 60 killed & wounded. The enemy's loss was much heavier.[8]

Just as the Md. Reg't. came up, & our line began to advance, Gen. Ashby, who was in front of the 58th Va. cheering the men forward, had his horse killed under him. He sprang to his feet & kept on, but had scarcely got ten paces from his horse, when in the act of turning to urge the men onward again, he was struck in the body by a rifle-ball. He fell instantly & died in a few seconds. His body & the equipments of his horse were brought off. The horse was a small bay, borrowed I think from Capt., now Col. Willis (12th Ga. Inf.)[9] & was the same on which Gen. Jackson was wounded at the 1st Manassas, where the horse was also wounded.

After burying our dead & bringing off our wounded, we marched to a camp a mile short of the future field of Cross Keys. June 7th we moved a mile or two and again camped. That evening an advance of the enemy was reported & Brig. Gen. Elzey[,] whose troops were nearest them, selected the position, in which we fought next morning.

About 10 A.M. of the 8th while in front with Gen'l Trimble, reconnoitreing, I heard guns toward Port Republic & soon rec'd an order to send my "best brigade" to report to Maj. Gen. Jackson at that point. The Louisiana Brigade of Gen. Taylor, being largest, was sent accordingly. About 11 A.M. the enemy advanced on my front, driving in the 15th Alabama, Col. Cantey,[10] from its post on picket. Col. Cantey however fell back so slowly as to give me full time to take up my position. I had been instructed to *fight* if attacked. The accompanying rude diagram will perhaps give you some idea of the ground. A is the road from Harrisonburg to Port Republic, the arrow pointing to Port Republic. B & C are roads coming from McGagheysville & Conrad's Store. Cross Keys is named from a tavern having the sign of two keys crossed, which formerly stood near the church.[11] In crossing the little creek, the road turns abruptly up the hill on which in a cleared field, my Art'y. was posted, supported by the 21st N.C. of Trimble's Brigade. The rest of his Brigade was on my right in the edge of a wood, across the creek. Gen. Geo. H. Steuart's Brigade was to the left of my Art'y. on the same ridge, in a wood, with a field in their front, Elzey in reserve behind my centre. Courtney's, Brockenborough's (Balto. Light Art'y) & Raine's batteries with a section of Lusk's, were, I think, all my Art'y. that was engaged.[12] The enemy's batteries were mostly opposite mine, near the church, & the artillery engagement began about noon.

After firing some time, the enemy advanced a brigade against Trimble's position. He allowed them to get within about 75 yards, when his brigade fired & charged, chasing the enemy across the open field in their front & capturing 75 prisoners. A second brigade which they brought up was likewise broken, one of their batteries nearly captured, it having barely time to get out of the way.[13]

Simultaneously with the enemy's attack on Trimble, they made another on my left, where *four* attacks, each as far as I can learn, by fresh troops, were steadily repulsed with much greater loss to the enemy than to us, our men fighting mostly behind trees. As Steuart's men gradually exhausted their ammunition, portions of Elzeys Brigade were moved over to their assistance.[14]

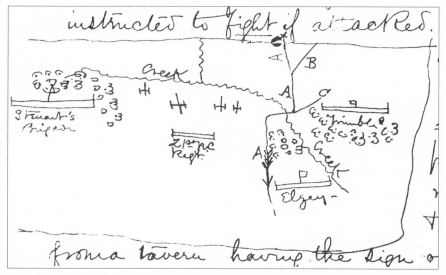

Campbell Brown's sketch of Cross Keys Battlefield. (Western Reserve Historical Society)

In repulsing the enemy's first attack, Gen. Trimble took a stand of colors.[15] The honor of its capture was claimed by both the 16th Miss. (Col. Carnot Posey)[16] & the 21st Ga. (Col. J. T. Mercer).[17] The enemy showed no disposition to attack Gen. Trimble again, & I was about to move my whole line forward, when Lt. Heinrichs,[18] Top'l Engineers sent to reconnoitre brought me word that there was a large column moving round our left flank to gain our rear. I sent the first Cavalry at my disposal (the 2d Reg't. Va. Cav. under Lt. Col. Watts)[19] to the left, who reported no signs of the enemy. [?][20] only staying five minutes. The La. Brigade of Gen. Taylor, not being needed, he[21] had sent it back, & I now placed it as soon as it came up behind Trimble, & sending one of the brigades[22] of Gen. Jackson's Div'n. which he had ordered up to support me, over to my extreme left, I ordered a general advance, which began just at dark. My left had got nearly within musket-range of the enemy's bivouac-fires near the church, & Gen. Trimble was about as close to them, when I rec'd. orders from Maj. Gen. Jackson to draw off as soon as possible & cross the river at Port Republic.[23] After burying my dead & bringing off all my wounded, except those "in articulo mortis,"[24] whom it w[ould]d only have been cruelty to disturb, I set out for[25] Port Republic about midnight, & crossed about daylight, my rear-guard (Gen. Trimble's Brigade) staying in front of the bridge till 8 or 9 o'clock, when upon Fremont's appearance, they crossed & burnt the bridge.[26]

My loss at Cross Keys was less than three hundred (300) all told. From the most reliable information I can get, the enemy buried at least (300) three hundred, besides some whom they threw into a well, as citizens state. We got seventy-five to one hundred (75 to 100) prisoners. Their total loss must have been over two thousand (2000), at which number they themselves stated it.[27]

Among our wounded were Gen. Geo. H. Steuart, severely in the neck; Gen. Elzey, slightly in the leg, & Col. Carnot Posey, 16th Miss., in the arm.[28] I was indebted to Gen. Elzey for valuable assistance in posting my Artillery.

From an Aide-de-Camp of Blencker's, killed by one of Gen. Trimble's men,[29] was taken Gen. Fremont's "order of march" for the day, showing his force to be composed of six (6) brigades of infantry (Blencker, Milroy, Stahel, Steinwehr,[30] commanding respectively) & one brigade Cavalry. I had three brigades, all small, & Elzey's & Steuart's especially so, they being chiefly composed of the troops before stationed at Allegheny Mtn. under Gen. Ed. Johnson, who were worn out by long marching.[31] Taylor did not come up in time to take part in the action. I am certain I had not five thousand muskets (5000) in the action.

The larger part of the enemy were Dutch or rather Germans, to which as well as to our superior position, is to be attributed the remarkable disproportion between their loss & ours.[32]

We fought here with a larger force than next day at Port Republic, and Yankee papers at first spoke of their loss as larger than on next day, though they afterwards attempted to hush up the matter in some degree.[33] Fremont was so severely checked that he did not get to the river next day, until Shields was defeated, & after 11 A.M., & made no attempt to cross or get at us. It is certain that but for the battle of Cross Keys there could have been no victory gained at Port Republic.

The account of this fight has been short & seemingly barren of incident, because the only movements made by us during its continuance were the transfer of Elzey's Brigade from the centre, where it was in reserve, to the left, & the forward move of both wings. My Artillery not only engaged the whole attention of the enemy's batteries, but annoyed every column that showed itself. About 5 P.M., the enemy attempted to charge it, but its infantry support being ordered up & our pieces giving them a few rounds of canister, they retired.

My men could not have behaved better than they did.

Very resp'y. Yours,

R S. Ewell

Lt. Gen.

1. This letter, although written by Ewell, is in Campbell Brown's hand. It is a copy of he one sent to Cooke.

2. Captain John Esten Cooke (1830–1886) served on Major General J. E. B. Stuart's staff successively as a volunteer aide-de-camp, ordnance officer, and assistant adjutant and inspector general. By war's end, he was assistant adjutant and inspector general for Brigadier General William Nelson Pendleton. After the war, Cooke wrote popular biographies of Robert E. Lee and Stonewall Jackson.

3. Turner Ashby commanded Jackson's cavalry during the 1862 Shenandoah Valley Campaign. He was killed in action at the Battle of Harrisonburg on June 6, 1862, just two weeks after being promoted to brigadier general.

4. Brigadier General George H. "Maryland" Steuart had commanded Ewell's cavalry earlier in the campaign. At this stage, he commanded a brigade of Virginia infantry. Steuart was wounded on June 8, 1862, at the Battle of Cross Keys. He survived his injury and led a brigade in the Army of Northern Virginia until the end of the war.

5. Sir Percy Wyndham, an English soldier of fortune, was leading the 1st New Jersey Cavalry when he was captured by Ashby near Harrisonburg, Virginia, on June 6, 1862. Lieutenant Colonel Joseph Kargé, Wyndham's successor, placed the total number of Union casualties in this affair at thirty-two.

6. Lieutenant Colonel Thomas L. Kane (1822–1883) commanded the 13th Pennsylvania Reserves (1st Pennsylvania Rifles). Commonly called the Bucktails, the men of the 13th Pennsylvania pinned deer tails to their caps to symbolize their hunting prowess. Taken prisoner at Harrisonburg, Kane was exchanged, promoted to brigadier general, and led a brigade in the Twelfth Corps until November 1863, when ill health compelled him to resign.

7. Ewell crossed out the words "a good many" here.

8. Ewell left no report of the Battle of Harrisonburg, an engagement in which the Confederacy lost 70 men. William Allan, citing a letter published in the *New York Tribune,* gave the Union's loss at Harrisonburg as 55 killed, wounded, and missing out of 125 men engaged. Allan, *History of the Campaign,* 143.

9. Edward S. Willis (1840–1864) served on Jackson's staff prior to December 13, 1862, when he was promoted to lieutenant colonel and assigned to the 12th Georgia Infantry. Bumped up to colonel just weeks later, Willis continued to lead the regiment until he received a mortal wound at Bethesda Church in May 1864.

10. Forty-three-year-old James Cantey had been a lawyer, planter, and Mexican War veteran in the antebellum South. Elected as colonel of the 15th Alabama

Infantry in 1861, he led the regiment through the Seven Days fighting, after which he returned to Alabama to take command of a brigade. He was promoted to brigadier general on January 8, 1863, and surrendered with the Army of Tennessee in April 1865.

11. Here, in parentheses, Ewell drew a symbol to represent Union Church: a Latin cross atop a blacked-in circle. The same symbol appears at the top of Brown's sketch of Cross Keys Battlefield (see accompanying illustration) to indicate the church's location.

12. The batteries Ewell mentions are the Courtney Artillery, commanded at Cross Keys by eighteen-year-old Lieutenant Joseph W. Latimer; Captain John B. Brockenbrough's Baltimore Light Artillery; Captain John A. M. Lusk's 2nd Rockbridge Artillery; and Captain Charles I. Raine's Lee Artillery. With the exception of Brockenbrough, each of the batteries was from Virginia.

13. Trimble routed Brigadier General Julius Stahel's brigade and then advanced in an effort to capture the four guns of Captain Frank Buell's West Virginia (Union) Battery C. The timely arrival of Brigadier General Henry Bohlen's brigade checked the Confederates long enough for Buell's guns to escape.

14. While Trimble successfully engaged Stahel's and Bohlen's brigades on the Confederate right, the brigades of Brigadier Generals Robert C. Schenck and Robert H. Milroy attacked Ewell's center and left, defended by George H. Steuart. Steuart's brigade successfully parried the Federal attacks, reinforced by Colonel John M. Patton's Virginia brigade, the 31st Virginia of Elzey's brigade, and the 7th and 8th Louisiana of Taylor's brigade.

15. Trimble identified the captured flag as belonging to either the 8th New York Infantry or the Pennsylvania Bucktails. He credited the capture to the 21st Georgia Infantry.

16. Carnot Posey (1818–1863) led the 16th Mississippi capably throughout the 1862 Shenandoah Valley Campaign, suffering a minor wound to the chest at Cross Keys. Promoted to brigadier general late in 1862, he led his brigade with mixed success until he suffered a mortal wound to the thigh at Bristoe Station on October 14, 1863.

17. Colonel John T. Mercer (1830–1864) graduated from West Point in 1854 and served as a lieutenant in the 1st U.S. Dragoons prior to the Civil War. He died in action at Plymouth, North Carolina, in April 1864.

18. Oscar Hinrichs (1835–1893), a Swedish immigrant, served as an engineering officer under Ewell and several other Confederate generals during the war. A lieutenant during the 1862 Shenandoah Valley Campaign, Hinrichs became a captain in October 1864.

19. James W. Watts (1833–1906) began the war as a lieutenant in the Second Virginia Cavalry but within a year rose to become its lieutenant colonel. A wound at Aldie, Virginia, in July 1863 rendered him unfit for further service in the field.

20. Someone scratched out two lines at this point in the letter.

21. Jackson.

22. Colonel John M. Patton's brigade consisted of the 21st, 42nd, and 48th Virginia regiments. The 21st Virginia did not participate in the battle.

23. The North and South rivers meet at Port Republic to form the South Fork of the Shenandoah River.

24. *"In articulo mortis"*—i.e., at the point of death.

25. Several words of the letter were crossed out here.

26. Trimble crossed the North River at Port Republic, burning the bridge after him.

27. Ewell's report of the Battle of Cross Keys appears in *OR* 12(1):781–83. It lists 288 casualties, nearly half of whom belonged to Trimble's brigade. Frémont, by contrast, admitted to 684 casualties: 114 killed, 443 wounded, and 127 captured or missing.

28. Steuart was struck in the shoulder by an artillery shell fragment that lodged in his back. He was out of action for a year, returning in time to command a brigade at Gettysburg. Elzey, too, was a victim of the heavy Union bombardment. Struck in the lower leg, he left the field on a stretcher but recovered in time to participate in the Seven Days fighting three weeks later. There he received a wound to the face that sidelined him for six months. Posey received a slight wound at Cross Keys and was soon back in action.

29. Brigadier General Louis Blenker lost two staff officers in the battle: a Captain Miser and Lieutenant E. Branderstein, both of whom were severely wounded in the action. Ewell may have been thinking of Captain R. Nicolai Dunka, an aide-de-camp to Frémont, who was killed while on an errand to the northern part of the field.

30. Ewell could not remember the commanders of the remaining Union brigades and left a space at this point in his manuscript, obviously intending to add them later. Frémont's six infantry brigade commanders were Colonel Gustave P. Cluseret and Brigadier Generals Julius Stahel, Adolph von Steinwehr, Henry Bohlen, Robert H. Milroy, and Robert C. Schenck. Colonel John A. Koltes commanded Steinwehr's brigade in the battle, while Brigadier General George D. Bayard led Frémont's cavalry. Brigadier General Louis Blenker commanded a division.

31. Six of the seven regiments in Elzey's and Steuart's brigades (the 12th Georgia and the 25th, 31st, 44th, 55th, and 58th Virginia) had fought under Edward Johnson in the Allegheny Mountains. Elzey's 13th Virginia had not.

32. Ewell had a low opinion of German-Americans, whom he referred to as "the Dutch."

33. Frémont "liberally" estimated that he had 10,500 men at Cross Keys, while Brigadier General Erastus B. Tyler, who commanded the Union forces at Port Republic on June 9, estimated his force at not greater than 3,000 men. Union losses at Port Republic were 1,018—48 percent greater than those reported by Frémont at Cross Keys.

119. To Benjamin Ewell

Feby 18. 64

Col. B. S. Ewell

Dear Ben;

If inaction without chance of doing anything is as hazardous as action with the chances of great results, the choice is plain. The enemy would collect his strength untill there would be as much loss as in taking the risk. We took the chances & are as well off as before the move.[1]

The enemy moved against Morton's Ford on the Rapidan picketed by my Corps. My Hd Qrts. are about 3 miles off & you may depend there was packing & racing & moving. The enemy did not succeed however in taking our lines & were pretty severely pressed by our men untill darkness stopped us. They crossed back again in the night (it was dark & drizzling) leaving 17 dead in our hands. Their reports or rather letters mention the names of 120 wounded & two killed—one Col. & two Lt. Col. We lost 4 killed & about 20 wounded, took 46 & lost 25 prisoners. So they made but little by that.[2] Col. Cabell who was on Magruder's Staff (Ord. Off.)[3] commands [an] Art'y Batt[alion]. on picket. He seems to be quite a gentleman & is here often. Do you remember him?[4] Col. Jeremiah Morton[,] who used to join us sometimes when there was a chance of catching a stray bullet, has sold the elegant place he owned at the beginning of the war & now lives at a small farm between Richmond & Danville of some one or two hundred acres. He is the author of some currency articles in the sentinel of recent appearance signed "the people." I am staying at his old place. Harriot has been trying to get Lizzie Ewell to come here but so far unsuccessfully.[5] Lizzie is wise I guess as the house is very cold without furniture

& tolerably dull. However Lizzie has an engagement with a dentist now about over & promises to take it into favorable consideration.

I am a little to[o] far from Orange Ct House to see much of the army. May be said to be on the out post.[6] Had I not been here there might have been a disaster the other day at Morton's Ford, but being on the spot as it were, I was able to give the necessary directions before the enemy had got a foothold. I asked Lizzie to write to ask you whereabouts was my gun. There were so many birds and our fare so bad I thought of trying to get some, but the winter is pretty much over & I dont believe the shot could have been had for reasonable rates. The enemy are in Culpepper chiefly extended from Stevensburg to Cedar Run Mtn (Slaughter Mtn.) & Rappahannock River.[7] They are said to be re-enlisting very rapidly but after receiving the bounty to be deserting as fast. The prisoners taken at Morton's Ford said but ten had returned out of 300 in one regt. Other sources corroborate this statement. We have now the coldest spell of the winter—clear & cold[—]& as the house is without carpets tolerably trying I guess to Lizinka & her daughter. Please give my respects to Genl Johnston.

Yours &—

R S. Ewell

1. Ewell may be referring to the Bristoe Station Campaign, the Army of Northern Virginia's most recent offensive operation. The October 1863 campaign resulted in a Confederate defeat.

2. On February 6, 1864, elements of Major General Gouverneur K. Warren's Second Corps crossed the Rapidan River at Morton's Ford. The purpose of Warren's demonstration was to divert Confederate attention from an advance by Major General Benjamin F. Butler up the Peninsula toward Richmond. Butler failed to make the advance, however, and Warren's troops recrossed after dark. Warren reported losing 255 men: 215 killed or wounded and 40 missing or captured. All but three of the casualties came from Brigadier General Alexander Hays's division. Among the Union casualties was Lieutenant Colonel J. H. Lockwood of the 7th West Virginia Volunteers. Hays reported capturing 30 Confederates during the initial crossing. Confederate figures are slightly different. Lee reported that the Federals left 17 men dead and 46 prisoners in their retreat, while his own army lost just 4 killed, 20 wounded, and 26 captured. Ewell wrote no report of the engagement.

3. Ordnance Officer.

4. Henry C. Cabell (1820–1889) commanded the Richmond Fayette Artillery before becoming chief of artillery for McLaws's division.

5. Lizzie was then staying in Richmond at the home of the Reverend Moses Hoge.

6. The Army of Northern Virginia had its headquarters near Orange Court House. Hill's corps held the left end of the line, from Liberty Mills to Clark's Mountain, and Ewell's corps held the right, from Clark's Mountain to Morton's Ford. It was approximately twelve miles from Ewell's headquarters at Morton's Hall to Orange Court House. A map showing the Confederate camps in April 1864 appears in Cowles, *Atlas,* plate 87, no. 4.

7. A map showing the Army of the Potomac's winter camps appears in Cowles, *Atlas,* plate 87, no. 2.

Five months of inactivity ended on May 4, 1864, when Confederate signalmen atop Clark's Mountain reported the Army of the Potomac moving toward Germanna Ford on the Rapidan River, beyond the Confederates' right flank. Lee immediately put his army into motion to meet the enemy, engaging them in a densely wooded region known as the Wilderness. For two days the fighting raged. Casualties were horrific—nearly thirty thousand men. Unable to break Lee's lines, Lieutenant General Ulysses S. Grant slid south toward Spotsylvania Court House. Again Lee blocked his path. Two more weeks of fighting ensued. The climax came on May 12 when Union troops broke Ewell's line in a dawn assault. The fighting centered around a turn in the Confederate logworks known as the "Bloody Angle." Both sides threw in everything they had, Grant to win, Lee to survive. In the end Lee held on, but it had cost his army sorely. Ewell escaped the battle unscathed, but his reputation did not. He mismanaged the fighting at Harris Farm on May 19 and lost his temper during the May 12 debacle, reinforcing Lee's poor opinion of him. Although Ewell might not have realized it, his days as Second Corps commander were numbered.

120. To Lizinka Ewell

16th[1] 9 P.M.

Mrs R S. Ewell

My Dear Lizinka;

Yours of the 15th just recd. You of course know why I have neglected writing to you. I felt my labors & exertions were all wanted for the occasion.[2] I picked up a Yankee horse so lame he was apparently ready to die, but I tried him just now & he is so recovered that I shall be able to ride him to morrow if

Ewell's map of Spotsylvania Court House and vicinity. (Polk-Brown-Ewell Papers, Southern Historical Collection, University of North Carolina)

necessary. Maj. Hamilton[3] gave me a delightful one in place of the black but he is a little thin but improving, so I am well off, but as a present from you I am extremely anxious to find the other & sending all over the Army. He ought to be advertised & hand bills struck off.[4] I started 2 hrs since to write you but C. had gone to look after a friend wounded & the Yankee skirmishers advancing.[5] I felt uneasy about him & could not write untill he returned which he did a few minutes since having discovered the trouble.[6] The Yankees have left their dead unburied. I have taken muskets enough from the enemy to pay for 100 cannon.[7] However if I am all right with you I dont care. Is it not an[n]oying that this army on which the fate of R[ichmon]d depends should be depleted at such a moment? Yet they have much of our cavalry &c.[8] I wont write military matters.

My health was never better.[9] C. does not sleep with me, as I am on the lines. He is a little way back with the Qmr Dept.[10] But he came up when T. was wounded & was in the thickest of the danger & is all day forward.[11] Remember me to Lizzie & Hattie.

Yours

R S.E

1. Ewell wrote this letter on May 16, 1864, during a lull in the Battle of Spotsylvania Court House.

2. The Overland Campaign had commenced on May 5, 1864, when the Army of the Potomac crossed the Rapidan River and engaged the Confederates in the Wilderness. After two days of inconclusive fighting, Grant shifted south to Spotsylvania Court House, but Lee anticipated the move and again blocked his path. Two more weeks of fighting followed. Ewell's corps was heavily engaged in both battles. His reports of those actions appear in *OR* 36(1):1069–75.

3. Major Samuel Prioleau Hamilton (1826–1897) began the war as a captain in the 1st Georgia Infantry. As a major at Sharpsburg and Fredericksburg, he commanded what later became Cabell's artillery battalion. In 1863 Hamilton was a judge advocate, but by the time Ewell wrote this letter he was again serving in Cabell's battalion.

4. Before the Battle of Spotsylvania Court House, Lizinka had given her husband a black horse. The animal ran off during the battle, prompting Ewell and his stepson, Campbell Brown, to conduct a vigorous search for it throughout the army. Brown asked his mother to look for the horse at auction sales in Richmond and in the city's livery stables. He also suggested that she advertise for the animal in the Richmond papers.

5. Apparently, Brown's friend lay wounded at the front, and Brown attempted to bring him in before advancing Federal forces overran the position.

6. For additional evidence of Ewell's anxiety about his stepson's safety, see Conner, *Letters,* 114–15, and RSE to BSE, undated letter (ca. Jan. 1864), folder 9, WM.

7. At dawn on May 12, 1864, Union troops broke through Ewell's line at Spotsylvania Court House, capturing twenty pieces of artillery and three thousand prisoners. Offsetting the loss in cannon was the Second Corps's rich harvest in small arms. In the Wilderness, Ewell's men collected nine thousand rifles from the battlefield, and it garnered eleven thousand more at Spotsylvania.

8. On May 9, 1864, Major General Philip Sheridan led three divisions of Union cavalry on a raid toward Richmond. Major General J. E. B. Stuart set out after him with three mounted brigades. He caught up with Sheridan at Yellow Tavern, north of Richmond, on May 11. In the ensuing battle, the Confederate commander received a mortal wound.

9. Campbell Brown confirmed Ewell's rosy assessment of his health. In a letter to his mother penned on May 16, Brown wrote: "So far the Gen'l. is unhurt & in excellent health, and has done an immense amount of work." Campbell Brown to Lizinka Ewell, 16 May 1864, FHS.

10. Jed Hotchkiss, the Second Corps's topographical engineer, noted that "Gen. Ewell sleeps & stays in the trenches, but he will not let any of his staff stay where there is danger if he can help it—sending them off as soon as they have done any duty he may require. He is very kind." Ewell's staff bivouacked with members of the Quartermaster Department at the J. Frazer house, approximately two miles from the front. Hotchkiss to wife, 19 May 1864, Hotchkiss Papers, LC; Hotchkiss, *Make Me a Map,* 204. For the location of the Frazer house, see Cowles, *Atlas,* plate 88, no. 3.

11. On May 10, 1864, while helping to repel Colonel Emory Upton's attack on Doles's Salient, Ewell's aide and future stepson Thomas Turner incurred a flesh wound in one leg and broke the tibia of the other. Campbell Brown discussed Turner's injuries and his own conduct during the battle in a May 11, 1864, letter published in Jones, *Campbell Brown's Civil War,* 251. Describing Turner's conduct at Spotsylvania, Ewell wrote that his aide-de-camp "was very efficient in rallying the fugitives, and was severely wounded while assisting in recapturing several pieces of artillery." *OR* 36(1):1072.

After two weeks of stubborn fighting at Spotsylvania Court House, Grant slid around Lee's right flank and drove toward Hanover Junction. Lee learned of the move and on May 21 raced south, reaching Hanover Junction ahead of the Union army. Ewell's corps led the march, followed by Richard Anderson (who had replaced the wounded Longstreet) and A. P. Hill. After a day and a half of hard marching, the Second Corps crossed the North Anna River and took up a defensive position around Hanover Junction. As his troops settled into their new position, Ewell found a few minutes to write the following letter to Lizinka. His comment on the condition of Grant's army reflects the general optimism felt in the Army of Northern Virginia at this time. Although the army's losses in the first three weeks of May had been high, Federal losses had been even higher—about twice as many. One day after Ewell wrote this letter, the Union army crossed the North Anna and engaged Hill's corps near Jericho Mills, adding more names to the campaign's already swollen casualty lists.

121. To Lizinka Ewell

Hanover Junction[1]
May 22d 64

Mrs R S Ewell

My Dear Lizinka

You see we are coming nearer—not because Grant drives us but because while keeping up a show in front, he tries to dodge around us. He got the start yesterday, but by marching all night & this morning I am again in front & the rest of the army well up. Anderson[2] next to me also in position. it seems to me that Grant has thrown away his chances by allowing us to unite with Beauregard.[3] C & myself are in capital health. I had a feast just now. Some sour milk, pone bread & cold chicken for nearly the first time since leaving Morton Hall. I was hungry & eat [*sic*] untill I felt the comfortable self complacency of satisfaction with myself & the world. Old Majr Doswell[4] has just brought me a lunch for supper: milk, ice, lamb &c. &c. Col. Pendleton speaks of running to Richmond untill tomorrow. C. will go if we remain quiet for a few days. I heard of an estray horse answering somewhat the description of the one you sent. am expecting to hear from the man sent to examine, but I rode Rifle to day who gets along pretty well. have still another horse & shall do very well.

Mr Holliday[5] near Orange sent me a b[a]rr[e]l of flour which is along & which I'll try to get to you. I am living on less than rations.

Turner writes in pretty fair spirits. I am very glad he can spare Withers.[6] It seemed almost like being with you to meet Mr Dibrell.[7] He is to take this letter. I feel in good spirits considering I was up all night. The position of Grant's army is this: Beaten, terrible losses, worn out. His chances are in his numbers that might stand killing untill we are worn out & he has still some left to use. But the chances are against this. I trust in Providence with the firm belief that the issue whatever it may be, will be to the best.[8]

I have had one letter from you since the march began.

I had like to have forgotten the main point in a small way. I am stewing down in my thick winter knit shirts & want you, if you can do so without more trouble than it is worth, to send me the flannel shirts—not knit[—]that are some where amongst my traps. These are what are called linsey I believe. As I am now[,] I fear I will melt entirely.

Remember me to Harriet & Lizzie.

Yours

R S Ewell[9]

1. Located twenty miles north of Richmond, Hanover Junction stood at the point where the Richmond, Fredericksburg, and Potomac Railroad crossed the Virginia Central Railroad.

2. Major General Richard H. Anderson (1821–1879) took command of the First Corps on May 7, 1864, after Lieutenant General James Longstreet was wounded in the Wilderness.

3. General P. G. T. Beauregard commanded the Confederate forces that confronted Major General Benjamin Butler's Army of the James, south of Richmond.

4. Thomas Doswell, who was then about seventy-one years old, owned a house just outside of Ewell's lines. He was a very wealthy man. Census records show that in 1860 he owned $50,000 in real property and $70,000 in personal property. For the location of his house, see Cowles, *Atlas,* plate 81, no. 7.

5. Waller Holladay (ca. 1830–?) was a dentist living in Orange County, Virginia.

6. Withers appears to have been one of Turner's horses.

7. Dibrell was a friend of the Ewell family. Ewell stayed at his residence, located on Main Street between First and Foushee streets, when he first transferred to Richmond. The 1860 U.S. census for Richmond, Virginia, identifies two men by this name, apparently a father and son: Edward Dibbrelle (b. ca. 1795) and R. H. Dibbrelle (b. ca. 1822). Edward kept a tobacco warehouse; his son was a tobacco merchant.

8. Grant had indeed taken heavy losses to that point. In the Wilderness, Union losses officially totaled 17,666, and at Spotsylvania they numbered 18,399. Confederate losses for the two battles are not known, but they are estimated to have been between 22,000 and 25,000.

9. Campbell Brown added a postscript to the letter: "You can imagine my disgust at not recognizing Mr. Dibbrell to-day. I thought I shd have known him anywhere, but I did not. Here we are & where the Yankees are, I don't know, but we are certain of one night's good rest, I think, & that is all we need much now. Wherever the Yankees are, we'll whip them on sight. I heard one of our men say 'Why old Lee can whip four such armies as Grant's', & this seems the universal feeling of confidence. Love to Sister G.C.B."

After a four-day standoff on the North Anna River, Grant broke contact again and shifted to his left. This time his objective was Totopotomoy Creek. The move came on the first anniversary of Ewell's marriage. Before leaving the North Anna line, Ewell scribbled a brief note to Lizinka, assuring her that he had not forgotten the importance of that date. With that happy recollection, however, came a prediction of more fighting and a hint, perhaps, that the South might not be able to meet the challenge.

122. To Lizinka Ewell

May 26. 1864

Mrs R S Ewell

My Dear Lizinka;

It just occured to me that this is the anniversary of our marriage.[1] I am a little unwell, not connected at all with my leg but bad diet &c. &c.[2] However I determined to take enough time to write if only to say that I wish you may regret as little as myself that day & that your happiness may have been as much increased as mine. I suppose one cannot change at any time of life & must continue as despondent &c as follows bad health &c, but it would be great happiness to be with you in the quiet pursuit of any business. We are still in juxtaposition with the Yankees—mutually watching—they entrenched so strongly as to make it impossible to attack any part of their lines on this flank, while they are equally afraid to[3] come against us. This will probably continue untill they take advantage of darkness to past [*sic*] across our flank when we will be forced to move back again to get in their front. We are getting too near Richmond for this to continue much more & one side or the other will have to change tactics & go at it "hammer & tongs." The idea of their reaching Richmond is too terrible to think of & unless the folly & incapacity of our managers interfere there is not much danger.[4]

But we ought to have several thousands more cavalry, but they are dissipated by some one & untill none have yet reached us. As at Newburne[5] they are risking the loaf for the crumbs. May God enlighten our councils & strengthen our army & protect you & yours.

Yours

R S. Ewell

I sent a telescope in the bundles & a lemon. You dont mention it. Did you open the bundle?

1. Ewell and Lizinka had been married by the Reverend Charles Minnigerode on May 26, 1863, at St. Paul's Episcopal Church in Richmond.

2. Ewell, by his own account, suffered from a "severe attack of diarrhea." Ironically, Brown had written his mother just one day earlier that "the Gen. never looked so well," adding, "Of course I am well, for he [General Ewell] had done twice the work I have—more than any man in the Army in the same time." *OR* 36(1):1074; CB to LCB, 25 May 1864, FHS.

3. Ewell mistakenly repeated the word "to."

4. Ewell's prediction was right on the mark. The very night this letter was written the Army of the Potomac abandoned its position on the North Anna River and marched downriver, crossing the Pamunkey River at Hanovertown and Hundley's Ford. Following a brief standoff at Totopotomoy Creek, Grant shifted to the left once again. On June 3 at Cold Harbor, he attacked "hammer and tongs," just as Ewell had predicted, and was severely punished for his efforts.

5. Union troops led by Brigadier General Ambrose E. Burnside had captured New Berne, North Carolina, on March 14, 1862. On three different occasions— March 1863, February 1864, and May 1864—the Confederates attempted to recapture the town. Each time they failed.

Upon leaving the North Anna River line, Ewell had a serious case of diarrhea that compelled him to relinquish command of the Second Corps to Jubal Early. He asked to be on reinstated on May 30, but Lee refused to do so on the grounds that Ewell had not yet sufficiently recovered his health and that it would be too dangerous to make a change in command with a battle pending. Ewell believed Lee was using his illness as a pretense to supplant him with Early, a suspicion that was confirmed on June 4 with the announcement of Early's temporary promotion to lieutenant general and his formal appointment to corps command.

123. To Lizinka Ewell

June 1. 1864

Mrs R S. Ewell

My Dear Lizinka;

I was sorry to hear from Capt. Hotchkiss[1] last night that you were occupied looking for rooms and without success. I had hoped you were settled at Dr H's.[2] I am sorry I did not send in the Ambulance last night that you or the girls[3] might use it, if needed. I am so entirely recovered that I shall be on horseback to day & so in case of any chance emergency will not need it. Please let me know when you will want to drive. You may wish to move.

I reported myself recovered yesterday & recd a letter last night, that the troops being in line of battle no change was deemed advantageous at this time, but the Genl[4] "recommended that as soon as I could move with safety that I go[5] to some place untill the impending battle is over to recuperate my health & restore my strength for future service." "To report for duty now would be to expose my life & health without corresponding advantages" &c.[6] I shall answer that I am as fit for duty as since I started & that unless my connection with this Army is permanently dissolved I shall remain here untill changes may make it proper[7] to restore me to command.[8] I anticipated this result & here at Hanover Junction did not report sick untill the move to new localities found me unable to make the necessary exertions. Say nothing of all this. I dont know that an engagement is imminent within a day or two. C. came in at twilight last night & went off early this morning. He is very well—angry at the note.[9] I have expected nothing else, it being Lee's habit.

Yours—

R. S. Ewell

P.S. C. will go to Richmond the first moment that he can do so with propriety. Though not particularly employed yet there is no saying when he may be wanted & though his presence may not be necessary his absence might be injurious.[10] Were it possible for you to come out here I would ask you, but besides

"Aunt Nicey," as she was known, was Benjamin Ewell's slave. She worked for General and Mrs. Ewell in 1864–65, when they resided in Richmond. (Courtesy Donald Pfanz)

the dust[,] movements of troops &c. &c. the possibility that at any moment we may be engaged is reason enough.[11]

Report says Early is promoted.[12] I would like to know as soon as possible if anything were meant injurious to me, in order that I might be prepared. I have neither influence nor intrigue[13] & at the earliest moment possible will have to give way to those that are. You should have thought of this before we were married. Love to Nicey & "staff."[14]

RSE—

1. Jedediah Hotchkiss was Ewell's topographical engineer. Although he held no formal rank in the Confederate army, he was referred to as captain, and later major, in official correspondence.
2. Dr. Francis Hancock of Richmond.
3. Hattie and Lizzie.
4. Robert E. Lee.
5. Ewell inserted the word "retire" above the word "go."
6. Copies of Lee's May 31, 1864, dispatch to Ewell are in folder 11, PBE, and in the Ewell Papers at the Library of Congress.
7. Ewell mistakenly repeated the word "proper" here.
8. A copy of Ewell's June 1, 1864, dispatch to Lee's adjutant, Colonel Walter Taylor is in folder 9, PBE. It reads:

    Colonel,

    The opinion of my Medl. attendent, Dr. McGuire and that of myself is that I am able for duty to-day as at any time since the campaign commenced. I am unwilling to be idle at this crisis, and with the permission of the Com'g Gen'l I would prefer to remain with this Army until circumstances may admit of my being replaced in command of my Corps.

    I am Col & etc.

    R S. Ewell Lt. Gen.

9. "The note"—i.e., Lee's response to Ewell's application to return to duty.
10. Campbell Brown, like the other members of Ewell's staff, served under Jubal Early during Ewell's leave of absence.
11. Reason enough for Lizinka to remain where she was.
12. Lee appointed Early to command the Second Corps in Ewell's absence on May 29. On June 4 he formally announced Early's temporary promotion to lieutenant general and his appointment to command the Second Corps.

13. Unlike many other officers, Ewell neither intrigued for promotion nor had influential friends in Richmond to look after his interests.

14. Nicey was a female slave owned by Benjamin Ewell. The 1860 census shows him as owning two slaves, a thirty-year-old male and a sixty-year-old female. Nicey was probably the latter. "Staff" appears to be a humorous reference to a comment that Lizinka had made in a recent letter, possibly in reference to other servants.

Although Lee refused to reinstate him to command of the Second Corps and urged him to retire to a place of safety to recover from his illness, Ewell refused to leave the army. Instead, he chose to remain nearby in case Lee summoned him to duty. He wrote the following two letters while waiting in vain for that call.

124. To Lizinka Ewell

June 2d 64

Mrs. R S. Ewell

My Dear Lizinka;

General Lee insists that he will make no changes while the troops are in line.[1] C. is highly indignant. Possibly all will come right, but while I only care about it on your account & knowing how ambitious you are, your letter of yesterday gives me no indication of the indignation I supposed you would feel. Fighting was heavy yesterday on our extreme right. the 2d Corps not engaged. the whole is[,] from what I can learn, cheerful for us. The Yankees will have to do now what they dodged at the Wilderness, Spots. Ct. H.[,] & H. Junction.[2] I am doing remarkably well—would be perfectly happy were I only with you & then the Yankees gone. Maj. Greene came in last night very happy. He had been on the extreme right & caught a spent minnie[3] through his Jacket & then between his watch & pocket book, both considerably damaged. Dont forget to ask him to show the marks. It didnt hurt him much & he is on duty to day.[4] Col. Richardson[5] unbended yesterday, sent us a quantity of potatoes & asparagus very nicely cooked. Offers me ice &c. &c. Should the chances justify it, I can send Lancaster to look at the horse, but he says my horse had a small white speck in the right flank & another on the neck near the withers.[6] Turner's wounded horse is in articulo mortis[7] having had tralismus[8] (I believe that is lock jaw) signs for several days. I doubt if the visits of young ladies would help him. C. is well—will go to town as soon as possible with propriety. is away all day, or I would send for you in spite of every thing. Col. Tyler (Enquirer)[9] was here yesterday. says he will leave with you some copies of the paper with letters about the war which I will want to help about my report.

The Cakes & Catchup from Mrs. Ray[10] were very acceptable, but you must cease to consider me an invalid & these attentions must be given to those really so. My case is, I was very sick for a day or two. Genl Lee moved the army and expecting a battle every moment will not[,] now I am well[,] risk the confusion &c. possible on a change of commanders. All this is in writing. I pray for protection to you & all that interests you.

Yours
R S. Ewell—

1. The Army of Northern Virginia was then confronting the Union army at Cold Harbor, Virginia, just outside of Richmond. Ewell had an interview with Lee on June 8, hoping to persuade Lee to restore him to corps command. A summary of their conversation appears in Hamlin, *The Making of a Soldier*, 128–30.

2. Ewell predicted that Grant, having run out of space for maneuver between Cold Harbor and the James River, would be forced to attack the Confederates' entrenched position head on. He was correct. The following day, June 3, 1864, Grant ordered a general assault on Lee's lines at Cold Harbor and was easily repulsed.

3. Minié balls were conical lead bullets fired from rifled muskets. They were named after their inventor, French gunsmith Claude E. Minié (1814–1879).

4. Green was the Second Corps's acting chief engineer at this time.

5. Colonel George W. Richardson owned a house near Ewell's headquarters. The house stood just north of Old Church Road, less than two miles from Mechanicsville. Richardson (b. 1819) was a lawyer by trade. He was a delegate to Virginia's Secession Convention in 1861 and served as colonel of the 47th Virginia Infantry from May 1861 to May 1862, when he failed reelection. Subsequent efforts by Richardson to secure a commission failed.

6. Ewell was still looking for a black horse that he lost during the Battle of Spotsylvania Court House in May. Apparently a horse roughly matching the description of the missing animal was reported in Richmond, prompting Ewell to consider sending "Lancaster" (possibly a slave) to identify it.

7. "*Articulo mortis*"—i.e., death throes.

8. Trismus is a condition in which the mouth is held shut by a sustained spasm of the jaw muscle, a condition often observed in tetanus, or lockjaw.

9. In 1860 Nathaniel Tyler (along with W. B. Allegre and O. Jennings Wise, the son of then-Governor Henry A. Wise) had purchased the *Richmond Enquirer.* When the war began, Tyler became lieutenant colonel of the 20th Virginia Infantry. That regiment disbanded in December 1862, and Tyler returned to his position as the newspaper's senior editor.

10. Unidentified.

125. To Lizinka Ewell

June 3. 64

Mrs. R. S. Ewell

My Dear Lizinka;

I heard from C. late yesterday in the way of vehement messages for something to eat & was able to dispatch early to day, as soon as there was a probability of finding him buttermilk, coffee &c. &c. I rode out yesterday to the right in hopes of finding him but he had shifted to the left with General Early.[1]

There does not seem much to day, so far, in our front, except artillery. There is no certainty as to where the storm will burst or within days, when. Possibly to day.[2] To allay as much as possible your anxieties, I promise you to let you know, as fast as a horse can go, in case anything should happen to C. & for that matter myself also, although it would require a very erratic miss[i]le to reach me, not being on duty.

We captured yesterday about 500 prisoners—chiefly Gordon. Rodes did hard fighting I hear. Doles killed.[3] Rosser had a brilliant cavalry affair at Ashland the other day.[4] Generally our affairs look cheerful. May God grant that you may not suffer more than you have already.

Yours
R. S. Ewell

1. Brown and the other members of Ewell's staff joined Early's staff during Ewell's illness.

2. The storm did indeed break that day when Grant hurled his army against Lee's entrenched lines at Cold Harbor, an action that resulted in thousands of Union casualties.

3. On June 2, 1864, the Second Corps attacked the Army of the Potomac's right flank near Bethesda Church. The divisions of Major Generals John B. Gordon and Robert E. Rodes took part in the fighting. A counterattack by Union re-

serves checked the Confederate advance and resulted in the death of Brigadier General George Doles.

4. On June 1, 1864, Brigadier General Thomas Rosser attacked Colonel J. B. McIntosh's Union cavalry brigade, which was employed in the destruction of the Richmond, Fredericksburg, and Potomac Railroad bridge over the Pamunkey River. McIntosh had completed this task and was tearing up tracks near Ashland, Virginia, when Rosser struck. McIntosh took shelter behind some nearby earthworks. Brigadier General W. H. F. ("Rooney") Lee later joined Rosser. Together they drove McIntosh from his works and pursued him toward Hanover Court House.

Chapter 10

Defender of Richmond, 1864–1865

Dissatisfied with Ewell's performance in the Overland Campaign, Lee had his subordinate transferred to the Department of Richmond. As the department's commander, it was Ewell's responsibility to defend the Confederate capital against attack, administer its military prisons, and maintain order. The troops that came with the command were decidedly substandard: inexperienced heavy artillery companies; reserve units composed of males either too old or too young for regular military service; and government clerks who, in an emergency, could be called away from their desks to man the city's defenses. It was a hodgepodge assortment of pseudo-soldiers, few in number, ill equipped, and badly disciplined.

None of that mattered much earlier in the war. Since McClellan's retreat in the summer of 1862, the Union army had been a distant threat. Except for an occasional cavalry raid, there had been little to disturb the day-to-day routine of city life. That all changed in May 1864, when the Union Army of the James, led by Major General Benjamin Butler, landed at Bermuda Hundred, a broad neck of land south of the city. Confederate troops, racing up from North Carolina, beat Butler to Richmond and succeeded in confining him to the peninsula. But no sooner was Butler under control than the Army of the Potomac threatened Richmond from the north, slowly pressing Lee's forces back on the Confederate capital. Unable to break Lee's lines at Cold Harbor, Grant boldly led the Army of the Potomac across the James River and lay siege to Petersburg. For the next nine months he would systematically sever supply lines leading into the city, slowly strangling Petersburg and Richmond into submission.

Throughout that period, Richmond was under constant threat of attack. In an effort to force Lee to extend the lines of his outnumbered army, Grant periodically sent Union troops north of the James River to menace the capital. It was Ewell's responsibility, as department commander, to support Army of Northern Virginia units defending Richmond until reinforcements could arrive from Petersburg.

The most serious threat took place in September 1864, when Butler made a determined lunge toward the capital with two Union corps. The move caught the

Confederates off guard, but a determined defense by Ewell and a few thousand troops at Fort Harrison kept the Federals at bay until reinforcements reached the battlefield. It was the greatest accomplishment of his career.

By then, however, the South was fighting a losing war. Short of men and supplies and pressed on every side, defeat became inevitable. For Ewell and his men, the end came in April 1865. On the first day of the month Grant captured Five Forks, a vital crossroads southwest of Petersburg. He followed up his success with a general assault on the city. The Confederate lines snapped, leaving Lee no choice but to evacuate Petersburg and head west. Ewell and the Richmond garrison joined the army in its retreat.

Grant aggressively pursued the Army of Northern Virginia toward Appomattox Court House. At Sailor's Creek, Union cavalry cut the Confederate column in two, isolating Ewell's and Anderson's corps from the rest of the army. Sensing victory, Northern infantry closed in for the kill. The Confederates made a gallant defense, but Union numbers prevailed. Just three days before Lee's surrender at Appomattox, Ewell and his men became prisoners of war.

126. To Benjamin Ewell

Richmond Va
July 20. 1864

Col. B. S. Ewell

Dear Ben;

I was at Chaffin's Farm[,][1] a military post some miles below here, last week & on my return to town heard of General J. E. Johnston's application for me. Unfortunately Lizinka went to see Bragg about it while I was away & learned that the authorities declined to make the transfer. I regretted her going very much as I wanted the chance to give the authorities a plain statement of my case & if developments authorized it, to hand in my resignation.[2]

I would at once have telegraphed to ask Genl Johnston for a command, on being relieved[,] but understood that Stewart had been appointed by Genl Johnston's request & of course it was too late.[3] My position here is without troops & merely a polite way of being laid on the shelf. For what reason I cannot tell, & had I have thought he wanted my services would have gone in spite of every thing.[4]

Genl Johnston's relief from command fell on every one like a thunderbolt, creating a great deal of anxiety.[5] I dont know anything about the situation of things out there—have regretted of course the abandonment of so large an ex-

During his tenure as the commander of the Department of Richmond, Ewell spent much of his time at the Chaffin Farm, near the front. (*Harper's Weekly*)

tent of country. I supposed that Genl Johnston knew what he was about & was afraid that he was thwarted by the authorities here, or as I had hea[r]d intimated that he was not allowed the command necessary to act. I was exceedingly anxious to resume my service under General Johnston—was willing to risk every thing under his guidance—but have always feared for the want of the entente cordiale[6] between him & the administration.[7] I repeat however that I would have resigned rather than not have joined him had I supposed he wanted me, before it was too late.

Maj Barbour says he is relieved because the balance of what is to do is of easy accomplishment.

I would be a Captain under him if he were Col. of a Regt. He was my only hope of regaining command.[8]

Yrs—

R S. Ewell

1. Chaffin's Farm stood on the left bank of the James River, opposite Drewry's Bluff, on the southern end of the Confederates' intermediate defensive line. For much of the summer and fall of 1864, Ewell had his headquarters there.
2. Following the Battle of Chattanooga, President Jefferson Davis relieved General Braxton Bragg as commander of the Army of Tennessee, appointing Joseph

Johnston to take his place. Bragg went to Richmond, where he acted as Davis's military advisor.

3. When Lieutenant General Leonidas Polk was killed in action outside of Atlanta, Georgia, on June 14, 1864, Johnston proposed that Ewell replace him. Robert E. Lee expressed his regard for Ewell but gave the opinion that his subordinate's health would be "unequal to his duties." President Davis chose Alexander P. Stewart to fill the vacancy instead. A division commander in Hardee's corps, Army of Tennessee, Stewart was promoted to lieutenant general and assigned to Polk's corps on June 23, 1864.

4. As commander of the Department of Richmond, Ewell commanded an assortment of second-rate troops consisting of heavy artillery units, Veteran Reserve regiments, and Local Defense Troops. On paper, at least, he commanded between four thousand and seven thousand men.

5. When Sherman advanced through northwest Georgia, Johnston fell back slowly toward Atlanta. He planned to strike Sherman at a point outside the city, but before he could do so President Davis on July 17, 1864, replaced him with General John B. Hood.

6. French, "good feeling."

7. Johnston had been on bad terms with President Davis since 1861, when Davis sent Johnston's name, along with those of Samuel Cooper, Albert Sidney Johnston, Robert E. Lee, and P. G. T. Beauregard, to the Senate for confirmation as full generals in the Confederate army. Joe Johnston's name was fourth on the list, making him subordinate to Cooper, Albert Sidney Johnston, and Lee. As Joe Johnston had outranked each of his rivals in the United States Army, he felt that Davis had slighted him. An angry letter by Johnston to Davis received a scornful reply, creating hard feelings on both sides.

8. The words "he" and "him" in the final three sentences of this letter refer to Joseph Johnston.

127. To Lizinka Ewell

29. July

Mrs R S. Ewell

My Dear Lizinka;

Anderson I am afraid did not meet with very decided success yesterday, nor indeed was the check he received a serious one. It showed the enemy to be in considerable force both of caval[r]y & Inty. I suppose all immediate cause for uneasiness is over as we probably are equal to the enemy.[1]

I gave Bob (is that better than Robin?) a hard ride yesterday. He is an excellent horse, being new to me is a little rough but that will wear off as I get used to him.[2] I hate to ride him while C. is on such a miserable wretch as his mare. I hope his horse will soon be fit for duty. I am very much in hopes that Early will draw off some of the Yankee troops from this or the other side of James River.[3] I suppose I will be soundly abused by the learned non-combatants of Richmond, but you ought not to mind that as I am hard at work & using I think the resources at my disposal to the best purpose. As I am not fighting for self, I am nearly satisfied if doing the best the circumstances allow.[4]

This is an amount of philosophy you wont credit me for, but I am chiefly in charge of the defense of Richmond. The movements of troops in the field are to a great degree directed by Genl Anderson under Genl Lee, it being a mixed sort of concern.[5]

Yours

R S. Ewell

1. In an effort to draw Confederate troops away from Petersburg, Grant sent Major General Winfield S. Hancock's Second Corps and two divisions of Major General Philip Sheridan's cavalry across the James River at Deep Bottom on July 27, 1864. Hancock attacked the Confederate defenses at New Market Heights and Fussell's Mill, while Sheridan swept around Hancock's right, advancing on Richmond by way of the Charles City Road. In response, Lee dispatched Lieutenant General Richard H. Anderson with three divisions of the First Corps to the north side of the James. Having accomplished their objective, Hancock and Sheridan recrossed the James River on the night of July 29 to take part in an assault on Petersburg.
2. Ewell acquired a horse named Robin, which Brown renamed Bob. The horse replaced a sorrel mare of Ewell's that had been killed on May 19, 1864, at Spotsylvania.
3. Following the Battle of Cold Harbor, Lee dispatched Jubal Early and the Second Corps to Lynchburg, Virginia, to head off a Union force led by Major General David Hunter. Early defeated Hunter on June 18, 1864, and then advanced down the Shenandoah Valley into Maryland, threatening Washington. Grant sent the Sixth Corps from Petersburg to defend Washington, and after a brief demonstration on July 12, Early withdrew to Virginia. Determined to crush Early once and for all, Grant reinforced the Sixth Corps with the Nineteenth Corps, two infantry and one cavalry division from Major General George Crook's Army of West Virginia, and two cavalry divisions drawn from the Army of the Potomac. He appointed Major General Philip Sheridan to command this force.

In a series of battles, Sheridan routed Early's army. By November he had effectively secured the Shenandoah Valley for the Union.

4. To repel this threat to Richmond, Ewell called out the Local Defense Troops, a body of men comprising clerks and mechanics who worked in the various government bureaus. Because their use threw government operations into confusion, Local Defense Troops were to be called out only in times of crisis for the actual defense of the city. Ewell determined that the Federal incursion constituted such a crisis and requested the secretary of war to activate the force. By the time they reached the front, however, the Federals had withdrawn, exposing Ewell to criticism.

5. As commander of the Department of Richmond, Ewell was in charge of protecting the city. When the Army of Northern Virginia arrived on the outskirts of Richmond, however, it assumed primary responsibility for the capital's defense, leaving Ewell in an ambiguous and largely supportive role.

128. To Lizinka Ewell

July 30. 64.

Mrs R. S. Ewell

My Dear Lizinka;

I will go up, you may depend, as soon as matters are in proper condition down here for me to be away.[1] The movements of the Yankees are incomprehensible on any grounds I can give, and I have a half sort of feeling with something of the ludricous [*sic*] as well as serious, that they are about to try some previously unheard of plan of taking Richmond, by balloons or under water, or that they may suddenly appear in some quarter impossible under every rule that usually governs troops. Why did Sheridan cross or why did he go back, or whether he went back or if he did not go back, where is he, are questions equally hard to answer.[2] People are planting potatoes. I would like to plant a bushel. Mr Connor[3] sent word from Morton's Hall that he would soon have a plenty for me but two strings to the bow—Turnips also.[4] Let Frank stay untill I telegraph. Why not put your name down for Family flour?[5] I may be up to-morrow. Why not put the[6] eggs in salt? Frank says "Mars Campbell & the gennem[7] eat his rations." I told him in future to keep his rations for himself or suffer consequences of hunger.[8]

---

1. Ewell then had his headquarters at the front, at the Chaffin farm. With Union forces apparently in retreat north of the James River, Lizinka hoped that her husband would be able to visit her in Richmond.

2. Having drawn three divisions of Lee's army north to defend Richmond, Hancock and Sheridan recrossed the James River on the night of July 29, 1864, to participate in a general assault on Petersburg. The attack's success hinged on the detonation of a mine placed under Elliott's Salient, east of the city. At 4:45 A.M., July 30, the mine exploded as planned, blowing a 170-foot-wide hole in the Confederate line. Union troops rushed into the smoking crater, only to be pinned down and slaughtered by Confederate reinforcements. Ewell's fears of an unorthodox attack, as expressed in this letter, reflect remarkable intuition, bordering on prescience.
3. Conner may have been a caretaker at Morton Hall.
4. Sometimes rendered "Two strings to the bow are better than one," this old proverb suggests the wisdom of having a backup plan in case the first alternative fails.
5. Grant's investment of Petersburg had reduced the already meager supply of food coming into Richmond, causing the price of flour to soar. Special supply stores created by the Richmond City Council provided food to the poor at reduced prices. In May 1864 the council had extended that privilege to "such officers and citizens as are prevented by military service from earning their usual support." Ewell may have been suggesting that Lizinka avail herself of that provision to obtain flour cheaply.
6. Ewell inadvertently added the word "in" here.
7. Gentlemen.
8. Frank was one of the Brown family slaves. He joined Campbell Brown in Jackson, Mississippi, in 1863 and remained with him throughout the rest of the war. Brown characterized him as "very active & efficient." Jones, *Campbell Brown's Civil War,* 183. For another reference to Frank, see LCB to David Hubbard, 4 January 1863, box 1, folder 3, Hubbard Papers, Tennessee State Library and Archives, Nashville.

129. Private Memorandum

Memoranda of the attack on North side James River 29th September /'64. I told you[1] when in Richmond that I would send you a short account of the attack on these lines on the 29th Sept. We had been directed to hold the line from Signal Hill to New Market[2] (Lilby's house 1/4 mile north of drill house) whence there was a line partly constructed to White Oak Swamp & marked out thence to the Chickahominy. From Signal Hill to New Market the line was naturally strong but not worked sufficiently to help the defence. All available means were at work & less than a week would have made it tenable with heavy batteries on

Signal Hill covering the enemy's canal at Dutch Gap.[3] Gen Lee could spare no troops & the Sec'ty of War [refused] to call out the Local Defence troops all that were available, or a part, unless[4] the city were in immediate danger.[5] The enemys works were within musket range of our picket line at Signal Hill & Deep Bottom & in fact along the most of this line of four miles.[6] While being for the whole distance close to the river the enemy could, whenever he pleased cross troops at any point without our being aware of it untill the attack. The line of four miles was held by less than 1500 muskets[7] & at Four A.M. on the 29th Sept. Thursday, I being at Chaffins[8] received notice that the enemy were crossing to the North of James River at Varina[9] & Deep Bottom. Notice was at once sent to Richmond & to Gen. Lee: but it requires hours to get out the Locals & Gen. Lee's disposable troops were near Petersburg. We were attacked at dawn at New Market & Johnsons Tenn. Brigade under Col. Hugh[s] at Signal Hill was turned on its left from Varina & driven back before overwhelming numbers[,] fighting as it retired. The Brigade had between 200 & 300 muskets.[10] A few moments after sunrise the enemy appeared in front of Fort Harrison, a commanding redoubt on the line running from Richmond below Chaffins & at the point where this line turns to approach the River. This redoubt was held by the gunners for its artillery; a portion of Hughs command & some of the artillery soldiers armed with muskets; a regt of Va reserves also guarded the fort: while Gen. Gregg's command consisting of his own & Benning's Brigade (under Col DuBose) were on the left extending towards New Market, covering those approaches to Richmond.[11] The enemy carried Fort Harrison with more than their usual bravery at some loss. Fortunately for us a screen of woods prevented their seeing that there was nothing between them & Chaffins Bluff & consequently Richmond. A very few extended to the left after a short time, but after time had been given to collect a few fugitives in Wise's old entrenchments[12] this looked like resistance & they satisfied themselves with occupying the next redoubt to Harrison as a work of advanced post towards the river.[13] Some of Stark's art.[14] was also as soon as time allowed placed on this line to make more show. The main column of the enemy turned to their right from Fort Harrison & attacked for[t] Field[15] a small work close to Harrison on the line towards Richmond. Here Gregg had collected his few hundred men & with some of Hardaway['s][16] & Stark['s] artillery drove them back with loss and this fight between 7 & 8 A.M. saved Richmond. The enemy marched up the Varina & New Market roads toward Richmond & about 12 M made a determined & formidable attack on Fort Gilmer[,] a strong enclosed work one & quarter miles from Ft Harrison on same line works. Some of their blacks got into the ditch but here Gregg again drove them back, with even greater loss than before.[17] Maj. Gen. Field[18] was by this time across the river with the balance of his division, consequently so much did not depend on this as on the attack at Ft Field. Brig. Gen. Gregg fell one week after in the attack on the enemy's right. He was a brave & able officer & no individual of his rank has been more directly instrumental in saving our capitol.[19] Gen. Lee ran a strong line cutting off the corner where the enemy held Ft. Harrison, a place of not much consequence to them, as the possession of Signal Hill gives them all the advantages in the way of command of the river &c. while they neutralize much force in holding it. Probably the moral effect in making our authorities active in getting out *some* who should have been in the ranks long since, is worth the place to us.[20] Some of our papers call the loss of Ft Harrison a surprise. This is absurd, as it is shown by my statements written & verbal to the Sec'ty of war it was in the enemy's power not only to have taken that place but Richmond. If all Gregg's force had been at once withdrawn to these lines, there would have been nothing to prevent the enemy from marching down the New Market road to R[ichmon]d; but they were held in check on the line from Ft Harrison to that road until their reverses at that fort made it necessary to withdraw everything to resist farther advances. When a place has more than the wonted garrison, has two hours notice, & uses all the means intended for its defence, its loss can hardly be called a surprise. When the authorities received due notice, When for months the almost certainty of such a movement by the enemy had been stated, When able officers who saw the position of affairs thought the fall of R[ichmon]d must follow the expected move of the enemy's[,] What sane person could be surprised that two army corps of the enemy[21] could, being able to fall on any point unexpectedly, of a line four miles in length held by less than 1500, be able to carry whatever they went against? It has been said; Why was not Ft Harrison more strongly guarded? It was held by more than its share of men & while to some degree Ft Harrison was the key to Rd we could not save the city for the key.

I write the above not for publication but that [the] history which you are compiling may have facts at its disposal. I dont suppose of course that all this will be copied or any portion, but it gives the general idea & I suppose will be used as suits the author. I send a map showing the position of the points.[22]

Resp.

Nov. 4./ '64.

1. This letter, although not in Ewell's hand, was obviously written by him for the benefit of someone in Richmond who was then writing a history of the war,

possibly Benson Lossing or Edward Pollard. The early date of this letter—less than six weeks after the Battle of Fort Harrison—makes it an important source of information on that subject. A detailed account of the battle appears in Sommers, *Richmond Redeemed,* 13–99.

2. Signal Hill overlooked the James River one mile upriver from Dutch Gap. The drill house stood directly north of Deep Bottom, just west of the junction of the Kingsland and New Market roads. New Market stood at the point where the Kingsland Road and the New Market (or River) Road met, approximately one mile north of Deep Bottom. The drill house appears in Cowles, *Atlas,* plate 92, no. 1, and plate 100, no. 2. A map showing Richmond's entire defensive system at this time appears in Sommers, *Richmond Redeemed,* 6.

3. To avoid Confederate batteries and obstructions on the James River, Major General Benjamin Butler on August 10, 1864, began construction of a canal across a narrow neck of land located at an oxbow in the river known as Dutch Gap. When completed the following year, the 174-yard canal reduced river navigation by nearly five miles.

4. Ewell inadvertently repeated the word "unless" here.

5. The Local Defense Troops constituted Richmond's last line of defense. Comprising city clerks and mechanics, this temporary force was only to be summoned to defend the city in cases of dire emergency. For Ewell's difficulties with Secretary of War James A. Seddon over the use of Local Defense Troops, see Pfanz, *Ewell,* 409.

6. Deep Bottom stood on the north side of the James River, approximately twelve miles southeast of Richmond and five miles east of Chaffin's Bluff, at a point where the river made a sharp bend. It was a favorite crossing point for Union troops throughout the Siege of Petersburg. For a sketch of Union defensive works there, see Cowles, *Atlas,* plate 67, no. 7.

7. This number included only the men in Ewell's department. It did not include nearly 2,900 Army of Northern Virginia veterans commanded by Brigadier General John Gregg, who manned the defenses at New Market. Gregg, while subordinate to Ewell in rank, was not in Ewell's department and normally operated independently of him.

8. Ewell's headquarters at this time were at the Chaffin Farm, approximately five miles west of Deep Bottom.

9. Varina, also known as Aiken's Landing, was just over a mile upriver from Deep Bottom. For maps of the area between Chaffin's Bluff and Deep Bottom, see Cowles, *Atlas,* plate 77, no. 3; plate 92, no. 1; and plate 100, no. 2.

10. Colonel John M. Hughs of the 25th Tennessee temporarily commanded Major General Bushrod R. Johnson's Tennessee Brigade, which at this time numbered no more than 400 men. Unlike Gregg's, Johnson's forces belonged to the Department of Richmond and reported directly to Ewell. Historian Richard J. Sommers characterized Hughs as "a brave guerrilla raider but a poor commander, whose negligence allowed [brigade] discipline to disintegrate." Sommers, *Richmond Redeemed,* 15.

11. Lieutenant John Guerrant's Goochland Artillery of Virginia manned nine guns in and around Fort Harrison. It was supported by five companies of 17th Georgia Infantry led by Major James Moore, Major James Strange's 1st Virginia Reserve Battalion, and portions of the 63rd Tennessee Infantry of Hughs's brigade. After falling back from New Market Heights, Gregg occupied the Intermediate Defense Line, north of Fort Harrison. Gregg commanded two brigades: his own Texas Brigade and Colonel Dudley M. DuBose's Georgia brigade.

12. This line of works ran west of and parallel to the Osborne Turnpike, near the Chaffin house.

13. After capturing Fort Harrison, Union troops moved south along the Diagonal Line, seizing Battery X and the White Battery before Confederate artillery fire from Forts Maury and Hoke blunted their advance.

14. Major Alexander W. Stark (1839–1898) commanded a battalion consisting of the Louisiana Guard Artillery, Mathews Artillery, and McComas Artillery.

15. Better known as Fort Johnson, this work stood two-thirds of a mile north of Fort Harrison, at the point where the Intermediate Line met the camp wall.

16. Lieutenant Colonel Robert A. Hardaway (1829–1899) commanded the 1st Virginia Light Artillery Battalion, which consisted of four Virginia batteries: the 3rd Richmond Howitzers, 1st Rockbridge Artillery, Powhatan Artillery, and Salem Flying Artillery.

17. Fort Gilmer stood five hundred yards north of the point where the Mill Road crossed the Intermediate Defense Line. Defended by Brigadier General Dudley DuBose's Georgians and others, the fort successfully withstood Union assaults by Brigadier General Robert S. Foster's and Brigadier General William Birney's divisions of the Tenth Corps. A small number of soldiers belonging to the 7th U.S. Colored Troops reached the fort moat, where they were slaughtered or forced to surrender.

18. As the morning progressed, Lee began to appreciate the serious nature of the attacks on Ewell's front. He dispatched Major General Charles W. Field with three brigades to reinforce Confederate troops north of the James. Fields's

leading brigade, Colonel Pinckney D. Bowles's Alabamians, arrived midway through the afternoon.

19. Brigadier General John Gregg (1828–1864) died on October 7, 1864, while leading the famous Texas Brigade in an engagement on the New Market Road.

20. The reference here may be to the Local Defense Troops.

21. Butler had attacked Fort Harrison with two corps, the Tenth and the Eighteenth.

22. No map was found with Ewell's draft of this memorandum.

On May 12, 1864, Ewell's corps had been attacked by an overwhelming Union force near Spotsylvania Court House. The Union assault succeeded in capturing most of Edward Johnson's division and threatened to destroy the rest of the Confederate army. To repair the breach, Ewell committed brigades sent to him from other portions of the line, among them Brigadier General Nathaniel Harris's Mississippi brigade. For about eighteen hours, Harris's men and others battled the Federals across breast-high logworks near a turn in the Confederate line that has come down to history as the Bloody Angle. Their determined stand gave Lee time to build a new set of logworks farther to the rear and saved the Confederate army from disaster. Ewell did not have time to properly thank Harris during the battle, and he was reassigned to the Department of Richmond a few weeks afterwards. He wrote the following letter belatedly to thank Harris for the gallant conduct of his brigade at Spotsylvania.

130. To Nathaniel Harris

Hdqrs. Dep't of Richmond, Va.,
December 27, 1864

General N. H. Harris, Commanding Brigade:[1]

General: I have omitted to acknowledge the valuable services rendered by your brigade on the 12th of May last at Spotsylvania not from any want of appreciation, but because I wish my thanks to rest upon the solid foundation of official reports.[2] The manner in which your brigade charged over the hill to recapture our works was witnessed by me with intense admiration, for men who could advance so calmly to what seemed and proved almost instant death. I have never seen troops under a hotter fire than was endured on this day by your brigade and some others. Major General Ed Johnson since his exchange has assured me that the whole strength of the enemy's army was poured into the gap caused by the capture of his command. He estimates the force engaged at this place on their side at forty thousand, besides Birney's command of perfectly fresh troops. Prisoners from all of their three corps were taken by us. Two divisions of my corps, your brigade and two others (one of which was scarcely engaged) confronted successfully this immense host and not only won from them nearly all the ground they had gained, but so shattered their army that they were unable again to make a serious attack until they received fresh troops.[3] I have not forgotten the Sixteenth Mississippi Regiment while under my command from Front Royal to Malvern Hill.[4] I am glad to see from a trial more severe than any it experienced while in my division that the regiment is in a brigade of which it may well be proud. Very respectfully your obedient servant,

Signed,   R. S. Ewell,

Lieutenant General.

1. Brigadier General Nathaniel H. Harris (1834–1900) commanded a brigade of Mississippi troops in Cadmus Wilcox's division of the Third Corps. On May 12, 1864, at Spotsylvania Court House, Harris led his brigade to the Muleshoe Salient to help repair a breach in the line made that morning by Union troops led by Major General Winfield S. Hancock.

2. Ewell's report for the Battle of Spotsylvania Court House is published in *OR* 36(1):1069–75. Written in March 1865, it glosses over the role of Harris's brigade and other units outside the Second Corps in a few brief sentences, a circumstance that caused some hard feelings among the troops in those units.

3. At dawn on May 12, 1864, Hancock's Second Corps attacked the Muleshoe Salient, a large outward bulge in the center of the Confederate line. Major General David B. Birney commanded a division in that attack. Hancock's men overran Major General Edward "Allegheny" Johnson's division, capturing twenty Confederate cannon and three thousand men, including Johnson and Brigadier General George H. Steuart. Major General Horatio G. Wright's Sixth Corps and two divisions of Major General Gouverneur K. Warren's Fifth Corps later supported the attack. In an effort to regain the works, Lee counterattacked with elements of four divisions. Harris's brigade, reaching the field around 7:30 A.M., charged past the McCoull house, crossed a draw, and captured a section of Confederate works just west of the Bloody Angle. It stubbornly held that position for the next eighteen hours, repulsing repeated Union attacks.

4. In the spring of 1862, the 16th Mississippi had fought in Brigadier General Isaac R. Trimble's brigade of Ewell's division.

By March 1865 the Confederacy was on the brink of collapse. General Robert E. Lee's outnumbered army had been stretched to the breaking point. With spring would come renewed Union attacks against Richmond and Petersburg, attacks that the Confederacy no longer had the power to resist. With the capital's capture almost certain, Ewell summoned a group of prominent Richmond citizens to discuss the creation of a special force to maintain order in the city in the event of the army's retreat. The group met on March 4. One day later, Ewell made the following notes about the meeting.

131. Private Memorandum

March 5. 1865

I will try to record important or interesting events that are brought to my notice. March 4th I called together a number of prominent citizens of my acquaintance or known to be men of eminence & explained to them that the necessities of General Lee's position would not let him post men here (in R[ichmon]d) & that to provide for contingencies that might happen it was necessary to have in the town a reliable body of men. This was appreciated by them but Dr Hc[1] suggested that as these men might be taken prisoners they should be recognized by the law & W. Robinson, James Lyons & N. Tyler were appointed a committee to have a bill passed [by] the Legislature.[2] They also apptd a committee of 5— Drs Burrows & Hoge, Mr Gwynne, Mr Kane[—]to organize sub-committees.[3] I met the committee of organization at 6 P.M. who asked if they should in electioneering exclude those who refused to go to the trenches & it was agreed that they should endeavor to raise one body of 500 merely for municipal duties & another for the entrenchments. I went with K[ane] to the Govr[4] to consult on organization who stated that as the bill passed by the legislature did not include over 50 yrs. all taken in by that would be added to Damforth & Evans Regt[s] of Va, 2d class militia[5] & declined to let Col. Kane try to raise another Regt.[6] This was written to Dr Hoge by me this morning. I found Ex-Govr & Genl Wise at the Gov's mansion who was exceedingly interesting. When in the Convention of 61. that took the state out of the Union, the Govr (Wise) said he found it very difficult to act on the Com,[7] 5 being for going out of the Union 16 against. That after many days of hard work without much apparent results & sick & in low spirits he met Imboden to whom when Govr he had loaned two cannon with the promise of their return when W. should demand it. Imboden kept his promise & told W. he should have them.[8] W[ise,] I[mboden,] two Ashbys & 9 others met at the Ex[change Hotel] & telegrams & persons were sent out to collect men at Gordonsville. 250 were so collected & sent by rail to Harper's Ferry, which the Yankees burned.[9] As soon as this party started from Gordonsville Wise informed the Va. Leg. of what was done, which stirred them a[s] the loss of Queen bee disturbs the hive, some insisting that as these men had voluntarily ran the risk they should incur the penalty. Wise's eloquent appeal however stirred them up & the bloody drama was decided on. One member was so carried away by W's eloquence that siezing his hand with tears declared that though he did not agree with all he said that he loved him &c. W. said this stage show more than his own carried the day. W. also spoke at Govr Smith's house a good deal of Clay & Scott.[10] spoke of a delightful supper party in Wash[ington]—at Wm. Cox's;[11] coming from the warm room Wise was attacked in the th[r]oat. Lay for days breathing through a tube while "Spanish leeches" were applied to reduce the inflammation &c. He was tenderly nursed by Botts. As W. recovered he would be visited by many persons & Botts was in the habit of having whist parties to relieve the tedium of sitting up. W. lay in an adjoining room with the door ajar & while under the influence of morphine was constantly annoyed by the "whining" "puling" frettings of Scott who came every night to play whist. W. associated S. with the images (horrible) of witches & hages.[12]

About this time, W. being well & present, at some convivial whist party, Clay came in flushed from a dinner party & stalking into the room asked in a loud sonorous tone, ["]Where's Scott. I want a game with Scott.["] Scott came up "fawningly". "here I am Mr Clay. I will be very glad to have a game with you Mr Clay when I am through this". "You have a game of your own have you Scott. Well S. play your game". C. played for a few moments. "Scott I want to bet you $5. on the point S." S declined & C. suddenly throwing up his hand re-commenced his taunts of S. [S]ome reply of S. made C. turn red & strike S. on the shoulder. S. shrunk & said "C you have stricken me on my wounded shoulder." "On your wounded shoulder, have I, Scott. I always knew you were rotten S!" The latter was taken away by his friends & did not return for 4 weeks. C. thought S. the author of the "triangular correspondence" that defeated him in the Harrisburg Convention.[13] (A writes to B. do something for Clay he has no friends here. B d[itt]o to C. C d[itt]o to A & B & in this way Clay was thrown out of the Convention as wanting strength.[)] Wise was with C. when the name of the nominee at H'g was sent on. C. was very much excited & after an hours swearing &c. strode up to W: "Were there two Henry C. one would make the other President." "No[,"] said W[,"] were there two C the continent could not hold both—one would destroy the other."

Whe[ne]ver Scotts name was mentioned to Jackson[14] even after the latter joined the Pres[byteria]n Church J. would swear & raise his hand proclaim him a coward. That a man with so hard a head could not be a great man[;] that. . . bullett struck him in the forehead & ploughed a mole track to the occiput". Wise spoke to Buchanan (whom he said some one compared to a great calf raised by two cows",) of Scott.[15] B. said he spoke to S. of the Mormon campaign, that S. at once lost all that puerility so habitual to him—showed himself able, powerful, fertile in resources, clear & in every respect a great man. W. quoted Genl Jackson's remark which made B. laugh. What a contrast between Smith & Wise.

1. Dr. Francis W. Hancock had been Ewell's medical director earlier in the war and subsequently was in charge of Jackson and Winder hospitals in Richmond.
2. Wirt Robinson and Nathaniel Tyler were civil engineers living in Richmond.
3. J. L. Burrows and Moses D. Hoge were prominent ministers in the city. Gwynne and Kane are unidentified.
4. William "Extra Billy" Smith (1796–1887) was governor of Virginia at this time. Earlier in the war he had commanded a brigade in Ewell's Second Corps.
5. Colonel John B. Danforth led the 1st Regiment of Second Class Militia, and Colonel Thomas J. Evans commanded the 19th Regiment of Virginia Militia.
6. Kane apparently wished to organize the emergency force into a separate regiment that he would command. Governor Smith opposed this, however, insisting that any men raised for a constabulary force be placed in existing militia units.
7. The Committee on Federal Relations.
8. John D. Imboden (1823–1895) practiced law and served two terms in the Virginia legislature prior to 1861. With civil war imminent, he organized and helped pay to equip the Staunton Artillery and was elected the battery's commander. Governor Wise loaned Imboden two guns from the state arsenal for use in this battery. Later Imboden commanded a cavalry brigade.
9. On April 16, 1861, with secession imminent, Wise met with several others—Imboden; Alfred M. Barbour, a former superintendent of the United States arsenal at Harpers Ferry; Captain John A. Harman of Staunton; railroad presidents Edmund Fontaine and John S. Barbour; Nat Tyler, editor of the *Richmond Enquirer;* and militia captains Turner Ashby, Richard Ashby, and Oliver R. Funsten—at the Exchange Hotel in Richmond to devise a plan for capturing the Harpers Ferry arsenal the moment the Secession Convention

voted the state out of the Union. The vote came on April 17, with eighty-eight delegates voting in favor of secession and fifty-five against. In a fiery speech prior to the vote, Wise announced to the convention that Virginia militia were even then moving to seize the Federal arsenal at Harpers Ferry. The following day Major General Kenton Harper did just that. Although a small guard loyal to the Union managed to destroy twenty thousand weapons, Harper and his militia succeeded in saving most of the arsenal's machinery. For a detailed account of the events leading to Harpers Ferry's capture, see Imboden, "Jackson at Harper's Ferry in 1861," 111–18.

10. Winfield Scott was the commanding general of the United States Army. Henry Clay (1777–1852) was one of America's foremost political figures. A representative of Kentucky, he served in both houses of Congress, where he became a leader of the "War Hawks" and a strong supporter of the American System, which advocated internal improvements and protective tariffs. On three different occasions he ran for president but each time suffered defeat.

11. Ewell may have been referring to Samuel Sullivan Cox (1824–1889), a long-term Democratic politician who represented Ohio, and later New York, in Congress.

12. Hags.

13. In 1839 Clay and Scott were rivals for the Whig Party's presidential nomination. The party held its convention in Harrisburg, Pennsylvania, that December. By then there were three candidates in the running: Clay, Scott, and William Henry Harrison. Clay held the lead after the first ballot, but he later lost when Scott's delegates threw their support to Harrison. Clay and Scott were together at the Astor Hotel in New York when the results came in. Disappointed by the outcome, an angry Clay struck Scott in the shoulder where the general had been wounded during the Battle of Lundy's Lane. Clay averted a duel by later apologizing for his actions.

14. Andrew Jackson, president of the United States from 1829 to 1837.

15. James Buchanan was president of the United States from 1857 to 1861, having been elected by a coalition of Northern and Southern Democrats, the "two cows" mentioned by Wise.

Chapter 11

Prisoner of War, 1865

After four years the Confederacy succumbed to the North's superior manpower and resources. Ewell recognized that the end was in sight. Early in 1865 his wife and stepdaughter slipped across the Potomac River and surrendered to United States authorities. However, Ewell and his stepson, Campbell Brown, remained at their posts to the end.

On April 2 Union troops shattered the Confederate lines at Petersburg, twenty-five miles south of Richmond, prompting the evacuation of both cities. Ewell, in charge of Confederate troops north of the James River, abandoned the capital that night. Mobs looted the doomed city. To add to the horror, Secretary of War John C. Breckinridge ordered Ewell to set fire to tobacco warehouses located on the city's waterfront so that they would not fall into Union hands. A strong breeze spread the flames to nearby buildings, and soon the entire business district was ablaze.

Ewell meanwhile led his makeshift corps toward Amelia Court House to join the Army of Northern Virginia in its retreat. From there, the reunited army staggered westward in an effort to escape Federal troops that were closing in around it. Union cavalry penetrated a gap in the retreating column near Little Sailor's Creek. Cut off and isolated from the rest of the army, Ewell surrendered himself and what remained of his corps on April 6. For the first time in his life, he was a prisoner.

Ewell's surrender at Sailor's Creek could not have come at a worse time. On April 15, news raced across the wires that Southern sympathizers had killed President Abraham Lincoln and wounded Secretary of State William Seward. A spirit of vengeance swept through the North. Realizing the dire consequences of Lincoln's assassination for himself and for the South, Ewell drafted a letter to General Ulysses S. Grant, repudiating the act.

Ewell and other general officers were incarcerated at Fort Warren in Boston Harbor. While there, he maintained a steady correspondence with Lizinka, who was under house arrest in St. Louis, Missouri. When Lizinka finally obtained her freedom, she journeyed to Washington to personally lobby President Andrew Johnson, Montgomery Blair, Ulysses S. Grant, and other influential officials for the freedom *of her husband and son. Her efforts paid off. On July 19, after three months of in-carceration, Ewell and Campbell were released on parole. The long war was finally over.*

132. To Ulysses S. Grant

Copy– Apl. 16th 1865[1]
Fort Warren

General

You will appreciate I am sure the sentiment which prompts me to address you. Of all the misfortunes wh[ich] c[oul]d. befall the Southern people or any Southern man, by far the greatest in my judgment would be the prevalence of the idea that they could entertain any other than feelings of unqualified indignation & abhorrence for the assassination of the Pres't. of the U.S. & the attempt to assassinate the Sec'y. of State. No language can adequately express the shock produced upon myself in common with the other Gen'l Offr's of the Confed. Army, confined with me, by the occurrence of this appalling crime, & by the seeming tendency in the public mind to connect the South & Southern men with it. Need we say that we are not assassins nor the allies of assassins, be they from the North or from the South? And that coming as we do from most of the States of the South we would be ashamed of our own people, were we not assured that (they)[2] will universally repudiate this crime.

Under the circumstances I could not refrain from some expression of my feelings. I thus utter them to a soldier who will fully comprehend them. The following officers, Maj. Genls. Edward Johnson of Virga[3] & Kershaw of So. Ca.,[4] Brig. Gen'ls. Barton,[5] Corse,[6] Hunton[7] & Jones[8] of Virga, DuBose,[9] Simms[10] & H. R. Jackson[11] of Ga, Frazier[12] of Ala., Smith[13] & Gordon[14] from Tennessee, Cabell[15] from Arks, & Marmaduke[16] of Missouri, & Commodore Tucker[17] of Va., all heartily concur with me in what I have said.[18]

R. S. Ewell

To Gen. Grant

1. The version of the letter published here is taken from a handwritten copy made by Campbell Brown. At first, Union authorities kept Brown and Ewell apart, but in May 1865 they transferred the young man to Ewell's casemate. Brown probably copied the letter at that time. Published versions of this letter appear in "Letter of General Richard S. Ewell," 4–5, and in *OR* 46(3):787. The letter

also appeared in newspapers of the time, including the May 8, 1865, edition of the *Richmond Commercial Bulletin.*

2. Ewell appears to have inadvertently omitted this word, which Brown added when he copied the letter.

3. Edward Johnson (1816–1873) commanded a division in Ewell's Second Corps before his capture on May 12, 1864, at Spotsylvania Court House. Exchanged a short time later, he was later recaptured at Nashville, Tennessee, while commanding a division in Lieutenant General Stephen Dill Lee's corps.

4. Joseph B. Kershaw (1822–1894) was commanding a division under Ewell when he was captured at Sailor's Creek. A veteran of Longstreet's First Corps, Kershaw was one of the Army of Northern Virginia's finest officers.

5. Seth M. Barton (1829–1900) had led a brigade in the West prior to his capture at Vicksburg in July 1863. Following his exchange, he served in North Carolina and Virginia and was eventually assigned a brigade in the Department of Richmond. Like Ewell, he was captured at Sailor's Creek.

6. Another general officer captured at Sailor's Creek, Montgomery Corse (1816–1895) fought with the Army of Northern Virginia from First Manassas through Petersburg.

7. Eppa Hunton (1823–1908) served the first half of the war as colonel of the 8th Virginia Infantry Regiment and the last half as a brigadier general in Pickett's division. Captured with Ewell at Sailor's Creek, Hunton in a privately published memoir criticized his superior for seeking to curry the favor of his Union captors.

8. A former brigade commander in the Army of Northern Virginia, John R. Jones (1827–1901) was charged with cowardice at the Battle of Chancellorsville and dismissed from the service. Captured at Smithsburg, Maryland, on July 4, 1863, he was incarcerated at Johnson's Island for several months before being transferred to Fort Warren.

9. Dudley M. Dubose (1834–1883) commanded the 15th Georgia Infantry Regiment for most of the war. In November 1864 he was promoted to brigadier general and led a brigade in Kershaw's division. He was captured at Sailor's Creek.

10. James P. Simms (1837–1888) fought with the 53rd Georgia Infantry until December 1864, when he was promoted to brigadier general and led a brigade in Kershaw's division. He surrendered with Ewell at Sailor's Creek.

11. Henry R. Jackson (1820–1898) was in command of a brigade when he was captured at Nashville on December 16, 1864. Before the war, he had been the

United States Minister to Austria and a judge on the Georgia Supreme Court. In 1885 President Grover Cleveland appointed him the United States Minister to Mexico.

12. John W. Frazer (1827–1906) led a brigade in eastern Tennessee and was in command of troops at the Cumberland Gap when he surrendered to Federal troops in September 1863. Perhaps because of this action, Frazer's nomination to brigadier general was rejected by the Confederate Senate on February 16, 1864.

13. Thomas B. Smith (1838–1923) commanded the 20th Tennessee Infantry Regiment and was leading a brigade in Major General B. Franklin Cheatham's corps when he surrendered to Union authorities at Nashville, Tennessee.

14. George W. Gordon (1836–1911) rose through the ranks of the 11th Tennessee Infantry to become its leader. He was wounded and captured at the Battle of Franklin, Tennessee, while serving as a brigade commander.

15. William L. Cabell (1827–1911) served as chief quartermaster to Generals P. G. T. Beauregard, Joseph E. Johnston, and Earl Van Dorn before being captured while leading a cavalry brigade at Marais des Cygnes, Kansas, on October 25, 1864. After the war he served four terms as the mayor of Dallas, Texas.

16. Like William Cabell, John S. Marmaduke (1833–1887) was captured at Marais des Cygnes, Kansas, in 1864. On March 18, 1865, while a prisoner at Fort Warren, he was promoted to major general, the last Confederate officer appointed to that rank. After the war, he was elected governor of Missouri on the Democratic ticket.

17. John R. Tucker (1812–1883) commanded the C.S.S. *Patrick Henry* during the Battle of Hampton Roads and later commanded the ironclad C.S.S. *Chicora* at Charleston, South Carolina. When Charleston fell in February 1865, he and his troops were assigned to duty at Drewry's Bluff, Virginia. In the retreat from Richmond, Tucker's seamen joined Ewell's corps and surrendered with him at Sailor's Creek.

18. Eppa Hunton later claimed that he and others opposed Ewell's sending this letter. In his *Autobiography,* Hunton wrote:

> One day I was asleep on my bed in my room, when I was aroused by an unusual commotion, and found that the twelve Confederate officers were holding a meeting. I inquired what it meant and was surprised and indignant to learn that it was a meeting called by General Ewell to declare by resolution that they had no complicity in the assassination of Abraham Lincoln and deplored the act. I was very much excited about it, and opposed to it with all

my might. I asked them if they thought it becoming for thirteen
gentlemen who were thought worthy to wear the stars of general
officers of the Confederate Army to declare to the world that they
were not assassins. By great exertions and the efforts of several
who came to my aid, the resolution was defeated.

Ewell cited Hunton as one of the officers endorsing the sentiments expressed
in the letter, suggesting that Ewell either added Hunton's name without his
knowledge or that his colleague actually supported the letter but altered his
story in later years. Hunton, *Autobiography,* 137.

133. To Rebecca Ewell

Fort Warren   April 18. 65
Miss R. L. Ewell

My Dear Sister;

　　Maj. Brown is confined in a different part of the Fort & though I see him
daily no intercourse is allowed. It would be better for us both were we together
but there is no authority here. Genl Officers are together. Others 3 to 400 including Brown are not allowed to communicate except by letter. I am sure this was
not what Genl Augur intended when he allowed Brown to come here. Still it is
infinitely better for him than Johnson's Island.[1] We could be quite comfortable

Ewell's baggage train fell into Union
hands in April 1865. Among the captured items was the sword carried by
his grandfather in the American Revolution. The Ewells later recovered the
weapon. (Courtesy Donald Pfanz)

During Richmond's evacuation, the city caught fire. Ewell disavowed any responsibility for the conflagration, adamantly insisting, "It was burned by the mob." (Library of Congress)

if together as our treatment is as gentlemanly & courteous as permitted by Regulations.

You spoke of coming here. As all intercourse is forbidden it would have been useless. I am abused for burning Richmond. It was burned by the mob.[2] There were no troops to keep order. I had told the principal citizens months before what would happen & urged them to form a constabulary force to keep order, but they would not, only 3 offering their services when there were hundreds doing nothing.[3] The Fire hose was cut & the Arsenal burnt by the mob.[4] I had taken every precaution possible & the people must blame themselves. To prevent lies in regard to our capture I would state that we were ordered to follow Anderson & that after driving back an attack on the wagons we found Anderson cut off from those of Lee's Army in front & the 6th Corps came after me attacking my troops.[5] Anderson failed after a trial, in breaking through those in his front & my men entirely surrounded, fighting over ten times their numbers[6] were all captured or slain. One Regt had 11 killed or wounded out of 12 Officers.[7]

I heard that Louis was well; if so, it is my decided preference that he should reside in Europe—England particularly.[8] I have not heard from Lizinka except that she is in Nashville.

For Ewell, the war ended on April 6, 1865, when Union forces surrounded and captured his command. For the first time in his life, he was a prisoner. (Library of Congress)

Should you meet Genl Hitchcock[9] or Augur do try to have Brown with the Genl Officers.[10] When you write to Ben, 3d Street between Clay & Leigh Richmond[,] ask him to find out th[r]ough Mr Edmunds[11] something about my baggage, particularly Grandfather's sword.[12] I suppose since the performances of that wretch Booth[13] that no indulgence for a time will be shown prisoners & it is useless to hope that my wishes will be gratified in regard to Brown. It would be useless at present to come here as no intercourse is allowed.

Yours &c—

R S. Ewell

1. Brevet Major General Christopher C. Augur (1821–1898) was in charge of the Department of Washington. Ewell and Augur had known each other since West Point, and when Ewell met Augur in Washington following his capture, he persuaded the Union general to have Campbell Brown imprisoned with him at Fort Warren instead of sending him to Johnson's Island, Ohio, with other officers of his grade. Upon reaching Fort Warren, however, Ewell and Brown were kept apart.

2. Prior to evacuating Richmond, Ewell had set fire to several tobacco warehouses at the orders of Secretary of War John C. Breckinridge. Embers from these fires ignited nearby buildings, causing a general conflagration. Newspaper editors blamed Ewell for deliberately firing the city. The general vehemently denied responsibility for the conflagration, arguing that he had set fire to the city's tobacco warehouses under orders and against his will. He steadfastly maintained

that vandals had set the fires that destroyed Richmond and that the warehouse fires had nothing to do with the general blaze.

3. Prior to the evacuation, Ewell had attempted to organize a police force made up of Richmond citizens for the purpose of maintaining order during the interval between the time that the Confederates pulled out of the city and the time that Union forces entered. Few volunteered.

4. The State Armory, or Arsenal, stood along the Kanawha Canal, between Fifth and Seventh streets.

5. On April 6, 1865, Lee's army struggled westward in an effort to escape its pursuers. James Longstreet's corps led the march, followed by Richard Anderson, Ewell, and John B. Gordon. The army's wagon train was between Ewell and Gordon. At Sailor's Creek, Union cavalry penetrated a gap that had developed between Longstreet's and Anderson's corps, cutting the retreating column in two. Ewell sent the wagons by a parallel road to prevent their capture. When Gordon followed the wagons, Ewell's corps became the army's rear guard. Anderson tried to clear the road ahead, but his attacks failed. Two divisions of the Union army's Sixth Corps meanwhile splashed across the creek and assailed Ewell's rear. Outnumbered and surrounded, Ewell surrendered his command.

6. The Army of the Potomac had approximately 30,000 men on the field at Sailor's Creek compared to Ewell's 3,000, but just 10,000 Union soldiers assailed Ewell's line. The rest confronted either Anderson or Gordon. In the brief battle, Ewell lost approximately 150 men killed or wounded and 2,800 captured.

7. Ewell may have been referring to the 18th Georgia Battalion, which lost 30 killed and 22 wounded in the battle—85 percent of its force.

8. Possibly a slave.

9. Major General Ethan Allen Hitchcock (1798–1870) was the North's commissioner for the exchange of war prisoners.

10. Rebecca L. Ewell sent a copy of this letter (minus the last two paragraphs) to General Hitchcock in Washington, adding the following paragraph:

> The above I copied from my brother's letter received yesterday. The letter was inspected before I received it. I hope Gen Hitchcock will have the extreme goodness to gratify my brother in having Brown with him. One reason that Brown was allowed to go was that he might render necessary assistance to Richard in his maimed state.

> Yours very truly
> R L Ewell

11. Unidentified.

12. Ewell's grandfather Colonel Jesse Ewell commanded a regiment of Virginia militia during the American Revolution. Dr. Jesse Ewell presented his cousin with their grandfather's sword in September 1862 during the general's convalescence at Dr. Ewell's home, "Dunblane." General Ewell carried the blade with him until the last week of the war, when it fell into Union hands. Benjamin tracked down the sword, and to this day it remains in the possession of the Ewell family.

13. Actor John Wilkes Booth (1838–1865) assassinated President Abraham Lincoln on April 14, 1865.

134. To Lizinka Ewell

April 20. 1865

Mrs L. C. Ewell

M. D. L.[1]

We have been pretty gloomy here since the murder of the Prest of the U.S. particularly. C. was to have been sent to Johnson's Island but Genl Auger made an exception in his favor, though on his arrival here the orders require[d] his separation from the Genl Off[icers]. I see him every day but only communicate by writing. He would be much better off with me & vice versa. We are treated with as much courtesy as the Regulations, which are strict, allow. In my retreat I was ordered to follow Anderson, but the wagon train, on same road, was attacked in rear & flank. After getting it through I found Anderson cut off from Lee & almost immediately large bodies of the enemy appeared in my rear. I formed to resist these while Anderson tried to break through those in his front. Anderson was badly whipped & the enemy broke through him & attacked my little handfull in front & rear capturing or dispersing the whole. Anderson got away. 3000 of his & mine were taken. I lost heavily. Colonel Crutchfield of S. Jackson memory, com'g Heavy Art'y Battalions (Inf'y) killed.[2] Stiles distinguished himself.[3] I thought we were entitled to terms off [*sic*] Lee's men, but I suppose must thank Boothe [*sic*] for that & numberless future woes.[4] E. Johnson is here & still talks of the Art'y on 12th of May.[5] I lost all my baggage as did C.[,] Buckskins too, but I suppose you will laugh at that.[6] Tell H.[7] Rifle was left at Hd Qr 6th Corps (Wright)[8] with many requests for kind treatment. He contrasted with the fat northern horses. I was not searched but treated with great courtesy. I came from N.Y. on [April] 15th to B.[9] & could hardly have believed that after the murder of so popular a Prest that a party of Con. Genls would be treated with such forbearance. Yours of the 8th came yesterday from Nashville & made the day bright. I had a letter from Tasker[10] at the Provost Marshall's in Wash. & saw your friends there. Writers from Richmond are eloquent on my burning of the City. Call me Drunken brute &c. You remember how I urged on the citizens to volunteer for a constabulary force explaining the riots certain to ensue on our leaving, but they were inert, three only volunteered where 300 were wanted & when we evacuated there were no troops to enforce order. Such a scene as the city presented the night[,] Sunday[,] of our leaving was never seen in this country before, I expect: Negroes, Women, Jews, were plundering first the public & then the private stores. They burned the Arsenal, cut the fire hose & set fire to the bridge[11] thereby endangering the capture of Breckinridge & all North of the James. The tobacco was burned by order of the govt but had the mob not interfered this would have been all. I was exceedingly averse to burning anything, but you know it was even contemplated to destroy the Capitol, but Houdin's statue prevented it.[12] But if we ever meet again I'll give you the whole story.

Yours—
[R. S. Ewell][13]

1. M. D. L. stands for "My dear Lizinka."
2. Colonel Stapleton Crutchfield (1835–1865) had been the Second Corps's chief of artillery under Stonewall Jackson. Like Jackson, Crutchfield was severely wounded at Chancellorsville, losing a leg there. When he returned to duty in 1865, he was put in charge of the Department of Richmond's artillery brigade, consisting of four battalions of heavy artillery. Armed as infantry, the brigade accompanied the army on its retreat from Richmond and fought at Sailor's Creek. Crutchfield died in that battle when a Union shell ripped through his thigh.
3. Major Robert Stiles commanded a battalion of artillerymen, armed as infantry, that was in Custis Lee's division during the retreat from Richmond. His gallant leadership at the Battle of Sailor's Creek elicited Ewell's praise. Stiles's memoirs, which include several anecdotes about Ewell, were later published under the title *Four Years under Marse Robert*.
4. The troops who surrendered with Lee at Appomattox Court House on April 9, 1865, were paroled and permitted to return to their homes. Those who surrendered with Ewell three days earlier were sent to prison camps in the North. When Ewell learned the terms of Lee's surrender, he wrote to Brigadier General

Orlando B. Willcox, commanding a division in the Union army's Ninth Corps, asking that the troops captured at Sailor's Creek receive the same terms accorded to the rest of Lee's army. Willcox forwarded Ewell's request to Army of the Potomac headquarters, but it was denied. Robert E. Lee pursued the same object two weeks later. Approaching Grant about the release of Confederate soldiers captured at Sailor's Creek, Lee wrote: "I see no benefit that will result by retaining them in prison; but, on the contrary, think good may be accomplished by returning them to their homes. . . . Should there, however, be objections to this course, I would ask that exceptions be made in favor of the invalid officers and men, and that they be allowed to return to their homes on parole. I call your attention particularly to General Ewell." Lee's efforts, like Ewell's, came to naught. *OR* 46(3):692–93, 1013.

5. Johnson had lost twenty cannon and three thousand men on the morning of May 12, 1864, when Union soldiers overwhelmed his division at Spotsylvania Court House.

6. Ewell apparently carried a pair of buckskins in his baggage, a relic from his days on the frontier.

7. Hattie, Lizinka's daughter.

8. Major General Horatio G. Wright (1820–1899) led the Union army's Sixth Corps during the final year of the war. Wright hosted Ewell at his headquarters the night of Ewell's capture.

9. Boston.

10. After serving on Major General George B. McClellan's staff in 1862, Ewell's cousin had been provost marshal in St. Louis, Missouri. When Lizinka surrendered to United States authorities in 1865, she was placed under house arrest and permitted to stay at Gantt's residence.

11. Confederate forces north of the James River retreated across Mayo's Bridge, at the foot of 14th Street. Just before reaching the bridge, the street passed over the James River and Kanawha Canal. Ewell claimed that incendiaries burned the canal bridge by pushing a burning canal barge against it.

12. Jean Houdin sculpted a famous statue of George Washington that stood in the Virginia state capitol. Fortunately, it survived the fire and is still there today.

13. Ewell's signature has been clipped from the original letter.

At some point in his imprisonment, Ewell wrote a letter to James D. McCabe Jr., in which he vehemently denied any responsibility for the burning of Richmond. A lawsuit by mill owners who had lost property in the fire may have prompted the letter.

Generals Joseph Kershaw (left) and Edward Johnson (right) commanded divisions under Ewell and were imprisoned with him at Fort Warren. (Library of Congress)

135. To James D. McCabe Jr.

Remember how hard I tried to organize a constabulary force in Richmond.[1] I knew nothing of the firing of the arsenal or cutting of the engine hose. These were the work of unauthorized persons or incendiaries. I had no force to stop the plundering which was going on all night. I made couriers and policemen of my staff, trying to prevent disorder and violence. Several fires were kindled before we left, and an attempt to burn Mayo's bridge frustrated by the daring of the engineer officers, who, at great risk, removed burning canal boats from under it. What I did was in obedience to positive orders that had been given me. Looking, with General Kershaw, towards Richmond, we saw building after building, at a distance from the river, ignite, evidently set on fire. I feel this matter very deeply. I see myself unjustly blamed. I did not exceed, but fell short of my instructions.[2]

Yours affectionately,
R. S. Ewell.

1. James Dabney McCabe Jr. (1842–1883), of Virginia, wrote early biographies of Stonewall Jackson (1863), Albert Sidney Johnston (1866), and Robert E. Lee (1867). Ewell wrote this letter to McCabe while a prisoner at Fort Warren. With or without Ewell's permission, McCabe submitted the letter to the *Rich-*

mond Republic, which published this excerpt of it on June 23, 1865. The *New York Herald* reprinted the article on June 26, and McCabe later published it in his book *Life and Campaigns of General Robert E. Lee,* 612fn.

2. Years after the war, Campbell Brown wrote to Lieutenant Colonel Charles S. Venable, who had served on General Robert E. Lee's staff:

> Gen. Ewell was so hurt at [the thought that] he would willingly injure any citizen of Virginia. . . . He was so distressed at the orders to burn cotton & tobacco—and so reluctant even to prepare for such a step—that I cannot bear the idea of his being blamed for it. I know how shocked we both were, when from Manchester Heights, we saw the Mills on fire. I knew the noble soul, the tender heart, the courage to suffer & be silent under wrong accusation from patriotic motives, in which no man could have surpassed Gen. Ewell. (Jones, *Campbell Brown's Civil War,* 311.)

136. To Lizinka Ewell

Fort Warren B H.[1]
May 5, 65

My Dear Lizinka;

Yours of April 8th, 28th & May 2d I have received. The two last are with C. who sent me to day some very nice tea (enough for two months) & two towels. I have asked Becca to get me some clothes & a few trifles, all I will want for some time. There is no occasion here for many things. I hate to think of the valuables[,] particularly papers, that were lost with my baggage & that cannot be replaced. The war however is like a horrid dream & I see little use in recalling that part of the last few years history. I recd quite a pleasant letter to day from Carroll's brother. He referred very kindly to the acquaintance between his Father & myself & his friendship for me, Offering to assist me in any way I may need.[2] I dont want anything that can be done for me here except to get C. in this part of the fort & that seems hopeless. I hope he is better off than he would be in the Old Capitol or at Johnson's Island.[3] At the former place however he would likely have a better chance to see you & Hattie. It seems to me Govt makes a great mistake in favoring those men in the South who have been governed by the apparent chance of success but in earnest on neither side. I would prefer to look for future faithful Citizens among those who have shown good faith even if against the U.S. Govt, than among such undecided characters. Faulkner's[4] arrival in Rich[mon]d was mentioned in a late paper.

A writer from R. mentions Anderson[,] J. R.[,][5] Macfarlane[,][6] Judge Lyons[,] Meredith[,][7] & "that jovial but rampant old Secesh Joe Mayo."[8] If you dont remember him Harriet will know how aptly he is described. Johnson has been repeating it about every ten minutes since getting the paper. There was nothing else to do[,] but what geese they made of themselves about leaving R[ichmon]d. I stopped Anderson & tried to stop others who would make a more dignified show now had they taken my advice instead of that of the women. You know no one had as able counsel as myself & yet I followed my own plans about my professional matters; if any one could have had an excuse it would have been myself.[9] You remember the Smith that would not be a courier at Orange Ct. House?[10] His family have sent many kind messages & made inquiries as to my rec'g a ring of which I am oblivious. He & his brother are in R[ichmon]d. The 2d brother is as prepossessing as the other. I saw Commodore Tucker making a very awkward effort at washing some napkins to day. He is mo[r]e of a dandy than any of us & is cook this week for his mess. I helped him by good advice in the washing. He could not spare them for the laundress. Some of my private letters to my annoyance have been published, which no one has a right to do without permission.[11] Remember me, please, to the family. I would write but my letters to you cover all that can be said & correspondence at present under the circumstances is not pleasant.

Yours

R S. Ewell

1. B.H. stands for Boston Harbor.
2. John Lee Carroll (1830–1911), the son of Colonel Charles Digges Carroll and the brother of Ewell's aide-de-camp Harper Carroll, was the governor of Maryland from 1876 to 1880.
3. Old Capitol Prison in Washington, D.C., and Johnson's Island Prison, near Sandusky, Ohio, were two Union prison camps. Brown probably would have been sent to Johnson's Island had Ewell not used his influence with Major General Christopher Augur to have him sent to Fort Warren.
4. Lieutenant Colonel Charles Faulkner had served as assistant adjutant general to both Jackson and Ewell. He resigned in the summer of 1863 as a result of his advanced age. He was fifty-seven years old at the time.
5. Joseph R. Anderson (1813–1892) owned Tredegar Iron Works in Richmond. He was one the city's wealthiest men, owning $480,000 of real estate and $275,000 of personal estate by 1860. When the war began, he was appointed brigadier general, serving in North Carolina and Virginia. When a wound at

Frayser's Farm disabled Anderson from further duty in the field, he resigned his commission and resumed management of the ironworks.

6. William McFarlane was a printer in the city.

7. Probably a reference to Judge John A. Meredith (b. ca. 1814). A tobacco factory manager named James D. Meredith also lived in the city at the beginning of the war.

8. Joseph Mayo (ca. 1795–1872) served as Virginia's commonwealth attorney from 1823 to 1853 and was mayor of Richmond from 1853 to 1865.

9. Apparently Ewell counseled Anderson and other prominent men to remain in Richmond when it surrendered to the Union army, but few took his advice. Although Ewell asserted that he followed his own judgment in professional matters, many felt that he too often deferred to the advice of others.

10. Unidentified.

11. Ewell may be referring to the letter he sent to General Ulysses S. Grant on April 16, 1865, deprecating the assassination of President Abraham Lincoln. On June 13, 1865, Ewell would write a letter to a former dragoon explaining his reasons for siding with the Confederacy. That letter also gained wide circulation.

137. To Rebecca Ewell

Fort Warren B.H.
May 8. 1865

Miss R. L. Ewell

My Dear Becca;

I foreshadowed lately the prospect of trouble to you in the way of sending me some things. If you can make arrangements by drawing on me here or otherwise for funds & are willing to trouble yourself I want you to send me a supply. Campbell & myself are finally in same part of Fort & are in a mess with several other officers. I wrote for a suit of clothes whi[c]h in addition to height & weight—5'10 1/2" & 140 lbs (supposing both legs present)[—]should have given size of waist 26 to 28 inches, say 28. If the tailor would fit the best made man of his customers with above dimensions he could not miss fitting me much (without any vanity).

We have to purchase at high prices every thing but meat & bread. We have two months supply of tea. It is not worth while to send such luxuries as canned fruits being expensive & bulky. In a month we use about 8 lbs of coffee, 12 to

16 of sugar[,] 12 of butter. A sapsago cheese would be good relish, a bottle of Anchovy sauce, D[itt]o of *best* olive oil for table, some mustard, about 12 lbs candles, 1/2 lb honey soap. You could send a few needles & buttons. I wish also you would send a bible of something about the same print as the prayerbook. They seem to have gone beyond that primitive book or at least it is scarce. The items I mention are suggestive. You might see some things that I know nothing of. Corn starch or something of the kind as we get no vegetables might be useful. No fish or cheese is wanted, except sapsago cheese. We buy potatoes & onions.

The things you bot. as we came along were very good & all duly recd. You gave no bill. If you will send a bill I can then arrange it with C.

I understand you have a permit to send these things. A bottle of tomatoe catchup would add to our diet, a little Cayenne pepper.

Things are much higher than the prices quoted in Newspapers. We draw from Govt bread & meat, occasionally baked beans or grits—are not allowed to visit Sutler's Store & when we give an order for articles we are furnished with such as suit his convenience.[1] I have been trying to buy a small earthenware teapot ever since I have been here. I have a very common mug that I had to pay 50 cts for. Ought you not to look after Stony[?][2]

Yrs—

R. S. Ewell

1. Ewell and other prisoners had to purchase goods from the post sutler, A. J. Hall. Having a monopoly on the prisoners' business, the sutler often provided poor-quality goods at high prices. For a list of some of Hall's prices, see Stephens, *Recollections,* 128–32.
2. Stony Lonesome.

138. To Lizinka Ewell

Fort Warren B.H.
May 12th 1865

Mrs L. C. Ewell

M. D. L;

I recd yours of the 4th yesterday & 8th to day. Many thanks for the draft but I have spent very little of the funds I brought from Richmond & when I want money will notify my friends. The oath has not been offered to us, nor do I see any indication that it will be soon. I signed the application to be placed on parole, made out by the General Officers here, because I thought that if I have to take the oath of allegiance (as I suppose will be the case with all who remain in the US. & in which case I can see not the slightest objection) it would be far better to do so away from apparent compulsion among one's own people.[1] I would not support in future a man who, whatever might have been his course during secession, provided of course it had been honest, who should not be a thoroughly patriotic citizen of the country. I am sick of halfway men. It is difficult to locate the different events of the last days at Richmond in reference to your leaving, but there were many things tending to shake ones belief in the patriotism of some of our leaders—I mean political—but I have not space to give details except to mention the efforts of some of them to prevent the blacks enlisting & to keep those that did from being useful. Some of the bl[ac]k soldiers were whipped, they were hooted at & treated generally in a way to nullify the law.[2] Amply sufficient men capable of bearing arms were around & in Richmond to have changed Pickett's defeat at 5 Forks to a victory. He lost 4000 prisoners there.[3] I could tell you a great deal that would tend to make you think it a mercy that the struggle came to a close without more useless loss of blood, that it ended as quickly as it did, that the coup de grace was so decided. I am with some Officers from the Trans Missi[ssippi] who give a lamentable picture of things as they were there some months ago.[4] I believe it is in the power of the Govt to make the South as truly patriotic & devoted to the Union as [any] portion of the country. But I would so like to talk to you & Tasker[5] as my stand point is not a very favorable one.

I should like very much to be doing something. The book store will be invaluable. We sent an order for some last week & C. is making out a list now—Chessmen &c.[6] An Officer said yesterday, "Genl Ewell your Chess Champion has been badly beaten." I told him I had only tried their calibre by sending Majr B.[7] & having taken their gauge would try them myself in a day or two. I have been well yesterday & to day for the first [time] almost since being here. have had several severe nervous attacks,[8] but there being 16 to suffer from my ill-humor[9] Campbell got off free. How J. E. Johnston looms up a head & shoulders above the crowd!

Did you tell H. about Rifle?

Love to the family.

Yours

R S. Ewell

1. In order to gain release from prison, Confederate soldiers had to be paroled or sign an oath of allegiance to the United States. With the war at an end and the Confederacy dissolved, Ewell saw no reason not to sign the oath, although he

preferred to do so as a free man so that it would not appear that he had signed it under compulsion. Union authorities did not give him that opportunity until July 19, 1865, the day of his release. The form that Ewell signed appears in the Richard Stoddert Ewell Papers at the Library of Congress. The body of the letter reads as follows:

> I, Richard Stoddert Ewell, of the County of Prince William, State of Virginia, do solemnly swear that I will support, protect, and defend the Constitution and Government of the United States against all enemies, whether domestic or foreign; that I will bear true faith, allegiance, and loyalty to the same, any ordinance, resolution, or laws of any State, Convention, or Legislature, to the contrary notwithstanding; and further, that I will faithfully perform all the duties which may be required of me by the laws of the United States; and I take this oath freely and voluntarily, without any mental reservation or evasion whatever.
>
> R. S. Ewell

2. With Southern manpower exhausted, the lower house of the Confederate Congress voted in favor of enlisting slaves into military service. The Senate defeated the measure. The Virginia legislature, on its own initiative, then passed a bill authorizing the use of black troops. Ewell supervised the enlistment and organization of the new units. In the end, he raised just two black companies, neither of which saw action.

3. On April 1, 1865, Union troops led by Major General Philip Sheridan routed Major General George E. Pickett's Confederate division at Five Forks, west of Petersburg, Virginia. Sheridan's victory led to the capture of the South Side Railroad, the last direct supply route into Petersburg, necessitating evacuation of city. Although Sheridan estimated that he took "at least 5,000 prisoners," he actually took fewer than 3,300 Confederates.

4. Brigadier Generals William L. Cabell and John S. Marmaduke were serving in the Trans-Mississippi Theater when they were captured at Marais des Cygnes, Kansas, on October 25, 1864.

5. Following her flight to the North, Lizinka traveled to Nashville, where she found her house occupied by the family of President Andrew Johnson, who had been a friend before the war. Lizinka offended Mrs. Johnson, prompting the president to place Lizinka under arrest and send her to St. Louis, where she remained under house arrest at the home of her cousin Colonel Thomas Tasker Gantt.

6. Apparently Ewell and other prisoners were allowed to order books and other articles from a vendor outside the fort.

7. "Majr B"—i.e., Campbell Brown.

8. Ewell suffered from periodic bouts of neuralgia.

9. Ewell refers here to the sixteen officers in his casemate.

139. To Montgomery Blair Sr.

Fort Warren May 14. 65[1]

Hon. M. Blair,[2] Washington—

Dear Sir,

Col. Gantt's letter endorsed by you reached me to-day.[3] I write to you rather than to him to save time, making your kindness my excuse.

On the surrender of Gen. Johnston,[4] considering the fall of the Confederate cause inevitable, I signed an application drawn up by the other Gen'l. Officers here to be placed on parole on the footing of Lee's & Johnston's armies. I thought that for all who expected to live in the country it was merely a question of time as to taking the oath of allegiance, but believed the effect on our own people would be better were we to return home on parole and take it there, as there would be less appearance of compulsion.[5]

I understand that the Superintendent of Prisoners at this post has reported that the officers generally are willing to take the oath & expects daily to receive directions on the subject. My mind is pretty well decided as to my course should the offer be made. What grounds he has for thinking Gen'l. Officers will be included in this offer I do not know. Can you enlighten me in this regard? Any influence I may have for good among the people I have been with for four years might be lost by unseemly haste in throwing off my allegiance to the Confederacy while a show of force in Texas is kept up. A few days more or less may make the difference between good and ill repute in my return and proportionably in my power for good, and though I may be satisfied that Kirby Smith can make no serious resistance, something may be due to form.

I have expressed myself as frankly as possible and ask as a personal favor of great importance your counsel with a view to action, whether to remain as I am until called upon to make my choice, or to apply to the Secy of War for permission to take the oath of allegiance.

Col. Gantt advises me to go to Europe. I see no necessity for this. My own judgement as at present advised would be to remain. If admitted to take the oath of allegiance—*it will be in good faith*—to become not a *passive* but a[n] *active* useful citizen.

I will not lose time in expressing my high appreciation of your kindness.

1. Ewell dictated this letter to Brown. Additions and deletions have been made, some in Brown's handwriting, some in Ewell's. The final paragraph of the letter was written by Ewell himself.

2. Montgomery Blair Sr. (1813–1883) had served as a judge on the Court of Common Pleas in St. Louis, Missouri, from 1845 to 1849. After running unsuccessfully as the Republican nominee for president of the United States in 1860, Blair accepted the position of postmaster general in Abraham Lincoln's first administration. Ewell had access to the Missouri politician through his cousin Tasker Gantt, a St. Louis attorney who knew Blair personally.

3. On May 4, 1865, Tasker Gantt wrote to Ewell, advising him to take the oath of allegiance and then go abroad for a few years. Blair added a postscript to the letter on May 10, likewise urging Ewell to take the oath.

4. Joseph E. Johnston surrendered the Army of Tennessee to William T. Sherman on April 26, 1865, near Durham, North Carolina, just seventeen days after Robert E. Lee surrendered the Army of Northern Virginia to Ulysses S. Grant at Appomattox Court House, Virginia. Grant and Sherman paroled their Confederate prisoners and permitted them to return to their homes. Officers were allowed to keep their sidearms and other personal property.

5. See also RSE to LCB, 12 May 1865, FHS (letter 138, this volume).

140. To Montgomery Blair Sr.

I enclose a letter from Mrs Ewell to her son,[1] which you will see has an important bearing on that of mine yours [*sic*] of .[2]

Confined here with me are two Officers from the Trans-Mississippi, Generals Marmaduke & Cabell, whose views in reference to the oath & parole are substantially such as were given by me in my letter of the .[3]

These Officers state that were they to take the oath of allegiance their motives would be liable to misconstruction, their families endangered & owing to want of correct information no good effect towards pacification would be produced. Probably they have as much or more influence as anyone with the troops they have been serving with & their presence there on parole, while it could not possibly injure the govt, would enable them, by giving true statements of the condition of things east of the Missi[ssippi], possibly to save that country much suffering & make the military operations of shorter duration.

Many Officers in other prisons & same Dept. write here to same effect. There being no mail facilities in that country, these Officers circulating among their friends would save much time in letting the true state of affairs be known.

Montgomery Blair Sr. served as post-master general in Lincoln's first administration. Ewell's cousin Tasker Gantt knew Blair and asked the Missouri politician to use his influence to have Ewell and his wife released from confinement. (Library of Congress)

Your former kindness to me & the peculiar circumstances of these Officers are my reasons for bringing this to your notice.

Resply &c—

R. S. Ewell

1. The draft of this letter is undated. An archivist later dated it May 16, 1865, which appears to be accurate.
2. Ewell left the date blank here. On May 16, 1865, Lizinka informed Campbell that Blair said that it would be better for the Ewells "to simply take the oath, go home, & attend quietly to business" rather than go to Europe. LCB to CB, 16 May 1865, FHS.
3. Again Ewell left the date blank. He wrote to Blair on May 14, 1865, indicating his willingness to take the oath of allegiance but suggested that it might be prudent for him to delay doing so until General E. Kirby Smith's army had surrendered. After his release, Ewell declared his intention to become an active and useful citizen of the country. RSE to Montgomery Blair, 14 May 1865, FHS (139).

141. To Lizzie Ewell

Fort Warren B H.
May 18th 1865

Miss Lizzy Ewell

Dear Lizzy;

Yours of 13th Ult came a few days since. The papers mentioned that the mail to Richmond was not in operation & so it was useless to write.

I have been expecting to hear from the Old man[1] but was doubtful about writing as I thought he might wish to be compromised as little as possible. C. & myself have been placed in same part of the Fort within the last two weeks. previously we had no intercour[s]e. Mrs Von Koppf[,] daughter of Mr Sam Smith of B[oston],[2] has written twice about a gold ring sent to me in Richmond. Do you know anything about it. She says there is a book in the library dedicated by Father to her grandfather Mr Robt Smith.[3]

I suppose you know Rifle was taken when I was. I expect when he got his fill of good oats & hay he thought the millenium had come. Prison life is not altogether as pleasant as might be, although we have every indulgence the law allows. I saw myself roundly abused in the papers for burning Rchd. There were two fires before we started, kindled by the mob. The Arsenal was set on fire & hose cut by irresponsible persons without authority.[4] In spite of our guards at the bridge it was set on fire by some one, evidently with a view to cut off our retreat. It was burnt by order after we crossed.[5] I see there is a Court of Equity to settle claims where contracts were made in Confederate money. I wish you would ask your Father to try to do something for my house rent. I am willing to pay a fair rent, on the *then* value in gold of Confederate money. After the cottage was rented, the most of the furniture was moved into the garret. Of course I have nothing to do with this. If the Old Man will arrange this matter for me I will not mind being liberal & standing treat when we meet.[6] I have suffered much from neuralgia since being here. One eye is partly closed in consequence a la Prize fighter. Are any of the ranking Officers allowed to take the oath? Remember me to the family.

[R. S. Ewell][7]

Respects to Miss M. Lloyds[8]

1. Benjamin Stoddert Ewell, Dick's brother and Lizzie's father.
2. Unidentified.
3. Ewell's father, Dr. Thomas Ewell, wrote several medical books.

4. One witness claimed that the arsenal caught fire when changing winds blew burning embers from the nearby Petersburg Bridge.
5. For details on the burning of the Mayo Bridge, see Sulivan, "The Fall of Richmond," 726.
6. Ewell had rented a house in Richmond during the war. He asked his brother Ben, who was then living in the city, to resolve the matter of his rent. Ewell was willing to pay rent for the period he had used the house, even in gold, so long as the rent charged was fair.
7. Ewell's signature has been cut out of this letter.
8. One of Lizzie's friends.

142. To Lizinka Ewell

Fort Warren
May 19 1865

M[rs] R. S. Ewell

M. D. L.

I send you a copy of [a] letter just recd from Judge Blair.[1] I write in a great hurry that the return mail may take this. I sent Tasker a copy of my letter—nearly. Remember that I am comparatively in the dark[—]may make mistakes—but I dont want[2] to work at cross purposes with you & Tasker.[3] Will send to-morrow full copy of my letter to Judge Blair. Excuse this scrawl. My eye is inflamed & can hardly see.[4]

Yrs &c
R S. Ewell

1. On May 17 Blair wrote to Ewell, advising him to remain in the country once he attained his freedom. Lizinka had suggested to President Johnson through intermediaries that the family might go abroad for a few years, in the belief that that might induce Johnson to free her husband and son. It did not. Johnson was provoked by the letter and its "want of national feeling." By contrast, Blair believed that Ewell's expressed intention of abiding in the country as a peaceable, law-abiding citizen would "produce a good effect" on the president. According to Blair, Ewell had written to him on May 13. Unfortunately, that letter has not been found. Montgomery Blair Sr. to RSE, 17 May 1865, FHS.
2. After the word "want," Ewell redundantly wrote the word "wish."
3. Ewell, Lizinka, and their cousin Tasker Gantt were each working through important friends in attempts to secure Ewell's and Campbell Brown's release.

Lizinka tried to use her influence with President Andrew Johnson, a former friend, while she, Gantt, and Ewell each corresponded with members of the Blair family.

4. While in prison Ewell suffered from neuralgia.

143. To Lizinka Ewell

Fort Warren B H.
May 21. 1865

Mrs L. C. Ewell

M. D. L.

I wrote a letter two days since but on receipt of Blair's burned it in order to send you his. I was in the dark as to your wishes or plans & was a little uneasy lest we should be at cross purposes. Were I a bachelor I should be as utterly purposeless as it is possible for any one to be. C. has signified his wish to take the oath. The quicker he gets out of this the better. it is neither good for mind or body & he ought to be at work—the balance of us too for that matter. He was cook last week & acquitted himself so well that the mutton chop story didn't make much impression.[1] They wont let me cook. We have grates but not cooking stoves proper. We keep up fires all the time. As the "wolf" got out why cannot you get the same for C.?[2] It would be none the worse for me here as far as trouble is concerned & probably better for me as far as matters away from here are concerned. I hope if you can do anything in this you will.

Mrs Reynolds writes "We were very sorry not to have a visit from Cousin Lizinka. I wrote to Hattie urging her to come with her Mother but I believe she never received the letter. I hope the time is not far distant when I shall have the pleasure of greeting her in the most cordial manner &c." She hopes to see Lizzy E. You are fortunate in having many friends beyond price. If you would number Mr Reynolds among them I dont think you would ever be sorry for it. I believe you know how highly I estimate his integrity, kindness &c.[3] Becca & Mrs R.[,] assisted by contributions from the young ladies[,] started us a box on the 17th. We are anxiously looking for it, more as an event than from need of the contents. I have improved my fare by getting my beef raw, which I cook a la Navajoe.

22d My box came today from Balt. Tea pot &c. All right except that they sent 12 lbs of candles. I wrote for 2.[4] I would hate to have to be a prisoner untill I burnt them all—regularly. More needles & thread than if I were to turn taylor. But the assortment is an excellent one—relishes &c. so as to go far without too much room en voyage.[5] C. has made himself look like "a little kid" by shaving clean. His excuse was that none of his family wore beard[s].

Tell Harriot I recd her letter with much pleasure. will answer it. She had better remember my sage remarks on independence.[6] I often think of my little "Goslings". As you say, "Bless um". I think of all unprofitable stock young womankind are the worst to raise as they are almost sure to be gobbled up as soon as they get to be useful. We have need of something in way of greens sometimes. Does Tasker know of any green Grocer in Boston with whom we might contract? The book business was such a success that C. suggests the latter idea.[7]

Remember me to the family.

Yours.
R S. Ewell

1. On May 8, Campbell wrote to his sister: "Marmaduke cooks [this] week—my turn, next. We live well. I have large undeveloped talents for cooking, and expect to astonish the mess." CB to Hattie Brown, 8 May 1865, PBE.
2. "The Wolf" is probably a reference to Lizinka's future son-in-law, Major Tom Turner, who had been released from Johnson's Island Prison on May 12. Turner had been an aide-de-camp on Ewell's staff and was captured with him at Sailor's Creek.
3. Although Mr. and Mrs. Reynolds lived in Baltimore, they remained loyal to the Union, a fact that soured Lizinka's opinion of them. Neither the general nor the Reynolds let political differences mar their friendship, however, and after the war Ewell hired the couple's son, Hugh, to manage his Mississippi cotton plantation.
4. On May 8 Ewell had written a letter to his sister Rebecca, requesting a number of items, including twelve pounds of candles. In the letter he also expressed his need of a teapot (137).
5. The idea here seems to be that the items Rebecca sent were relatively small in size but would provide the prisoners enjoyment for a long time.
6. Ewell's advice to Hattie regarding independence, womankind, and so on was undoubtedly prompted by the recent announcement of her engagement to Tom Turner.
7. Ewell and the other prisoners had successfully purchased books by mail from a Boston book dealer, and they now sought a similar arrangement with a local grocer.

144. To Lizinka Ewell

Fort Warren B.H.
Saty. May 27. 65

Mrs L. C. Ewell

M. D. L.

C. made his appearance on the rampart Thursday afternoon with the "Tenant of Wildfell Hall," which I finished yesterday (Friday) which is pretty well for my age without specs.[1]

Since the arrival of some State prisoners, our grounds for exercise have been changed to top of the Rampart, corresponding to removing one's walk from cellar to roof. Hitherto our walk was in the Fort surrounded by walls where nothing but Garrison events could be seen. From the Ramparts we have a fine view of the Ocean, Shipping & harbor. I liked the novel but was disappointed in finding any particular, distinctively peculiar traits of character in common with the one in question. I thought her vastly superior to Mr Markham.[2] I could draw a character much more similar in many respects, but I could not help liking her very much & when she handed the candle to burn the drunkard's fingers in her own narrative, I thought was the first point of similarity. She is a head & shoulders above Markham in the last scene of all. But there is nothing very peculiar in being tall & graceful & wearing black & misfortune & devotion to children. Self sacrifice, long-suffering & forgiving of injuries are in common, but the fact is I read it in too much of a hurry & am going to read it more carefully, for the more I think of it the more points of resemblance I make out & the more highly I think of her. My last letter from you is the 18th. I would not like John Frame enough to write for him.[3] The best servant (Colored) I ever had was Frank, except when in Richmond & had it not been for his wife & had I not been obliged to stay at Chaffin's my vanity makes me think I could have managed him there, by devoting my mind to it, as the man said about his cravat tie.[4] I find a decided improvement since giving up coffee for tea. It is curious to hear the rest dictating to me how tea is to be made & in consequence wasting more than used to keep us going. Earle[5] sent over his card the other day but I received a box from Baltimore with a suit of clothes & mixed assortment generally.[6] I contemplate getting a Canary bird—have sent for a geranium & rose bush. Have written to Parson Stoddert without an answer.

We are daily expecting some announcement of conditions on which we can take the oath & as each successive paper has a different version of what they will be, the spirits of some of the party rise & fall in proportion. One who is habitually persuaded of the certainty of the more dire events said the other day that there was nothing left but to "die gracefully". It is curious to see how the same prognostic of some ignorant "penny-a-liner" will be interpreted by one man as altogether favorable & another as shutting out all hope.[7] Remember me to the family.

Yours
R. S. Ewell

1. Anne Brontë's novel *The Tenant of Wildfell Hall* first appeared in 1848. In the story, the protagonist, Helen Graham, flees an alcoholic husband and seeks refuge at Wildfell Hall, the property of her brother.
2. Ewell is referring here to Helen Graham and Gilbert Markham, characters in *The Tenant of Wildfell Hall*.
3. John Frame was a black servant who accompanied Ewell during the war. One person described him as "a Colored French gentleman." Another described him as an "elegant" man and "a very dignified personage." Ewell, *A Virginia Scene*, 64–65. For additional references to Frame, see Pfanz, *Ewell*, 258, 261, 521; and Jones, *Campbell Brown's Civil War*, 132, 158.
4. For additional information on this valued servant, see RSE to LE, 28 May 1865 (letter 146, this volume).
5. A Boston vendor.
6. This box was probably sent by the Reynolds family.
7. The pessimistic officer was Brigadier General Henry R. Jackson.

145. To Rebecca Ewell

May 27. 1865

Miss R. L. Ewell

My dear Becca;

I intended to write on receipt of box but you owe me several letters & I have been a little unwell with neuralgia. I did not write for tea but it was lucky you sent it, as I cannot drink coffee & find my health better since taking tea alone. I am very much obliged to you for the trouble you have taken & if it is any gratification to you to know it, the contents are conducive to health of purse & body.[1]

I dare say some of the contents seemed extravagant but in fact are not so much so as they appear as a few drops of sauce or catchup will change the whole flavor of the dishes which are very uniform in character. Where you can choose variety from the whole market it is not so important to have these flavoring elements. You must not think I attach more importance to eating than other things but I have the misfortune to know that I have a stomach & not an accommodating one.[2]

I have read a novel lately, "Tenant of Wildfell Hall[,]" with much interest. Have you read it & what do you think of the heroine?

I have not worn the clothes yet as the old ones are warmer & summer has not yet arrived. I eat the dried fruit just so, as it saves cooking & goes farther. Campbell is experimenting to day on a rice pudding which is to be made of such ingredients as were in the box. We have a better walk & a more extensive prospect than was given us before & enjoy it prodigiously. We can go during the day, on the ramparts—quite an improvement.

Were I in your place I would try to get an agent to look at Stony Lonesome & if possible have grass, guano & love dust sowed there this fall. There was a good deal of love dust as well as phosphate of lime put on the ground in winter of 61. I have never heard with what result. Miss Mary Balch[3] went to see me in Richmond last winter & after very absurd precautions about having no one by said she wanted to purchase some wood. I told her I had sold out my interest in the farm 15 yrs since & that she ought to see you, that the dead wood was not worth much. But the great demand now will be for grass & it is the best permanent improvement of the soil.

The mania for farming is as strong with me as ever & I am trying to get some shrubs—Rose & Geraniums—to set in the window. Why dont you get permission to come & see us & bring on Cousins Rosanna & Sophia?[4] It would be pleasant to see the "hub of the universe"[5] & it is a beautiful harbor.

Please remember me to Mr Reynolds & the family.

You said nothing about accounts &c. I am in hope C. will get out before long & I want to settle accounts before he leaves.[6]

Yrs truly
R S. Ewell

1. Rebecca had sent her brother a box containing food and a variety of useful articles, including a teapot, candles, needles and thread. Dick received the box on May 22.
2. Ewell suffered from dyspepsia, what modern doctors might diagnose as an ulcer.
3. Mary Balch (ca. 1842–1899) lived at "The Manse," a house just five hundred yards from Stony Lonesome. The house still stands at 10214 Lonesome Road.

4. Sophia Reynolds was Rosanna's daughter.

5. Boston.

6. Ewell and Campbell wished to pay Rebecca for the food and other items that she had sent them, but Rebecca had not sent them a bill.

146. To Lizzie Ewell

Fort Warren,
May 28, 1865.

Dear Lizzie:

I wrote a long letter to "Pop"[1] the other day, chiefly about Governor Pierpont.[2] Authorities differ as to the spelling of his name. The darkies have it Pierpoint. I hear that "Pop" has gone back to Williamsburg. I do hope that he will recover the fine old wine I hid away and buried. I suppose you are very anxious to get back to the old place.[3] I had a letter from Parson Stoddert, who says that from personal experience he can assure me that hanging is not so painful after all.[4]

Tell Frank I heard with much pleasure of his efforts to help you. If he had been along when I was taken prisoner, he might have saved my property. He was the best darkie that ever waited on me out of Richmond. If I ever get out of this and can give him employment, I will be glad to do so.[5] You sneer in your letter to Major Brown at the idea of Stony Lonesome blossoming like a rose. It is not to be compared to a sand bank, but if this war had let me alone I would have owned it. I would have had a place you would have been proud to visit— and far more lively than bricks and dirty streets.[6]

A lady who saw my daguerrotype the other day wanted to know if I were really as fine a looking specimen as that appeared to represent. When one remembers that that kind of likeness never flatters, it is almost enough to make me vain.

Remember me to Dr. Hoge, and tell him I am glad to hear of his return. I want him to remember how hard I tried to get up a constabulary force in Richmond. I knew nothing of the burning of the Arsenal or the cutting of the engine hose, which were the work of incendiaries and unauthorized persons. I had no force to stop the plundering that was going on all night, and against which I made my staff and couriers go on police duty. Several fires were kindled before we left, and an attempt to burn Mayo's Bridge was frustrated by the personal daring of the Engineer officers, who at great risk removed burning canal boats from under it. I acted merely in obedience to previous orders. General Kershaw and myself looking on from the river saw buildings ignite at a distance from the river and apparently burned by the ill will of some of the mob. I have this matter very deeply at heart. I repeatedly see myself blamed. I rather fell short of than exceeded my instructions. Tell the Doctor I have heard no preaching since my capture. I wish he were able to better our conditions in that respect.

Major B. would be very glad if he ever had a chance to employ Frank, Josam, and Willis.[7]

The other day a young lady of three years sent me her "Ferrotype"—we live in an iron age—a very nice child. Please send me a little present for her, a book or something as you may judge best.[8]

I suppose you know Rifle was taken when I was. I expect when he got his fill of good oats and hay, he thought the millenium had come.

Remember me to the young ladies and the family.

Yours,

R. S. Ewell

1. Benjamin Ewell.
2. Francis H. Pierpont (1814–1899) was Virginia's Unionist governor, having been unanimously elected to that post by a convention of Virginians loyal to the Union at Wheeling in June 1861. When Virginia's western counties organized themselves into the State of West Virginia in 1863, Pierpont moved to Union-held Alexandria, Virginia. He continued in office until 1868.
3. Ben and Lizzie had a house just outside of Williamsburg that they had left upon the arrival of the Union army in 1862. The building is now the office of Williamsburg Memorial Park.
4. In 1863, shortly after leaving the service of the Confederate army, William took the oath of allegiance to the Union. He kept the oath so well, wrote his cousin Tasker Gantt, that he was *"half hanged"* by Confederate bushwhackers. TTG to RLE, 6 June 1865, folder 11, WM.
5. Frank was a black servant who lived with the Ewells in Richmond during the last year of the Civil War. When Ewell fled the city in April 1865, Frank apparently went to live with Benjamin Ewell and his daughter, Lizzie, later accompanying them to Williamsburg. After the war, Ewell employed Frank and his wife at Lizinka's farm in Spring Hill, Tennessee.
6. A reference to Lizzie's hometown of Williamsburg, Virginia.
7. Slaves owned by Lizinka or her son. Willis accompanied Brown during the war. Nothing is known of Josam. Jones, *Campbell Brown's Civil War*, 87.
8. The little girl was Mabel Appleton, the daughter of Fort Warren's commander, Major John W. M. Appleton.

147. To Lizinka Ewell

Fort Warren B. H.
May 28th 1865

Mrs L. C. Ewell

M. D. L.

I answer yours of 23d & 4th by return of mail. Of course that man Russell is an impostor as there was no such person on my Staff. He ought to have been called on for his orders.[1]

I am afraid your health will suffer in St Louis if you remain there during the warm weather. I have known Genl Grant for many years. our relations have always been pleasant & I think he would be friendly disposed.[2]

General Sherman was a classmate at West Point. We were also on friendly terms while there, though I have not met him since. The papers speak of his being assigned to the Dept. of Miss. Would you think it advisable for me to write to Sherman, to state your case & ask that you may either be released from arrest or informed what the charges against you are & be allowed an opportunity to meet them.[3] There is no time lost in referring to you as Genl Sherman will be, so the papers say, several days in N.Y. & his Hd Qrts. are not yet determined on. Nashville is spoken of among other places. Some of your friends know him better than I do & it is possible you may have already taken steps in this direction.

Major General William T. Sherman had been a friend and classmate of Ewell's at West Point. At least one man thought the two officers resembled one another. (Library of Congress)

Please remember me to Col. Gantt & family. Yrs &c

R S. Ewell

1. Lizinka had sent Ewell a clipping from the May 23, 1865, *St. Louis Republican* describing the disreputable behavior of a Major Russell, a man who claimed to be on Ewell's staff. Russell had gotten drunk at the Lindell Hotel and created a ruckus. A provost guard took him to prison. The imposter had paid Lizinka a visit prior to the incident.

2. Ewell and Grant had attended West Point together for one year. Ewell was in the Class of 1840 while Grant graduated in the Class of 1843. The two men crossed paths again in the United States Army on at least two occasions, at Jefferson Barracks and in Mexico. According to her daughter, Lizinka later visited General Grant while in Washington and secured a promise from him to "do what I can for my old friend Ewell." Turner, "Recollections of Andrew Johnson," 175.

3. Lizinka fled north early in 1865 and had taken refuge with her cousin Colonel Thomas Tasker Gantt in St. Louis. She was placed under house arrest but was set free on March 25 after taking the amnesty oath. Lizinka immediately set out for Nashville, where she proceeded to offend President Andrew Johnson's wife, who was then residing in Lizinka's house near the capitol. Johnson placed Lizinka under arrest and sent her back to St. Louis. Although no charges were brought against her, she remained under house arrest until June 22.

148. To Andrew Johnson

FORT WARREN, MASS., *May 30, 1865.*

His Excellency ANDREW JOHNSON,

President of the United States of America:

SIR: I hereby apply to be allowed to take the oath of allegiance prescribed in your proclamation of 29th instant and to be released. I am excluded, as having been educated at the U.S. Military Academy, on account of my rank as lieutenant-general in the Confederate service, and as being now a prisoner of war, and on no other grounds.[1]

R. S. EWELL.

1. Johnson's amnesty proclamation appears in *OR,* series 2, 8:578–80. It granted pardon and the restoration of property rights to individuals who had taken part in the rebellion. Several classes of Southerners were excluded from the pardon because of their high economic, political, or military standing. Ewell's exclu-

As governor of Tennessee, Andrew Johnson had been Lizinka's neighbor and friend. As president of the United States, he would be her jailor. (Library of Congress)

sion was based on the three criteria listed in this letter. He was also ineligible on a fourth count, having resigned from the service of the United States Army to enlist in the rebellion. Those, like Ewell, who did not qualify for Johnson's blanket amnesty had to apply individually for pardons.

149. To Lizinka Ewell

Fort Warren B.H.
May 31st 65

Mrs Lizinka C. Ewell

My dear Lizinka;

I was puzzled how the anniversary of May 26th being in 63 on Tuesday could come on Friday in 65 & thought I must be mistaken somewhere untill C. made the explanation of Leap Year having intervened.[1]

He & myself applied yesterday in consequence of the proclamation of the 29th & I wrote to day to Judge Blair to say I had done so.[2] Yesterday brought me yours of the 25th. I am anxious about your health, particularly if required to remain in St Louis during the Summer. The fact that so many are so much worse off does not lessen my concern as regards yourself, though if released before the warm weather there will not be so much harm done. We find it much more pleasant here since being allowed to go on the ramparts. The Fort is so far out that it never gets very warm I understand.

My own health is a great deal better than when I was first confined. Still it would be a great relief to be allowed to go to work again & I think I could work right hard. You would have to realize it though, to know how hard it is to fix the mind on any thing like books or what does not concern the present. Every one now is in a state of excitement about the Amnesty proclamation[,] some having been in for nearly two years. After writing about John Frame & Frank the other day I thought you may suppose I think of hiring the latter, but there is no such notion. I want very little assistance & except that it takes more time, get along nearly as well as any one else.

Yours,

R S. Ewell

1. The Ewells had been married at St. Paul's Church in Richmond on May 26, 1863.
2. Like Ewell, Brown was ineligible for the blanket amnesty offered to the Confederates and had to apply individually for a pardon. Brown was ineligible because he was then a prisoner and because he had personal wealth in excess of $20,000.

150. To Lizinka Ewell

Fort Warren June 5. 65

Mrs L. C. Ewell

My dear Lizinka;

Your last was of the 1st. I am much obliged to Tasker for his suggestion to you as to frequent letters. I thought you would know that to receive letters must be the greatest pleasure here. The number I write is the best proof that that portion of a correspondence is pleasant. They are very kind to us here about our letters as indeed in every thing that the U.S. Officers are allowed any limit.

I said nothing to you about writing, knowing that you dont care to do so when you have nothing, or think you have nothing, to say. I regret that my letters are so much longer in reaching you, than yours in return—about double the time—I suppose owing to the time taking up there in examining them—unnecessary precaution as it is done here[,] & there is no chance for sending any except th[r]ough the regular channels.

The "Piedmont" country includes all along the base of the Mountain (Blue Ridge) by Warrenton through to the Potomac. Tasker most likely referred to Fauquier & Loudoun Counties, which are the best. Kinloch where Maj. T was born is in the Fauquier part.[1]

I am more anxious for C's release that you may make your plans for the future than on any other account. The winters though, in the section you speak of would be too cold for you. You forget that when I went to Millborough I was on my back, as well as when I returned[,] & saw nothing but the top of the baggage car.[2] In your debates as to your future plans, I place my vote in your hands. I cannot see in the past that any particular locality had anything to do with happiness. The mere moving of any particular section of country to my Frontier posts would not have made me more happy. There was as little exterior charm about Morton's Hall[3] to attract as possible, yet I was as contented there, except the war, as I could be & removing that deep tragedy I would be at a loss to combine more of what is essential to my happiness than were collected there. I have every thing here—dont expect to be hung for treason, it is pleasant weather, magnificent prospect & no care—but I would be happier out. I write this to illustrate that you must judge. When the war broke out I was preparing Stony Lonesome to live at for the rest of my life & you know that is not considered the most desirable locality & am now advising Becca about guano, grass &c. I am provoked excessively with myself at times at my depression of spirits & dismal way of looking at every thing, present & future & may be next day considering the same things as all "Couleur de rose," but though I know it is physical yet my conduct is governed to a certain extent by these transient fits & I fear sometimes may have to repent.

Genl Cabell told me the other day I ought to be with you who would take care of me & "make me behave myself." I forget what had been the subject of dispute.

Yours
R. S. Ewell

---

1. Kinloch is nestled between the Bull Run Mountains and The Plains, Virginia. Ewell and his attendants stopped at the house on September 18, 1862, after fleeing Dunblane. Tom Turner, Ewell's aide-de-camp and Lizinka's future son-in-law, was born there around 1842.
2. Ewell was wounded on August 28, 1862, at Groveton and was taken by train to Millborough, Virginia, to recuperate. He remained there until November, when he moved to Richmond. Millborough (now spelled Millboro) is located in the Allegheny Mountains, west of Staunton.

3. Ewell had made his headquarters at Morton's Hall near Orange, Virginia, in the fall and winter 1863. Lizinka had joined him there. Although the couple had then been married for more than three months, the war had kept them apart. The house therefore became the Ewells' honeymoon bower.

151. To Lizinka Ewell

June 8th 65 —

Mrs L. C. Ewell

My dear Lizinka;

Harriots of the 2nd came yesterday & yrs. of the 1st several days before. I have not recd Willm Stoddert's letter.[1] I sent you a copy of Judge Blair's letter about Genl Grant's asking for my parole.[2] Nothing more has been heard on the subject, but I would far prefer being released now on the oath of allegiance with restoration to rights of citizenship than to take the release on parole. Of course should the parole come I would not delay, but leave and renew at once my application for the oath.[3] I venture to predict that the portion of the community in future who will return with most alacrity & good faith to their duties will be the class now held up to most opprobrium; i.e. Ex-Officers of the Old U.S. Army & Navy.

The only one I remember to have heard spoken of as a violent advocate of secession & all that, remained in the Army & has been active in suppressing the South. It is all right, but still it seems strange to hear one's self denounced while some of the class that did most harm are highly honored. I mean the Pre-Adamite Secessionists.[4] I for one had everything to lose & nothing to gain. Had I been ambitious there was not much cause for expecting favor from Mr Davis as at the end of the Mexican War he caused the promotion of Northrop[,] a Citizen[,] to the Captain's vacancy to which I was entitled, Though I was Brevetted for services in Mexico while in the previous 12 years Northrop had been two yrs. a citizen & ten an Officer on sick leave.[5] All my hopes of ease & quiet for the future were sacrificed when with regret I took my course. Though after events made a change, there were not any elements but of pain in the calculation or prospect. I saw yesterday a large Ocean Steamer passing, on her way to Liverpool, The China I believe. being the first of the kind I had seen I enjoyed the sight excessively. She was crowded with passengers & I felt very much in the humor of joining. I had a letter the other day from an old New Mexican friend, Govr D. Merew[e]ther of Louisville, K'y.[6] As your reference to the Alderney cow came about same time & the Govr seemed very anxious to do something for me, I was tempted to get him to buy one for me at Alexander's sale,[7] but C. thought they could be had on better terms almost anywhere else. I think your fancy in that respect will be gratified, even if we have to rent Stony Lonesome as you suggest in a recent letter.[8] You have said nothing more about that man Russell. I hope it was stated in the papers that he was no Staff Officer of mine. I at least had gentlemen about me. I am sick of the constant discussions I hear daily of Amnesty Oath, Oath of Allegiance &c. &c. I for my part am heartily anxious to become a law-abiding member of the community, if allowed & would be the best one to be found, either to put down guerillas or stop the mouths of demagogue talkers of sedition—the worse of the two—provided the govt establishes such an office. I am willing to take either Amnesty or Allegiance, as I have seen nothing yet that one with these views should object to.[9] Excuse a dull letter & if barren of incidents please remember that circumstances are unfavorable to much variety.

Yours—

R. S. Ewell[10]

1. Lizinka, Harriot, and William Stoddert were all staying at Tasker Gantt's house in St. Louis at this time.

2. Not found.

3. Ewell told Montgomery Blair that he did not want to take the oath of allegiance while General E. Kirby Smith's Confederate army was still in the field, lest he appear to be disloyal to the South. By like token, he preferred to take the oath while on parole rather than while in prison, for fear that if he took it in prison, the people of the South might think that he did so under compulsion. Smith's surrender on June 2, 1865, changed the situation. With all organized resistance in the South now at an end, Ewell wanted to take the oath as soon as possible so as to have his rights of citizenship restored. However, if the Federal authorities refused to let him take the oath and offered him parole instead, he would take that.

4. The term Pre-Adamite Secessionists may refer to those who advocated secession prior to the bombardment of Fort Sumter.

5. In 1839 Lieutenant Lucius B. Northrop (1811–1894) accidentally shot himself in the knee while serving as a first lieutenant in the 1st U.S. Dragoons. For much of the next decade, he was on leave of absence and took no part in the Mexican War. During that time he studied and briefly practiced medicine, an activity that resulted in the army dropping him from its rolls. Northrop appealed this action to Senator Jefferson Davis of Mississippi, who used his

influence in Congress to have his old friend not only reinstated but promoted to captain. Ewell felt particularly aggrieved by this development because it delayed his own promotion. In 1861 Davis appointed Northrop Commissary General of the Confederacy, a position he held until February 1865, when he was forced to resign.

6. David Meriwether (1800–1893) was born in Virginia but moved to Kentucky at an early age. As a teenager, he engaged in trading in the West, later returning to Kentucky to farm and practice law. He held several high political offices during his life, including the Kentucky House of Representatives (1832–45, 1858–85), secretary for the State of Kentucky (1851), United States senator (1852), and governor of the New Mexico Territory (1853–55). While in the latter office, he became a friend of Ewell's. In 1865, Meriwether was serving in the Kentucky House of Representatives.

7. Unidentified.

8. Alderneys, imported from the English Channel island of the same name, were small dairy cows known for producing large quantities of rich milk and yellow cream. Smaller than Guernseys but larger than Jerseys, they had in-turned horns, deep chests, and short legs. Lizinka purchased two Alderneys in Baltimore in April 1867 and shipped them to Tennessee. She paid the princely sum of $1,000 dollars for the pair. They were the first cattle of that type introduced into the state.

9. The amnesty oath read as follows:

> I (name) of (place of residence) do solemnly swear, in the presence of Almighty God, that I will henceforth faithfully support, protect and defend the Constitution of the United States, and the Union of the States thereunder, and that I will, in like manner, abide by and faithfully support all laws and proclamations which have been made during the existing rebellion with reference to the emancipation of slaves, so help me God.

The oath of allegiance, or loyalty oath, took several forms. One version read:

> I (name) of the county of (county name), state of (state name), do solemnly swear, in presence of Almighty God, that I will henceforth faithfully support, protect, and defend the Constitution of the United States, and the Union of the States thereunder; and that I will, in like manner, abide by and faithfully support all acts of Congress passed during the existing rebellion with reference to slaves, so long and so far as not repealed, modified or held void by Congress, or by decision of the Supreme Court; and that I

will, in like manner, abide by and faithfully support all proclamations of the President made during the existing rebellion having reference to slaves, so long and so far as not modified or declared void by decision of the Supreme Court: So help me God.

10. Campbell Brown added the following footnote:

> I wrote Sister yesterday of a queer letter from Aunt Susan. Look-
> ing over it, I am convinced she is hurt by either yours or Sister's
> fancied neglect, not meaning there is any ground for the fancy.
> As for my own personal matters she mentions, I am a little shy
> of discussing them by letter. Will give you any information you
> want, when we meet; that is, that I possess myself.
>
>   Yrs. Affecy   C. Brown

152. To Lizinka Ewell

11th 65[1]

Mrs L. C. Ewell

My dear Lizinka;

Yrs of 7th & 2d came yesterday. You speak of applying to the Secty of
War. I think it would be the best thing you could do. He released Mrs Hough[2]
& some one else in Richmond. The point of most anxiety now to both C. &
myself is your arrest.[3] If you were allowed to go to a healthier place we would
feel much better satisfied & would wait patiently the action of the Government.
Moreover it is perfectly evident that in my own case at least we will have to wait
in spite of anything that can be done. Now what I want you to do is to urge
some mitigation of your arrest not bringing anything else into question. If you
succeed in regard to yourself I still wish you not to take any steps in regard to
me either by writing or personal application. I think I have pretty good reasons
for this wish, but they are too long &c. to give here. By placing your case on
its own merits (unintention of offence, danger to health &c. &c.) you may at
least be able to get a change of locality unless the spirit of the govt has changed
very much in the last few years. We did not keep soldiers in arrest in my time
over Eight days without giving them a copy of their charges. I think it is safe to
calculate that C. will be in prison for some weeks & that I shall have to remain
longer. Further that in my case nothing can be done by importunity—certainly I would prefer its not being tried, at the risk of keeping you in statu[s]
quo & for many other reasons, nor would my views be changed by your release
in regard to the expediency of any effort.

A Meeting of Doctors is going on in Boston & some hundreds of them paid a visit to the Fort a day or two since.[4] Before the guard could stop them, they crowded into the prisoners rooms like bees & some of them asked me in regard to action in bringing on the war. I told them I was absent in Arizona in 60, & had to come in sick in the Spring of 61, that I was quite unwell in a secluded part of Va & found the war suddenly inaugurated, that on one side I had a handsome position, good pay & some means saved from long years service. All this I forfeited by going South, but that I had to fight with or against my state & did what the people of Mass. would have done & which I should have done at forfeit of my head. They agreed somewhat with my views & I saw myself published in the Boston papers as hurrying in from Arizona to take part in the war & many other like absurdities, the greatest being that I did not regret being taken p[r]isone[r]! I preferred captivity to being killed but I owe the loss of liberty & of much property to not being able to get away. We were in a pretty dangerous position & the result was doubtful. in this much I felt I had made a narrow escape in myself & others getting off safe. However the notice was gratuitous in the papers for nothing was said on the subject with the Doctors.

We sometimes find our greatest misfortunes turn into benefits, but if there were anything I had to dread & regret in 61 it was this war. I was too sick & too busy sowing guano & timothy &c. to think much about it, but I clung to the last ray of hope like a drowning man to straws. I had only received benefits from the U.S. The greatest act of injustice I had experienced was the making North[r]op a Captain over my head from civil life, but this several years before & by our leading man. Certainly I had nothing to tempt me into secession either from Ambition or hope.

But the consequences were unexpected.

I hope to hear that H. has taken the trip to Narragansett, mentioned in your last.[5] I wont answer her letter untill I know whether she has gone. In case she does, you must make up your mind to write daily tho. between the two places you will be kept busy. Why not send T.[6] after yr. baggage in Va? I dont know anything about it. It may be safer where it is. I lost the daguerreotype with the baggage I presume.[7] Cannot you send me another? You remember what style I thought most suitable or rather becoming. It is impossible that I should be released out of my turn. I am excluded by rank & former status & it would be unjust to others. So it is only loss of time to try it.

Yours

R S. Ewell

1. June 11, 1865.

2. Unidentified. Perhaps the same as "Mrs. Hoof" mentioned in RSE to LCB, 20 Dec. 1863, PBE (115).

3. President Johnson had ordered Lizinka's arrest after learning that she was in Nashville demanding rents of blacks who had thrown up shanties on some of her town lots. This, together with other evidence, convinced Johnson that Lizinka was not truly repentant, and on April 21, 1865, Secretary of War Stanton ordered her to be arrested and sent back to St. Louis.

4. The American Medical Association held its annual meeting in Boston. On June 8, 1865, the group took a cruise of the harbor, stopping for an hour at Fort Warren, where, according to a newspaper reporter, some of them got a glimpse of "Gens. Ewell, Marmaduke, Kershaw and other noted rebels confined there. The bands which accompanied the excursion discoursed national music to the prisoners who gathered in the open court and on 'Dixie' their shouts were long and loud. They did not appear as well pleased with 'We'll hang Jeff Davis, etc.'" One physician who saw Ewell described him "as a thin, nervous-looking man, resembling somewhat the pictures of Gen. Sherman." "Annual Meeting of the American Medical Association," *Boston Post,* 9 June 1865; "Excursion of Physicians Down the Harbor," *Boston Daily Evening Traveller,* 9 June 1865.

5. The Reynolds family owned "Narragansett," a house situated six or seven miles from Kingston, Rhode Island. Lizinka stayed at the house the following month while awaiting the release of Dick and Campbell from Fort Warren.

6. Thomas Turner.

7. Ewell had lost all of his baggage, including Lizinka's daguerreotype, at Sailor's Creek.

153. To Joseph Lewis

FORT WARREN, BOSTON HARBOR,[1]

June 13, 1865.

Dear Sir[2]—I was highly gratified at the receipt of yours of the 30th ult. Long experience has given me very different views in regard to the responsibilities of an officer, from those with which I left West Point, where a few mathematical formulas, never used afterwards, and abstruse branches of sciences were dwelt upon, to the utter exclusion of the duties and responsibilities that were to occupy our lives. It is therefore highly gratifying that I have the testimony of one companion in arms, that I made some friends among the soldiers, a portion of humanity where the treatment of the best is measured often by what the worst deserve, and whom it is easier to govern by the harshest rules than to take the trouble to discriminate between good and bad, and to make the profession easier when possible.

After the time of which you write my health suffered terribly for years, not much to the improvement of my temper, and I remember with regret much harsh language and conduct towards men who showed themselves better able to control themselves than I could control myself. However, I always tried to be just in the long run, and while the discipline and good behavior of my company was notorious, I hope I may say no man was made worse by service with me, and many of the boys discharged from my company became valuable and industrious citizens. I never heard of one turning out badly during many years in New Mexico, and I learned that kindness gives a far more perfect control over the human, as well as brute races, than harshness and cruelty.

That you may have as little as possible to be ashamed of serving with me, I will give you a short account of how I came into the Southern cause.

I came from Arizona, sick, in the spring of 1861. Stayed in the country, in Virginia, my State, trying to get well, and found the war, to my bitter regret, was being started. All the highest United States army officers were resigning, except Gen. Scott, and he published a letter that the United States would divide into four parts, thus showing that he thought all was over.[3] A United States Senator said he would march a Northern regiment to help the South for every one sent against her. Nothing was done with either of these men or with others, whose deeds were treasonable. A member of Congress from California made a public speech calling upon the South to resist the election of Mr. Lincoln.[4]

Now, I found myself forced to fight against my brothers and all my nearest and dearest relatives, against my own State, when many abler men than myself contended she was right. By taking up the side of the South I forfeited a handsome position, fine pay and the earnings of twenty years hard service. All the pay I drew in four years in the South was not as much as one year's pay in the old army. The greatest political favoritism against me I ever had was from Mr. Davis, after the Mexican war.[5]

It is hard to account for my course, except from a painful sense of duty; I say painful, because I believe few were more devoted to the old country than myself, and the greatest objection I had to it was because of my predilection for a strong one.[6] Now I see persons who did what they could to bring about the war in high favor in the North, holding high office. It was like death to me.

En route here from New Mexico, 1861, I volunteered my services to fight the Texans, threatening a United States post,[7] and was careful to do nothing against the United States before resigning.

I have asked to be allowed to take the oath of allegiance and return to my duties as a citizen. I see, though, that many persons active in the first steps in bringing this war about are at liberty, while I am here with no very good prospect of getting out, while my wife is under arrest in St. Louis, and has been since April, but up to this time has utterly failed even to find out why she is arrested. Neither she or myself have the slightest idea of the cause of her arrest.[8]

I have given you a long letter about myself, because of the friendly tone of your letter, and because I feel naturally drawn toward those with whom I have served. I remain, very respectfully, &c.,

R. S. Ewell

1. This letter was taken from an anonymous newspaper clipping found in box 1, folder 15, PBE. It was also published in Williams, "General Ewell to the High Private in the Rear," 157–60.

2. Ewell wrote this letter in response to a friendly letter he received from Joseph Lewis, a soldier who had served under him in the dragoons more than twenty years earlier. Lewis had the letter published in the *St. Paul Pioneer,* and it was later picked up by the *New Orleans Times,* the *New York World,* and other newspapers throughout the country. An excerpt of Lewis's letter appears in Hamlin, *"Old Bald Head,"* 195–96. Lewis replied to Ewell's letter on June 20, 1865, describing how he had suffered long-term effects from a saber blow inflicted by Captain Burdette A. Terrett, the post commander, which fractured Lewis's skull. This letter is archived in the Brown-Ewell Papers at the Filson Historical Society in Louisville, Kentucky. Lewis had been discharged from the army at Fort Scott on October 15, 1843.

3. On October 29, 1860, on the eve of the presidential election, General Winfield Scott had written to President James Buchanan suggesting that, rather than engage in fratricidal civil war, the United States be partitioned into four separate federations that would remain under the larger umbrella of the United States government.

4. In the opinion of historian T. Harry Williams, the senator referred to by Ewell is probably Joseph Lane of Oregon, who was outspoken in his support of the South. The congressional delegate from California may have been Senator William M. Gwin or Representative Charles L. Scott. Williams, "General Ewell to the High Private in the Rear," 159 n7.

5. A reference to the promotion of Lucius B. Northrop.

6. Ewell's meaning here is unclear. He may have meant to say that his strongest objection to secession was his preference for a strong central government.

7. The post in question may have been either the army supply depot or the United States armory near San Antonio. General David Twiggs surrendered these and other U.S. installations to Benjamin McCullough and the Texas Rangers in February 1861, at just the time Ewell would have been passing through.

8. For the circumstances surrounding Lizinka's arrest, see Turner, "Recollections of Andrew Johnson," 174.

154. To Andrew Johnson

Fort Warren, Boston Harbor,
June 16th 1865

His Ex[ellen]cy Andrew Johnson,
President of the United States

Sir: I have the honor to forward herewith the oath prescribed in your proclamation of the 29th Ult: and to apply for pardon.

For three months, Ewell was confined at Fort Warren in Boston Harbor. His favorite visitor during that time was three-year-old Mabel Appleton, daughter of the post commander. (*Harper's Weekly* and courtesy Filson Historical Society)

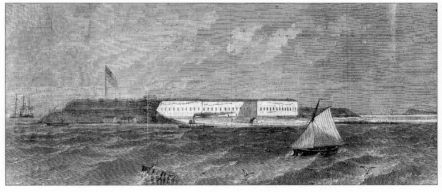

I belong to the excepted classes as I graduated at the U.S. Mil. Academy, resigned an appointment in the U.S. Army, and when taken prisoner on the 6th April last, held the rank of Lieut: Gen'l: in the C.S. Army.

This oath is the strongest proof I can give of my wish to become a loyal citizen and, as far as in me lies, to do my duty to the country.

Respy &c.

R S. Ewell

Pris: of War

[*Enclosure*]

I Richard S. Ewell do solemnly swear in presence of Almighty God that I will henceforth faithfully support and defend the constitution of the United States and the Union of the States thereunder and that I will, in like manner, abide by and faithfully support all laws and proclamations which have been made during the existing rebellion with reference to the emancipation of slaves, so help me God.

R S. Ewell

Sworn and subscribed to before me at Fort Warren, Boston Harbor, Mass. this 16th day of June 1865

Wm Ray

1st Lieut. 1st Battn Hvy. Arty. M V.

Post Adjt.[1]

1. The cover letter was written by someone other than Ewell but was signed by him. The amnesty oath that follows was written in a neat hand by Ewell himself and signed by him. The postscript was written by Lieutenant William Ray, who administered the oath.

155. To Lizinka Ewell

17th 65[1]

Mrs L. C. Ewell

My dear Lizinka;

I commenced a letter on the 14th & have been writing a little almost ever since & to day decided to write another. I dare say I had more pleasure in writing than you would have had in decyphering.

349

Yesterday in accordance with a circular from the Attorn[e]y General we renewed our applications for pardon accompanying the letter with our oaths in accordance with the proclamation of the 29th. There has been much confusion & more talk in this debating club[2] on the question of not what to do but *how,* as every one is perfectly willing like Capt Allen's Company of Regulars in the old Army; "to swear to anything the Captain pleases."[3] I am satisfied special applications in my own case, are useless, as I belong to an excepted class that will probably be the last to receive any Executive clemency. You will therefore merely lose time & trouble to try for my release & had I my choice between the two I would prefer seeing you out of trouble.

I have no right to complain under any Circumstances but in your case as far as I can understand it, there seems to be an exercise of arbitrary power that is calculated to make one fret, to say the least. Ben in a "sui generis"[4] letter asks if I would not have preferred less rank—curious when he credited rank in former times with so much! I heard from Wm who seems absorbed in Ten. He informs me in a postscript that hanging is not so painful & not much to be dreaded as far as this world is concerned.[5] I read the N.Y. Tribune with most pleasure. it seems at least to be honest & I believe the best thing the south could do, would be to give suffrage under certain restrictions (educational & financial) regardless of color. Otherwise it may have to be universal. It looks very much like the old question of fighting them for us or not & refusing to do so because the black soldiers would be in the way after the war & on other equally strong grounds.[6] People seem unable to accept the situation.

My letter in reference to St. Louis was as much interrogatory as anything else as I suspected more delay than Judge Blair seemed to anticipate. Taking Judge Underwood's indictment into consideration it hardly seems advisable to leave these "Deep solitudes and awful cells" without a pardon. Particularly for Va.[7]

Yours

R S. Ewell[8]

1. Ewell's reference to applying for a pardon identifies this letter as having been written on June 17, 1865.
2. A sarcastic reference to those imprisoned with him.
3. Ewell may be referring to Captain James Allen of the 1st U.S. Dragoons, who died on August 23, 1846, at Fort Leavenworth, Kansas.
4. *"Sui generis"*—i.e., unique. From a Latin expression meaning "of its own kind."
5. In 1863, shortly after leaving the service of the Confederate army, William took the oath of allegiance to the Union. He kept the oath so well, wrote his

cousin Tasker Gantt, that he was *"half hanged"* by Confederate bushwhackers. In June 1865 "Parson Stoddert" left the Gantt household in St. Louis, Missouri, where he had been staying, and moved to Giles County, Tennessee, where, as Campbell Brown informed his aunt, "He is half farmer, half preacher, and does a little bit of amateur school-teaching." TTG to RLE, 6 June 1865, folder 11, WM; CB to Rebecca Hubbard, 7 Sept. 1865, Hubbard Papers, Tennessee State Library and Archives, Nashville.

6. Ewell advocated that the South permit African-Americans to vote so long as they passed certain financial or educational requirements. If the South did not bend to that degree, he felt, the United States Congress might give the vote to all blacks regardless of their qualifications. Ewell likened the situation to the question, raised late in the Civil War, of whether to arm slaves to fight for the Confederacy. In both instances, Ewell took the pragmatic approach that it was better to grant blacks certain privileges and have them as allies rather than attempt to restrict them and have them as opponents.

7. John C. Underwood (1808–1873) was a magistrate of the United States Circuit Court. Appointed judge of the District Court of Virginia during the Civil War, he was vigorous in his enforcement of Federal laws and his support of civil rights for black citizens. He likewise supported the confiscation of Southern property, a practice from which he, or at least his family, profited. In a private letter written after General Ewell's death, Campbell Brown wrote: "After the war closed, there were a number of insurance suits for losses at that time, and I remember it was important for one side, in order to avoid liability, to show that the town was burned by the military authorities. On this point there was some correspondence between Col. Ewell on one hand & Gen. Ewell & myself on the other—and for a time I expected to be called as a witness, or to have my deposition taken. But our testimony would have damaged, instead of helping, the defendants—and we were not called on." Judge Underwood may have been in charge of these proceedings. Jones, *Campbell Brown's Civil War*, 311.

8. Campbell Brown added the following postscript:

> P.S. Send us twenty-five dollars apiece. We don't want to spend our gold. Does the new Constitution affect you? It seems to be adopted.
>
> C. Brown

For amendments made to the Tennessee State Constitution in 1865, see Laska, *The Tennessee State Constitution: A Reference Guide.* For a St. Louis attorney's opinion on the fairness and legality of the vote on the this measure, see Thomas Tasker Gantt to Montgomery Blair, 6 June 1865, Blair Family Papers, Library of Congress.

156. To Lizinka Ewell

Fort Warren B.H.
June 18th 1865.

Mrs L. C. Ewell

My dear Lizinka;

I had a letter from a Mrs Archer,[1] who had been engaged I believe, by Becca in my behalf. She seemed confident of effecting my release on condition of the amnesty oath. I informed her that I had signed this & it was in [the] hands of the Com'g Officer for transmission through proper channels to the Prest. I went on to say that I thought that there was but little chance for myself out of the excepted class to which I belong, that they would be acted on together, but that I would avail myself of her offer to ask her assistance in your case, which I described. Gov Meriwether of Ky had sent me offers of assistance, written twice & had also written to the Prest for me. I answered his letter also by reference to you & asking his aid if his judgement decided it to be advisable to do so. I dont care about being released merely to go to Va. to Stony Lonesome or some other equally lively place, you being under arrest in St. Louis. I would be worse off in every respect than I am here, where are books, music[,] papers &c. I should be more troubled by far than at present besides the additional chance of being arrested on Judge Underwood's indictment and being placed in civil confinement. I also mentioned to both, that I did not expect you to try to visit this Post in case of your release, as this might be a difficulty and I wanted your application to stand on its single merits and not to be mixed with other favors & thereby lose some of its strength. There are such difficulties in the way of a visit here, that the effort to come would not be advisable untill it shall appear that my sojourn is likely to be longer than the information we have at present warrants us to think. C. has a very good prospect of release when the prisoners now going, are disposed of.

Should I get out before you do, I will try to make some arrangement with Becca & Wm to sow some grass at Stony Lonesome, this fall or to carry on the experiment begun in 1861.[2] Yesterday brought me your letter of the 13th. I dont hope much from your letter to Mrs Lee (neé Blair)[3] as it applies to the same class of influences already tried. This month began on Thursday, which as I am superstitious & Thursday during the war has been my unlucky day is my only reason for being afraid to hope for you in June.[4] I have turned my attention to geraniums, not as yet with any decided success beyond giving me something to do. I have heard a rumor of changes in the garrison, which interest us a good deal as we have been very kindly treated by the Battalion of Volunteers now here (who do military duty more strictly than I ever saw Regulars) and dont care to risk a change.[5] C. writes but I did not have a chance to explain fully about the arrest & wanted to give you correct information & it is not much trouble to read two letters, as you know my hand by this time.

Yours
R S. Ewell

1. Unidentified.
2. Rebecca and William were joint owners of Stony Lonesome. Dick had sold his interest in the farm to William in 1850. At the time the Civil War began, Ewell was on leave of absence at Stony Lonesome, putting the farm in order and experimenting with the use of guano, love dust, and lime as fertilizer.
3. Elizabeth Blair Lee (1815–1906) was the daughter of Francis Preston Blair and the wife of Admiral Samuel Phillips Lee of "Sully," in Fairfax County, Virginia. Postmaster General Montgomery Blair and Major General Frank P. Blair were her brothers.
4. Thursday had indeed been an unlucky day for Ewell. He was shot in the leg on Thursday, August 28, 1862, at Groveton; his lines at Spotsylvania were overrun on Thursday, May 12, 1864; he had lost Fort Harrison to the Federals on Thursday, September 29, 1864; and he was captured at Sailor's Creek on Thursday, April 6, 1865.
5. The 1st Battalion, Massachusetts Heavy Artillery, garrisoned Fort Warren throughout Ewell's incarceration.

157. To Lizinka Ewell

June 22d 65

Mrs L. C. Ewell

My dear Lizinka;

Yesterday's mail (yours, T & Mrs Turner)[1] cured me of a headache which prevented my writing. It was the first severe one I have had for several weeks but you see it yielded at once to remedies. Your letter was [*sic:* of] the 18th mentioned that your suit had been postponed untill the fall.[2] I am too much in the dark about your affairs to know whether this is much of an annoyance, but I hope not. I think it likely C. will be out in a few weeks; indeed Mrs T. has been making efforts that may lead to his release at any moment. We[,] the Pris.[,] also have interested Senator Wilson in our behalf & it is possible he may go to Washington in person to present our applications.[3] I dont wish, at this time, were I at liberty, to go to Richmond. I should prefer of all things to go with you as mentioned in a late letter to some of the Va. Springs. If you are still to be in St. Louis I would prefer to stay here, to going to Stony Lonesome, provided I had a little more liberty. If I could get on a boat & try the fishing it seems to me I should exhaust the delights of this section. The weather is delightful & but for the idea of the warm weather in St Louis & regret for you & Harriot's not being able to enjoy it, I would say it is the most delicious Summer temperament I ever felt. In fact I feel ashamed sometimes at receiving so much commisseration when in fact as far as exteriors are concerned we are very well off. C. however is the only one (except Gordon of Ten.) who turns his confinement to any account. He C. is studying Spanish quite diligently & I should judge is making rapid progress. I expect he knows more of the grammar & science of the language than I do.[4] He has no trouble in reading it & pronounces well enough to carry on an ordinary conversation. Gordon is a very young man from Giles I believe & is reading, studying French & will improve himself.[5] Most of the balance dawdle around, read novels, wait for the mail or speculate on what the govt will do. I saw some nice horses advertised in Boston the other day. I have never driven you out with any fine horses yet. If we should have to go to Stony Lonesome we will have to content ourselves for a time, with the old kind—Safe but slow. I dont suppose it is necessary to tell you to use Louis[6] if it suit[s] you to do so. Becca sent me some geraniums, but not understanding them killed the first plants. The 2d lot came on in better order & C. has one finely under way. I expect to hear him boast of superior skill without duly crediting the superior condition of the plant when received. However he has the merit of letting it alone more than I have.[7] He asks me to say that he will write to Richmond concerning the safety of your trunks & be governed by the answer. I have just received a present, a Ferrotype of a beautiful young lady with a lock of her hair. Miss Mabel Lander Appleton aetat[8] 3 years[,] one of the young belles of the garrison & the one I believe I wrote to you of sending to C's prison when across the way under pretence of seeing a cat with no tail. She created quite a sensation among the crowd of prisoners & apparently shocked the Major & her Mother by the proceeding. I suppose a little akin to what it would have been had she ventured into a menagerie. One enthusiastic Lieut. at once sent for a lb of candy. Bye the bye I asked you for a daguerreot[y]pe as yrs. was most likely lost with my baggage. If you have done nothing that way, yet, & dont object to the trouble there are other ways of taking likenesses that seem better. this Ferrotype for instance is very pretty & has not the hard look of the others.[9] Have you read Reverdy Johnson's argument befor[e] the Military Commission? Our Lawyers here think it conclusive. I was very sorry when the commission was summoned.[10] Tompkins my old acquaintance of Fairfax Ct. House is one of the members, I think. You remember his "cutting his way through 1500 Inty & killing 27.["] There were less than 50 Int'y & one Officer was killed by accident some hundreds of yards from the ground where they skirmished. This & my wound & one or two prisoners were our losses. This may not be the same Officer.[11]

I received a very acceptable present of strawberries from Mrs Salter[,] sister of Geo. H. Steuart, as well as several books &c.[12] If C. gets out of this before I do I will try by his aid to have larger limits. I shall require more when he leaves as we are together more than with other prisoners & they are not as patient as he is. The fact is it is a great advantage to him to have to exercise forbearance & patience & I fear he will miss me to his disadvantage when he gets out. We are strong when we exercise our strength. Probably he will be married some of these days & may find the use[13] of preparatory trials. Seriously though he has a wonderful amt. of endurance. He is much liked among the Pris.[,] is cook for our mess this week & very busy. we always fare better when he or Gordon officiate. I have written a very dry letter I fear, but the circumstances are unfavorable.

Yours

R. S. Ewell

1. "T" refers to Tom Turner. Mrs. Turner may be his mother.
2. One of several lawsuits initiated by Lizinka in an effort to retrieve property confiscated from her by the Federal government.
3. Henry Wilson (1812–1875) was a member of the Massachusetts state legislature and editor of the *Boston Republican* before his election to the United States Senate in 1855. He sat in the Senate for eighteen years, during which time he served on the Committee of Military Affairs, often as its chairman. From 1873 until his death in 1875, he served as vice president to Ulysses S. Grant.
4. Ewell had picked up some Spanish in the Mexican War and during his subsequent service in the Southwest.
5. Brigadier General George Washington Gordon (1836–1911) of Giles County, Tennessee, commanded a brigade at the Battle of Franklin, where he was wounded and captured. After the war, he studied law, held numerous public offices (including a seat in the House of Representatives), and became commander-in-chief of the United Confederate Veterans.
6. A horse.

7. Brown informed his mother: "Gen. E. & I are diligently cultivating rival geraniums. He is all the time nursing them and gives them [too] much water. . . . Mine is the let-alone system of Bo-Peep." Jones, *Campbell Brown's Civil War,* 292.

8. Aetat is an abbreviation of the Latin word *aetatis* meaning "of the age."

9. Unlike daguerreotypes, which were produced on silver-coated copper plates, ferrotypes used thin iron plates.

10. Reverdy Johnson (1796–1876) was one of the finest lawyers in America, his most notable case being his successful suit in the Dred Scott case. After four years in the U.S. Senate, Johnson resigned his seat to become attorney general under Zachary Taylor. Although sympathetic to the South, he opposed secession and strove to keep his native state of Maryland in the Union. During the war, he again served in the Senate as a moderate Democrat. At the end of the war, he sat on a committee that drafted Reconstruction policy, using his influence to fight arbitrary imprisonment and other infringements of individual freedoms. President Grant appointed Johnson to be minister to Great Britain in 1868, after which Johnson returned to the United States and resumed his law practice.

11. Lieutenant Charles Tompkins, Company B, 2nd United States Cavalry, led the attack on Ewell's Fairfax Court House outpost before dawn on June 1, 1861. In his report of the skirmish, Tompkins claimed to have encountered more than one thousand Confederates and to have killed and wounded twenty-five of them. Ewell's force actually consisted of two inexperienced cavalry companies, which fled at the first sign of trouble, and one infantry company, altogether a force of perhaps 200 men. Ewell's losses appear to have been 1 killed, 1 wounded, and 5 captured. Captain John Quincy Marr of the Warrenton Rifles was the sole fatality.

12. Abby W. Salter (b. ca. 1813) of Massachusetts, was married to Dr. Richard H. Salter. She was not related to Brigadier General George H. Steuart.

13. "Use"—i.e., usefulness.

158. To Mrs. M. Ringgold Archer

Fort Warren B.H.
June 23, 1865

Mrs. M. Ringgold Archer[1]

My dear Madam;

Your favor of the 19th is just received. I wrote on the 17th a second letter to which you dont refer & lest it may have escaped you I re-copy from a letter of

Mrs Ewell's of the 13th showing her anxiety & the reasons for my preference that your efforts should rather be on her account. I think no special cases will be made in regard to my class of Prisoners & your efforts for two in place of one, more likely to fail.[2] Mrs E. writes "I have just finished a long letter to Mrs Lee, Judge Blair's sister. We were warm friends once & I have asked her to find out the cause of my arrest & to ask for my release & she will do it if she can. It is a mystery & is beginning to have on my mind the evil effect of a ghost story, something unseen & dreadful because you cannot get hold of it. I have been so careful & quiet, not even writing the kindest people for fear of giving offence or getting into trouble that I feel injured & indignant as well as mortified & provoked."[3] A letter received to day speaks of applying to the Military authority in St. Louis for permission to visit Washtn which was declined. She asked that permission might be given her to go there or to know the cause of her arrest. I feel a thousand times worse on her account than on my own. I am accused & held to account, but here is a person pardoned by Mr Lincoln & restored to rights but afterwards arrested & kept in arrest to this time without reason being given, sent from her home & property with no prospect even of getting what is allowed to the blackest criminal, a hearing. Her health is endangered & I cannot but think the President when made aware of the case will take some action in the matter. I have no right to complain for myself & do not but I wish she could at least have a hearing.

Yrs, in haste—

R S. Ewell

P.S.

    I stated nothing in my letter about property not being within the limit.[4] I enclose copy of my oath & letter.   RSE–

1. Unidentified.
2. Mrs. Archer had offered to use her influence to try and free both Ewell and his wife. Ewell urged Mrs. Archer to focus her efforts on Mrs. Ewell's release alone.
3. The letter quoted here was written by Lizinka on June 13, 1865, and is now among the Brown-Ewell Papers at the Filson Historical Society in Louisville, Kentucky.
4. As Lizinka's husband, Ewell's wealth alone would have made him ineligible for President Johnson's March 29, 1865, blanket pardon. In his letters to Johnson and others, Ewell never cited this wealth as a barrier to his freedom. Apparently, he did not consider himself as sharing in Lizinka's wealth, at least not in a legal sense. Indeed, on the day of his marriage, he had executed a legal document disclaiming any rights to his wife's property.

159. To Lizinka Ewell

Sat.y 24. 1865[1]

Mrs L. C. Ewell

My dear Lizinka;

I have been waiting in much trepidation since the arrival of C.'s scolding for my dose. It was such a gentle "roar" however as not to have required the preliminary notice & if I get off as easily it will be a strong instance of anticipation being worse than reality. Your notice of an application to & through Genl Pope came yesterday. I am anxiously waiting the result.[2]

We are not so very badly off when compared to some others. The privilege of hearing so often is very highly prized & the climate is delicious and our position as far as the material world is concerned could hardly be better. You write very truly that, being under arrest & away from home you are best where you are, there being no danger from the climate. I fear you are mistaken in the latter however.[3] What a contrast the acct. in Napoleons Life of Caesar [of] the sacrifices & devotion & unselfishness shown by the Roman Senate & Nobility, Page 97 &c. makes to our Congress & Legislatures in the Confederacy. 80 Roman Senators perished in the ranks in one battle. Instead of ours doing anything so rash, they were intriguing for office to keep out of the Army & it was difficult to keep a quorum when bullets were heard. Yet I daily hear of the failure being the fault of the people, when I know how willingly they poured out blood & property as long as there was proper use made of them, & untill it became evidently nothing but pouring water into sand. To abuse the people is as reasonable as to expect horses in a field to harness themselves & draw off the wagons without drivers. I only bring up these painful subjects because I am excessively annoyed at times to hear our Officers abusing the people & when any thing is said of the selfishness & incapacity of the government to hear of "kicking the dead lion" &c. The Tribune after devoting columns to darkie Suffrage, has a few lines in one corner of 1000 released Rebel prisoners at the Battery,[4] sick, without medical treatment &c. & suggests that if anyone were to send them a few strawberries they would be received. I was very glad to see by to-day's papers that those rebels that had gone to Mexico had sided with the Empire.[5] Better not to go at all, but the very worst thing is to join one of the vicious, thieving factions so long as no foreign powers helps [sic] them. I have seen much of Mexican Revolutionists.[6] Genl Raymond Lee has taken very active measures for the release of the Genl Officers confined here & has interested Senator Wilson & others of the Officials of this State. He must have forgiven the harsh treatment you speak of.[7] I am more patient on my own account in remembrance of the vast importance of the measures before the Govt & thankfulness for the mercies already shown. I understood after I was captured that Capt. Carr (or Ker) my Ordi Officer lost his leg or worse, just before we were taken & it seemed strange that more did not suffer.[8] To have been insured then of nothing more serious than the present status (as far as I know) would have seemed very fortunate.[9]

I am reading "Clever women of the family" with much interest[10]—am going to re-read "Tenant of W.H." Genl Marmaduke said the other day he felt better when he go[t] up from reading of that "sweet, noble woman Mrs Graham.["] I read the book so hastily that I could not appreciate it properly.

Yrs. of 21st just recd. am delighted so far.

Yours—

R. S. Ewell

No time to look over

RSE

Dont ask anything for *me.*

1. This letter was written either on Friday, June 24, 1865, or Saturday, June 25, 1865.
2. On April 21, 1865, President Andrew Johnson had ordered General George H. Thomas to arrest Lizinka in Nashville and send her back to St. Louis, Missouri. For two months she remained under house arrest at the home of her cousin Tasker Gantt, not knowing who had ordered her arrest or why. On June 19, Lizinka applied to the local commander, Major General John Pope, for permission to go east. Pope granted her request, the only restriction being that she could not go to Nashville.
3. More than once, Ewell had expressed concern for Lizinka's health if she remained in St. Louis during the hot summer months. He had contracted malaria while in that part of the country many years before, and he feared that his wife would likewise become ill.
4. The Battery is located at the southern end of Manhattan.
5. Upon the collapse of the Confederacy, many Southern officers, such as Jubal Early, had fled to Mexico rather than remain in the United States and face arrest.
6. While serving in the Southwest, Ewell had entertained guests from Sonora, a Mexican state roiled in political intrigue.
7. Brevet Brigadier General William Raymond Lee (ca. 1804–1891) was captured at Ball's Bluff in October 1861. While in prison, he and thirteen other Union officers were held as hostages by Confederate Provost Marshal John H. Winder,

who threatened to put them to death if Federal authorities executed the crews of two Confederate privateers who had been captured and convicted of piracy. Fortunately, the Confederates' convictions were overturned, and the privateer crew members were treated as prisoners of war. Campbell Brown wrote to his mother that "Gen'l. Raymond Lee is more of a *man,* to judge from his letters, than one of ten thousand. What you tell me of Winder's treatment of him is the first I had heard. It could never have been imaged from the contents of his notes. I don't see how Senator Wilson's or Gen'l. Lee's influence in your favor can do you harm." CB to LCB, 23 June 1865, PBE.

8. Captain James Ker (1836–1896) had been appointed the chief ordnance officer for the Department of Richmond on June 18, 1864, and continued in that capacity until his capture at Sailor's Creek. Ker was paroled on April 20, 1864, in Richmond. The fact that he was not sent to a prison camp in the North suggests that he may indeed have been wounded, although there is no evidence of that in his record. Robert E. L. Krick, in his reference book *Staff Officers in Gray* (p. 193), lists a second officer, Captain John Kerr, as serving on Ewell's staff as an ordnance officer at the same time as James Ker. The similarity in the two men's names coupled with their identical position and rank suggests that they may be the same person.

9. Ewell's parenthetical note, "as far as I know," clearly shows that he remained worried about his ultimate fate.

10. *The Clever Women of the Family,* written in 1865 by Charlotte M. Yonge (1823–1901), follows the life of a fictitious young social reformer named Rachel Curtis.

160. To Elizabeth Ewell Jr.

Fort Warren B. H.
June 25th 1865

Miss E. S. Ewell

My dear Elizabeth;

The Revd Father Fulton[1] brought over your letter a few weeks since. He asked to see me & any of this batch of Pris. that chose. Some five or six of us went up & saw him for 5 or 10 minutes, the boat not giving him longer time. If the "Bowl had been stronger &c."[2] I observed to him none of the party were Catholics but like myself had relations in it, or words to that effect.[3] He came over since but only sent for Campbell Brown[,] an old student, but C. said he would have been glad to see us but did not feel authorised to give the trouble. I was as the rest pleased enough with the acquaintance. He made some suggestions as to the weather in the winter, which rather startled us as a hint that he thought our sojourn during the next winter, likely. I dont know whether he spoke from knowledge or not but I concluded next day to send for some geranium plants as a defence against bad odors, tobacco &c. and a little amusement.[4] Brown proposed that we should write to ask him to buy us some plants & a canary bird but I did not like to take such a liberty with him & Becca sent me some plants by express. Not being very fresh when they arrived & not having experience & unable to get instruction the last of that invoice has just done & died. A few days after, however[,] brought a fresh lot better secured & they are flourishing[,] putting out shoots & give fine promise. We have not yet perpetrated the canary bird for want of a good opportunity to get it here & other reasons that make it inadvisable at present.

I intended to write to you before but remember the difficulty of introducing any subject that did not involve a lecture & even the harmless geranium may suggest the sin of wasting time on trifles that might be devoted to more important matter[s]. I did not tell the Revd Father that none were Catholics of the crowd in any offensive spirit or manner but only because I thought he would like to know & might not like to ask. Mrs Salter a lady in Boston has sent B[5] & myself several acceptable presents of books & strawberries & the last was accompanied with the respects of the Revd Father Fulton that she was commissioned to send to him & myself. I believe she is related to General Stuart[6] of Balt. who was a Refugee in the South & whose son was in the service. The Father did not take any part in the war of course but I presume wanted to be near his son.

I am very much obliged for the offer in regard to the spectacles but my eyes are pretty fair still & I have no trouble in reading yet. I take a good deal of care of them—avoid reading after meals, put cold water in them &c.[7]

Please remember me to cousin Francis if he does not object to acknowledging relationship with a "Repentant Rebel." They say Tasker's Pastor[,] Revd Mr Elliott[,] Unitarian[,] is so zealous an Union man that he objects to the verse "Let a repentant Rebel live.["][8] Lizinka is expected in W[ashington] D.C. about this time.[9]

Yrs &c
R S. Ewell

1. Based on Ewell's later comment, the Reverend Fulton appears to have been Campbell Brown's former tutor.
2. A line from an English folksong, "Three Wise Men of Gotham," which went as follows:

Three wise men of Gotham,
Went to sea in a bowl;
And if the bowl had been stronger,
My song would have been longer.

3. Elizabeth and Rebecca Ewell were Catholics.

4. According to his stepdaughter, Harriot, "Gen. Ewell never touched tobacco and smoke nauseated him at all times." Turner, "The Ewells of Virginia," 49.

5. Campbell Brown.

6. Major General George Hume Steuart (1790–1867) had served in the War of 1812 and was wounded at the Battle of North Point. His eldest son and namesake became a brigadier general in the Confederate army and served under Ewell.

7. Hydrotherapy was common at that period, one of its most famous practitioners being Stonewall Jackson.

8. William Greenleaf Eliot (1811–1887) founded the Church of the Messiah in St. Louis, Missouri, the first Unitarian Church west of the Mississippi River. A strong Unionist and reformer, he supported abolition, prohibition, and women's suffrage. Poet T. S. Eliot was his grandson. "Let a repentant rebel live" is a line from the hymn "Show Pity, Lord."

9. Lizinka received permission to leave St. Louis on June 21, 1865. She and her daughter traveled to Baltimore, arriving there by train three days later.

161. To Rebecca Ewell

June 28th 1865

Miss R. L. Ewell

My dear Sister;

Harriot wrote to her brother a few days since that you had some things you wished to send. The best way is to direct the box to Lt. W. H. Woodman U S.A. care of Majr H. H. Allen,[1] Fort Warren & put a paper inside directed to me & as all boxes are opened, he will see the paper & send it to me. I would like say half a dozen cans of tomatoes, 10 lbs of white sugar[,] three papers of corn starch, three cans condensed milk & 8 or 10 lbs of rice. Dont care about more cheese. have some tea. I would be glad if you would send me two white Pocket H[an]dk[erchie]fs. I wrote of two nightshirts. What I want is something in way of vegetables & the tomatoes are the best—go farthest & most pleasant. It matters not whether more or less of these come. I mess with half-a-dozen & a can of tomatoes will season a dish for several days, whereas of peaches it would be eat[en] up at once & be nowhere (I have the one half left—red pepper.)

Mark the Hdkfs &c. as my Laundress lost one for me. They are to be kept & ought to be good quality as cheapest.[2] We have enough cooking utensils. The Dr said I might send for a bottle of whiskey, but I dont care about it now. I can pay out of the funds I have here, if you can draw on me.[3]

A young lady of three yrs sent me her "Ferrotype" (we are in an iron age) very nice child. please put in a little present for her—a book or something of the kind, as you may judge best, or oranges.

You had better send five or six lbs of green coffee & 1 of tea. I would not send up fine qualities because they are not made with much skill and the finer qualities are no better than others. I did not intend to write for these things just now, but in consequence of H's letter & on mature deliberations.

Tell Cousin Rosanna I will answer her letter in a few days. I write in a hurry. If it come[s] in your way to send me about 1 1/2 feet (18 inches) of wire about size of telegraph wire & not much trouble please do so. I want to bend it and any material with that quality will do. One use is to make a gridiron for my stove. Tomatoes are almost the only important article in above menu.

With remembrances to the family.

Yrs

R S. Ewell

1. Major Harvey Abner Allen of the 2nd United States Artillery was commander of the post. Lieutenant William H. Woodman had been a boot maker in Randolph, Massachusetts, prior to the Civil War. After serving for three months in the 4th Massachusetts Infantry, Woodman enlisted in the 1st Battalion, Massachusetts Heavy Artillery, becoming a first lieutenant on March 16, 1863.

2. Ewell intended to keep the handkerchiefs; therefore, he advised his sister to buy ones of good quality, as they would be cheaper in the long run.

3. Ewell wished to reimburse Rebecca for her expenses in sending him these goods using funds that were in his prison account.

162. To Lizinka Ewell

June 29th 1865

Mrs L. C. Ewell

My dear Lizinka;

A letter was recd last night from Genl Raymond Lee to the effect that after consultation with Senator Wilson they had concluded that at this time no good would arise from pressing our petitions for pardon, that the administration is occupied with matters of great national importance &c. in short giving the same advice that I have written to you as regards myself. He gives hopes in the future. I thought that all your efforts concentrated in one direction—your own arrest & interests—would be more likely to succeed & that I could not be helped.

The Herald of the 27th[1] refers to a letter that I have written, winding up its remarks by "led to believe that a dissolution of the Union was inevitable & therefore, though very reluctantly, resigned his commission in the National Army & entered that of Jeff Davis." The mode of expression is the Heralds. Never since being here have I written a word for publication. But it looks like the merest truism to say that one regretted to resign the result of 25 yrs hard service & I suppose no human being would say otherwise at any time than that the necessity for doing so was a matter of regret & not be liable to accusations of untimely or unseemly admissions. While one's conscience was helped by the fact that resigning involved the loss of every thing worldly, this loss & the havoc of war were necessarily to be regretted. But this is not saying what was right or wrong as things then were, or is regret to be confounded with repentance (under the lights then existing).

I almost feel ashamed to write in this way but Campbell attaches so much more importance to the paper than I do & fearing lest you may misunderstand it (tho' I have precious little mistrust on this score) I write this explanation. It is, I think unfortunate to have letters, that are intended to be private & therefore not so guarded, quoted or referred to in the papers as they are so liable to misconstruction. Still these things seem such truisms that I wonder they are thought worth re-producing. I have your letters of the 22 & 23d & have seen one from Harriot in Balt. (24th I think). My greatest anxiety concerns you. I am so much afraid that I may be the cause of loss to yourself or H. I have a pernicious habit of accusing myself, amt'g to nervousness, that as I have no property to lose for myself & every one says that we will be attended to after a few months, the greatest favor would be to relieve me from a great source of anxiety by getting yourself out of trouble.[2] More than one of this party thinks that when released it will be on condition of leaving the country.

I had a very pleasant letter from Mrs Turner. I hope you will meet her & I feel almost satisfied you will like her as well as I do. I have a plenty of funds on deposit here & hardly know why Campbell asked for the checks—something in connection with the price of gold I believe. You will find Mr Reynolds a very devoted Pres[by]t[eria]n. If you will go to Church with him, I can, judging from my experience, promise a fine sermon. Mrs Hough has a pew in St. Pauls.[3] Remember me to Mr R. & family.

Yours
R.S. Ewell

1. The editor could not find this reference; however, the June 26, 1865, edition of the *New York Herald* contained Ewell's letter (ca. June 1865) to James D. McCabe regarding the burning of Richmond. The article was favorable to the Confederate officer, stating that "General Ewell, after taking every precaution in his power to prevent mischief, did what every soldier is bound to do— obeyed orders. They were, it is true, outrageous, but for them the Confederate Congress is responsible."

2. Fellow prisoner Brigadier General Eppa Hunton wrote that Ewell "seemed to be possessed with the idea that the property of his wife 'Mrs. Brown,' would be confiscated. It was very large." Hunton, *Autobiography,* 129.

3. Probably a reference to St. Paul's Protestant Episcopal Church in Baltimore. The church, which was rebuilt in 1856 following a fire, still stands at 233 Charles Street. Mrs. Hough may be the mother of Miss Anna Hough, an acquaintance of Lizzie Ewell. See RSE to LE, 16 May 1858, LC (letter 63, this volume).

163. To Lizinka Ewell

July 1st 1865

Mrs L. C. Ewell

My dear Lizinka;

In your letter of the 27th to Campbell you accuse yourself of selfishness after seeing the letter I wrote to Mrs Archer.[1] I dont think there was any selfishness in the whole business. as matters stood you were the one whose release was of consequence. neither of us had any immediate business to attend to and not being able to go to St. Louis & you not able to leave there, I certainly had no choice. This place was as good as any other. Now the case is different.

You would have no pleasure in visiting us at the Fort. The boat is but a few minutes at the wharf and the few moments allowed to meet our friends in the Office are so hurried that it must be anything but pleasant to either party. There have been but one or two instances even of this since I have been here.

Have not you sufficiently recovered from you sojourn at Dr Hancock's[2] to be bold enough to tell Mrs Reynolds that you prefer green to black tea? I would be tempted to write to her of your preference, but suppose Becca has informed her by this time. I think I know both her & Mr R. well enough to say they would feel hurt if you did not freely express your preferences. When a person cares for nothing beyond green tea, bread & butter it is a pity not to get those. It is provoking to see notices of the sales of so many Govt horses & mules that would be so necessary and to have Campbell shut up here, unable to take advantage of the chance. Mules are quoted as averaging $65 (about $40 in gold I suppose) in N.Y. at govt sales.[3]

I was in hopes that many of the reg[ula]t[io]n[s] governing Pris. of War now that the reduced number makes these rules no longer necessary, would be relaxed, but so far there seems no prospect. The 25 or 30 here have to be under the same surveillance as when there were nearly 400, & the rules as regards intercourse are as strict as when the Southern Confederacy was in full feather. Time I suppose is the only certain panacea.

The release of Mr Trenholm gives me more satisfaction than of Bruce.[4] They are both wealthy however & permission for some less conspicuous & poorer rebels to go home & try to support their suffering families would be still better. The release of persons, powerful in bringing about the war & who gave it all possible support by influence & council in contrast with others in penal confinement who merely risked their persons & had nothing to do with its inception, may well puzzle clearer brains than are in this crowd when the abstract question of criminality is concerned. "Who struck first?" is asked in children's squabbles. Certainly in Va. there were a good many blows struck by persons now at large, before I came into the struggle. Yesterday & to-day are the first decidedly warm weather we have had. I hope our health does not suffer. This is the coolest place I ever spent the summer in except among some of the Rocky Mtns. Sultry, gloomy weather is my excuse for a stupid letter. Your last letter was to me of 25. C. of 27.[5]

Yours

R S. Ewell

1. RSE to Mrs. M. Ringgold Archer, 23 June 1865, LC (158).
2. Lizinka had resided with the Hancocks in Richmond during Ewell's convalescence there in 1863.
3. Soldiers returning to their farms after the war needed horses and mules to plough their fields.
4. George Alfred Trenholm (1807–1876) owned a successful fleet of blockade runners during the war. On July 18, 1864, he succeeded Christopher Memminger as the Confederate secretary of the treasury. He remained in Richmond when the capitol fell to the North and was imprisoned for several months. Eli M. Bruce (1828–1866) represented Kentucky in the Confederate Congress. He served on both the Committee on Military Affairs and the Committee on Ways and Means.
5. Lizinka had written her husband a letter on June 25. She had written Campbell on the June 27.

164. To Lizinka Ewell

July 2d 1865—

Mrs L. C. Ewell

My dear Lizinka:

I sincerely hope by this time your expectations given in yrs. of the 28th are filled & that as far as you are concerned the war is really over.[1] With all trouble removed with respect to you I should be comparatively quiet. On the 16th Ult. Tasker wrote to me "You can do no more, and I am assured by my mediators that this is enough to secure the most favorable hearing and adjudication that is possible; *not* that it will insure your wishes in full, but if not, then that nothing will." He speaks of other means also. So you see it is useless to bother yourself to push my cause. I would prefer as far as that above is concerned that you with every thing before you, should judge of the field before us & determine what is best for the future. I have implicit confidence in your judgement when you exercise it untrammeled. I dread the risk of new phases—the past, except as affected by public events & the certainty of new & vital changes, seems to have had the elements of perfect happiness and I look back with great longing. I am uneasy about any changes. Cannot bear the thought of losing a star from the galaxy. Campbell has a very decided improvement in spirits since there is a prospect of getting out. Harriot in a letter to him regrets not going to Nar[r]agansett.[2] I dont know what detains you. If it is for want of funds I should be very sorry. There are about $300 of mine here in gold & I can send it by Campbell if it affects your going at all or you can repay at leisure.[3] I spend next to nothing here. It would be such a pity for her to miss the trip. Your health too would be very much improved by the cool sea breezes. It would be some satisfaction that you are nearer even by that much, if I should be turned out. I feel so confident of your success in regard to your affairs that the disappointment would be very severe if the mail bring notice that you have failed. I was glad to read your encomiums on Tasker. I have known him longer than you have & have never been tempted to waver for a single moment in my faith in his high integrity. Not having been, of late years[,] so much with him as you, I have seen little or nothing of the harshness that you mention, but men are able to get out of each other's way when[4] the "wind is in the east" much better then women can avoid the one who is "rageous." When I did not feel sociable or he seemed in same way there were many ways of relief without showing any apparent effort to avoid the other. In much of my early life Brook Grove was far more pleasant than my own home & he was only second to his Mother among those I wanted to see. Our intercourse of later years has been (the war excepted) calculated to strengthen my earlier feelings & in the war he was acted upon by conscientious motives, I presume[,] & where he has had power has used it mercifully. At all events the cry as far as the war is concerned is against me, as my side is the losing one & so held responsible for the misery. I venture one remark in regard to the offending note[5]—that nothing is so likely to exasperate as the want of appreciation of favors, though I know nothing to warrant an opinion as to whether any were conferred on you while in Dixie.

I mentioned that one of our Officers had expressed his willingness to spend the balance of his life in prison provided this would secure his property to his children. This is a good place to form fancies & to nourish them and it seems to me I would have the same feeling stronger in regard to any possible effect my release might have on your property than this Officer above quoted on his family. He might have made his money—at least there was less reason for his anxiety than my care that all your efforts should be directed towards your own interests. Time is the panacea for me, but is the element of danger where you are concerned. I was very much annoyed this morning at seeing a letter published that I had written for no such purpose, to a private individual & will in future pledge all persons either not to publish anything I write or will write only to you.[6] Of course I know nothing of the merits of the difficulty in Nashville but the non appreciation of favors is the most calculated of anything to mortify & give offense. There may have been no favors conferred but that seems to have been the case as far as I can judge with my limited information.

Yours— R S. Ewell

1. Lizinka had traveled to Washington in late June for an interview with President Johnson. Although he refused to grant General Ewell a pardon at that time, he indicated that he would sign a pardon for Lizinka and Campbell. Officials at the Attorney General's Office assured Lizinka that all Confederate officers would soon be released and that no one would be tried for treason. For a second-hand account of Lizinka's interview with the president, see Turner, "Recollections of Andrew Johnson," 175.

2. Narragansett was the Reynolds' summer house. It was located six or seven miles from Kingston, Rhode Island. The Reynolds family had invited Lizinka and Hattie to stay with them there.

3. Although they were husband and wife, Dick and Lizinka kept their financial accounts strictly separate. They occasionally loaned each other money, but they never mixed their funds.

4. Ewell repeated the word "when" here.

5. Lizinka owned one of the nicest houses in Nashville. When she returned to the house in 1865, she discovered it occupied by President Johnson's family. With a distinct want of tact, she sent Mrs. Johnson a note that read: "Dear Madam, I reached this place a week ago & avoided troubling you hoping for the arrival of Gov. J. but my young daughter wishes to join me here & I have no place in which to receive her. If not inconvenient to you will you (do me the favor to) allow me the use of one or two rooms in my own house[?]" That note, together with other actions, convinced President Johnson that Lizinka was unrepentant, and on April 21 he ordered her to be sent back to St. Louis under arrest. PBE; Turner, "Recollections of Andrew Johnson," 174.

6. This was probably the June 13, 1865, letter that Ewell had written to a former comrade-in-arms, Joseph Lewis. Lewis published the letter in the *St. Paul (MN) Pioneer,* and it was reprinted by other newspapers throughout the North. See letter 153, this volume.

165. To Lizinka Ewell

Tuesday 11th 65[1]

Mrs L. C. Ewell

My dear Lizinka;

Jackson[2] who was released on Saturday promised to ask for you at the Revere House.[3] I hope you met him. We have not heard from you since you left but take it for granted that[4] you have gone to Narragansett.[5] I had a little head ache Sat'y & much to my astonishment was roused up by the sight of the bird which has created quite a sensation. He has not sung any yet, but makes himself very much at home & is the handsomest bird I think I ever saw. He is evidently more at home.[6] Yrs. of the 9th just came & I will not write a long letter in order to get this off to day.

I had no ill effects from the fall.[7] When I get out of this I must[,] I think, go to some Springs as want of exercise &c has debilitated me & if I dont revive at Nar[raganse]tt I will try the Mtns. C. asked me the other day to wake him up early. He only tried it once but *I* was roused the other morning by hearing him work at the bird & he has been taking the greatest interest in it ever since. I have no time to write more except a letter from Gantt of the 6th who writes hopefully of our release. Remember me to Mrs Turner & family.

Yours—

R S. Ewell

P.S. Stigma was not exactly the very word I wanted.[8]

1. July 11, 1865.
2. Henry R. Jackson had been released on a $2,000 bond.
3. A Boston hotel where Lizinka had stayed during her visit to Fort Warren.
4. Ewell repeated the word "that" here.
5. Lizinka and Hattie received permission to visit Fort Warren and paid a brief visit to Ewell and Campbell there during the first week of July. Hattie attributed that privilege to the kindness of General Grant rather than that of President Johnson.
6. During her visit to Fort Warren, Lizinka had brought Ewell a canary in a wooden cage.
7. Shortly after Lizinka's visit, Ewell fell in his casemate but was not injured.
8. In a letter that can no longer be found, written in early July 1865, Ewell wrote to Lizinka of being under a stigma, possibly for being a high-ranking officer in the Confederacy. "Do get over your delusion about a stigma," she chided him in reply, "it is a queer idea. Read the 46th Psalm." LCB to RSE, 9 July 1865, PBE.

166. To Lizinka Ewell

Thursday 13. 65[1]

Mrs L. C. Ewell

My dear Lizinka;

Yrs. of the 10th has been received. The bird is very playful, chirps & twitters at a great rate but has not commenced singing yet. I think there is no doubt it is a male. I am almost as much amused at C's interest in it as in the bird itself. He said it is worth 300 geraniums. I cant imagine how the equipage (cage &c) could be improved. Mrs Salter is sister of Col. Ives.[2] She is constantly sending little things over to us. I gave one grape a piece to the crowd & "wisely she kept the remainder herself." They are peculiarly grateful [for] the grapes, & I shall send for more.

Genl Jackson[3] writes back very hopefully in regard to our release—to be patient &c. &c. Thinking of his gloomy views of "dying gracefully[,]" "life imprisonment[,]" "perpetual banishment[,]" one concludes that matters look very differently from different sides of the prison walls. However this and other letters, one from General Hancock[,][4] have turned the corners of the mouths of the Prisoners as the man in the Pilot says, from their necks to their eyebrows.[5]

They are all to the tune of "Few days," & as I have heard nothing of the box or Becca either I very much fear she is under the same influence. Over two weeks since I could not restrain her impatience to ship it & the subsequent deliberation is excessive. However there are only one or two articles in it I want just now. Should the fates keep me here next winter I shall get a cooking stove & mess by myself, Supposing of course C. will be out. I have seen small affairs[6] to cook in, advertised in such flattering style that one might almost expect them to cook themselves. I regret very much that you did not meet Jackson. He is a very superior man: eloquent, earnest & powerful. His military views whether original or not, are such as to show the highest talent & perception of our position. In military matters though, there is possible to be the widest line between theory & practice, the practice requiring so many qualities. Jackson's practice, I believe, in his limited sphere was highly creditable. certainly no practice could be good without correct theory.

I take the Tribune, which I believe to be as truthful as Greeley's prejudices permit.[7] I have thought of taking another paper to keep myself posted in events. C. & myself were discussing the propriety of another paper & knowing nothing of the "World"[—]I thought it had stopped—thought of taking the Daily News.[8] He agrees with me in thinking it as well to ask you to send us one of the two as you may select. There is one advantage in different papers, that we get a wider view, but this is not so important as the respective merits. I cut out what may be worth keeping, so you must decide.

Mrs Prout[9] wrote in March—it seems as though it were years ago—asking you to go to her house & professing kindness. I have heard nothing of her since, except her move to Brooklyn. The letter was a kind one. Have you seen a circular[10]. . . the Knights of the G. C.[11] giving a[12]

P.S. Please remember me to Mrs Turner & Kearney.[13] Tell H. to write a song for our case to tune of "Few days" & if her nerves will stand "Old John Brown."[14] I want to hear it on the harp for the tune is a good one as played on our band.[15]

RSE[16]

1. July 13, 1865.
2. Colonel Joseph C. Ives (1829–1868) graduated from West Point in 1852 and was a first lieutenant in the United States Ordnance Department when the Civil War began. He resigned in 1861 to become a colonel of engineers in the Confederate army and later joined President Jefferson Davis's personal staff. Mrs. Salter was not Colonel Ives's sister.

3. General Henry R. Jackson had been imprisoned with Ewell at Fort Warren until his release on July 8.

4. General Winfield S. Hancock (1824–1886) of the Union army led the Second Corps for much of the war. At this time he was in command of the Middle Military Division.

5. In chapter 18 of James Fenimore Cooper's seafaring novel *The Pilot* (1823), the coxswain says: "Let the riptyles clew up the corners of their mouths to their eyebrows now!"

6. Stoves.

7. Horace Greeley (1811–1872) was the influential editor of the *New York Tribune*. He ran unsuccessfully against Ulysses S. Grant in the 1872 presidential campaign.

8. The *New York World* newspaper operated from 1860 to 1931. The *Daily News* has not been identified.

9. Ann Gantt Prout (b. ca. 1813) was Dick's and Lizinka's first cousin. She had married Jonathan Prout of Washington, D.C.

10. Half a line of the letter was cut out here.

11. The Knights of the Golden Circle was a secret order of Southern sympathizers living in the North at the time of the war. Composed largely of Peace Democrats, it had its strongest support in the Midwest.

12. The rest of this page has been destroyed.

13. Mrs. Turner may be a reference to the wife of Henry S. Turner, a former officer in the 1st United States Dragoons. Mrs. Kearny was Mary Radford Kearny, a stepdaughter of General William Clark and the widow of General Stephen Kearny. Ewell became acquainted with the Kearnys while stationed at Jefferson Barracks in the 1840s.

14. By "Old John Brown" Ewell probably means "John Brown's Body," a popular tune early in the war. Julia Ward Howe later gave the song new lyrics, and it became famous as the "Battle Hymn of the Republic."

15. Hattie's harp is in the collection of the Museum of the Confederacy in Richmond, Virginia.

16. Here Campbell Brown added the following postscript:

> I enclose a letter from Cousin Becca, just rec'd. *You might get* Mr. Blair *to go with you.*
>
> C. Brown

Lizinka may have been planning another trip to see President Johnson about the release of her husband and son. In this postscript, Campbell Brown suggests that his mother take Montgomery Blair with her to the interview. Lizinka started to Washington on July 14 after receiving a message from Johnson indicating that he was ready to pardon both Ewell and Brown.

167. To Lizinka Ewell

July 16. 65

Mrs L. C. Ewell

My dear Lizinka;

Yours of 14th notified us yesterday of your Journey. I am as anxious on your as on my account that your hopes will not be disappointed. You make some strange mistakes. dont you see if you give bail for C. and myself it will be you that will have to walk straight and not we & on the first provocation we can cause a forfeiture of the bonds that you suppose are to be given by you & the trouble will be yours?[1] C. had a letter from H. to day who writes that a letter to Balt. will reach you & I take the chance that wishes for success may not be thrown away.

My box arrived yesterday & we have been enjoying some of the contents to day. I have not yet gone into much of an examination. I suppose C. has written to you of Mrs Salter's continued kindness [?][2] views &c. &c. She is the most perseveringly kind person to strangers I ever saw. I wish you had seen her. If so disposed & you return to Boston & choose to[,] let her know of your whereabouts. She lives at No. one Stamford Street.[3]

You wrote on the 14th [and] said "The worst is over. pecuniary loss is nothing & there may be less of that than we apprehend." I dont know to what you refer or how our release is connected with pecuniary loss, but I *would not accept* my release at a sacrifice of property on your part. I believe such a thing would be illegal & wrong in every respect. C. as well as myself shuddered at the thought of disappointment after such sanguine hopes as you showed in your letter. I think it more than likely you will succeed in C's case, but I doubt if anything more than promises will be had in regards to me. I made up my mind to trust to time & had I commenced by preparing for a years siege it would have been best.[4] The attractions of Wakefield are not enhanced by quiet. I am as regards that in the same state as the negro, according to Greel[e]y with reference to good advice. I have more than I want & a little of the reverse would be a blessing.

I want to fly around generally & am mentally in the state as those suspended by the hands, alias, crucified. Some faculties as some muscles are unnaturally strained and the greatest relief would be the exercise of the balance.

So after trying Wakefield a time I will begin my plan if the nervous system is not relieved.[5]

You see I am not at all sanguine about my release & if you fail I want you to remember that I am not troubled much, not having expected much. If C. & yourself are pardoned and a third one is not required, it will save time & trouble just to proceed at once for your future arrangements.

The bird has not sung as yet but I still think it a male & will sing after a time. It has seemed on the point of breaking out every minute but is so quiet to day, one might almost think it keeping Sunday.

Yours

R S. Ewell

P.S.

Please tell Becca I am very thankful for the box. I would like to see her. I shall apply for some relaxation of the rules if you fail in respect.

Excuse a dull letter but the wind is in the east.

R. S. Ewell

1. On July 7 President Johnson sent a telegraph to Lizinka that read: "If you will visit Washington on tomorrow or Monday, I will see if some arrangement cannot be made in reference to the release of General Ewell and your son." Unaware that Lizinka was then in Rhode Island, Johnson sent the telegram to the Reynolds' residence in Baltimore. Consequently, the letter did not catch up with her until July 13. The following day she boarded a train for Washington. She was giddy with delight at the prospect of her loved ones' release. "Probably—almost certainly—I am required to give bond & security for the good behaviour of you both," she wrote to them, "& *won't* you have to walk straight & give an account of yourselves every evening." To secure Ewell's freedom, Lizinka had to put up a $10,000 bond. When Ewell later learned that other general officers incarcerated with him at Fort Warren had had to post bonds in the amount of just $2,000, he wrote to General George Meade's adjutant general, asking that his bond be reduced to a like sum. Meade granted the request. Andrew Johnson to LCB, 7 July 1865, PBE; LCB to RSE, 14 July 1865, FHS.
2. Unintelligible word.
3. Boston directories indicate that Mrs. Salter lived at No. 1 Staniford Street.
4. Johnson was true to his word. Both Ewell and Brown were released from prison on July 19.
5. Lizinka and Hattie were then residing with the Reynolds family at Narragansett, their house near Wakefield, Rhode Island. Lizinka wished to bring

her husband and son there once she effected their release in the belief that the home's quiet setting would help them recover from their prison ordeal. Ewell was willing to go, but he argued that exercise, rather than rest, would be the best tonic for his health. After sitting in a prison cell for three months, he was ready to get back to work.

Chapter 12

Gentleman Farmer, 1865–1872

After his release from Fort Warren, Dick Ewell and his family returned to Virginia. He had no career, no home. For the first time in his life, he was at loose ends. The Ewells settled temporarily in Warrenton while Campbell Brown searched the countryside for a suitable farm on which the family could settle. Nothing suited, however, and in October 1865 they moved to Tennessee, occupying Lizinka's thirty-eight-hundred-acre plantation near Spring Hill. Hattie did not accompany them there. In October the twenty-one-year-old woman married Ewell's aide-de-camp Tom Turner and went to live with him at his farm outside of St. Louis, Missouri.

For three years Ewell worked tirelessly to restore Lizinka's farm. He planted wheat, barley, and potatoes; he bred cattle, sheep, and mules; he harvested grapes and cut timber. He rose before dawn and worked until sunset and in the process made Spring Hill one of the finest stock farms in the state.

But Ewell was not satisfied. Spring Hill was Lizinka's farm; he wanted a place of his own. In Mississippi, fortunes were being made in cotton. Fortunes were also being lost. Flooding, boll weevils, labor shortages—many things could destroy a crop and ruin its owner. But when it came to matters of finance, Ewell was a gambler. He plunged into the high-risk enterprise without hesitation. Using his own money, Ewell leased a 412-acre plantation called "Tarpley," located on the banks of the Mississippi River. Lizinka and Campbell owned a larger plantation called "Melrose," a few miles upriver.

For the next three years, Ewell shuttled back and forth between Spring Hill and Tarpley in an effort to manage both farms. He was not entirely successful. Although he recorded a profit at Tarpley each of the three years that he rented it, Spring Hill suffered as a result of his prolonged absence. His frequent trips to Mississippi likewise put a strain on his marriage. In December 1871, when his lease on Tarpley ran out, he did not renew it.

Ewell's lease on life ran out a few weeks later. In January 1872 he contracted a virulent contagion and was put to bed at Spring Hill. The disease spread throughout the household, infecting no fewer than eight people. Lizinka contracted the disease *while nursing her husband and died on January 22. Three days later, Ewell, broken in health and in spirit, followed her to the grave.*

The letters that follow represent but a small fraction of the dozens penned by Ewell during the final years of his life. Many letters from this period were written during his frequent trips to Mississippi; nearly all of them focus on farming and finances. While these topics were important to Ewell, they would be tedious, not to say incomprehensible, to the modern reader. In the interests of space, most of these letters have been left out. Those that remain provide a glimpse of Ewell's final years of life as a gentleman farmer.

168. To Benjamin Ewell

Balt. Sept 19. 65

Pro. B. S. Ewell

Dear Ben;

L. H[1] & myself came here last night, Becca remaining in Warrenton to attend to her estates. We came because of the approaching affair in Octr[2] clothes &c. & expect to return in a few days. I received yr. letter just before starting, in which you caution me against going to see Mr Johnson too often. I met when here last a Ten[nesse]an one legged man (before the war as regards the leg) friend of L. in old times, who asked me why I didnt go to see the Prest that he liked to see the Genls &c. & so I asked permission in my next weeks report to visit Md & the D.C. for the purpose of seeing the Prest. &c. & I recd a permit to visit them for 15 days.[3] As L. up to a few days since was still kept out of her money in St. Louis it was important that no feeling of animosity should be sowed or rather that impressions should be favorable.[4] Sat'y week Campbell wrote word that the Freedmen's bureau had siezed her property in Ten. except her house kindly occupied by Govr Brownlow & others[5] our means being reduced to a few hundred dolls. in gold deposited in bank here & about $1000 of hers & mine together in Mr Reynolds hands of which we invested, in a moment of confidence, $700 in a barouche[6] & pair of horses & harness, thereby leaving matters in a very interesting aspect as regarded pecuniary matters, for a time. In fact[,] though we were living very economically in Warrenton, the present available means were running very low & it was absolutely necessary not to raise any antagonism with the powers. However, it never rains but it pours & simultaneously with the withdrawal of the suit in St. Louis comes the order for the restoration of her property in Ten. and she has received remittances from both places & will be able to pay Harriott her fortune[7] as soon as the accts are settled. But what affects me more directly, Tasker encloses a note[8] for my signature which he thinks in view of the near approach of my pardon can be presented for payment amounting to some $4000, which he thought I held in my possession "untill he came across it accidentally" & says he supposes I have others, which I have not.[9] The long & short of it is that I am tolerably flush as well as is Lizinka & you must be sure & come to the wedding & borrow, if necessary, the money from either of us. I left Lizinka about two hrs. since but the truth is she & H. are a little mortified about Lizzie Ewell who was to have been one of the bridesmaids, but they found a letter here from her in which she says she must "decline the melancholly pleasure." I dont know about the etiquette in such cases but I believe to decline is very uncommon unless for good reasons & Lizzie gives none. I told Lizinka I thought it possible she had not the funds & would not give that excuse from delicacy, but the fact is I thought both were mortified—H & Her Mother.

They are very warm in their feelings towards Lizzie & you must come as a balm. Lizinka told me that H. would write to Miss Ingersoll[,] "her nearest available female relative," to be bridesmaid.[10] Lizinka had authorized Lizzie to draw for her travelling expenses $25.00. If you will come & draw for your expenses on Mr Reynolds, if you require it for your journey or any other purpose, you will remove the little soreness caused by the unexplained refusal of Lizzie more than can be done by any other mode.

Lizinka likes you very much & feels a little mortified.

She does not know the tenor of this letter—will not see it and will not see your answer if you should prefer it, so you need not hesitate to say why Lizzie refuses, if you know.

I will write again soon. Yrs &c

R S. Ewell

Write to Warrenton[11]

1. "L. H"—i.e., Lizinka and Hattie.
2. Harriot was engaged to be married to Ewell's former aide-de-camp Captain Thomas Turner in October.
3. As a condition of his parole, Ewell had to remain in Virginia and report weekly to the military authorities in his district.
4. Despite Lizinka's pardon, the United States government had frozen her assets in St. Louis, Missouri. At President Johnson's order, the agency dropped the suit against her on September 15, 1865, after she agreed to pay $400 in legal fees.
5. Although the United States District Court for the District of Middle Tennessee had released a few of Lizinka's landholdings in that state, the Freedman's

Bureau continued to maintain control of her most important properties. Her Maury County plantation was rented out to a carpetbagger, while her house in Nashville, lately occupied by President Johnson's family, had now become the residence of Tennessee's governor, William G. "Parson" Brownlow.

6. A horse-drawn carriage that featured a driver's seat, two passenger seats facing one another, and a folding top.

7. "Fortune"—i.e., dowry.

8. "Note"—i.e., bank note or check.

9. Tasker Gantt and William Reynolds acted as Ewell's financial agents both before and after the war.

10. Susan Campbell Ingersoll (b. 1829) was the married sister of Lizinka's first husband, Percy Brown. In a note to Lizinka written on September 25, Ewell indicated that Mrs. Ingersoll would not be able to attend the wedding.

11. Warrenton is in Fauquier County, Virginia.

169. *To Andrew Johnson*

Warrenton Fauquier Co Va
Sept 23d 1865

His Ex[cellenc]y
Andrew Johnson
President of the U.S.

Sir;

I beg leave to ask your attention to the enclosed copies of the Paroles required at Fort Warren of the General Officers confined with me and of that required, four days previous to theirs, of me and to ask that I may be placed on the same footing with them.[1] Some of these officers entered the service of the late Confederate States with higher rank than I had & were instrumental in bringing about the secession. The list includes graduates of West Point and every feature that could be waged against me with the single exception that when taken prisoner I held the rank of Lieut. General, a rank I received solely because I did my duty to the best of my ability. I think nothing can be alleged against me that calls for harsher treatment than others in like condition.

I take the liberty of applying directly to you because I see by the papers that the Secy of war is absent and fear in the accumulation of business that my application may be lost as some time has elapsed without hearing from a similar application sent to the War Dept.

I remain very respectfully
Yours &c.
R. S. Ewell
Prisoner of war

1. Unlike the other officers with whom he had been imprisoned, the terms of Ewell's parole restricted his movements to Virginia, required him to post a $10,000 bond, and obliged him to report weekly to the secretary of war.

170. To Lizinka Ewell

Wed. Sept. 27. 65—

Mrs L. C. Ewell

My dear Lizinka;

Monday there was a collision[1] near Washington & no mail & Tuesday I went to see Dr Ewell[2] & returning this afternoon found yours of 24th & 25, (Sunday & Monday). I was not altogether unprepared, as I thought from Harriott's appearance & the prescription & advice of the Doctor that the case was serious but had no idea that Dyptheria was expected.[3] Becca went with me & I took

Love blossomed even amid war. In October 1865, Ewell's aide-de-camp, Lieutenant Thomas Turner, took Lizinka's daughter, Hattie, as his wife. (Courtesy *St. Louis Post-Dispatch* and Stan Aylor)

the letters to her. She speaks of going down tomorrow but I dont know what she will do.[4]

Our boiler on the Warrenton branch[5] has become unfitted & if she wants to go & the train does not run I will take her in the carriage. Would go to Alexandria so as to be nearer but think there is a better chance to hear where I am. I wrote on Saturday in as strong terms as I could to the Prest asking to be placed on same terms as the other General Officers in prison with me, sending copies of mine & of their paroles. I hope to hear to-morrow.[6] As I have given my "Sacred word of honor" to refrain to, and remain in Va. it is out of the question for me to do otherwise. It wants 33 hrs. of the 15 days allowed me and I was reserving these so as to insure my being present at Harriot's wedding.[7] I was so much in hopes of hearing something favorable to my going down that I hurried to Dr Ewells, expecting that H. would only have a bilious attack. Should she become worse & you want me I will spend that time there, or if you see proper to write to Mr Johnson I see no particular objection to it. I was more particularly opposed to your going to see him on my account. There is reason now that justifies your writing, disagreeable as it is to do so. I have not had time to hear from my application yet, nor will it be untill the end of the week.[8]

I sent Mr J. the copies of the two paroles on Saturday the 23d. It is doubtful if Hancock recd my letter as he was in Balt. So William Reynolds says. 28th Should you write to Mr J., which, if H. is continuing to improve may not be necessary, you had better state that I had applied to be placed on same footing as the other General Officers confined with me at Fort Warren.[9]

One or two persons have spoken of buying the carriage & horses. as C. is probably in Balt. by this time, you can let me know your conclusion. Willis might take it to Tennessee for not over $50. Of course when people force a sale they must sacrifice, but we could not have got along without it.[10] Why didnt you send for Juleps to a bar—they make them best—but that sort of thing must be drunk at once, it deteriorates by keeping. Old Madeira wine is the best thing I ever drank for a constancy. Toddy keeps better than Juleps.

The mail will come to day I expect. When you buy grapes be sure to get those raised under glass & by taking off the skin [&] removing the few seed there is nothing but liquid to swallow. I send a letter from C. stating that he expects to start the 25th & will go to Balt, also one to H. from Phila. Tell Wm Reynold[s] there is a dispute in reference to the farm between the old & new owners. Spillman holds it at $35. Maj. Helm has written to Stuart Buchanan & Co.[11] Ben writes from Wmburg that he is very busy—cannot leave.[12]

I will make all my arrangements so as to leave the moment I receive permission. Mr Helm is in the D.C. to buy cattle. I will send or take down the butter knife. I had some repair done to the carriage in Buckland.[13] 11. A.M. The mail brought me yours of the 26th. Becca spoke yesterday of going down. I told her to do what suited herself, that you would prefer that (I remember what you said about Aunt Rebecca.). I will stop to renew my letter to Gen. Hancock which I will send to Wm Reynolds.

Yrs—

R. S. Ewell

P.S. I believe Becca has decided to go & I enclose the letters by her, & one for Genl Hancock which, it will facilitate matters for William to hand in.[14]

RSE—

1. A train collision.
2. Dr. Jesse Ewell III of "Dunblane" (1802–1897) owned a house near Manassas, Virginia. The general had stayed at his kinsman's house in September 1862 following his wounding at Groveton.
3. A few days earlier, Ewell had accompanied his wife to Baltimore to attend Hattie's wedding. When the nuptials had to be postponed due to the bride's illness, Ewell returned to Virginia. Lizinka remained in Baltimore to nurse her daughter back to health.
4. At the time he wrote this letter, Ewell may have been staying with his sister Rebecca, who owned property in Warrenton.
5. The Warrenton Branch Railroad served the town of Warrenton, where the Ewells were living at this time. It joined the Orange and Alexandria Railroad at Warrenton Junction (modern Calverton), Virginia.
6. See RSE to Andrew Johnson, 23 Sept. 1865, PBE (letter 169, this volume).
7. Ewell had been granted permission to travel to Washington, D.C., and Maryland for a fifteen-day period beginning on September 15.
8. Ewell had applied for permission to return to Baltimore and from there to proceed to Tennessee. When he received no reply, he resubmitted the application.
9. The terms of Ewell's parole had been harsher than those given to the other general officers with whom he had been imprisoned. Earlier Ewell had written to President Johnson through Major General Winfield S. Hancock, commander of the Middle Military Division, requesting that the terms of his parole be changed to bring them in line with those of the other prisoners. He enclosed a copy of his own parole and that of another officer with the request. When he learned that Hancock was in Baltimore, Ewell sent a copy of his request directly to the president.

10. Upon arriving in Virginia, the Ewells had purchased a barouche and two horses. Now that they were planning to move to Tennessee, they wished to sell them. If they could not get a fair price, Ewell suggested having his black servant, Willis, take the carriage to Tennessee.

11. The Ewells had been looking to purchase a farm in Virginia. Spillman and Helm have not been identified.

12. A week earlier, Ewell had written to his brother urging him to attend Hattie's wedding, but Ben replied that he was too busy trying to get the College of William and Mary back in operation to make the trip.

13. Buckland was a village located on the Warrenton Turnpike, approximately two miles west of Gainesville.

14. When he learned that his sister Rebecca was going to travel to Baltimore, Ewell decided to send with her this letter and the one to Hancock. She was to give Hancock's letter to William Reynolds, who would deliver it personally to the general. See RSE to E. W. Clark Jr., 28 Sept. 1865, PBE (letter 171, this volume).

171. To E. W. Clark Jr.

Warrenton Fauquier Co.
Va. Sept. 28th 1865

Capt. E. W. Clark Jr
A.A.G. Middle Milty Div.
Hd Qrts Genl Hancock;

Capt;

I enclose copies of the paroles required of me & of the other Genl Officers confined with me at Fort Warren.[1] I have forwarded copies of these to the Prest and to the Secty of War asking to be placed on same footing as the others, but nothing has been heard from them. I had permission to visit Md & the D. C. for 15 days but that time has expired except a day & a half. I was obliged to leave some of my family very ill in Balt. & return to Va, Applying at same time to Genl Hancock for permission to remain longer, if in his power to grant this, directing my letter to Washington where I supposed him to be. I beg leave to renew my application to him for such extension of my parole as may be in his power to grant.

My immediate want is to go to Baltimore where one of my family is very ill, but it is my wish to accompany them to Tennessee where circumstances require their presence.

I would be exceedingly favored by as prompt attention to this as circumstances admit.

I have gone into detail in this matter in order to let the General know all the circumstances of the case.

Resply &c
R. S. Ewell

P.S. I would beg leave to add that I know nothing of any orders referring to paroled prisoners & if such exist as to make this an unnecessary intrusion on the General's time, that it is owing to my inability to find such notices.

R S. E.

1. As the other officers' paroles were identical, Ewell presumably accompanied his parole with just one of theirs.

172. To Lizzie Ewell

Spring Hill Maury Co
Tenn. Jany 7th 65 [*sic:* 66]

Miss E. Ewell

Dear Lizzie;

Yrs of 27 ult came duly to hand. I am as usual fretting my soul away because of the darkies who wont see that 12.50 & rations are any particular reasons for working hard.[1] In fact they think they are conferring a favor on us. The other day I sent one who was hauling rails to leave the load on another part of the fence. he left them where there were more new rails than anywhere else. I told him to take the next load farther on. he said he was "hungry" hadnt eat[en] since breakfast. it was 12M. He didnt like to be working for nothing. I told him to leave them where I had directed & he did so. As I left they asked permission[2] to put some wood on the wagon to bring to the house to burn & I consented. After an hour I went back & found them loading up having forgotten their hunger, when working for themselves. I merely told them to come on. In the evening when returning to work this same driver stopped his wagon on the road & went to work to load a horse pistol & placed it capped in his belt. As it was not a proper equipment for a teamster I told him to leave it. he said he wasnt going to hurt no one with it. I told him[3] to put it down or leave the farm. He still hesitated when Campbell rode up to him & pulled out a pistol & threatened to shoot him when he concluded to give it up. I was told afterwards he was subject to almost fits of insanity & when the soldier of an United Country[4] had shot at his Lieutenant besides other like capers. The fact is they are crazy half the time and are constantly apparently trying to see if they are really free.

Willis poor fellow is very sick. I wrote a long letter to Dr Hancock in which I made several inquiries about Frank & other matters but have heard nothing from him & am afraid he did not get my letter. I would be obliged to you to ask him about the letter when next you see the Doctor.[5]

I suppose you know we are not in very brilliant society out here. In fact there is very little society. The people seem torpid from the war, and except drinking whiskey dont do much. I am sick of it. dont see much in the future. No darkie will do half a day's work & corn & pork are very dear[6] although I dont see much chance of raising them to profit. I had rather be back in Va I believe.

Tell Becca we are packed away like herrings in a barrel but talk of building a new house, one room of which is for her.[7] I would give anything to hear some music. But she musnot [*sic*] think I want her here for music alone.[8]

Lizinka is quite unwell having been worried with darkies & cows & bread that wouldnt rise untill she is used up. Harriot made some mince pies which her mother enjoyed as she said they were the first she had been able to eat as the others were so rich, while Capt. T. said they were made of the pork left from breakfast.[9] Lizinka constantly speaks of your coming out. They are all in bed. Love to all.

Yrs &c   R. S. Ewell

1. Ewell paid his black laborers $12.50 per month in wages along with rations. Privates in the Union army, by comparison, had received $13.00.
2. Ewell redundantly wrote "they asked leave" here.
3. Ewell mistakenly repeated the word "him" here.
4. Although Ewell wrote "of a United Country," he may have meant "of the United States" or "of Union cavalry."
5. Willis and Frank were former slaves of the Brown family. Willis had accompanied Ewell and his wife to Tennessee, and Ewell was hoping to bring Frank there too. Dr. Francis Hancock had been the medical director of Ewell's division in the early part of the Civil War. At the time of this letter, he was practicing medicine in Richmond.
6. Corn and pork made up a large part of the rations that Ewell distributed to his laborers.

7. On several occasions, Dick invited his sister to come live with his family in Tennessee, but she declined. In 1867, after his wedding to Susan Polk, Campbell Brown made some improvements to the Ewell's Tennessee house, which he called "Sutherland." Lizinka made additional improvements to the structure in 1870.

8. Both of Ewell's sisters were accomplished musicians.

9. Hattie and her husband were visiting the Ewells at Spring Hill.

173. To Benjamin Ewell

Nashville
Jan'y 25. 65—[1]

Prof B S. Ewell

Dear Ben;

I found yours of the 17th here to day & recd the one in reference to the Sthn Un'y[2] a week or two since. Bishop Quintard stopped with us & I showed it to him as it best explained itself & complimented the Bishop besides. He has Suwanee on the brain, is building a cottage there as are some others & he expects there will be quite a crowd of people escaping the summer heats. He insists there will be society but failed to get Lizinka to go unless you have a cottage there & she can take two rooms with you. The Bishop did not say much about the place except that he did not expect to have it in full blast for a year or two but a smaller affair at first[,] that he had written to some other Bishop & I understood had referred to you in the letter. I did not think it delicate to say anything myself, merely to listen.[3] Lizinka is more anxious that you should go to Columbia to open an Academy[—]has written to the head of the girl's institute of that place about yr. having it for a time untill the girls can start again, but has recd no answer as yet.[4]

Aunt Rebecca made several valuable suggestions to the B[ishop] in the course of the conversation such as the style of the buildings & told him that you had an elder sister who from her experience & accomplishments would be a capital person to open an establishment for young ladies at some place. I suppose she meant Becca[5] though as she had expressed no wish on the subject Lizinka thought it would have been better to have consulted her first. I expect from what I hear that Suwanee is healthy & the B. thinks that the college & cheapness would bring society.[6] I am very busy planting for cotton but as there is no fencing hardly & scarcely any improvements of any kind, it is like opening an entirely new farm. There are strong indications of petroleum. there is a great deal of slate that bu[r]ns with a very bright light similar to that from pe[t]r[o]-leum. it would seem as if the slate were saturated with the oil which burns with-out[7] reducing the slate. I was told to day that there are some kinds of this slate that give 50 gallons of oil by distillation from a ton of the material.[8]

We are troubled to know what to bring to the farm besides cotton, to make money. It is probable that the crop of corn will be large & the most obvious use would be to turn it into Pork, but the Cholera (hog), is so prevalent that it seems useless.[9] I am getting a few sheep.[10] I am in this place to attend a large sale of Government buildings tomorrow to see if it wont be the cheapest way of getting lumber. At Spring Hill I am so tired after running all day after the darkies that I cannot write with any satisfaction.

Love to the family.[11]

P.S. The gun is in elegant order & very complete in all the accoutrements. I am very glad of it.[12]

1. Ewell meant to write 1866.
2. Southern University—i.e., the University of the South.
3. Charles T. Quintard (1824–1898) had been both a chaplain and medical officer of the 1st Tennessee Infantry Regiment. After the war, he moved to Nashville and was appointed a bishop in the Episcopal Church. He was instrumental in reestablishing the University of the South at Sewanee, Tennessee, and served as its vice chancellor.
4. After the Civil War, Lizinka took an active interest in improving the educa-tion of Southern women. In 1871 she purchased the Columbia Institute and prepared to open a female academy of her own. Her death in January 1872 cut short that endeavor. Columbia is ten miles south of Spring Hill.
5. Ewell's sister Rebecca Ewell, not to be confused with Rebecca Hubbard, his aunt, mentioned in the previous sentence.
6. The University of the South, located in Sewanee, Tennessee, was founded in 1866 by representatives of the Episcopal Church. Its founders included General E. Kirby Smith, General (and Bishop) Leonidas Polk, and Bishop James H. Otey.
7. Ewell repeated the word "without" here.
8. That summer Campbell Brown erected an oil derrick on the farm. He did not hit oil, but at a depth of 550 feet he did strike a vein of marble.

9. Ewell contemplated raising corn and using it to feed hogs, which he could then sell at market. A cholera epidemic among Tennessee's hog population rendered his plan unfeasible, however.

10. Ewell purchased a herd of sheep on May 3, 1866. Within three months, he had upwards of 860 animals.

11. A thief clipped Ewell's signature from this letter.

12. Ben had Dick's rifle at his home in Williamsburg. At Dick's request, he sent it to Tennessee.

174. To Jedediah Hotchkiss

Spring Hill Maury Co.[1]
Tenn. March 14th 1866.

Maj. Jed. Hotchkiss

Dear Sir;

I have heard with much pleasure & interest that you & Col. Allen are about to publish a work illustrating the Battle fields of Va.[2] As Chief topographical Engineer on the Staff of Genl Jackson to the time of his death, in the same capacity in the 2nd Corps first under my command & then under that of Genl Early it was your especial duty to make yourself acquainted with the topographical features of the country where this portion of the Army of Northern Va. always took so conspicuous a part. Your opportunities for preparing a work of the kind were peculiar and I can testify to the good use you made of them. Before hearing of this enterprise I was anxious that you as better qualified than any one I knew should undertake something of the kind.

Your association with Col. Allen, Ordnance Officer to the same command, I consider a fortunate feature. It was his duty to keep himself advised of the position of the troops in action while all who know him will be satisfied that his superior intellect & judgment will give value to whatever he undertakes.

I wish to express in the strongest manner my appreciation of the services rendered by Maj. Hotchkiss Topographical Officer of the Corps, probably one of the very best Officers of that branch of service. I never repented the confidence I always placed in his zeal and judgement and his activity & energy were incomparable.

1. This is a draft of a letter that appears in roll 49 of the Hotchkiss Papers at the Library of Congress, Washington, D.C. It comes from box 6, folder 1, in the

Campbell Brown and Richard S. Ewell Papers at the Tennessee State Library and Archives in Nashville, Tennessee.

2. In 1867 Jedediah Hotchkiss (1828–1899) published *The Battle-Fields of Virginia, Chancellorsville; Embracing the Operations of the Army of Northern Virginia from the Final Battle of Fredericksburg to the Death of Lieutenant-General Jackson* in partnership with Lieutenant Colonel William Allan, the Second Corps's chief of ordnance. Ewell probably drafted this endorsement of the book at Hotchkiss's request.

175. To Lizzie Ewell

Spring Hill Maury Co.
Tenn. April 22. .66

Miss Lizzie Ewell

Dear Lizzie;

I am not certain whether I owe you a letter or not but I have not heard from you or your Aunt or Father for some time & I am getting uneasiness. Becca makes it a point not to answer letters & "Pop" never was a very good hand.[1]

We are hard at work renewing a farm of large size utterly destroyed, with no means but hired labor. it is somewhat trying but we are making good progress in crops & fencing. There is a great deal of worry & I have had several severe attacks—neuralgic[—]& I have very seldom been entirely free from the boils that commenced on me in 64 while exposed to the malaria below Richmond.[2] Fort Warren did not agree with me. I had several very severe attacks while there & in consequence my eyes are still much affected.[3] After being asleep a while I expect the appearance on waking is somewhat ludicrous as I only open one eyelid.

May—12th I began this letter, took it to Nashville my inkstand leaking out all the ink on the road[,] brot it back & have been putting off sending it untill "Tomorrow" & tomorrow has reached today[,] Sunday evening[,] & we are going to N. again tomorrow & I have determined to finish it this time.[4]

Lizinka speaks of going to St. Louis in a few days to see Harriot, when I will probably go to Kentucky for a short time.[5]

We are farming with the usual complaints. Cut worm destroyed all the corn & cotton has come up badly &c. &c. I have a good deal of disagreeable feeling at times—Stretchy & nervous[—]that make me disinclined to [do] anything.[6] Four or five days since I recd your Father's letter of the 2nd & several days after Lizinka one of the 1st. I will write to him soon, but you can tell him that

I have a report of the Valley yet for J. E. J. & of Rich[mon]d Defense for Lee[7] & some more for a Mr Lossing author of the Field book of the Rev[olu]t[io]n who is writing a history of this war & wants a true account of the burning of Richmond &c.[8] so that I cant tell when I shall be able to write what he wants & have a great mine [*sic:* mind] to bundle up & forward all I have to him.

We want to see you all. Parson Stoddert is a few miles (30) from here. What he is doing I cant tell.[9]

There seems to be a big darkie named Johnson who has taken the place of old Mr Marsteller, Mr Balch D. D. & all his other pastors and masters.[10] Lizinka & myself are chiefly employed in visiting a store 4 miles off where are a h[an]dk[erchie]f full of goods, eggs &c[,] & taking salt to the cattle when she thinks it necessary to bawl "Cow wench" at all she sees & claim all that are strayed to the farm[,] marked or not. Love to all.

Yours &c

R S. Ewell

1. Rebecca Ewell was then living with Ben and Lizzie in Williamsburg.
2. Ewell had developed boils under his arms and on the stump of his amputated limb in the summer of 1864.
3. Ewell suffered from neuralgia while at Fort Warren.
4. This letter has a large ink blot in the center of the second page.
5. Lizinka and Ewell traveled together to St. Louis later that month, stopping at Louisville, Kentucky, en route.
6. For Ewell's nervous condition, see RSE to Dr. Samuel Jackson, 21 May 1866, Milligen Collection, Maryland Historical Society (letter 177, this volume).
7. Generals Joseph E. Johnston and Robert E. Lee were Ewell's superior officers at different times in the war. Ewell probably meant to say that he intended to send Johnston his report for the First Battle of Manassas rather than for the 1862 Shenandoah Valley Campaign. He had submitted reports of his actions in the 1862 Shenandoah Valley Campaign to his immediate superior, Stonewall Jackson, back in June and July 1862. Those reports appear in *OR* 12(1):778–87. Ewell's report covering the evacuation of Richmond and the subsequent Battle of Sailor's Creek appears in *OR* 46(1):1292–95. He did not submit a report on First Manassas to Johnston in 1861 but rectified that omission by sending it to him on August 15, 1866.
8. Benson J. Lossing (1813–1891) of New York was a historian, editor, and engraver. He gained fame in 1852 with the publication of his popular history, *Pictorial Field-Book of the Revolution*. He later published a three-volume companion

piece, *Pictorial History of the Civil War in the United States of America*. While preparing the latter work, Lossing wrote to Ewell for information about the First Battle of Manassas and the 1865 burning of Richmond. Ewell complied, and Lossing quoted an excerpt from one of his letters in volume 3, pp. 545–46fn. See RSE to Benson Lossing, 29 Apr. 1866, PBE (letter 176, this volume).

9. In September 1865 Campbell Brown reported to his great aunt Rebecca Hubbard that William Stoddert was residing in Giles County, Tennessee: "He is half farmer, half preacher, and does a little bit of amateur school-teaching, having as scholars two returned soldiers whom he is trying to prepare for the University of Va. He is now very popular and widely known, round the country, and has had several churches offered him. . . . It is probable Parson Stoddert will move to Maury next year & rent some of Mother's land." CB to Rebecca Hubbard, 7 Sept. 1865, David Hubbard Papers, Tennessee State Library and Archives, Nashville.

10. The Marstellars had been friends of the Ewells in Virginia. Arellan L. Marstellar was a teacher in Prince William County prior to the Civil War. For information on Thomas Balch, see note 4 to letter 60, this volume. Johnson has not been identified.

176. To Benson Lossing

Nashville
29th April 1866[1]

To B. J. Lossing Esq.

Dear Sir

I beg leave to state in answer to your request that Genl Beauregard in an official letter to me a few days after the first battle of Manassas wrote that the order to advance had been sent to Genl Holmes[2] & that that officer had informed him it was never received.

Genl Beauregard stated at the same time that he had no copy of the order & it was not known who carried it.[3]

Genl Holmes had just arrived & was encamped about one mile in rear of my position.[4]

My Division[5] moved twice that day: once when I learned the movement previously contemplated had been begun by the commands to my left when I put my Division in motion reporting to Genl Beauregard but was ordered to resume my former position & again in the afternoon when I marched across the river to attack a position nearly opposite McLean's ford but from which I was recalled to the Stone Bridge.[6] It was never contemplated that I was to make any movement looking to intercepting the retreat of the U.S. forces. Our plans had been to move forward the right wing & attack & it was the failure to carry out this plan that formed the groundwork for much discussion at the time & the orders for which were sent to Genl Holmes.[7]

No other failure of orders in reference to my command was spoken of on that day.

1. This letter is a draft of the one that Ewell wrote to Lossing. The actual letter was put up for auction in lot 331 of the September 4, 2003, edition of *The Rail Splitter,* a website describing itself as "A Journal for the Lincoln Collector and Market for Buying and Selling Historical Americana" (http://www.railsplitter. com/main.htm).

2. Major General Theophilus H. Holmes (1804–1880) commanded a brigade at the Battle of First Manassas. Promoted to lieutenant general in October 1862, the elderly Holmes commanded the Trans-Mississippi Department until July of the following year, when he was transferred to North Carolina to take charge of that state's reserves.

3. For a copy of the correspondence that passed between Ewell and Beauregard after the battle, see *OR* 51(2):198–99; and Campbell Brown, "General Ewell at Bull Run," 259–60fn.

4. At First Manassas, Ewell held a position at Union Mills, on the far right flank of the Confederate army.

5. Ewell actually commanded a brigade in the battle.

6. At 7:00 A.M., Beauregard ordered Ewell to advance across Bull Run and attack the Union army's left flank, supported by Brigadier General David R. Jones on his left and Holmes in his rear. The order to Ewell miscarried, however, apparently because the courier entrusted with it fled in fear from the battle-field. When Ewell belatedly learned about the order, he led his brigade across the river, only to be recalled to the south side of the stream by Beauregard, whose own left flank was then under attack. At 3:00 P.M. Beauregard ordered him to cross the stream again, this time to attack a Union battery overlook-ing McLean's Ford. Again Ewell's brigade splashed across the run, but again it was recalled, this time to reinforce Confederate troops at the stone bridge. By the time Ewell's men reached the bridge, the Union army was in full retreat and the battle was over. For accounts of Ewell's actions in the battle, see *OR* 2:536–37; Johnston, "Responsibilities of the First Bull Run," 250–51; Brown, "General Ewell at Bull Run," 259–61; and Pfanz, *Ewell,* 135–41.

7. Holmes remembered that at about 9:00 A.M. he received an order from Beauregard directing Ewell "to hold himself in readiness to take the offensive at a moment's notice, to be supported by my brigade. This order caused me to move nearer to Ewell's position, where, after waiting about two hours, another order was received through Ewell to resume our former places." *OR* 2:565.

177. To Dr. Samuel Jackson

Spring Hill Maury Co.
Tenn. May 21st 66.

Dr Samuel Jackson

Dear Sir;

I received your kind letter last winter but was daily expecting some original letters of Genl T. J. Jackson (Stonewall) which only arrived to day.

Hotchkiss who is writing a guide book to the Va. Battle grounds was copying them for data for his work. I was led in this way to postpone my reply for such an unpardonable time.

I hope Mrs Jackson will accept the enclosed. I hesitated between this & one written by Genl J. E. Johnston to which Jackson had written a hasty sort of postscript, but the latter is hastily written & is hardly a fair specimen.[1]

My health is slowly improving & I have not had any severe attacks of pain lately. I used your remedy for my last nervous attack & beneficially I expect, but under your directions was not able to avail myself of the other prescription as living in an almost semi-savage manner I could not comply with the conditions.[2]

The political condition here is wonderful. I presume you have seen some notice of the high handed measures of our legislature, many of whom would be as ultra as any in Congress. Justice to the negro requires that I should say he does better than the false friends who come to take care of him, would have him do[3] & if the Southern people can exercise patience & forbearance [&] the abolitionists would let him alone he might become a valuable assistant. I try to become interested in sheep & other rustic interests but it is very difficult to keep one's mind from boding over the past or trying to guess the future. Please dont attribute my silence to any want of recognition of your kindness, but there has been much worry &c. Excuse such a long letter. Mrs Ewell joins me in remembrances to yourself & family.

Resply &c   R. S. Ewell

1. Mary Anna Jackson, Stonewall Jackson's widow, was collecting documents written by her husband. Whether she was collecting these for her own benefit or to sell in order to raise funds for a charitable cause is uncertain.

2. Ewell suffered from painful bouts of neuralgia around the eyes. His habit of working in all types of weather may have exacerbated the condition.

3. During Reconstruction, men of abolitionist principles flooded the defeated South seeking profit or power. Called "carpetbaggers" (if from the North) or "scalawags" (if from the South), they befriended the freed slaves in order to secure political power.

178. To Joseph E. Johnston

August 15th 1866

Genl Joseph E. Johnston

General;

For some weeks previous to the battle of Manassas General Beauregard had repeatedly explained to the Brigade Commanders his plan of meeting the enemy's attack. i.e. of crossing his right & as much of his centre as circumstances allowed & attacking the enemy.[1]

On the morning of the 21st about daylight I received a notification from him to hold myself in readiness to move at a moments warning to carry out the previous plan, with cautions in reference to my flank & rear.[2] About 9 or 10. A.M. I learned from Genl D. R. Jones on my left that he had been ordered to commence the movement & I at once started my Brigade across Bull Run reporting the fact to Genl Beauregard & also that I had received no further orders.[3] The reply was "In consequence of the impediments in the front the troops will resume their former positions."[4] Nothing further until after one P.M. when Col. Lucy[5] brought orders to attack a battery of the enemy near McLean's Ford.[6] The crossing was by two narrow footpaths one at the R.Rd Bridge, the other 400 yds below at the Ford & was necessarily slow.[7] The two leading Regts were crossed & pushed nearly to the enemy's outposts. The arrangements for the attack were made & only waited the closing up of the third Regt nearly in position when a staff officer brought me orders to move to the Stone Bridge, Genl Holmes my supporting force having already started. Supposing the case imminent I moved back as rapidly as possible & without delaying a moment reached your Hdqts a few moments before sunset I being in advance of the troops.[8] Information considered reliable had been brot to Genl B. that the enemy in considerable force had occupied my position on Bull Run & were threatening Manassas Junction & in consequence he ordered my immediate return.[9] Before reporting to you Col Preston of S.C.[10] met me & said that a force of the enemy were in ambuscade near Bull Run Bridge & wanted me to move my command to that point but your glass shewed [*sic*] that our troops were in pursuit beyond the point. As my troops were much fatigued having been under arms or moving since daylight I asked & received permission from you to meet & take them back to the RRd Crossing which they reached sometime after dark to find it a false alarm. The necessity had been thought so pressing that some of the Infantry had been mounted behind the Cavalry to get them back quicker. My Command consisted of a squadron of Cavalry—(Gov's Guard Capt. Cabell, Rappahannock Cavalry Capt Shack Green) commanded by Col Jennifer, Ross' Battery of the Washington Artillery[,] Rodes Regt (5th Ala— Infantry)[,] Seibel's (6th Ala) & Seymour's (6th La) in all about 1800 men & officers.[11] A few days after the battle finding myself violently assailed in the papers for disobedience of orders & unnecessary delay in moving based upon the fact, positively stated, that I had been ordered to cut off the enemy's line of retreat I wrote to Genl Beauregard to enquire what orders had been sent me, sending copies of the preceding. He replied in substance that he had not sent orders to me except those referred to, but had sent orders to move across the run & attack to Genl Holmes, who had informed him they had never been received, that in the hurry he had kept no copy of the orders & did not know by what courier. He reiterated that they had been sent to Holmes & not to me. Yet I see in his report of the battle he three times refers to these orders as having been sent to me.[12] The most violent of the attacks on me was over the signature P. W. A. in a Georgia paper & being present his statements received more credit as he blended truth with error & was supposed to have derived his information from Genl Beauregards Hdqs & there was enough of truth to give plausibility to his insinuations of bad faith or want of willingness.[13] Dr Dabney's Life of Jackson[14] gives an entirely erroneous view of the movements of the day in this respect, & these errors have been general. I hope General you will not think my request unreasonable that you will set this matter clear for the future, you being the one best qualified to do so.[15] I have not a copy of my correspondence with Genl Beauregard at this place, but there are two present besides myself who have seen it[16] & if you wish I will forward from Tenn. a copy or certified statements if the papers have been destroyed. In this correspondence Genl Beauregard made a request in pencil in a postscript, that I would not publish as it might do injury to the cause & he would set it all right in his report, which would appear in a few days.[17]

Report of
Manassa to
Genl Johnston

1. In his report of the battle, Beauregard wrote that his plan was to make "a rapid, determined attack with my right wing and center on the enemy's flank and rear at Centreville, with due precautions against the advance of his reserves from the direction of Washington." "In anticipation of this method of attack," he later wrote, "and to prevent accidents, the subordinate commanders had been carefully instructed in the movement by me, as they were all new to the responsibilities of command." *OR* 2:487; Beauregard, "The First Battle of Bull Run," 205.

2. *OR* 2:486, 536.

3. When Ewell did not receive orders from Beauregard to advance, he sent staff officers to Generals David R. Jones, on his left, at McLean's Ford, and General Theophilus Holmes, in his rear, asking if they had received any orders. In reply, Jones sent Ewell a dispatch that he had received from Beauregard at 7:10 A.M., in which Beauregard stated that he had ordered Ewell "to take the offensive upon Centreville." Ewell promptly advanced his brigade across the run. *OR* 2:537; Fitzhugh Lee to CB, 17 Dec. 1884, PBE; Jones, *Campbell Brown's Civil War,* 30.

4. Beauregard's dispatch read: "On account of the difficulties of the ground in our front it is thought advisable to fall back to our former positions." Quoted in Beauregard, *A Commentary,* 115. Compare Jones, *Campbell Brown's Civil War,* 30.

5. No Colonel Lucy has been found. In *OR* 2:536, Ewell identifies this officer as an aide-de-camp named Colonel Terry. Brown thought that the message was brought by either Captain Fitzhugh Lee, Ewell's assistant adjutant general, or Captain Charles H. Rhodes, Ewell's assistant quartermaster. Technically, he was correct. The courier delivered the order to Lee, who in turn delivered it to Ewell. Jones, *Campbell Brown's Civil War,* 30.

6. McLean's Ford was one mile upstream from Ewell's position at Union Mills.

7. Union Mills stood at the point where the Orange and Alexandria Railroad crossed Bull Run.

8. Johnson's headquarters were at the Lewis house, "Portici."

9. *OR* 2:477, 499.

10. John S. Preston, a Harvard alumnus and South Carolina state senator, served as volunteer aide to Beauregard during the battle. He and other members of

Beauregard's staff assisted Johnston throughout the day. Preston held a variety of administrative posts during the war, and by the time it ended he was a brigadier general.

11. At First Manassas, Ewell's brigade consisted of Colonel Robert E. Rodes's 5th Alabama Infantry, Colonel John J. Seibels's 6th Alabama Infantry, Colonel Isaac G. Seymour's 6th Louisiana Infantry, Captain Thomas L. Rosser's battery of the Washington Artillery, and four companies of Virginia cavalry led by Lieutenant Walter H. Jenifer. Among the companies in Jenifer's squadron were the "Governor's Mounted Guard," which became Company I, 4th Virginia Cavalry, and the Rappahannock Cavalry, which became Company B of the 6th Virginia Cavalry. Captain John Grattan Cabell commanded the former unit, and Captain John Shackleford Green the latter.

12. The text of Ewell's letter, dated July 25, 1861, and Beauregard's response appear in Brown, "General Ewell at Bull Run," 259–60fn. Beauregard's report of the battle was published in *OR* 2:484–504.

13. The article appeared in the *Columbus (GA) Sun.*

14. Robert L. Dabney's *Life and Campaigns of Lieut.-Gen. Thomas J. Jackson (Stonewall Jackson)* was published by Blelock & Co. of New York in 1866.

15. After the war, Johnston wrote an article entitled "Responsibilities of the First Bull Run," in which he sought to refute statements made by Jefferson Davis in his book *The Rise and Fall of the Confederate Government.* In that article, Johnston defended Ewell against criticisms leveled by Beauregard in his November 1884 article, published in *The Century.* Both articles were republished in *Battles and Leaders of the Civil War.*

16. The two men in question were Ewell's aide-de-camp Campbell Brown and Captain George F. Harrison of the Goochland Light Dragoons (later Company F, 4th Virginia Cavalry). Harrison resigned in October 1861. "Before I left," he recalled, "General Ewell sent for me to his quarters. 'Captain,' said he, 'handing me some papers, 'I learn that some of the newspapers in the far South are imputing responsibility to me for the failure of our army to make the attack at Manassas as contemplated. Now, of course, I can publish nothing at this time. But you are going home, through Richmond, and may, sooner or later, hear the subject discussed. Have an accurate copy made of this correspondence between General Beauregard and myself, and take it with you, that you may have it in your power to vindicate me.'" Both Brown and Harrison later used the correspondence to defend Ewell from insinuations made by Beauregard that Ewell had been negligent in not making the morning attack. Brown's defense of Ewell appears in an article titled "General Ewell at Bull Run" in *Battles and*

Leaders of the Civil War, 1:259–61. Harrison's article, "Ewell at First Manassas," appears in the *Southern Historical Society Papers* 14 (1886): 356–59.

17. Beauregard's postscript to Ewell read as follows: "Do not publish until we know what the enemy is going to do—or reports are out—which I think will make it all right." Brown, "General Ewell and Bull Run," 260fn.

179. To Elizabeth Ewell Jr.

Spring Hill
Oct. 28. 66

Miss E. S. Ewell

Dear Elizabeth;

I have just recd your letter and was gratified that the important ceremonies &c of your Church had not turn[e]d your head. In regard to the severe test you expect of your musical talents I expect you can take the same consolation I did in the army[—]i.e. that as deficient as I might be, I did not know where they could better themselves.[1] I am unusually busy just now. Brown & his friend Bayliss[2] are both absent & I am the only one here who represents the interests of the place. We have an excellent manager but no one has as many eyes as the owners.[3] Lizinka worries herself very much about the house.[4] there is more than one person can attend to, and if there were an assistant to give out things & look after what was going on occasionally it would relieve her very much. I shall be disappointed if Lizzie does not come out. more pains have been taken to get her here than L. has taken with any one but Becca and a failure to come would give great disappointment. Lizinka is afraid to be too pressing even where she is very anxious. I have just had a severe nervous head ache which has left me somewhat exhausted & stupid. Our Cotton crop is better than we expected at one time or indeed at any time during the Spring & early Summer. Labor of every kind is scarce & high. there is so much to be done that every one is behind & one owes high wages and personal obligations for what is done.

I wrote to Becca a few days since at Mr Meredeths.[5] I asked if the Waverly place is still for sale. Please communicate this to her if in your vicinity. I talked to her about that place & she sent off Young Marsteller[6] to examine some stiff clayey land a long way off that would not be as desirable as Stony Lonesome. Please remember me to cousin Frances.[7] Write soon.

Yrs &c
R S. Ewell

1. Elizabeth played the organ at Holy Trinity Catholic Church in Georgetown, District of Columbia.

2. Captain Wyatt Bayliss had served in the 7th Battalion, Mississippi Infantry. After the war, he worked for a time at Spring Hill.

3. Spring Hill's manager was a man named Porter.

4. In April 1866 Campbell Brown had announced his engagement to Susan Polk, the daughter of Brigadier General Lucius Polk. "I suspect I am delighted but am not sure[;] am afraid I'm indifferent[,] possibly a little mortified at not having a nice house in which to receive her," Lizinka confided to Lizzie Ewell. The wedding occurred on September 12, 1866. While the Browns were on their honeymoon, Lizinka undertook renovations to the Spring Hill house. LCB to LE, 25 Apr. 1866, WM.

5. This may be a reference to John T. Meredith, a wealthy Kentucky-born farmer who lived near Bristoe, Virginia.

6. Young Marstellar may be Arellan L. Marstellar's son, Lewis, who was seventeen years old in 1866.

7. Francis Lowndes lived in Washington, D.C.

180. To Benson J. Lossing

My efforts were useless.[1] The Legislature thought it inhuman to make old men perform any military service (I thought some were afraid of their popularity), and they would do nothing more than authorize any persons to volunteer into an organization for city guards that chose, while the citizens were only active in trying to get others to volunteer. The result was that only three men volunteered.[2] . . . Many buildings were fired by the mob, which I had carefully directed should be spared. Thus the arsenal was destroyed against my orders. A party of men who proceeded to burn the Tredegar Iron Works, were only deterred by General Anderson's arming his employees and threatening resistance. The small bridge on Fourteenth Street, over the canal, was burnt by incendiaries, who fired a barge above[3] and pushed it against the bridge. . . . I left the city about seven in the morning, and, as yet, nothing had been fired by my orders, yet the buildings and depot near the bridge were on fire, and the flames were so close as to be disagreeable as I rode by them.[4]

1. In November 1866, in response to a request for information, Ewell wrote to historian Benson Lossing about his efforts to raise a constabulary force to maintain order in Richmond when and if the Confederates had to abandon it.

Again, he took pains to deny any responsibility for the fires that subsequently destroyed the city's business district. Lossing quoted this excerpt from Ewell's letter in a footnote that appeared in volume 3, pp. 545–46, of his book *Pictorial History of the Civil War in the United States of America.*

2. Recognizing the evacuation of Richmond to be inevitable, Ewell recommended that the city raise a constabulary force to maintain order from the time the Confederate army evacuated until the time the Union army entered. A few weeks later he proposed drafting men between the ages of fifty and sixty to supplement the South's dwindling manpower supply. Nothing came of either suggestion, and mobs ransacked the city when Confederate troops pulled out.

3. "Above"—i.e. upriver.

4. Concerning Ewell's letter, Lossing added:

> He also mentions seeing from the hills above Manchester, the flames burst through the roof of a fire-proof mill, "on the side farthest from the large warehouses;" and he was informed that Mr. Crenshaw found his mill full of plunderers, who were about the burn it, and he saved it by giving them all the flour. Ewell was offered, by the "Ordnance Department," turpentine to mix with the tobacco, to make it burn more fiercely, but he refused to use it because it would endanger the city. After considering all the facts and circumstances, the writer is impressed with the belief, that the humane Ewell never issued the prescribed order for firing the warehouses, but that the work was done by a less scrupulous hand, connected with the "War Department." Ewell had specially advised care in keeping the fire-engines in order, in the event of a conflagration. "These," he said, "were found to be disabled." (Lossing, *Pictorial History,* 3:546fn 2.)

181. To Elizabeth Ewell Jr.

Spring Hill Tenn
Jan'y 8th 1867

Miss Elizabeth S. Ewell

Dear Elizabeth;

Yours of the 1st came to day. You had been so long in my debt that I began to think something was the matter. This has been decidedly one of our dark days for Maj. Brown & his wife went to Charlottesville Va or rather started for that place to day where he proposes to study law for five or six months. As usual his Mother is made sick by the separation though I think there is no doubt that he will return here at the end of the Session.[1] Harriots letters dont come near as often since she has added to the number of sinners, but this was to be expected as formerly she must have spent a large percentage of her time in writing. I expect there will be some brilliant maneuvering over the scion of the two houses in regard to her future religious education, rivalling the struggles over the body of Achilles' friend. Protestant or Catholic is the question & I feel more inclined to think highly of the chances of the latter just now.[2] I remember some essay on the respective strength of Francis & Philip[3] and I think a parallel case could be made of the present. One Grandam has more brilliancy of intellect but the other has more coolness & self possession with solid sense & good assistants. One is on the spot but then this is met again by the Mother's presence and as if too much advantage might be taken of this there is the Father a Catholic, fond of his wife & not very zealous.[4] You would probably compare it to the Angel & Evil one fighting for the body of Moses.[5]

By the way I heard you quoted as saying that none but ladies were admitted to the black veil. Did you mean at the Convent in Georgetown or over the church? I rather denied this as I was told of a convent in Balt where blacks were nuns. They might be ladies but not in the sense most probably in which you were quoted. It was not so much in reference to their moral qualities as their position that you were understood as expressing yourself. Did you mean that a woman who might have been in a menial or "poor but honest" walk of life could not take the black veil? Can any one who takes the white & deports herself properly take the bl[a]ck? Are the conditions those of birth or if a woman, who was born in the lower walks of life but raised no question of her zeal & sincerity[,] whose piety was unquestioned, wished to take the black veil is there no place for her? If she has money is the case altered, & if so what is the minimum[?]

Compare your answer with what I have written & make as decided & positive answer as possible.[6] Remember me to Cousin Francis.

Yrs—   R S. Ewell

1. Campbell attended just one session at the University of Virginia Law School, returning to Spring Hill in May 1867. He later passed the bar examination and opened his own law practice. During that period he lived at "Glen Oak," one of his mother's properties in Nashville.

2. Harriot had given birth to her first child, Lizinka Campbell Turner, on November 15, 1866, in St. Louis, Missouri. Ewell likened the struggle over the

baby to Achilles' struggle with the Trojans over the slain body of his friend Patroclus, a legend described in Homer's epic *The Iliad,* book 18.

3. Unidentified.

4. Lizinka wanted her granddaughter to be raised a Protestant, while Hattie's mother-in-law, a Roman Catholic, wished the child to be raised in that faith. The elder Mrs. Turner had an advantage over Lizinka inasmuch as she lived close to the child and would therefore have more influence over the family. However, Ewell thought that Hattie, being a firm Protestant, would offset that advantage. Her husband, a Catholic, was apparently not rigid in his convictions and would presumably side with his wife in the matter. Ewell reported this to his sister Elizabeth, who had converted to Catholicism in 1839.

5. Here Ewell refers to a biblical passage found in the Book of Jude: "But when the archangel Michael, contending with the devil, disputed about the body of Moses, he did not presume to pronounce a reviling judgment upon him, but said, 'The Lord rebuke you.'" Jude 9, Revised Standard Version.

6. Women wishing to join a convent had to pledge themselves to God and had to undergo a year-long trial period, called a novitiate. The apprenticeship began with a ceremony in which novices received a white veil. During the probationary period that followed, novices could leave the monastery, if they chose to do so, or they could be dismissed by their superiors if the superiors deemed them unsuitable to that calling. At the end of the one-year period, novices confirmed their earlier vows and became formal members of the religious order, replacing their white veils with black ones.

182. To Elizabeth Ewell Jr.

April 7. 67—

Miss E. S. Ewell

Dear Elizabeth;

I have been busy, dyspectic & generally out of sorts & so have not written. Please tell Cousin Francis that the melon seed will receive great care & if they dont come up to anything of the kind I ever eat my disappointment will be very great.[1] Our winter since the middle of Feb'y has been wonderful for the amount of rain & the cold. The grass has hardly yet begun to grow, although this time last year the animals were fattening on it. As we had a good many cattle the extraordinary season has been unfortunate in the way of keeping them poor.

I sold a good many by way of precaution & though at a profit, not as large as if we had had an average winter I expect. Harriot & her baby went away ten

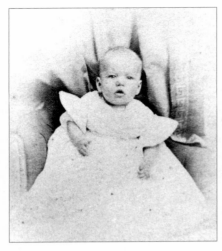

Hattie named her first daughter Lizinka in honor of her mother, although the little girl was commonly known as Lily. "She has the sensitive nature & loving disposition that characterized mother," Hattie later wrote of the child, "& is also like her in being more than usually clever." (Tennessee State Library and Archives)

days since after a short visit. her baby is a remarkably quiet little affair, owing I presume to its very good health.[2] Harriot is very proud of it & there was always a summons to the female part of the community to see it bathed, to see it dressed, to see it sleeping & then a general summons to come see "the baby which was awake now."

I am working now without any overseer & am pretty busy as the darkies think it necessary to a day's work that the white man should be present. Otherwise their instincts make it incumbent that they must stop & look out for him. Tell Cousin Frances [*sic*] that I have not time even to go fishing for a short time.

We are half expecting a visit from Lizzy Ewell who has been talking of coming out before long.

As Aunt Rebecca expects to go into her new house before long & Harriot & Campbell are both away it is a good time as far as Lizinka is concerned for her to come.[3]

Lizinka would be exceedingly anxious to see Becca if there were any hope of getting her out here, but we have written for her untill it seems useless to try any more.[4]

Wm was on a visit her[e] for a day several weeks since but he does not write & we hear of him as seldom as you do I expect.[5]

I write in a great hurry for the mail.

Lizinka wrote a few days since about some cause which she has since concluded is a humbug.

Love to Cousin Francis.

Yrs &c

R. S. Ewell

1. Ewell's cousin had apparently sent him some melon seeds.

2. Harriot's child, Lizinka Campbell Turner, had been born on November 15, 1866, and was nearly five months old.

3. Rebecca Hubbard and her husband had moved to Spring Hill following the war. They lived under the same roof as the Ewells until 1867, when they moved into a new house nearby. By the time Ewell wrote this letter, Harriot had returned to St. Louis and Campbell was attending law school in Virginia.

4. Ewell's eldest sister, Rebecca, was living with Ben and Lizzie in Williamsburg. She died there four months later, on August 9, 1867, following a short bout of bilious dysentery. She is buried in an unmarked grave in the College Cemetery on the grounds of the College of William and Mary.

5. After visiting the Ewells at Spring Hill in February, William had returned to his home in Giles County, Tennessee.

183. To Elizabeth H. Brown

Spring Hill Maury Co
Tenn. April 14. 67—

Mrs E. H. Brown[1]

My dear Madam;

I hardly know how to explain my neglect of your letter of December the 10th 66, & will only say that every attempt to write an autograph letter for the purpose desired, called up such painful recollections of the past that after several efforts I gave it up.[2]

Whose autograph of those Officers can be more than a testimony to the bravery, devotion & sacrifice of those who for the most part are denied the most ordinary resting place? Their conduct was so heroic that there seems even a disposition on the part of our conquerors to fear them when dead.[3]

Curiosity may be gratified by my autograph simply, which I enclose. Will you excuse the liberty I take of enclosing the small check you will find in this & use it as your judgement may direct either for the cemetary or for the destitute living?[4] Will you have the kindness to remember me to Dr Hoge & the family? Please tell the Doctor that I often think of him when trying to interest myself about the many interests and duties of the farm as at other times.

Somehow the Dr's name brings more vividly to mind than almost any other, the lives & all the indelible recollections of the war of .64 around Richmond.[5]

Mrs Ewell is well & would join me in remembrances if she knew I am writing.

Very Resp'ly—

R S. Ewell

P.S. I have a little headache which accounts in part for a rather confused letter.

RSE

1. Elizabeth Brown was the sister of Captain James Power Smith, Ewell's former aide-de-camp.

2. Ewell apparently wrote this letter in response to a request he had received from Mrs. Brown for an autographed letter. Mrs. Brown intended to sell the letter to raise money for one of the many Confederate cemeteries being established throughout the South.

3. Immediately after the war, the United States government spent approximately $2.5 million interring the remains of Union soldiers in newly created national cemeteries throughout the country. The remains of the Southern dead were interred in Confederate cemeteries at private expense.

4. In addition to raising money for Confederate cemeteries, Southerners were raising money to help support the widows and orphans of their deceased soldiers. Widows and orphans in the North received pensions from the United States government.

5. Ewell and his wife saw a great deal of the Hoge family during the final year of the war, when Ewell was in command of the Department of Richmond.

Ewell occasionally corresponded with former military colleagues. In most cases the letters were genial, but there were exceptions. In the following letter, Colonel John M. Patton wrote to Ewell about an incident that took place during the Battle of Cross Keys. Patton commanded a small brigade in that battle, and when he brought his regiments onto the field, he experienced firsthand the hot temper and impatience that Ewell often exhibited in combat. In his anger, Ewell apparently spoke harshly to Patton and made some comment that Patton believed reflected badly on his courage. Ewell forgot the incident, but Patton did not. Five years later he wrote to Ewell, complaining of the treatment he had received. Ewell crafted the following response, showing that he could be as diplomatic in peace as he was fierce in war.

184. To John M. Patton Jr.

May 12 –67

Col. Jno. M. Patton[1]

Dear sir;

I take your suggestion to endorse my answer on your letter & will retain the duplicate untill the arrival early in June of my Aide on that field (Maj. C.B). His recollection may recall facts to my mind that are now forgotten. Your account agrees with my recollection as far as my memory goes of the events of the fight at Cross Keys.[2] On the 3d Page you refer to some temper shown by me in reference to a discussion as to the position of one of your Regts.[3] I forget it & think it more than likely the chief cause was my habitual annoyance during a fight when my attention was called from important points on which it was necessary to act. Having to decide promptly on the most important steps it was impossible for me to discuss coolly unimportant occurrences.

Trimble, in accordance with his own suggestion was to attack with the right flank, the left as accessory not a condition to make a diversion. He did not attack though the left flank did[,] but not being supported by the right & in small force, without particular results. for this you were in no way responsible.[4] When ordered to withdraw my troops you were selected to remain. You remonstrated on the grounds of your small command but did not change my intention. Trimble saw Genl Jackson & had his own command left behind in addition as you state, but with no result, as I had anticipated, beyond depriving the command of too few to fight Fremont & too many to take from the field of Port Republic.[5]

We must distinguish between the caution of a commander & mere personal fear. I saw in you the first but not a circumstance, not a shadow of anything to detract from the highest appreciation of your personal courage, but the contrary. Differing from you in opinion I might have expressed such a difference but never anything reflecting in the slightest degree on your courage. I regret this occurrence & hope for the sake of the past it will be set at rest.

I never relieved you from command, or substituted Col. Morton[6] or any one else, either in camp or on the battle-field on the march or any where else. Nor were you ever guilty of conduct under my observation subjecting you to the charges alleged or of conduct unbecoming an Officer or forfeiting my respect.[7]

I have the honor—

to remain &c—

R S. Ewell—

1. Colonel John M. Patton Jr. (1826–1898) at Cross Keys led a brigade consisting of the 21st, 42nd, and 48th Virginia regiments and the 1st Virginia (Irish) Battalion.
2. Cross Keys lies approximately six miles south of Harrisonburg, Virginia. On June 8, 1862, Confederate forces led by Ewell defeated a larger Union force led by Major General John C. Frémont at Cross Keys in one of the last battles in Stonewall Jackson's 1862 Shenandoah Valley Campaign.

After the war Ewell divided his time between Lizinka's farm near Spring Hill, Tennessee (shown here), and "Tarpley," a cotton plantation that he rented in Mississippi. Lizzie wed Beverly S. Scott at Spring Hill in December 1867. (Courtesy Donald Pfanz and Stan Aylor)

3. Patton's brigade was camped not far from the village of Port Republic when the fighting at Cross Keys began. Upon reaching the battlefield, he sent the 48th Virginia and the Irish Battalion to shore up Ewell's left flank. Ewell sent the 42nd Virginia to the far right to assist General Isaac Trimble, who was then driving forward in an effort to capture a Union battery. After just a few minutes, however, the regiment's commander received orders to move to the left, where it ultimately reunited with the rest of the brigade. It was probably the movement of the 42nd Virginia that sparked Ewell's harsh comments to Patton, comments that the junior officer interpreted as questioning his bravery.

4. The first two sentences of this paragraph contain many deletions and insertions making their reconstruction problematic and rendering their meaning questionable.

5. The night of the battle Jackson ordered Ewell to break contact with Frémont and march to Port Republic. Jackson planned to join forces with Ewell and attack the leading elements of Major General James Shields's division north of Port Republic the following morning. Ewell ordered Patton to remain at Cross Keys to delay the advance of Frémont's army toward Port Republic. Jackson later ordered Trimble to join Patton in that task.

6. There was no Colonel Morton. Ewell was probably referring to Lieutenant Colonel William Martin, commander of the 42nd Virginia Infantry, one of the regiments in Patton's brigade.

7. It is unclear who made these accusations against Patton, but Ewell felt compelled to deny them.

185. To Lizzie Ewell Scott

Spring Hill
March 4. 68—

Mrs Beverly Scott
Care of Pro. Ewell

Dear Lizzie;

I have been intending to write to you for some time but Mrs Ewell has been writing so diligently, that there has been no necessity except for form's sake. Please imagine that this is of some months earlier date & full of all sorts of congratulations &c.[1]

You would have felt quite well pleased with yourself had you known what a favorable impression you made on all especially Mrs Ewell who although always very fond of you yet never expressed herself so warmly or constantly or strongly in your favor as on this occasion. In fact she seems to think you were unreasonable in taking yourself away when you were so pleasant & agreeable.

I understand you made a conquest of a Dr Gordon in Giles, so as a mark of appreciation when your Uncle William notified me that there was a great demand for mules in Giles & that among others Dr Gordon wanted one, I sent the best bargain I had in that line. I hope he will pay cash.[2]

Mrs Ewell "worried considerable" about losing Mr Scott's likeness but I dont think you sent another as promised.

Mrs Turner (Harriot) has just paid a visit here. She was not very well & so was especially severe on every body & every thing. In fact I thought it was about as well for all parties when she left. Since then she has been writing faster & faster & more of letters expressing her regret at making herself so disagreeable.[3] Every thing is pretty much as you left it. Except that the cattle are poorer & sheep have their numbers swelled by sundry little lambs.

I direct this as advised by my better half. Wm Stoddert was here for a day or two last week. Some complain that his preaching without salary & keeping the Church in order is ruining his congregation.[4] George Campbell came from him, to take down mules.[5] I am very much afraid that my happening to open the Vicar of Wakefield at the part where Moses trades the Colt for the spectacles, was phrophetic.[6]

Please give my respects to Mr Scott & tell him how glad we would be to see him here.

Yours &c
R S. Ewell

1. Lizzie had married Beverly S. Scott of Prince Edward County, Virginia, on December 12, 1867, at the Ewell's Spring Hill, Tennessee, home. Scott (ca. 1845–1906) had been wounded in the leg at Port Walthall Junction, Virginia, on May 18, 1864, while serving as a private in the 34th Virginia Infantry Regiment. One year later, he was captured at Farmville, Virginia, during Lee's retreat to Appomattox and imprisoned at Newport News. His military service records describe him as being six feet tall with light hair and blue eyes.

2. Dr. David C. Gordon (b. ca. 1834) had been a private in the 13th Tennessee Cavalry in the Civil War. Lizzie may have met Gordon during a visit to her uncle William Stoddert, who lived in Giles County.

3. This is among the first references to Hattie's emotional instability. As she grew older, Lizinka's daughter increasingly exhibited signs of anger, violence, and de-

pression. At times she was suicidal. In 1873, Hattie was committed temporarily to an asylum, and she was receiving medical treatment as late as ten years later. She died in 1932.

4. According to one source, Ewell's brother was "a most successful preacher, popular lecturer and esteemed teacher in Tennessee." Hayden, *Virginia Genealogies,* 349.

5. Several men named George Campbell appear in the 1870 census. The most probable matches are farmers George Campbell of Wilson County, Tennessee, and George Campbell of Davidson County, Tennessee.

6. In Oliver Goldsmith's eighteenth-century novel *The Vicar of Wakefield,* the vicar's son, Moses, is sent by his parents to sell the family colt and buy a horse. The naive boy instead is taken in by a pair of swindlers and returns with a gross of worthless green spectacles.

186. To Lizinka Ewell

Vicksburg Feby 14th 70[1]

Mrs L. C. Ewell

M.D.L;

I found on visiting the sales stables in Mobile that prices asked for mules were higher than I had seen anywhere & I was satisfied that it was best to hold ours over. Admiral Semmes[2] told me they had been twice offered [and] though the lot was liked people objected to their age. Two of the four sold were of the smallest but purchasers took them for four years old.[3] It is possible they were. His son took them to his farm 40 miles above & turned them on cane where they are costing us nothing. It seems likely they will be sold about the time that plowing begins late in March as people dont want to have them on hand. If not they will keep over untill fall & bring a good price as dray mules. They have no Cholora there so I can see but little risk in keeping them over. The mules I saw were all called 4 yrs old, as fat as pork hogs & I thought a poor lot—held at from $165 to 175. It is evident that it is a small & uncertain market. S's son[,] not the one who went to Tenn, told me they tried to raise the money to buy the whole lot on speculation.[4] Campbell can get them cheaper & better from Memphis, where are the cheapest I've seen anywhere.

I went from Mobile to N.O.[5] chiefly attracted by the vapor bath[6] which pleased me as much as before & was to leave Saty evening but saw so many friends in N.O & it was so much more pleasant there than on the boat that I waited for the Sunday evening train & here I am being ahead of the 2 boats that left Saty.

I take 1st boat for Bolivar, where I will give C. the $500, visit Tarpley & decide either to return at once to Tenn or wait to get the cotton to market.[7] Among other cards left for me was one from Genl Longstreet, who left another for me Sunday asking me to take a seat with him in his Pew at Trinity Church. I started out for the cars with Genl Wilcox, C.S.A.[,][8] who introduced me to Dr Joseph Jones of the N.O. Infirmary, formerly of Nashville Medical College but driven out with Messrs Eve, Jennings &c. He was very pleasant & agreeable, a savant, & Secty of the Historical Society of the South of N.O.[9] He, on learni[n]g where I was going seemed to hesitate at first, but finally though on his way to another Church, without any solicitation on my part, joined me & we went to L.'s pew in a very handsome church, formerly Bishop Polk's.[10] Longstreet & Mrs L. were in & shook hands very cordially. The regular Priests were not there but some one who served during the war on some one's Staff officiated. From the Church Dr J. & myself walked a short distance to Mrs Polk['s]. A diminutive little maid threw open the door & stood at attention like a soldier as we filed past. I walked in, mentioning my name, & shook hands with Miss Polk who laughed & said it was not Miss Polk but very much like her. Miss Susan came in afterwards & I remained very much puzzled untill we left after 15 or 20 minutes when Dr Jones told me it was Mrs Blake.[11] They all looked well & in good spirits, But seemed surprised when I told them I had been in L[ongstree]t's pew although they acknowledged that the principles he advocated were those being adopted by all, only L. was the first. The fact is most people seem to want to quarrel with some one & dont know with whom. I thought I could see a good many scowling glances thrown at me in church, taking me I suppose for a Northern Officer. All in talking of Longstreet regret that people took the course they did in tabooing him & I believe if it were to go over again they would not follow the same plan as regards him.[12]

Tell Miss Lizinka C. Turner that people down here say it was Ellen that had the little lamb.[13] I have asked at all the book stores for "My Enemy's daughter" and all have just sold out.[14] Love to Harriot. Yours—   R. S. Ewell

1. Ewell penned this letter from Vicksburg, Mississippi, where he had gone after visiting Mobile, Alabama, and New Orleans, Louisiana, on business.
2. Rear Admiral Raphael Semmes (1809–1877) was the celebrated commander of the C.S.S. *Alabama,* which captured or sank dozens of United States ships until June 1864, when it was destroyed in battle off the coast of France. Semmes

survived the fight, made his way back to Virginia, and commanded the James River Squadron during the final months of the war.

3. Ewell had sold Admiral Semmes four mules on February 11.

4. Semmes had two sons: Samuel Spencer Semmes (1838–1912) and Judge Oliver John Semmes (1839–1918).

5. New Orleans.

6. While in New Orleans, Ewell visited a public sauna.

7. From Vicksburg, Ewell planned to travel up the Mississippi River to Bolivar County, Mississippi, where the Browns owned a cotton plantation called "Melrose" and where Ewell himself had leased a neighboring plantation called "Tarpley." Once there, he planned to give Campbell Brown the money he had gained from the sale of the mules and then return to Lizinka in Tennessee.

8. Major General Cadmus M. Wilcox (1824–1890) had commanded a division in the Army of Northern Virginia's Third Corps.

9. Joseph Jones (1833–1896), a college professor and doctor, had served in the Confederate medical department. After the war, he taught at the University of Louisiana and from 1880 to 1884 served as the president of the state's board of health. A member of several medical societies, Jones also helped organize the Southern Historical Society. Paul Fitzsimons Eve (1806–1877), also a surgeon, practiced medicine in both the United States and Poland. Settling in Augusta, Georgia, he helped organize the Medical College of Georgia and was professor of surgery there. In 1851 he took a position as professor of surgery at the University of Nashville, holding that position until the Civil War, when he received an appointment as surgeon-general of Tennessee. He later became chief surgeon of the Army of Tennessee. After the war, Eve served as president of the American Medical Association and wrote hundreds of articles on topics of health and medicine. By the time of his death, he was widely regarded as not only the leading surgeon but also the leading professor of surgery in the South. Jennings has not been identified.

10. Lieutenant General Leonidas Polk (1806–1864) commanded a corps in the South's Army of Tennessee until June 14, 1864, when he was struck and killed by an artillery shell outside of Atlanta, Georgia. Prior to the war, he had been a bishop of the Episcopal Church in Louisiana. Polk had preached at New Orleans's Trinity Episcopal Church.

11. Frances A. Devereux (1807–1875) had married Leonidas Polk in 1830. Their third daughter, Sarah (b. 1840), had married Francis Daniel Blake in 1866.

12. After the war, Longstreet was decried in the South for becoming a "Black Republican." He supported his friend Ulysses S. Grant in his bid for president and

later accepted a number of federal appointments from him. Animosity toward Longstreet increased still more when he later published articles critical of General Lee's leadership at Gettysburg.

13. Ewell is referring to the children's song "Mary Had a Little Lamb," which the children in New Orleans had apparently changed to "Ellen had a Little Lamb."

14. Justin McCarthy's *My Enemy's Daughter* (1869) was published in three volumes by Tinsley Brothers of London.

Bibliography

Manuscripts

College of William and Mary. Williamsburg, VA.

"Buildings and Grounds—College Cemetery." Subject file.

Chapman, Anne West. "Benjamin Stoddert Ewell: A Biography." Ph.D. dissertation, 1984.

Ewell, Benjamin Stoddert, Papers.

Turner, Harriot Stoddert. "The Ewells of Virginia, Especially of Stony Lonesome."

Duke University, Durham, NC.

Ewell, Richard Stoddert, Letter Book.

———, Papers.

Ewell, Benjamin Stoddert, and Richard Stoddert Ewell Papers.

Johnson, Bradley Tyler, Papers.

Filson Historical Society. Louisville, KY.

Brown-Ewell Family Papers.

Fredericksburg and Spotsylvania County Battlefields Memorial National Military Park, VA.

Mann, Jonathan Taylor, Papers.

Smith, James Power, Papers (Cat. no. 3477).

Library of Congress. Washington, DC.

Campbell, George Washington, Papers.

Ewell, Richard Stoddert, Papers.

Hotchkiss, Jedediah, Papers.

Maryland Historical Society. Baltimore, MD.

Milligen Collection (Ms. no. 590).

National Archives and Records Administration. Washington, DC.

    United States Census records, 1830–70.

    Compiled Service Records of Confederate Generals and Staff Officers, and Nonregimental Enlisted Men, Record Group 109, Microcopy 331.

Pfanz, Donald. Fredericksburg, VA.

    Tyner, Mildred. Letter to Pfanz, February 22, 2007.

    Prince William County Land Deeds Office. Manassas, VA.

    Deed Books L2 and V3.

Tennessee State Library and Archives, Nashville.

    Brown, Campbell, and Richard S. Ewell Papers.

    Chancery Court Minutes.

    Hubbard, David, Papers.

University of North Carolina, Chapel Hill. Southern Historical Collection.

    Allen, William, Papers.

    Polk-Brown-Ewell Papers.

Virginia Historical Society.

    St. Paul's Church (Protestant Episcopal), Richmond, VA. Records, 1828–1963

Newspaper Articles

"Annual Meeting of the American Medical Association," *Boston Post,* June 9, 1865.

"The Burning of Richmond," *New York Herald,* June 26, 1865.

"Excursion of Physicians Down the Harbor," *Boston Daily Evening Traveller,* June 9, 1865.

"Gen. R. S. Ewell," *Charlotte (NC) Southern Home,* Feb. 5, 1872.

"General Jackson's Death—Particulars of the Event," *Lynchburg (VA) Daily Republican,* May 15, 1863.

"History of the 107th Regiment New York Volunteers," originally published in *Canisteo (NY) Valley Times.* An unidentified newspaper reprinted this article on December 4, 1869; the clipping is on file at Fredericksburg and Spotsylvania County National Military Park.

"Letter from Rebel General Officers on the Assassination," *Richmond (VA) Commercial Bulletin,* May 8, 1865.

"Poet Laureate Chose the Pen over the Sword," *Hampton Roads (VA) Virginian-Pilot,* June 18, 1995.

"Skirmish at Fairfax Court House," *Richmond (VA) Enquirer,* June 7, 1861.

"The Southern Press and Gen. Jackson," *Newark (NJ) Daily Advertiser,* May 16, 1863.

"The Subscriber," *Alexandria (VA) Gazette,* Sept. 14, 1839.

Published Works

Acuña, Rudolph F. "Ignacio Pesqueira: Sonoran Caudillo." *Arizona and the West* 12 (1970): 139–72.

Allen, William. *History of the Campaign of Gen. T. J. (Stonewall) Jackson in the Shenandoah Valley of Virginia.* 1880. Repr., Dayton, OH: Morningside Bookshop, 1987.

Altshuler, Constance W., ed. *Latest from Arizona! The Hesperian Letters, 1859–1861.* Tucson: Arizona Historical Society, 1969.

Andrews, J. Cutler. *The South Reports the Civil War.* Princeton, NJ: Princeton University Press, 1970.

Barnes, Will C. *Arizona Place Names.* Revised by Byrd H. Granger. Tucson: University of Arizona Press, 1960.

Barron, Earle P. *Ewell's March Home.* Kearney, NE: Morris Publishing, 1999.

Bean, William G. "Stonewall Jackson's Jolly Chaplain, Beverley Tucker Lacy." *West Virginia History* 29, no. 2 (Jan. 1968): 77–96.

Beauregard, Pierre G. T. *A Commentary on the Campaign and Battle of Manassas of July, 1861.* New York: G. P. Putnam's Sons, 1891.

———. "The First Battle of Bull Run." In Johnson and Buell, *Battles and Leaders of the Civil War,* vol. 1: 196–227.

Bell, William Gardner. *Secretaries of War and Secretaries of the Army: Portraits and Biographical Sketches.* Washington, DC.: Center of Military History, 1992.

Blair, William. *Virginia's Private War: Feeding Body and Soul in the Confederacy, 1861–1865.* New York: Oxford University Press, 1998.

Boatner, Mark M. *The Civil War Dictionary.* Revised edition. New York: David McKay Company, 1988.

Boyd, David F. *Reminiscences of the War in Virginia.* Edited by T. Michael Parish. Austin, TX: Jenkins, 1989.

Brown, Campbell. "General Ewell at Bull Run." In Johnson and Buell, *Battles and Leaders of the Civil War,* vol. 1: 259–61.

Browne, J. Ross. *Adventures in the Apache Country: A Tour through Arizona and Sonora, with Notes on the Silver Regions of Nevada.* New York: Harper & Brothers, 1869.

Bunn, Alfred. *Old England and New England: In a Series of Views Taken on the Spot.* 2 vols. London: Richard Bentley, 1853.

Calkins, Christopher M. *From Petersburg to Appomattox.* Farmville, VA: The Farmville Herald, 1983.

————. *Thirty-Six Hours before Appomattox.* Farmville, VA: The Farmville Herald, 1980.

Clarke, Dwight L. *William Tecumseh Sherman: Gold Rush Banker.* San Francisco: California Historical Society, 1969.

Connelley, William E., ed. "A Journal of the Santa Fe Trail." *Mississippi Valley Historical Review* 12 (Sept. 1925): 249–55.

Conner, James. *Letters of James Conner, C.S.A.* Edited by Mary Conner Moffett. Columbia, SC: R. L. Bryan Company, 1950.

Cowles, Calvin D., comp. *Atlas to Accompany the Official Records of the Union and Confederate Armies.* Washington: Government Printing Office, 1891–95.

Cullum, George W. *Biographical Register of the Officers and Graduates of the U.S. Military Academy at West Point, New York, Since Its Establishment in 1802.* Supplement, Vol. 6-A (1910–20). Edited by Colonel Wirt Robinson. Saginaw, MI: Seemann & Peters, 1920.

Dabney, Robert L. *Life and Campaigns of Lieut.-Gen. Thomas J. Jackson (Stonewall Jackson).* New York: Blelock & Co., 1866.

Davis, William C., ed. *The Confederate General.* 6 vols. Harrisburg: National Historical Society, 1991.

Donohoe, John C. "The Fight near Front Royal, Va." *Confederate Veteran* 22, no. 7 (July 1914): 308–9.

Dorris, Jonathan T. *Pardon and Amnesty under Lincoln and Johnson.* Chapel Hill: University of North Carolina Press, 1953.

Dowdey, Clifford, and Louis H. Manarin. *The Wartime Papers of R. E. Lee.* Boston: Little, Brown and Company, 1961.

Driver, Robert J., and Kevin C. Ruffner. *1st Battalion Virginia Infantry, 39th Battalion Virginia Cavalry, 24th Battalion Virginia Partisan Rangers.* Lynchburg, VA: H. E. Howard, 1996.

Drumm, Stella M., ed. *Down the Santa Fe Trail and into Mexico: The Diary of Susan Shelby Magoffin, 1846–1847.* Lincoln: University of Nebraska Press, 1982.

Durham, Walter T. *Nashville: The Occupied City.* Nashville: Tennessee Historical Society, 1985.

Dwight, Charles S. *A South Carolina Rebel's Recollections*. Columbia, SC: The State Company, n.d.

Early, Jubal A. *Autobiographical Sketch and Narrative of the War between the States*. Philadelphia: J. B. Lippincott & Co., 1912.

Eberlein, Harold D., and Cortlandt V. Hubbard. *Historic Houses of George-Town and Washington City*. Richmond, VA: Dietz Press, 1958.

Eckenrode, H. J., and Bryan Conrad. *James Longstreet: Lee's War Horse*. Chapel Hill: University of North Carolina Press, 1986.

Eisenhower, John S. D. *Agent of Destiny: The Life and Times of General Winfield Scott*. New York: The Free Press, 1997.

————. *So Far from God: The U.S. War with Mexico, 1846–1848*. New York: Doubleday, 1989.

Elliot, Charlotte C. *William Greenleaf Elliot: Minister, Educator, Philanthropist*. Boston: Houghton, Mifflin and Company, 1904.

Elliott, George. "The First Battle of the Confederate Ram 'Albemarle.'" In Johnson and Buell, *Battles and Leaders of the Civil War*, vol. 4: 625–27.

Evans, Clement A., ed. *Confederate Military History: A Library of Confederate States History . . . Written by Distinguished Men of the South*. 13 vols. Atlanta: Confederate Publishing Co., 1889.

Ewell, Alice M. *A Virginia Scene or Life in Old Prince William*. Lynchburg, VA: J. P. Bell Company, Inc., 1931.

Flournoy, Henry W., ed. *Calendar of Virginia State Papers and Other Manuscripts from January 1, 1836, to April 15, 1869; Preserved in the Capitol at Richmond*. 11 vols. Richmond, VA: R. F. Walker, 1893.

Foote, Shelby. *The Civil War: A Narrative*. 3 vols. New York: Random House, 1958–74.

Forbes, Robert H. *The Penningtons, Pioneers of Early Arizona*. N.p.: Arizona Archaeological and Historical Society, 1919.

Frazier, Robert W. *Forts of the West: Military Forts and Presidios and Posts Commonly Called Forts West of the Mississippi River to 1898*. Norman, OK: University of Oklahoma Press, 1965.

————. *Forts and Supplies: The Role of the Army in the Economy of the Southwest, 1846–1861*. Albuquerque: University of New Mexico Press, 1983.

Fremantle, James A. L. *Three Months in the Southern States: April to June 1863*. New York: J. Bradburn, 1864.

Gallagher, Gary W. *Stephen Dodson Ramseur: Lee's Gallant General.* Chapel Hill: University of North Carolina Press, 1985.

Garrett, Jill K., ed. *Confederate Soldiers and Patriots of Maury County, Tennessee.* Columbia, TN: Cpt. James M. Sparkman Chapter of the U.D.C., 1970.

Goldsmith, Oliver. *The Vicar of Wakefield.* 1766. Repr., New York: Washington Square Press, 1965.

Gordon, John B. *Reminiscences of the Civil War.* New York: Charles Scribner's Sons, 1903.

Graf, Leroy P., Ralph W. Haskins, and Paul H. Bergeron, eds. *The Papers of Andrew Johnson.* 16 vols. Knoxville: University of Tennessee Press, 1967–2000.

Grant, Ulysses S. "General Grant on the Siege of Petersburg." In Johnson and Buell, *Battles and Leaders of the Civil War*, vol. 4: 574–79.

———. *Personal Memoirs of U. S. Grant.* 2 vols. New York: Charles L. Webster & Company, 1886.

Grunder, Charles S., and Brandon H. Beck. *The Second Battle of Winchester, June 12–15, 1863.* Lynchburg, VA: H. E. Howard, Inc., 1989.

Hamlin, Percy G., ed. *The Making of a Soldier: Letters of General R. S. Ewell.* Richmond, VA: Whittet & Shepperson, 1935.

———. *"Old Bald Head" (General R. S. Ewell): The Portrait of a Soldier.* Strasburg, VA: Shenandoah Publishing House, 1940.

Handerson, Henry E. *Yankee in Gray.* Cleveland, OH: Press of Western Reserve University, 1962.

Harrison, George F. "Ewell at First Manassas." *Southern Historical Society Papers* 14 (1886): 356–59.

Harrison, Fairfax. *Landmarks of Old Prince William: A Study of Origins in Northern Virginia.* Berryville, VA: Chesapeake Book Company, 1964.

Hart, B. H. Liddell. *Sherman: Soldier, Realist, American.* New York: Dodd, Meade, & Co., 1929.

Hassler, William W., ed. *The General to His Lady: The Civil War Letters of William Dorsey Pender to Fanny Pender.* Chapel Hill: University of North Carolina Press, 1965.

Hayden, Horace Edwin. *Virginia Genealogies.* Wilkes-Barre, PA: E. B. Yordy, 1891.

Heitman, Francis B. *Historical Register and Dictionary of the United States Army.* 2 vols. Washington, DC.: U.S. Government Printing Office, 1903.

Hennessy, John. *Return to Bull Run: The Campaign and Battle of Second Manassas.* New York: Simon and Schuster, 1993.

Howard, McHenry. *Recollections of a Maryland Confederate Soldier and Staff Officer under Johnston, Jackson and Lee.* Baltimore: Williams & Wilkins Co., 1914.

Hotchkiss, Jedediah. *Make Me a Map of the Valley: The Civil War Journal of Stonewall Jackson's Topographer.* Edited by Archie P. McDonald. Dallas: Southern Methodist University Press, 1973.

Hughes, Nathaniel C., Jr., and Roy P. Stonesifer Jr. *The Life and Wars of Gideon J. Pillow.* Edited by Gary W. Gallagher. Chapel Hill: University of North Carolina Press, 1993.

Hunt, Roger D., and Jack R. Brown. *Brevet Brigadier Generals in Blue.* Gaithersburg, MD: Olde Soldier Books, 1990.

Hunton, Eppa. *Autobiography of Eppa Hunton.* Richmond, VA: William Byrd Press, 1933.

Imboden, John D. "Jackson at Harper's Ferry in 1861." In Johnson and Buell, *Battles and Leaders of the Civil War,* vol. 1: 111–25.

Jackson, Mary Anna. *Memoirs of Stonewall Jackson.* Louisville, KY: Prentice Press, Courier Journal Job Printing Co., 1895.

Johnson, Allen. *Dictionary of American Biography.* 20 vols. New York: Charles Scribner's Sons, 1929.

Johnson, Allen, and Dumas Malone, eds. *Dictionary of American Biography.* 20 vols. New York: Charles Scribner's Sons, 1928–36.

Johnson, Charles. "Attack on Fort Gilmer, September 29th, 1864." *Southern Historical Society Papers* 1 (1876): 438–42.

Johnson, John L. *The University Memorial: Biographical Sketches of Alumni of the University of Virginia Who Fell in the Confederate War.* Baltimore: Turnbull Brothers, 1871.

Johnson, Robert U., and Clarence C. Buel, eds. *Battles and Leaders of the Civil War.* 4 vols. New York: The Century Company, 1887–88.

Johnston, Joseph E. "Responsibilities of the First Bull Run." In Johnson and Buell, *Battles and Leaders of the Civil War,* vol. 1: 240–59.

Jones, Terry L., ed. *Campbell Brown's Civil War: With Ewell and the Army of Northern Virginia.* Baton Rouge: Louisiana State University Press, 2001.

Jones, John William. "The Career of General Jackson." *Southern Historical Society Papers* 35 (1907): 79–98.

Jordan, David M. *Winfield Scott Hancock: A Soldier's Life.* Bloomington: Indiana University Press, 1988.

Krick, Robert E. L. *Staff Officers in Gray*. Chapel Hill: University of North Carolina Press, 2003.

Krick, Robert K. *Conquering the Valley: Stonewall Jackson at Port Republic*. New York: William Morrow and Co., 1996.

————. *Lee's Colonels: A Biographical Register of the Field Officers of the Army of Northern Virginia*. Dayton, OH: Morningside Bookshop, 1991.

Laska, Lewis L. *The Tennessee State Constitution: A Reference Guide*. Westport, CT: Greenwood Press, 1990.

"Letter of General Richard S. Ewell to General Grant." *Southern Historical Society Papers* 39 (1914): 4–5.

Long, E. B. *The Civil War Day By Day: An Almanac, 1861–1865*. 1971. Repr., New York: Da Capo Press, 1985.

Lossing, Benson J. *Pictorial History of the Civil War in the United States of America*. 3 vols. Hartford, CT: Thomas Belknap, Publisher, 1877.

Mansfield, Edward Deering. *Life and Services of General Winfield Scott: Including the Siege of Vera Cruz, the Battle of Cerro Gordo, and the Battles in the Valley of Mexico, to the Conclusion of Peace, and his Return to the United States*. New York: A. S. Barnes & Co., 1852.

Matter, William D. *If It Takes All Summer: The Battle of Spotsylvania*. Chapel Hill: University of North Carolina Press, 1988.

McCabe, James D., Jr. *Life and Campaigns of General Robert E. Lee*. Atlanta: National Publishing Company, 1866.

McGuire, Judith W. *Diary of a Southern Refugee during the War*. Richmond: J. W. Randolph & English, 1889.

McPherson, James M. *Battle Cry of Freedom: The Civil War Era*. New York: Oxford University Press, 1988.

McDonald, Archie P., ed. *Make Me a Map of the Valley*. Dallas: Southern Methodist University Press, 1973.

The Medical and Surgical History of the War of the Rebellion. 6 vols. Compiled by George A. Otis and D. L. Huntington. Washington, DC.: U.S. Government Printing Office, 1883.

Miller, William J. *Mapping for Stonewall: The Civil War Service of Jed Hotchkiss*. Washington, DC.: Elliott & Clark Publishing, 1993.

Moore, Edward A. *The Story of a Cannoneer under Stonewall Jackson*. New York: Neale Publishing Company, 1907.

Moseley, Edward H., and Paul C. Clark Jr. *Historical Dictionary of the United States–Mexican War.* Lanham, MD: Scarecrow Press, 1997.

Mowry, Sylvester. *Arizona and Sonora.* New York: Harper & Brothers, 1864.

North, Diane M. T. *Samuel Peter Heintzelman and the Sonora Exploring & Mining Company.* Tucson: University of Arizona Press, 1980.

Northrop, Jerrold N. *Confederate Commissary General: Lucius Bellinger Northrop and the Subsistence Bureau of the Southern Army.* Shippensburg, PA: White Mane Publishing Co., 1996.

Oates, William C. *The War between the Union and the Confederacy and Its Lost Opportunities.* New York: Neale Publishing Company, 1905.

"The Opposing Forces in the Chancellorsville Campaign." In Johnson and Buell, *Battles and Leaders of the Civil War,* vol. 3: 233–38.

Owen, Thomas McAdory. *History of Alabama and Dictionary of Alabama Biography.* 4 vols. 1921. Repr., Spartanburg, SC: The Reprint Company, 1978.

Pappas, George S. *To the Point: The United States Military Academy, 1802–1902.* Westport, CT: Praeger Publishers, 1993.

Parrish, T., Michael. *Richard Taylor: Soldier Prince of Dixie.* Chapel Hill: University of North Carolina Press, 1992.

Partin, John W., ed. *A Brief History of Fort Leavenworth.* N.p.: The U.S. Combined Arms Center and Fort Leavenworth, Kansas, n.d.

Patrick, Rembert W. *The Fall of Richmond.* Baton Rouge: Louisiana State University Press, 1960.

Pfanz, Donald C. *Richard S. Ewell: A Soldier's Life.* Chapel Hill: University of North Carolina Press, 1998.

Polk, William M. *Leonidas Polk, Bishop and General.* 2 vols. New York: Longman's, Green & Co., 1893.

Powers, Tracy. *Lee's Miserables: Life in the Army of Northern Virginia from the Wilderness to Appomattox.* Chapel Hill: University of North Carolina Press, 1998.

Report of the Adjutant General of the State of Kentucky, Confederate Kentucky Volunteers, War 1861–65. 2 vols. Utica, KY: McDowell Publications, n.d.

Rhea, Gordon C. *The Battles for Spotsylvania Court House and the Road to Yellow Tavern, May 7–12, 1864.* Baton Rouge: Louisiana State University Press, 1997.

Roman, Alfred. *The Military Operations of General Beauregard.* 2 vols. New York: Harper & Brothers, 1884.

Rouse, Parke, Jr. "'Old Buck: A Hero in Spite of Himself," *The Alumni Gazette* (A publication of the College of William and Mary), vol. 50, no. 6 (Jan.–Feb. 1983): 18–20.

Scheina, Robert L. *Latin America's Wars: The Age of the Caudillo, 1791–1899.* Dulles, VA: Brassey's, Inc., 2003.

Serven, James E. "The Military Posts on Sonoita Creek." *The Smoke Signal*, no. 12 (Fall 1965): 26–48.

Sifakis, Stewart, *Who Was Who in the Civil War*. New York: Facts on File, 1988.

Smith, Eugenia B. *Centreville, Virginia: Its History and Architecture*. Fairfax, VA: Fairfax County Office of Planning, 1973.

Smith, Everard, ed. "The Civil War Diary of Peter W. Hairston, Volunteer Aide to Major General Jubal Early, November 7–December 4, 1863." *North Carolina Historical Review* 67 (Jan. 1990): 59–86.

Smith, Justin H. *The War with Mexico*. 2 vols. New York: Macmillan, 1919.

Smith, William. "An Eye-Witness Account of the Skirmish at Fairfax Courthouse." In *Fairfax County and the War Between the States*, 1–10. Vienna, VA: Fairfax County Civil War Centennial Commission, 1961.

Sommers, Richard J. *Richmond Redeemed: The Siege of Petersburg*. Garden City, NY: Doubleday, 1981.

Sorrel, Gilbert M. *Recollections of a Confederate Staff Officer*. New York: Neale, 1917.

Starr, Stephen Z. *The Union Cavalry in the Civil War*. 2 vols. Baton Rouge: Louisiana State University Press, 1981.

Stephens, Alexander H. *Recollections of Alexander H. Stephens*. Edited by Myrta Lockett Avary. New York: Doubleday, Page & Company, 1910.

Stiles, Robert. *Four Years under Marse Robert*. New York: Neale Publishing Company, 1903.

Sulivan, Clement. "The Fall of Richmond." In Johnson and Buell, *Battles and Leaders of the Civil War*, vol. 4: 725–26.

Tanner, Robert G. *Stonewall in the Valley*. Garden City, NY: Doubleday, 1976.

Taylor, Richard. *Destruction and Reconstruction*. New York: Appleton, 1879.

Tevis, James H. *Arizona in the '50's*. Albuquerque: University of New Mexico Press, 1954.

Thomas, Emory M. *The Confederate State of Richmond: A Biography of the Capital*. Baton Rouge: Louisiana State University Press, 1998.

Trudeau, Noah A. *Out of the Storm: The End of the Civil War, April–June 1865.* Boston: Little, Brown, 1994.

Turner, Harriot S. "Recollections of Andrew Johnson." *Harper's Monthly Magazine* 120 (Jan. 1910): 168–76.

United States Department of Justice. *Attorneys General of the United States, 1789–1985.* Washington, DC: Government Printing Office, 1985.

United States War Department. *Official Records of the Union and Confederate Navies in the War of the Rebellion.* 27 vols. Washington, DC.: Government Printing Office, 1894.

———. *The War of the Rebellion: A Compilation of the Official Records of the Union and Confederate Armies.* 128 vols. Washington, DC.: Government Printing Office, 1880–1901.

Utley, Robert M. *Frontiersmen in Blue: The United States Army and the Indian, 1848-1865.* New York: Macmillan, 1967.

Wallace, Lee A., Jr. *A Guide to Virginia Military Organizations, 1861–1865.* Lynchburg, VA: H. E. Howard,1986.

Warfield, J. D. *The Founders of Anne Arundel and Howard Counties, Maryland.* Baltimore: Kohn & Pollock, 1905.

Watehall, E. T. "Fall of Richmond, April 3, 1865." *Confederate Veteran* 17, no. 5 (May 1909): 215.

Weddell, Elizabeth W. *St. Paul's Church.* 2 vols. Richmond: William Byrd Press, 1931.

White, James T. *The National Cyclopedia of American Biography.* New York: James T. White & Co., 1909.

Wilcox, Cadmus M. *History of the Mexican War.* Washington, DC.: Church News Publishing Co., 1892.

Williams, T. Harry. "General Ewell to the High Private in the Rear." *Virginia Magazine of History and Biography* 54, no. 2 (Apr. 1946): 157–60.

Wilson, James Grant, and John Fisk, eds. *Appletons' Cyclopaedia of American Biography,* 6 vols. New York: D. Appleton and Co., 1889.

Woodward, C. Vann, ed. *Mary Chesnut's Civil War.* New Haven, CT: Yale University Press, 1981.

Wright, Mike. *Richmond under Siege: Richmond in the Civil War.* New York: Cooper Square Press, 2002.

Other

Niles' National Register (Baltimore, Washington, DC, and Philadelphia), 1811–1849.

United States House of Representatives, 52nd Congress, 1st Session, Report No. 344.

United States Senate, 51st Congress, 1st Session, Report No. 95.

Index